(ISC)²®

CCSP® Certified Cloud Security Professional

Official Study Guide

Third Edition

(ISC)²®

CCSP® Certified Cloud Security Professional

Official Study Guide

Third Edition

Mike Chapple, Ph.D. CCSP, CISSP

David Seidl, CISSP

Acknowledgments

The authors would like to thank the many people who made this book possible. Thanks to Jim Minatel at Wiley Publishing, who helped us extend the Sybex certification preparation franchise to include this title and has continued to champion our work with the International Information Systems Security Certification Consortium (ISC)². Thanks also to Carole Jelen, our agent, who tackles all the back-end magic for our writing efforts and worked on both the logistical details and the business side of the book with her usual grace and commitment to excellence. Sharif Nijim and Charles Gaughf, our technical editors, pointed out many opportunities to improve our work and deliver a high-quality final product. John Whiteman, our technical proofreader, and Judy Flynn, our copy editor, ensured a polished product. John Sleeva served as our project manager and made sure everything fit together. Many other people we'll never meet worked behind the scenes to make this book a success, and we really appreciate their time and talents to make this next edition come together.

The publisher and (ISC)² would like to acknowledge and thank the previous edition author Ben Malisow for his dedicated effort to advance the cause of CCSP and cloud security education.

About the Authors

Mike Chapple, Ph.D. CCSP, CISSP, is an author of the best-selling *CISSP (ISC)² Certified Information Systems Security Professional Official Study Guide* (Sybex, 2021), now in its ninth edition. He is an information security professional with two decades of experience in higher education, the private sector, and government.

Mike currently serves as teaching professor of IT, Analytics, and Operations at the University of Notre Dame's Mendoza College of Business. He previously served as senior director for IT Service Delivery at Notre Dame, where he oversaw the information security, data governance, IT architecture, project management, strategic planning, and product management functions for the University.

Before returning to Notre Dame, Mike served as executive vice president and chief information officer of the Brand Institute, a Miami-based marketing consultancy. Mike also spent four years in the information security research group at the National Security Agency and served as an active duty intelligence officer in the U.S. Air Force.

Mike has written more than 30 books, including *Cyberwarfare: Information Operations in a Connected World* (Jones & Bartlett, 2021), *CompTIA Security+ SY0-601 Study Guide* (Wiley, 2021), and the *CompTIA Cybersecurity Analyst+ (CySA+) Study Guide* (Wiley, 2020) and *Practice Tests* (Wiley, 2020).

Mike earned both his BS and PhD degrees from Notre Dame in computer science and engineering. He also holds an MS in computer science from the University of Idaho and an MBA from Auburn University. His IT certifications include the CISSP, Security+, CySA+, CISA, PenTest+, CIPP/US, CISM, CCSP, and PMP credentials.

Mike provides books, video-based training, and free study groups for a wide variety of IT certifications at his website, CertMike.com.

David Seidl, CISSP, is vice president for information technology and CIO at Miami University. During his IT career, he has served in a variety of technical and information security roles, including senior director for Campus Technology Services at the University of Notre Dame, where he co-led Notre Dame's move to the cloud and oversaw cloud operations, ERP, databases, identity management, and a broad range of other technologies and services. He also served as Notre Dame's director of information security and led Notre Dame's information security program. He has taught information security and networking undergraduate courses as an instructor for Notre Dame's Mendoza College of Business and has written books on security certification and cyberwarfare, including coauthoring the previous editions of *CISSP (ISC)² Official Practice Tests* (Sybex, 2021) and *CompTIA CySA+ Study Guide: Exam CS0-002, CompTIA CySA+ Practice Tests: Exam CS0-002, CompTIA Security+ Study Guide: Exam SY0-601,* and *CompTIA Security+ Practice Tests: Exam SY0-601,* as well as other certification guides and books on information security.

David holds a bachelor's degree in communication technology and a master's degree in information security from Eastern Michigan University, as well as CISSP, CySA+, Pentest+, GPEN, and GCIH certifications.

About the Technical Editor

Sharif Nijim is an associate teaching professor of IT, Analytics, and Operations in the Mendoza College of Business at the University of Notre Dame, where he teaches undergraduate and graduate business analytics and information technology courses.

Before becoming part of the Mendoza faculty, Sharif served as the senior director for IT service delivery in the University of Notre Dame's Office of Information Technologies. In this role, he was part of the senior leadership team for the Office of Information Technologies, overseeing data stewardship, information security and compliance, learning platforms, product services, project management, and enterprise architecture. Prior to Notre Dame, Sharif co-founded and was a board member of a customer data integration company catering to the airline industry. He also spent more than a decade building and performance-optimizing enterprise-class transactional and analytical systems for clients in the logistics, telecommunications, energy, manufacturing, insurance, real estate, healthcare, travel and transportation, and hospitality sectors.

About the Technical Proofreader

John L. Whiteman is a security researcher for Intel Corporation with over 20 years experience. He is a part-time adjunct cybersecurity instructor for the University of Portland and also teaches the UC Berkeley Extension's Cybersecurity Boot Camp. He holds multiple security certifications including CISSP and CCSP. John holds a MSCS from Georgia Institute of Technology and a BSCS from Portland State University.

Contents at a Glance

Contents

Introduction

The Certified Cloud Security Professional (CCSP) certification satisfies the growing demand for trained and qualified cloud security professionals. It is not easy to earn this credential; the exam is extremely difficult, and the endorsement process is lengthy and detailed.

The *CCSP (ISC)² Certified Cloud Security Professional Official Study Guide* offers the cloud professional a solid foundation for taking and passing the Certified Cloud Security Professional (CCSP) exam.

The more information you have at your disposal and the more hands-on experience you gain, the better off you'll be when attempting the exam. This study guide was written with that in mind. The goal was to provide enough information to prepare you for the test, but not so much that you'll be overloaded with information that's outside the scope of the exam.

This book presents the material at an intermediate technical level. Experience with and knowledge of security concepts, operating systems, and application systems will help you get a full understanding of the challenges that you'll face as a security professional.

We've included review questions at the end of each chapter to give you a taste of what it's like to take the exam. If you're already working in the security field, we recommend that you check out these questions first to gauge your level of expertise. You can then use the book mainly to fill in the gaps in your current knowledge. This study guide will help you round out your knowledge base before tackling the exam.

If you can answer 90 percent or more of the review questions correctly for a given chapter, you can feel safe moving on to the next chapter. If you're unable to answer that many correctly, reread the chapter and try the questions again. Your score should improve.

 Don't just study the questions and answers! The questions on the actual exam will be different from the practice questions included in this book. The exam is designed to test your knowledge of a concept or objective, so use this book to learn the objectives behind the questions.

CCSP Certification

The CCSP certification is offered by the International Information System Security Certification Consortium, or (ISC)², a global nonprofit organization. The mission of (ISC)² is to support and provide members and constituents with credentials, resources, and leadership to address cybersecurity as well as information, software, and infrastructure security to deliver value to society. (ISC)² achieves this mission by delivering the world's leading information security certification program. The CCSP is the cloud-focused credential in this series and is accompanied by several other (ISC)² programs:

- Certified Information Systems Security Professional (CISSP)
- Systems Security Certified Practitioner (SSCP)
- Certified Authorization Professional (CAP)
- Certified Secure Software Lifecycle Professional (CSSLP)
- HealthCare Information Security and Privacy Practitioner (HCISPP)

The CCSP certification covers six domains of cloud security knowledge. These domains are meant to serve as the broad knowledge foundation required to succeed in cloud security roles:

- Cloud Concepts, Architecture, and Design
- Cloud Data Security
- Cloud Platform and Infrastructure Security
- Cloud Application Security
- Cloud Security Operations
- Legal, Risk, and Compliance

The CCSP domains are periodically updated by (ISC)². The most recent revision in August 2022 slightly modified the weighting for Cloud Data Security from 19 to 20 percent while changing the focus on Cloud Security Operations from 17 to 16 percent. It also added or expanded coverage of emerging topics in cloud security.

Complete details on the CCSP Common Body of Knowledge (CBK) are contained in the Exam Outline (Candidate Information Bulletin). It includes a full outline of exam topics and can be found on the (ISC)² website at www.isc2.org.

Taking the CCSP Exam

The CCSP exam is administered in English, Chinese, German, Japanese, Korean, and Spanish using a computer-based testing format. Your exam will contain 150 questions and have a four-hour time limit. You will not have the opportunity to skip back and forth as you take the exam: you only have one chance to answer each question correctly, so be careful!

Passing the CCSP exam requires achieving a score of at least 700 out of 1,000 points. It's important to understand that this is a scaled score, meaning that not every question is worth the same number of points. Questions of differing difficulty may factor into your score more or less heavily, and adaptive exams adjust to the test taker.

That said, as you work through the practice exams included in this book, you might want to use 70 percent as a goal to help you get a sense of whether you're ready to sit for the actual exam. When you're ready, you can schedule an exam at a location near you through the (ISC)² website.

Questions on the CCSP exam use a standard multiple-choice format where you are presented with a question and four possible answer choices, one of which is correct. Remember to read the full question and *all* of the answer options very carefully. Some of those questions can get tricky!

Computer-Based Testing Environment

The CCSP exam is administered in a computer-based testing (CBT) format. You'll register for the exam through the Pearson Vue website and may take the exam in the language of your choice.

You'll take the exam in a computer-based testing center located near your home or office. The centers administer many different exams, so you may find yourself sitting in the same room as a student taking a school entrance examination and a healthcare professional earning a medical certification. If you'd like to become more familiar with the testing environment, the Pearson Vue website offers a virtual tour of a testing center:

```
https://home.pearsonvue.com/test-taker/Pearson-Professional-
Center-Tour.aspx
```

When you take the exam, you'll be seated at a computer that has the exam software already loaded and running. It's a pretty straightforward interface that allows you to navigate through the exam. You can download a practice exam and tutorial from the Pearson Vue website:

```
www.vue.com/athena/athena.asp
```

 Exam policies can change from time to time. We highly recommend that you check both the (ISC)² and Pearson VUE sites for the most up-to-date information when you begin your preparing, when you register, and again a few days before your scheduled exam date.

Exam Retake Policy

If you don't pass the CCSP exam, you shouldn't panic. Many individuals don't reach the bar on their first attempt but gain valuable experience that helps them succeed the second time around. When you retake the exam, you'll have the benefit of familiarity with the CBT environment and the CCSP exam format. You'll also have time to study the areas where you felt less confident.

After your first exam attempt, you must wait 30 days before retaking the computer-based exam. If you're not successful on that attempt, you must then wait 60 days before your third attempt and 90 days before your fourth attempt. You may not take the exam more than four times in any 12-month period.

Work Experience Requirement

Candidates who want to earn the CCSP credential must not only pass the exam but also demonstrate that they have at least five years of work experience in the information technology field. Your work experience must include three years of information security experience and one year of experience in one or more of the six CCSP domains.

Candidates who hold the CISSP certification may substitute that certification for the entire CCSP experience requirement. Candidates with the Certificate of Cloud Security Knowledge (CCSK) from the Cloud Security Alliance (CSA) may substitute that certification for one year of experience in the CCSP domains.

If you haven't yet completed your work experience requirement, you may still attempt the CCSP exam. An individual who passes the exam is a designated Associate of (ISC)² and has six years to complete the work experience requirement.

Recertification Requirements

Once you've earned your CCSP credential, you'll need to maintain your certification by paying maintenance fees and participating in continuing professional education (CPE). As long as you maintain your certification in good standing, you will not need to retake the CCSP exam.

Currently, the annual maintenance fees for the CCSP credential are $125 per year. This fee covers the renewal for all (ISC)² certifications held by an individual.

The CCSP CPE requirement mandates earning at least 90 CPE credits during each three-year renewal cycle. Associates of (ISC)² must earn at least 15 CPE credits each year. (ISC)² provides an online portal where certificate holders may submit CPE completion for review and approval. The portal also tracks annual maintenance fee payments and progress toward recertification.

What Does This Book Cover?

This book covers everything you need to know to pass the CCSP exam:

Chapter 1: Architectural Concepts

Chapter 2: Data Classification

Study Guide Elements

This study guide uses a number of common elements to help you prepare:

Summaries   The summary section of each chapter briefly explains the chapter, allowing you to easily understand what it covers.

Exam Essentials   The exam essentials focus on major exam topics and critical knowledge that you should take into the test. The exam essentials focus on the exam objectives provided by (ISC)².

Chapter Review Questions   A set of questions at the end of each chapter will help you assess your knowledge and whether you are ready to take the exam based on your knowledge of that chapter's topics.

Additional Study Tools

This book comes with a number of additional study tools to help you prepare for the exam. They are described in the following sections.

Go to www.wiley.com/go/Sybextestprep to register and gain access to this interactive online learning environment and test bank with study tools.

Sybex Test Preparation Software

Sybex's test preparation software lets you prepare with electronic test versions of the review questions from each chapter, the practice exam, and the bonus exam that are included in this book. You can build and take tests on specific domains or by chapter, or cover the entire set of CCSP exam objectives using randomized tests.

Electronic Flashcards

Our electronic flashcards are designed to help you prepare for the exam. Over 100 flashcards will ensure that you know critical terms and concepts.

Glossary of Terms

Sybex provides a full glossary of terms in PDF format, allowing quick searches and easy reference to materials in this book.

Audio Review

Mike Chapple provides an audiobook version of the exam essentials from this book to help you prepare for the exam.

> Like all exams, the CCSP certification from (ISC)² is updated periodically and may eventually be retired or replaced. At some point after (ISC)² is no longer offering this exam, the old editions of our books and online tools will be retired. If you have purchased this book after the exam was retired, or are attempting to register in the Sybex online learning environment after the exam was retired, please know that we make no guarantees that this exam's online Sybex tools will be available once the exam is no longer available.

CCSP Exam Objectives

(ISC)² publishes relative weightings for each of the exam's domains. The following table lists the six CCSP objective domains and the extent to which they are represented on the exam.

Domain	% of Exam
1. Cloud Concepts, Architecture, and Design	17%
2. Cloud Data Security	20%
3. Cloud Platform and Infrastructure Security	17%
4. Cloud Application Security	17%
5. Cloud Security Operations	16%
6. Legal, Risk, and Compliance	13%

CCSP Certification Exam Objective Map

How to Contact the Publisher

If you believe you have found a mistake in this book, please bring it to our attention. At John Wiley & Sons, we understand how important it is to provide our customers with accurate content, but even with our best efforts an error may occur.

In order to submit your possible errata, please email it to our Customer Service Team at wileysupport@wiley.com with the subject line "Possible Book Errata Submission."

Assessment Test

1. What type of solutions enable enterprises or individuals to store data and computer files on the internet using a storage service provider rather than keeping the data locally on a physical disk such as a hard drive or tape backup?

   A. Online backups

   B. Cloud backup solutions

   C. Removable hard drives

   D. Masking

2. When using an infrastructure as a service (IaaS) solution, which of the following is not an essential benefit for the customer?

   A. Removing the need to maintain a license library

   B. Metered service

   C. Energy and cooling efficiencies

   D. Transfer of ownership cost

3. _____focuses on security and encryption to prevent unauthorized copying and limitations on distribution to only those who pay.

   A. Information rights management (IRM)

   B. Masking

   C. Bit splitting

   D. Degaussing

4. Which of the following represents the correct set of four cloud deployment models?

   A. Public, private, joint, and community

   B. Public, private, hybrid, and community

   C. Public, internet, hybrid, and community

   D. External, private, hybrid, and community

5. Which of the following lists the correct six components of the STRIDE threat model?

   A. Spoofing, tampering, repudiation, information disclosure, denial of service, and elevation of privilege

   B. Spoofing, tampering, refutation, information disclosure, denial of service, and social engineering elasticity

   C. Spoofing, tampering, repudiation, information disclosure, distributed denial of service, and elevation of privilege

   D. Spoofing, tampering, nonrepudiation, information disclosure, denial of service, and elevation of privilege

6. What is the term that describes the assurance that a specific author actually created and sent a specific item to a specific recipient and that the message was successfully received?

   A. PKI

   B. DLP

   C. Nonrepudiation

   D. Bit splitting

7. What is the correct term for the process of deliberately destroying the encryption keys used to encrypt data?

   A. Poor key management

   B. PKI

   C. Obfuscation

   D. Crypto-shredding

8. What is the process of replacing sensitive data with unique identification symbols/addresses?

   A. Randomization

   B. Elasticity

   C. Obfuscation

   D. Tokenization

9. Which of the following represents the U.S. legislation enacted to protect shareholders and the public from enterprise accounting errors and fraudulent practices?

   A. PCI

   B. Gramm–Leach–Bliley Act (GLBA)

   C. Sarbanes–Oxley Act (SOX)

   D. HIPAA

10. Which of the following is a device that can safely store and manage encryption keys and is used in servers, data transmission, and log files?

    A. Private key

    B. Hardware security module (HSM)

    C. Public key

    D. Trusted operating system module (TOS)

11. What is a type of cloud infrastructure that is provisioned for open use by the general public and is owned, managed, and operated by a cloud provider?

    A. Private cloud

    B. Public cloud

    C. Hybrid cloud

    D. Personal cloud

12. What is a type of assessment that employs a set of methods, principles, or rules for assessing risk based on nonnumerical categories or levels?

    A. Quantitative assessment

    B. Qualitative assessment

    C. Hybrid assessment

    D. SOC 2

13. Which of the following best describes the *Cloud Security Alliance Cloud Controls Matrix (CSA CCM)*?

    A. A set of regulatory requirements for cloud service providers

    B. A set of software development lifecycle requirements for cloud service providers

    C. A security controls framework that provides mapping/cross relationships with the main industry-accepted security standards, regulations, and controls frameworks

    D. An inventory of cloud service security controls that are arranged into separate security domains

14. When a conflict between parties occurs, which of the following is the primary means of determining the jurisdiction in which the dispute will be heard?

    A. Tort law

    B. Contract

    C. Common law

    D. Criminal law

15. Which of the following is *always* available to use in the disposal of electronic records within a cloud environment?

    A. Physical destruction

    B. Overwriting

    C. Encryption

    D. Degaussing

16. Which of the following takes advantage of the information developed in the business impact analysis (BIA)?

    A. Calculating ROI

    B. Risk analysis

    C. Calculating TCO

    D. Securing asset acquisitions

17. Which of the following terms best describes a managed service model where software applications are hosted by a vendor or cloud service provider and made available to customers over network resources?

    A. Infrastructure as a service (IaaS)

    B. Public cloud

    C. Software as a service (SaaS)

    D. Private cloud

18. Which of the following is a federal law enacted in the United States to control the way financial institutions deal with private information of individuals?

    A. PCI DSS

    B. ISO/IEC

    C. Gramm–Leach–Bliley Act (GLBA)

    D. Consumer Protection Act

19. What is an audit standard for service organizations?

    A. SOC 1

    B. SSAE 18

    C. GAAP

    D. SOC 2

20. What is a set of technologies designed to analyze application source code and binaries for coding and design conditions that are indicative of security vulnerabilities?

    A. Dynamic Application Security Testing (DAST)

    B. Static application security testing (SAST)

    C. Secure coding

    D. OWASP

Answers to Assessment Test

1. **B.** Cloud backup solutions enable enterprises to store their data and computer files on the internet using a storage service rather than storing data locally on a hard disk or tape backup. This has the added benefit of providing access to data should infrastructure or equipment at the primary business location be damaged in some way that prevents accessing or restoring data locally. Online backups and removable hard drives are other options but do not by default supply the customer with ubiquitous access. Masking is a technology used to partially conceal sensitive data.

2. **A.** In an IaaS model, the customer must still maintain licenses for operating systems (OSs) and applications used in the cloud environment. In PaaS models, the licensing for OSs is managed by the cloud provider, but the customer is still responsible for application licenses; in SaaS models, the customer does not need to manage a license library.

3. **A.** Information rights management (IRM) (often also referred to as digital rights management, or DRM) is designed to focus on security and encryption as a means of preventing unauthorized copying and limiting distribution of content to authorized personnel (usually, the purchasers). Masking entails hiding specific fields or data in particular user views in order to limit data exposure in the production environment. Bit splitting is a method of hiding information across multiple geographical boundaries, and degaussing is a method of deleting data permanently from magnetic media.

4. **B.** The only correct answer for this is public, private, hybrid, and community. Joint, internet, and external are not cloud models.

5. **A.** The letters in the acronym STRIDE represent spoofing of identity, tampering with data, repudiation, information disclosure, denial of service, and elevation (or escalation) of privilege. The other options are simply mixed up or incorrect versions of the same.

6. **C.** Nonrepudiation means that a party to a transaction cannot deny they took part in that transaction.

7. **D.** The act of crypto-shredding means destroying the key that was used to encrypt the data, thereby making the data essentially impossible to recover.

8. **D.** Replacing sensitive data with unique identification symbols is known as tokenization, a way of hiding or concealing sensitive data by representing it with unique identification symbols/addresses. While randomization and obfuscation are also means of concealing information, they are done quite differently.

9. **C.** The Sarbanes–Oxley Act (SOX) was enacted in response to corporate scandals in the late 1990s/early 2000s. SOX not only forces executives to oversee all accounting practices, it also holds them accountable for fraudulent/deceptive activity. HIPAA is a U.S. law for medical information. PCI is an industry standard for credit/debit cards. GLBA is a U.S. law for the banking and insurance industries.

10. B. A hardware security module (HSM) is a device that can safely store and manage encryption keys. These can be used in servers, workstations, and so on. One common type is called the Trusted Platform Module (TPM) and can be found on enterprise workstations and laptops. There is no such term as *trusted operating system module*, and public and private keys are used with asymmetric encryption.

11. B. This is the very definition of public cloud computing.

12. B. A qualitative assessment is a set of methods or rules for assessing risk based on non-mathematical categories or levels. One that uses mathematical categories or levels is called a quantitative assessment. There is no such thing as a hybrid assessment, and an SOC 2 is an audit report regarding control effectiveness.

13. C. The CCM cross-references many industry standards, laws, and guidelines.

14. B. Contracts between parties can establish the jurisdiction for resolving disputes; this takes primacy in determining jurisdiction (if not specified in the contract, other means will be used). Tort law refers to civil liability suits. Common law refers to laws regarding marriage, and criminal law refers to violations of state or federal criminal code.

15. C. Encryption can always be used in a cloud environment, but physical destruction, overwriting, and degaussing may not be available due to access and physical separation factors.

16. B. Among other things, the BIA gathers asset valuation information that is crucial to risk management analysis and further selection of security controls.

17. C. This is the definition of the software as a service (SaaS) model. Public and private are cloud deployment models, and infrastructure as a service (IaaS) does not provide applications of any type.

18. C. The Gramm–Leach–Bliley Act targets U.S. financial and insurance institutions and requires them to protect account holders' private information. PCI DSS refers to credit card processing requirements, ISO/IEC is a standards organization, and the Consumer Protection Act, while providing oversight for the protection of consumer private information, is limited in scope.

19. B. Both SOC 1 and SOC 2 are report formats based on the SSAE 18 standard. While SOC 1 reports on controls for financial reporting, SOC 2 (Types 1 and 2) reports on controls associated with security or privacy.

20. B. Static application security testing (SAST) is used to review source code and binaries to detect problems before the code is loaded into memory and run.

Chapter 1

Architectural Concepts

THE OBJECTIVE OF THIS CHAPTER IS TO ACQUAINT THE READER WITH THE FOLLOWING CONCEPTS:

Cloud computing is everywhere. The modern business depends upon a wide variety of software, platforms, and infrastructure hosted in the cloud, and security professionals must understand how to protect the information and resources used by their organizations, wherever those assets reside.

In this chapter, we introduce the basic concepts of cloud computing and help you understand the foundational material you'll need to know as you begin your journey toward the Certified Cloud Security Professional (CCSP) certification.

Cloud Characteristics

Cloud computing is the most transformative development in information technology in the past decade. Organizations around the world are retooling their entire IT strategies to embrace the cloud, and this change is causing disruptive impact across all sectors of technology.

But what is the cloud? Let's start with a simple definition: cloud computing is any case where a provider is delivering computing to a customer at a remote location over a network. This definition is broad and encompasses many different types of activity.

There are some common characteristics that we use to define cloud computing:

- Broad network access
- On-demand self-service
- Resource pooling
- Rapid elasticity and scalability
- Measured, or "metered," service

These traits are expressed succinctly in the NIST definition of cloud computing.

NIST 800-145 Cloud Computing Definition

The official NIST definition of cloud computing says, "Cloud Computing is a model for enabling ubiquitous, convenient, on-demand network access to a shared pool of configurable computing resources (e.g., networks, servers, storage, applications, and services) that can be rapidly provisioned and released with minimal management effort or service provider interaction."

These characteristics are also similar to how cloud computing is defined in ISO 17788 (www.iso.org/iso/catalogue_detail?csnumber=60544).

Let's explore these characteristics in more detail.

- **Broad network access** means services are consistently accessible over the network. We might access them by using a web browser or Secure Shell (SSH) connection, but the general idea is that no matter where we or our users are physically located, we can access resources in the cloud.

- **On-demand self-service** refers to the model that allows customers to scale their compute and/or storage needs with little or no intervention from or prior communication with the provider. This means that technologists can access cloud resources almost immediately when they need them to do their jobs. That's an incredible increase in agility for individual contributors and, by extension, the organization. Before the era of on-demand computing, a technologist who wanted to try out a new idea might have to spec out the servers required to implement the idea, gain funding approval, order the hardware, wait for it to arrive, physically install it, and configure an operating system before getting down to work. That might have taken weeks, while today, the same tasks can be accomplished in the cloud in a matter of seconds. On-demand self-service computing is a true game changer.

- **Resource pooling** is the characteristic that allows the cloud provider to meet various demands from customers while remaining financially viable. The cloud provider can make capital investments that greatly exceed what any single customer could provide on their own and can apportion these resources as needed so that the resources are not underutilized (which would mean a wasteful investment) or overtaxed (which would mean a decrease in level of service).

- **Rapid elasticity and scalability** allows the customer to grow or shrink the IT footprint (number of users, number of machines, size of storage, and so on) as necessary to meet operational needs without excess capacity. In the cloud, this can be done in moments as opposed to the traditional environment, where acquisition and deployment of resources (or dispensing old resources) can take weeks or months. In many cases, this scaling can occur automatically, using code to add and remove resources as demands change.

- **Measured service,** or metered service, means that almost everything you do in the cloud is metered. Cloud providers measure the number of seconds you use a virtual server, the amount of disk space you consume, the number of function calls you make, and many other measures. This allows them to charge you for precisely the services you use—no more and no less. This is the same model commonly used by public utilities providing commodity services such as electricity and water. The measured service model is a little intimidating when you first encounter it, but it provides cloud customers with the ability to manage their utilization effectively and achieve the economic benefits of the cloud.

Real World Scenario

Online Shopping

Think of retail demand during the pre-holiday rush toward the end of the year. The sheer volume of customers and transactions greatly exceeds all normal operations throughout the rest of the year. When this happens, retailers who offer online shopping can see great benefit from hosting their sales capability in the cloud. The cloud provider can apportion resources necessary to meet this increased demand and will charge for the increased usage at a negotiated rate, but when shopping drops off after the holiday, the retailers will not continue to be charged at the higher rate.

Elasticity vs. Scalability

Many people use the terms *elasticity* and *scalability* interchangeably, but they are actually subtly different concepts.

Strictly speaking, *scalability* refers to the ability of a system to grow as demand increases. This growth does not need to be automated, but it does need to be possible. Scalability may come from using the automated scaling features of a cloud provider, or it may come from adding physical hardware to a system.

Elasticity refers to the ability of a system to dynamically grow and shrink based upon the current level of demand. Administrators may set up a system to automatically add storage, processing power, or network capacity as demand increases and then release those resources when demand is lower. This provides tremendous cost efficiency by only purchasing expensive computing resources when they are actually needed.

Business Requirements

In most businesses, the IT department is not a profit center; it provides a support function that allows other business units to generate a profit. Cybersecurity teams definitely fit into this category—they generally don't do anything that generates revenue for the business, and from the perspective of business leaders, they represent a sunk cost that reduces efficiency by lowering profits. In fact, security activities often hinder business efficiency (because, generally, the more secure something is, be it a device or a process, the less efficient it will be). This is why the business needs of the organization drive security decisions and not the other way around.

A successful organization will gather as much information about operational business requirements as possible; this information can be used for many purposes, including several functions in the security realm. (We'll touch on this throughout the book, but a few examples include the business continuity and disaster recovery effort, the risk management plan, and data categorization.) Likewise, the astute security professional needs to understand as much as possible about the operation of the organization. Operational aspects of the organization can help security personnel better perform their tasks no matter what level or role they happen to be assigned to. Consider the following examples:

- A network security administrator has to know what type of traffic to expect based on the business of the organization.

- The intrusion detection analyst has to understand what the organization is doing, how business activities occur, and where (geographically) the business is operating to better understand the nature and intensity of potential external attacks and how to adjust baselines accordingly.

- The security architect has to understand the various needs of the organizational departments to enhance their operation without compromising their security profile.

- Security leaders must not only understand the technologies used by the organization but also the associated risks and how to appropriately manage them.

Functional requirements: Those performance aspects of a device, process, or employee that are necessary for the business task to be accomplished. Example: A salesperson in the field must be able to connect to the organization's network remotely.

Nonfunctional requirements: Those aspects of a device, process, or employee that are not necessary for accomplishing a business task but are desired or expected. Example: The salesperson's remote connection must be secure.

As organizations consider their distribution of resources between the cloud and on-premises computing environments, they must select a mix that is appropriate for their needs. This is not a decision made lightly, and the business requirements must be supported by this transition. There are also different cloud service and delivery models of cloud computing, and an organization must decide which one will optimize success.

Understanding the Existing State

A true evaluation and understanding of the business processes, assets, and requirements are essential. Failing to properly capture the full extent of the business needs could result in not having an asset or capability in the new environment after migration to the cloud.

At the start of this effort, however, the intent is not to determine what will best fulfill the business requirements but to determine what those requirements are. A full inventory of assets, processes, and requirements is necessary, and there are various methods for collecting this data. Typically, several methods are used jointly as a means to reduce the possibility of missing something.

Here are some possible methods for gathering business requirements:

- Interviewing functional managers
- Interviewing users
- Interviewing senior management
- Observing employees doing their jobs
- Surveying customers
- Collecting network traffic
- Inventorying assets
- Collecting financial records
- Collecting insurance records
- Collecting marketing data
- Collecting regulatory mandates

After sufficient data has been collected, a detailed analysis is necessary. This is the point where a *business impact analysis (BIA)* takes place.

The BIA is an assessment of the priorities given to each asset and process within the organization. A proper analysis should consider the effect (impact) any harm to or loss of each asset might mean to the organization overall. During the BIA, special care should be paid to identifying critical paths and single points of failure. You also need to determine the costs of compliance—that is, the legislative and contractual requirements mandated for your organization. Your organization's regulatory restrictions will be based on many variables, including the jurisdictions where your organization operates, the industry the organization is in, the types and locations of your customers, and so on.

 Assets can be tangible or intangible. They can include hardware, software, intellectual property, personnel, processes, and so on. An example of tangible assets would be things like routers and servers, whereas intangible assets are generally something you cannot touch, such as software code, expressions of ideas, and business methodologies.

Cost/Benefit Analysis

Once you have a clear picture of what your organization does in terms of lines of business and processes, you can get a better understanding of what benefits the organization might derive from cloud migration as well as the costs associated with the move. Conducting a *cost/benefit analysis* helps you understand this trade-off in clear financial terms.

Obviously, the greatest driver pushing organizations toward cloud migration at the moment is perceived cost savings, and that is a significant and reasonable consideration. The next few sections describe some aspects of that consideration.

Reduction in Capital Expenditure

If your organization buys a device for use in its internal environment, the capacity of that device will either be fully utilized or (more likely) not. If the device is used at its fullest capacity, then it's quite likely that the function for which it is needed may experience inefficiencies at some point. Even a small uptick in demand for that device will overload its capacity. However, if the device is not fully utilized, then the organization has paid for something for which it is getting less than full value. The unused or excess capacity goes to waste. In effect, the organization has overpaid for the device unless it uses the device to the point where it is dangerously close to overload—you cannot buy just part of a device.

Moreover, tax benefits that can be realized from the purchase of a device have to be accrued over years of operation, as depreciation of that device/asset. With a paid service (such as cloud), an operational expenditure, the entire payment (perhaps monthly or quarterly) is tax deductible as an expense.

In the cloud, however, the organization is only paying for what it uses (regardless of the number of devices, or fractions of devices, necessary to handle the load) and no more. This is the *metered service* aspect described earlier. As a result, the organization does not overpay for these assets. However, cloud providers do have excess capacity available to be apportioned to cloud customers, so your organization is always in a position to experience increased demand (even dramatic, rapid, and significant demand) and not be overwhelmed (this is the *rapid elasticity* aspect described earlier).

One way an organization can use hosted cloud services is to augment internal, private data center capabilities with managed services during times of increased demand. We refer to this as *cloud bursting*. The organization might have data center assets it owns, but it can't handle the increased demand during times of elevated need (crisis situations, heavy holiday shopping periods, and so on), so it rents the additional capacity as needed from an external cloud provider. See Figure 1.1.

Therefore, with deployment to a cloud environment, the organization realizes cost savings immediately (not paying for unused resources) and avoids a costly risk (the possibility of loss of service due to increased demand).

Cloud Governance

Cloud services can quickly spring up all over an organization as individual business units make adoption decisions without coordinating with the IT department or other business units.

Cloud governance programs try to bring all of an organization's cloud activities under more centralized control. They serve as a screening body helping to ensure that cloud services used by the organization meet technical, functional, and security requirements. They also provide a centralized point of monitoring for duplicative services, preventing different business units from spending money on similar services when consolidation would reduce both costs and the complexity of the operating environment.

Building a centralized governance program also helps organizations avoid the use of *shadow IT*, where functional units discover and provision cloud services on their own to satisfy unmet technical needs.

FIGURE 1.1   Rapid scalability allows the customer to dictate the volume of resource usage.

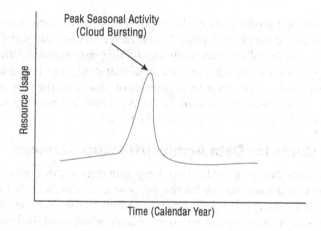

Reduction in Personnel Costs

For most organizations (other than those that deliver IT services), managing data is not a core competency, much less a profitable line of business. Data management is also a specialized skill, and people with IT experience and training are relatively expensive (compared to employees in other departments). The personnel required to fulfill the physical needs of an internal IT environment represent a significant and disproportionally large investment for the organization. In moving to the cloud, the organization can largely divest itself of a large percentage, if not a majority, of these personnel.

Reduction in Operational Costs

Maintaining and administering an internal environment takes a great deal of effort and expense. When an organization moves to the cloud, the cost becomes part of the price of the service, as calculated by the cloud provider. Therefore, costs are lumped in with the flat-rate cost of the contract and will not increase in response to enhanced operations (scheduled updates, emergency response activities, and so on).

Transferring Some Regulatory Costs

Some cloud providers may offer holistic, targeted regulatory compliance packages for their customers. For instance, the cloud provider might have a set of controls that can be applied to a given customer's cloud environment to ensure the mandates of the payment card industry (PCI) are met. Any customer wanting that package can specify so in a service contract instead of trying to delineate individual controls à la carte. In this manner, the cloud customer can decrease some of the effort and expense they might otherwise incur in trying to come up with a control framework for adhering to the relevant regulations.

 We will go into more detail about service-level agreements, or service contracts, in later chapters.

While it is possible to transfer some of the responsibilities and costs to service providers or insurance companies, it simply isn't possible to transfer all responsibility to external providers. If your organization collects *personally identifiable information (PII)*, you remain ultimately responsible for any breaches or releases of that data, even if you are using a cloud service and the breach/release results from negligence or attack on the part of the cloud provider. You might be able to transfer some of the financial risk, but you still may be subject to regulatory and/or reputational risk in the wake of a breach.

Reduction in Costs for Data Archival/Backup Services

Offsite backups are standard practice for both long-term data archival and disaster recovery purposes. Having a cloud-based service for this purpose is sensible and cost-efficient even if the organization does not conduct its regular operations in the cloud. However, moving operations into the cloud can create an economy of scale when combined with the archiving/backup usage; this can lead to an overall cost savings for the organization. It can enhance the business continuity and disaster recovery (BC/DR) strategy for the organization as well.

Intended Impact

All of these benefits can be enumerated according to dollar value: each potential cost-saving measure can be quantified. Senior management—with input from subject matter experts—needs to balance the potential financial benefits against the risks of operating in the cloud. It is this cost-benefit calculation, driven by business needs but informed by security concerns, that will allow senior management to decide whether a cloud migration of the organization's operational environment makes sense.

 Return on investment (ROI) is a term related to cost-benefit measures. It is used to describe a profitability ratio. It is generally calculated by dividing net profit by net assets.

A great many risks are associated with cloud migration as well. We will be addressing these in detail throughout this book.

Cloud Computing Service Categories

Cloud services are often offered in terms of three general categories, based on what the vendor offers and the customer needs and the responsibilities of each according to the service contract. (ISC)[2] expects you to understand these three models for testing purposes. These categories are *software as a service (SaaS)*, *infrastructure as a service (IaaS)*, and *platform as a service (PaaS)*, as shown in Figure 1.2. In the following sections, we'll review each of them in turn.

FIGURE 1.2   Cloud service categories

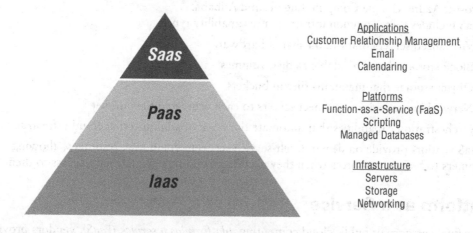

Some vendors and consultants demonstrate a lot of zeal in capitalizing on the popularity of the "cloud" concept and incorporate the word into every term they can think of in order to make their products more appealing. We see a broad proliferation of such labels as networking as a service (NaaS), compliance as a service (CaaS), and data science as a service (DSaaS), but they're mostly just marketing techniques. The only service categories you'll need to know for both the exam and your use as a practitioner are IaaS, PaaS, and SaaS.

Software as a Service

In *software as a service (SaaS)* offerings, the public cloud provider delivers an entire application to its customers. Customers don't need to worry about processing, storage, networking, or any of the infrastructure details of the cloud service. The vendor writes the application, configures the servers, and basically gets everything running for customers, who then simply use the service. Very often these services are accessed through a standard web browser, so very little, if any, configuration is required on the customer's end.

Common examples of software as a service application capability types include email delivered by Google Apps or Microsoft Office 365 and storage services that facilitate collaboration and synchronization across devices, such as Box and Dropbox. SaaS applications can also be very specialized, such as credit card processing services and travel and expense reporting management.

Infrastructure as a Service

Customers of *infrastructure as a service (IaaS)* vendors purchase basic computing resources from vendors and piece them together to create customized IT solutions. For example, IaaS vendors might provide compute capacity, data storage, and other basic infrastructure building blocks. The four largest vendors in the IaaS space are Amazon Web Services (AWS), Microsoft Azure, Google Compute Engine, and Alibaba.

IaaS includes these common infrastructure capability types:

- Virtualized servers that run on shared hardware
- Block storage that is available as disk volumes
- Object storage that maintains files in buckets
- Networking capacity to connect servers to each other and the internet
- Orchestration capabilities that automate the work of administering cloud infrastructure

IaaS vendors provide on-demand, self-service access to computing resources, allowing customers to request resources when they need them and immediately gain access to them.

Platform as a Service

In the final category of public cloud computing, *platform as a service (PaaS)*, vendors provide customers with a platform where they can run their own application code without worrying about server configuration. This is a middle ground between IaaS and SaaS. With PaaS, customers don't need to worry about managing servers but are still able to run their own code.

Function as a service (FaaS) is a common PaaS capability where the customer creates specialized functions that run either on a schedule or in response to events. Examples of FaaS offerings include AWS Lambda, Microsoft Azure Functions, and Google Cloud Functions.

Platform capability types also include cloud-based database engines and services as well as "big data"–style services, such as data warehousing and data mining. The provider offers access to the back-end engine/functionality, while the customer can create/install various apps/APIs to access the back end.

Cloud Deployment Models

Cloud deployment models describe different approaches to the way that organizations might implement cloud services. Essentially, they describe the place where the assets are hosted and who has access to them. The major cloud deployment models are private cloud, public cloud, hybrid cloud, multi-cloud, and community cloud.

Private Cloud

Organizations using the *private cloud* model want to gain the flexibility, scalability, agility, and cost effectiveness of the cloud but don't want to share computing resources with other organizations. In the private cloud approach, the organization builds and runs its own cloud infrastructure or pays another organization to do so on its behalf.

A private cloud is typified by resources dedicated to a single customer; no other customers will share the underlying resources (hardware and perhaps software). Therefore, private clouds are *not* multitenant environments.

Public Cloud

The *public cloud* uses the multitenancy model. In this approach, cloud providers build massive infrastructures in their data centers and then make those resources available to all comers. The same physical hardware may be running workloads for many different customers at the same time.

Hybrid Cloud

Organizations adopting a *hybrid cloud* approach use a combination of public and private cloud computing. In this model, they may use the public cloud for some computing workloads but they also operate their own private cloud for some workloads, often because of data sensitivity concerns.

Multi-Cloud

While many organizations pick a single public cloud provider to serve as their infrastructure partner, some choose to adopt a *multi-cloud* approach that combines resources from two or more public cloud vendors. This approach allows organizations to take advantage of service and price differences, but it comes with the cost of added complexity.

Community Cloud

Community clouds are similar to private clouds in that they are not open to the general public, but they are shared among several or many organizations that are related to each other in a common community. For example, a group of colleges and universities might get together and create a community cloud that provides shared computing resources for faculty and students at all participating schools.

Gaming communities might be considered community clouds. For instance, the PlayStation network involves many different entities coming together to engage in online gaming: Sony hosts the identity and access management (IAM) tasks for the network, a particular game company might host a set of servers that run information rights management (IRM) functions and processing for a specific game, and individual users conduct some of their own processing and storage locally on their own PlayStations. In this type of community cloud, ownership of the underlying technologies (hardware, software, and so on) is spread throughout the various members of the community.

A community cloud can also be provisioned by a third party on behalf of the various members of the community. For instance, a cloud provider might offer a FedRAMP cloud service, for use only by U.S. federal government customers. Any number of federal agencies might subscribe to this cloud service (say, the Department of Agriculture, Health and Human Services, the Department of the Interior, and so on), and they will all use underlying infrastructure that is dedicated strictly for their use. Any customer that is not a U.S. federal agency will not be allowed to use this service, as nongovernmental entities are not part of this particular community. The cloud provider owns the underlying infrastructure, but it's provisioned and made available solely for the use of the specific community.

Exam Tip

When you take the exam, you should remember that no one cloud deployment model is inherently superior to the others. Organizations may wish to use a public cloud–heavy approach to achieve greater cost savings while others may have regulatory requirements that prohibit the use of shared tenancy computing.

Multitenancy

The public cloud is built upon the operating principle of multitenancy. This simply means that many different customers share use of the same computing resources. The physical servers that support our workloads might be the same as the physical servers supporting your workloads.

In an ideal world, an individual customer should never see the impact of multitenancy. Servers should appear completely independent of each other and enforce the principle of isolation. From a privacy perspective, one customer should never be able to see data belonging to another customer. From a performance perspective, the actions that one customer takes should never impact the actions of another customer. Preserving isolation is the core crucial security task of a cloud service provider.

Multitenancy allows cloud providers to oversubscribe their resources. Almost all computing workloads vary in their needs over time. One application might have a high CPU utilization for a few hours in the morning, while another uses small peaks throughout the day and others have steady use or different peaks.

Oversubscription means that cloud providers can sell customers a total capacity that exceeds the actual physical capacity of their infrastructure because, in the big picture, customers will never use all of that capacity simultaneously. When we fit those workloads together, their total utilization doesn't ever exceed the total capacity of the environment.

Multitenancy works because of resource pooling. The memory and CPU capacity of the physical environment are shared among many different users and can be reassigned as needed.

Of course, sometimes this concept breaks down. If customers do suddenly have simultaneous demands for resources that exceed the total capacity of the environment, performance degrades. This causes slowdowns and outages. Preventing this situation is one of the key operational tasks of a cloud service provider, and they work hard to manage workload allocation to prevent this from happening.

Cloud Computing Roles and Responsibilities

In the world of cloud computing, people and organizations take on different roles and responsibilities. As a cloud security professional, it's important that you understand these different roles. The two primary roles in the world of cloud computing are those of the cloud service provider and the customer.

The *cloud service provider* is the business that offers cloud computing services for sale to third parties. The cloud service provider is responsible for building and maintaining their service offerings. Cloud service providers may do this by creating their own physical infrastructure, or they might outsource portions of their infrastructure to other cloud service providers. In that case, they are also cloud customers!

Customers are the consumers of cloud computing services. They use cloud services as the infrastructure, platforms, and/or applications that help them run their own businesses.

The relationship between the cloud service provider and the customer varies depending upon the nature, importance, and cost of the service. A customer may never interact with employees at a cloud provider, purchasing services only on a self-service basis, or a cloud provider may have dedicated account representatives who help manage the relationship with different customers.

Cloud service partners play another important role in the cloud ecosystem. These are third-party companies that offer some product or service that interacts with the primary offerings of a cloud service provider. For example, a cloud service partner might assist a company in implementing a cloud application, or it might offer a security monitoring service that provides operational assistance with using a cloud infrastructure product. Large cloud service providers commonly have a certification program that designates third-party vendors as official partners.

Regulators also play an important role in the cloud ecosystem. Different regulatory agencies may have authority over your business depending upon the locations where your organization does business and the industries in which you operate. Make sure you consult the rules published by different regulators to ensure that your use of cloud computing resources doesn't run afoul of their requirements.

Finally, the last role that we'll discuss is that of the *cloud access security broker (CASB).* These are cloud service providers who offer a managed identity and access management service to cloud customers that integrates security requirements across cloud services. We'll talk more about CASBs later in this book.

When organizations use public cloud resources, they must understand that security in the public cloud follows a shared responsibility model. Depending upon the nature of the cloud service, the cloud service provider is responsible for some areas of security while the customer is responsible for other areas. For example, if you purchase a cloud storage service, it's your responsibility to know what data you're sending to the service and probably to configure access control policies that say who may access your data. It's the provider's responsibility to encrypt data under their care and correctly implement your access control policies.

Cloud Computing Reference Architecture

The International Organization for Standardization (ISO) publishes a *cloud reference architecture* in its document ISO 17789. This document lays out a common terminology framework that assists cloud service providers, cloud service customers, and cloud service partners in communicating about roles and responsibilities.

Exam Tip

Before we dive in, it's important to note that the cloud reference architecture concepts are a helpful framework but there are no reference architecture police. You should feel free to use whatever terms and framework make sense for your organization. That said, the CCSP exam does explicitly cover the cloud reference architecture, so be sure you're familiar with it.

The reference architecture defines different cloud computing activities that are the responsibility of different organizations in the cloud ecosystem.

Let's begin by talking about the responsibilities of the cloud service customer. The reference architecture says that the following activities are the responsibilities of the customer:

- Use cloud services
- Perform service trials
- Monitor services
- Administer service security
- Provide billing and usage reports
- Handle problem reports
- Administer tenancies
- Perform business administration
- Select and purchase service
- Request audit reports

Cloud service providers have many more responsibilities:

- Prepare systems and provide cloud services
- Monitor and administer services
- Manage assets and inventories
- Provide audit data
- Manage customer relationships and handle customer requests
- Perform peering with other cloud providers
- Ensure compliance
- Provide network connectivity

Finally, cloud service partners have varying activities depending upon the type of partner:

- Design, create, and maintain service components
- Test services
- Perform audits
- Set up legal agreements
- Acquire and assess customers
- Assess the marketplace

In the real world, these activities may shift around depending upon the nature of each organization and the cloud services being provided. However, the reference architecture provides us with a starting point.

Virtualization

The world of enterprise computing has changed dramatically over the years. The advent of virtualization is one of those transformative changes and is the driving force behind cloud computing infrastructure.

It was only a few decades ago that enterprise computing was confined to the world of the data center and its mainframe. Dozens of computing professionals carefully tended to this very valuable resource that served as the organization's electronic nerve center.

Then, in the 1980s and 1990s, the enterprise IT landscape shifted dramatically. We moved away from the world of monolithic mainframes to a new environment of client-server computing. This shift brought tremendous benefits. First, it put computing power right on the desktop, allowing users to perform many actions directly on their machines without requiring mainframe access. Centralized computing improved also, by allowing the use of dedicated servers for specific functions. It became much easier to maintain data centers with discrete servers than to tend to a cranky mainframe.

Over the past decade, we've seen another shift in the computing landscape. The client-server model served us well, but it also resulted in wasted resources. Data center managers realized that most of the time, many of their servers were sitting idle, waiting for a future burst in activity. That's not very efficient. Around that same time *virtualization* technology became available that allows many different virtual servers to make use of the same underlying hardware. This shared hardware platform makes it easy to shift memory, storage, and processing power to wherever it's needed at the time. Virtualization platforms like VMware and Microsoft Hyper-V make this possible.

At a high level, virtualization platforms involve the use of a *host machine* that actually has physical hardware. That hardware then hosts several or many *virtual guest machines* that run operating systems of their own.

Hypervisors

The host machine runs special software known as a *hypervisor* to manage the guest virtual machines (VMs). The hypervisor basically tricks each guest into thinking that it is running on its own hardware when, in reality, it's running on the shared hardware of the host machine. The operating system on each guest machine has no idea that it is virtualized, so software on that guest machine can function in the same way as it would on a physical server.

There are two different types of hypervisors, as shown in Figure 1.3.

In a *Type 1 hypervisor*, also known as a bare metal hypervisor, the hypervisor runs directly on top of the hardware and then hosts guest operating systems on top of that. This is the most common form of virtualization found in data centers.

In a *Type 2 hypervisor*, the physical machine actually runs an operating system of its own and the hypervisor runs as a program on top of that operating system. This type of virtualization is commonly used on personal computers. Common hypervisors used in this scenario are VirtualBox and Parallels.

FIGURE 1.3   Type 1 and Type 2 hypervisors

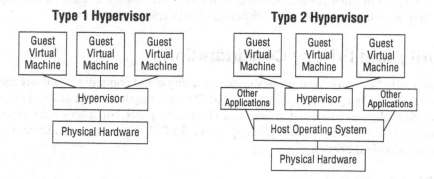

Virtualization Security

From a security perspective, virtualization introduces new concerns around VM *isolation*. In a physical server environment, security teams know that each server runs on its own dedicated processor and memory resources and that if an attacker manages to compromise the machine, they will not have access to the processor and memory used by other systems. In a virtualized environment, this may not be the case if the attacker is able to break out of the virtualized guest operating system. This type of attack is known as a *VM escape* attack.

Virtualization technology is designed to enforce isolation strictly, and the providers of virtualization technology take seriously any vulnerabilities that might allow VM escape. Security professionals working in virtualized environments should pay particular attention to any security updates that affect their virtualization platforms and apply patches promptly.

There's one other security issue associated with virtualization that you should be aware of when preparing for the exam. Virtualization makes it incredibly easy to create new servers in a data center. Administrators can usually create a new server with just a few clicks. While this is a tremendous convenience, it also leads to a situation known as *VM sprawl*, where there are large numbers of unused and abandoned servers on the network. This is not only wasteful, it's also a security risk because those servers are not being properly maintained and may accumulate serious security vulnerabilities over time if they are not properly patched.

One of the major benefits of virtualization is that it allows an organization to adopt an *ephemeral computing* strategy. *Ephemeral* just means temporary, or lasting for a short period of time. Ephemeral computing means that you can create computing resources, such as servers and storage spaces, to solve a particular problem and then get rid of them as soon as you no longer need them. If you tried to do this in the physical world, you'd be installing and removing equipment as needs change. With virtualization, you can create and destroy servers and other computing resources with the click of a button.

Cloud Shared Considerations

As you decide the appropriate ways for your organization to make use of the cloud, you should keep a set of other considerations in mind. Let's take a look at some of the important factors that organizations must consider during cloud deployment efforts.

Security and Privacy Considerations

At a high level, the security and privacy concerns facing cloud computing users are the same as those faced by any cybersecurity professional. We have the three main goals of cybersecurity: confidentiality, integrity, and availability. These three goals, commonly referred to as the CIA triad, are shown in Figure 1.4. We supplement the CIA triad with an additional goal of protecting individual privacy.

FIGURE 1.4 The CIA triad

- *Confidentiality* seeks to protect assets (information and systems) from unauthorized access.
- *Integrity* seeks to protect those same assets against unauthorized modification.
- *Availability* seeks to ensure that assets are available for authorized use when needed without disruption.

Privacy adds another dimension to these requirements by ensuring that we respect the rights of confidentiality not only of our own organization but also of the individuals whose personal information we store, process, and transmit. The presence of these goals is nothing new. We worry about the confidentiality, integrity, availability, and privacy of information wherever we use it. The only thing that changes in the world of cloud computing is that we may have more partners to include in our security planning work. This introduces three new concerns: governance, auditability, and regulatory oversight.

Cloud computing *governance* efforts help an organization work through existing and planned cloud relationships to ensure that they comply with security, legal, business, and other constraints. Most organizations set up a cloud governance structure designed to vet potential vendors, manage relationships, and oversee cloud operations. These governance structures are crucial to organizing cloud efforts and ensuring effective oversight.

Auditability is an important component of governance. Cloud computing contracts should specify that the customer has the right to audit cloud providers, either directly or through a third party. These audits may take place on a scheduled or unplanned basis, allowing the customer to gain assurance that the cloud vendor is meeting its security obligations. The audits may also include operational and financial considerations.

Finally, *regulatory oversight* exists in the cloud world, just as it does in the realm of on-premises computing. Organizations subject to HIPAA, FERPA, PCI DSS, or other cybersecurity regulations must ensure that cloud providers support their ability to remain compliant with those obligations. Some regulatory schemes include specific provisions about how organizations ensure that third-party providers remain compliant, such as using only certified providers or requiring written agreements with providers that the provider's handling of data will be consistent with regulations.

Operational Considerations

Just as the cloud raises security considerations that organizations must take into account through their governance structures, it also raises operational concerns. As with the security concerns we discussed, the operational considerations for cloud computing are quite similar to those that we encounter during on-premises operations. Let's look at a few of these considerations.

Availability and Performance

First, we mentioned availability as a security consideration, but it is also an operational consideration. One of the core measures of cloud performance is that service's availability. What percentage of the time is the service up and running and meeting customer needs?

We can increase availability by increasing our *resiliency*. Resiliency is the ability of the cloud infrastructure to withstand disruptive events. For example, we can use redundant servers to protect against the failure of a single server and we can use multiple cloud data centers to protect against the failure of an entire data center.

Performance is a closely related concept. How well can the cloud service stand up to the demands that we place on it? If we encounter an extremely busy period, will the service continue to respond at an appropriate rate?

All three of these considerations: availability, resiliency, and performance, are crucial issues to cloud operations. Customers should negotiate specific service levels with vendors during the contracting process and then document those service levels in written agreements called *service-level agreements (SLAs)*. SLAs specify the requirements that the vendor agrees to meet and commonly include financial penalties if the vendor fails to live up to operational obligations.

Maintenance and Version Control

IT teams around the world also know the importance of scheduled maintenance and *version control*. Managing change is a difficult issue in enterprise IT, and those concerns don't go away in the cloud. In fact, they become more complex because IT teams must not only coordinate their own maintenance schedules but also consider the maintenance schedules of cloud providers. Does the provider have scheduled maintenance periods? If so, IT teams must consider how those periods will impact business operations.

Version control allows organizations to manage the development of software by tracking different versions being worked on by different developers. It is an essential component of any software development program. Version control may also be used to track the configuration of systems and applications.

Outsourcing Issues

Moving to the cloud also introduces some cloud-specific operational considerations that come as a result of outsourcing parts of our IT operations. Let's talk about three of these concerns.

First, organizations moving to the cloud or between cloud vendors should consider the importance of *reversibility*. What if something goes wrong operationally, technically, or financially? How difficult would it be to restore the original operations and reverse the move? Organizations should make rollback plans part of every transition plan.

Similarly, organizations should strive to avoid *vendor lock-in* whenever possible. Portability is a design principle that says workloads should be designed so that they don't leverage vendor-specific features and may be more easily shifted between cloud providers. This isn't always possible, but it is a good design practice.

Each vendor relationship should also provide the ability to export data when required. The vendor relationship will eventually come to an end and the organization will need the ability to retrieve any business data stored with the cloud provider to support a transition to another provider or data archive.

Finally, organizations should consider the *interoperability* of cloud providers whenever adopting a new cloud solution. This is especially important for SaaS and PaaS products. IT teams are called upon to integrate solutions regularly, and the ability of a vendor to support those integrations is crucial. Imagine the impact if your expense reporting system couldn't interoperate with your financial system, or if your storage provider didn't interoperate with your web content management solution. Interoperability is crucial.

Emerging Technologies

As you prepare for the CCSP exam, you need to be familiar with a set of emerging technologies that are especially significant in the world of cloud computing.

Machine Learning and Artificial Intelligence

Machine learning is a technical discipline designed to apply the principles of data science and statistics to uncover knowledge hidden in the data that we accumulate every day. Machine learning techniques analyze data to uncover trends, categorize records, and help us run our businesses more efficiently.

Machine learning is a subset of a broader field called *artificial intelligence (AI)*. AI is a collection of techniques, including machine learning, that are designed to mimic human thought processes in computers, at least to some extent.

As we conduct machine learning, we have a few possible goals:

- *Descriptive analytics* simply seeks to describe our data. For example, if we perform descriptive analytics on our customer records, we might ask questions like, what proportion of our customers are female? And how many of them are repeat customers?

- *Predictive analytics* seek to use our existing data to predict future events. For example, if we have a dataset on how our customers respond to direct mail, we might use that dataset to build a model that predicts how individual customers will respond to a specific future mailing. That might help us tweak that mailing to improve the response rate by changing the day we send it, altering the content of the message, or even making seemingly minor changes like altering the font size or paper color.

- *Prescriptive analytics* seek to optimize our behavior by simulating many scenarios. For example, if we want to determine the best way to allocate our marketing dollars, we might run different simulations of consumer response and then use algorithms to prescribe our behavior in that context. Similarly, we might use prescriptive analytics to optimize the performance of an automated manufacturing process.

Cloud computing has revolutionized the world of machine learning. Many of the applications where we apply artificial intelligence techniques today simply wouldn't have been possible without the scalable, on-demand computing offered by the cloud. Cloud providers now offer very specialized services designed to help organizations design, build, and implement machine learning models.

Blockchain

The second emerging technology that you'll need to understand for the CCSP exam is *blockchain* technology. The blockchain is, in its simplest description, a distributed immutable ledger. This means that it can store records in a way that distributes those records among many different systems located around the world and do so in manner that prevents anyone from tampering with the records. The blockchain creates a data store that nobody can tamper with or destroy.

The first major application of the blockchain is *cryptocurrency*. The blockchain was originally invented as a foundational technology for Bitcoin, allowing the tracking of Bitcoin transactions without the use of a centralized authority. In this manner, blockchain allows the existence of a currency that has no central regulator. Authority for Bitcoin transactions is distributed among all participants in the Bitcoin blockchain. While cryptocurrency is the blockchain application that has received the most attention, there are many other uses for a distributed immutable ledger, so much so that new applications of blockchain technology seem to be appearing every day, as in the following examples:

- Property ownership records could benefit tremendously from a blockchain application. This approach would place those records in a transparent, public repository that is protected against intentional or accidental damage.

- Blockchain might also be used to track supply chains, providing consumers with confidence that their produce came from reputable sources and allowing regulators to easily track down the origin of recalled produce.

- Blockchain applications can track vital records, such as passports, birth certificates, and death certificates. The possibilities are endless.

Cloud computing enables blockchain by providing computing resources that are scalable, economically efficient, and globally distributed.

Internet of Things

The *Internet of Things (IoT)* is the third emerging technology covered on the CCSP exam. *IoT* is a term used to describe connecting nontraditional devices to the internet for data collection, analysis, and control. We see IoT applications arising in the home and workplace.

On the home front, it's hard to walk around your house or the local consumer electronics store without seeing a huge number of devices that are now called "smart this" or "smart that." We can now have in our homes a smart television, a smart garage door, and even a smart sprinkler system. All that *smart* means is that the devices are computer controlled and network connected.

IoT technology began by taking some of the more common computing devices in our homes, such as game consoles and printers, and making them first network connected and then wireless. Manufacturers quickly realized that we wanted connectivity to enable multi-player games and printing without cables and then brought this technology into the home. From there, the possibilities were endless and wireless smart devices spread throughout the home, and even into the garage with the advent of smart cars that expose in-vehicle computing systems to the drivers and passengers.

All of these devices come with security challenges as well. First, it is often difficult for the consumer to update the software on these devices. While the device may run slimmed-down versions of traditional operating systems, they don't always have displays or keyboards, so we don't see that our so-called "smart" device is actually running an outdated copy of Windows 95!

Second, these devices connect to the same wireless networks that we use for personal productivity. If a smart device is compromised, it can be a gateway to the rest of our network.

Finally, smart devices often connect back to cloud services for command and control, creating a potential pathway onto our network for external attackers that bypasses the firewall.

Containers

Containers are the next evolution of virtualization. They're a lightweight way to package up an entire application and make it portable so that it can easily move between hardware platforms.

In traditional virtualization, we have hardware that supports a hypervisor and then that hypervisor supports guest virtual machines. Each of those guest machines runs its own operating system and applications, allowing the applications to function somewhat independently of the hardware. You can move a virtual machine from hardware to hardware, as long as the machines are running the same hypervisor. One of the downsides to traditional virtualization is that virtual machines are somewhat heavy. Each one has to have its own operating system and components. If you're running 10 different Windows virtual servers on a hypervisor, you have the overhead of running 10 different copies of Windows at the same time.

Containerization seeks to reduce this burden by building more lightweight packages. Containers package up application code in a standardized format so that it can be easily shifted between systems. Instead of running a hypervisor, systems supporting containers run a containerization platform. This platform provides a standard interface to the operating system that allows containers to function regardless of the operating system and hardware. The major benefit of containers over virtual machines is that they don't have their own operating systems kernel. The containerization platform allows them to use the host's operating system kernel.

From a security perspective, containers share many of the same considerations as virtualized systems. The containerization platform must strictly enforce isolation to ensure that containers cannot access the data or resources allocated to other containers. As long as this isolation remains intact, containers are a highly secure option for lightweight virtualized computing.

Quantum Computing

Quantum computing is an area of advanced theoretical research in computer science and physics. The theory is that we can use principles of quantum mechanics to replace the binary 1 and 0 bits of digital computing with multidimensional quantum bits known as qubits.

Exam Tip

Quantum computing is one of the emerging technologies that you need to be familiar with for the CCSP exam, but honestly, there's not much that you need to know. That's because, as of today, quantum computers are confined to theoretical research. Nobody has yet developed a practical implementation of a useful quantum computer.

If practical quantum computers do come on the scene, they have the potential to revolutionize the world of computer science by providing the technological foundation for the most powerful computers ever developed. Those computers would quickly upend many of the principles of modern cybersecurity. For example, it is possible that a quantum computer could render all modern cryptography completely ineffective and require the redesign of new, stronger quantum cryptography algorithms. But that's all theory for now. Unless you're a research physicist, there won't be much impact of quantum computing on your world for the foreseeable future.

Edge and Fog Computing

The emergence of the Internet of Things is also dramatically changing the way that we provision and use computing. We see the most dramatic examples of the Internet of Things in our everyday lives, from connected and semiautonomous vehicles to smart home devices that improve the way we live and travel.

However, many of the applications of the Internet of Things occur out of sight. Industrial applications of IoT are transforming manufacturing. We're seeing the rise of microsatellites that bring scientific instruments and other devices into Earth orbit and beyond. Even agriculture is changing dramatically with the sensors, information, and analytics that IoT makes possible.

The cloud computing model doesn't always fit these applications. When your sensors are far away from cloud data centers and either not connected to a network or connected by very low bandwidth connections, the model starts to break down. It simply doesn't make sense to transfer all of the data back to the cloud and have it processed there.

Edge computing is an approach that brings many of the advances of the cloud to the edge of our networks. It involves placing processing power directly on remote sensors and allowing them to perform the heavy lifting required to process data before transmitting a small subset of that data back to the cloud.

Fog computing is a related concept that involves placing gateway devices out in the field to collect information from sensors and perform that correlation centrally, but still at the remote location, before returning data to the cloud. Together, edge and fog computing promise to increase our ability to connect IoT devices and the cloud.

Confidential Computing

Confidential computing is a new and emerging focus for organizations operating in extremely secure environments, such as the military and defense sector. It extends security throughout the entire computing process.

Let's take a look at what this means. In a normal client-server computing model, we have a client that might want to request that a server take some action on the client's behalf. That server might have to access some data that is maintained in a separate storage environment and then perform some processing on that data.

In a traditional computing model, we know that we need to add some security to this process. We apply encryption to the data that is kept on the storage devices so that unauthorized individuals can't access it. That's called protecting data at rest. We also add encryption to network communications to prevent eavesdropping attacks between the client and the server and between the server and storage. That's called protecting data in motion.

However, we generally don't worry about the data that's being actively processed by the server. We don't apply encryption to data in memory, which is known as data in use.

Confidential computing adds protection for code and data in memory. It does this by offering *trusted execution environments (TEEs)*. These trusted environments guarantee that no outside process can view or alter the data being handled within the environment. That provides an added assurance that data is safe through all stages of the computing lifecycle.

DevOps and DevSecOps

IT organizations around the world are quickly embracing the *DevOps* philosophy to improve the interactions between software developers and technology operations teams. The DevOps movement seeks to combine two worlds that have often found themselves in conflict in the past.

Software developers are charged with creating code: building applications and integrations that meet the needs of customers and the business. They are motivated to rapidly release code and meet those demands.

IT operations staff are charged with maintaining the infrastructure and keeping the enterprise stable. They are often wary of change because change brings the possibility of instability. This makes them nervous when developers seek to rapidly deploy new code.

The DevOps movement seeks to bring these two disciplines together in a partnership. DevOps seeks to build collaborative relationships between developers and operators with open communication. The DevOps movement embraces automation as an enabler of both development and operations. DevOps practitioners seek to create the environment where developers can rapidly release new code, while operations staff can provide a stable environment.

The DevOps philosophy is often tightly linked to the *agile software development methodology*. While they are two different concepts, they are deeply related to each other. Developers following these strategies seek to implement a continuous integration software development approach where they can quickly release software updates, creating multiple software releases each day, sometimes even releasing hundreds of updates in a single day.

Cloud computing is one of the enabling technologies for DevOps environments. Specifically, DevOps shops embrace a concept known as *infrastructure as code (IaC)*. In this approach, operations teams no longer manually configure servers and other infrastructure components by logging in and modifying their configurations directly. Instead, they write scripts that specify how to start with a baseline configuration image and then customize it to meet the specific requirements of the situation. For example, an organization might have a standard baseline for a Linux system. When someone needs a new server, they write a script that starts a server using the baseline configuration and then automatically configures it to meet the specific functional needs.

Infrastructure as code separates server configuration from specific physical or virtual servers. This has some clear advantages for the organization.

- **IaC enables scalability.** If the organization needs more servers, the code can create as many as necessary extremely rapidly.

- **IaC reduces user error through the use of immutable servers.** This means that engineers don't ever log into or modify servers directly. If they need to make a change, they modify the code and create new servers.

- **IaC makes testing easy.** Developers can write code for new servers and spin up a fully functional test environment without affecting production. Once they've verified that the new code works properly, they can move it to production and destroy the old servers.

The DevOps approach to IT provides many different benefits to the organization. Security teams can also benefit from this approach by using security automation techniques. There's no reason that cybersecurity teams can't embrace the DevOps philosophy and build security infrastructure and analysis tools using an infrastructure as code approach.

When DevOps is used in a cybersecurity program, it is often referred to as *DevSecOps* and introduces a "security as code" approach to cybersecurity. As organizations move to DevOps strategies, cybersecurity teams will need to evolve their practices to provide value in this new operating environment.

Summary

In this chapter, we have examined business requirements, cloud definitions, cloud computing roles and responsibilities, and foundational concepts of cloud computing. This chapter has provided an introductory foundation for these topics. We will explore each of them in more detail as we move ahead.

Exam Essentials

Explain the different roles in cloud computing.   Cloud service providers offer cloud computing services for sale. Cloud service customers purchase these services and use them to meet their business objectives. Cloud service partners assist cloud service customers in implementing the services they purchase from providers. Cloud access service brokers offer an intermediary layer of security for cloud users. Regulators define requirements for operating in the cloud with sensitive data.

Identify the key characteristics of cloud computing.   The key characteristics of cloud computing are on-demand self-service, broad network access, multitenancy, rapid elasticity and scalability, resource pooling, and measured service.

Explain the three cloud service categories.   The three cloud service categories are software as a service (SaaS), infrastructure as a service (IaaS), and platform as a service (PaaS). In a SaaS offering, the provider runs a complete application in the cloud that is sold to customers.

In IaaS offerings, the provider sells technology building blocks to customers, who assemble their own solutions. In PaaS offerings, the provider sells an environment where customers may run their own code.

Describe the five cloud deployment models.   Public cloud deployments use multitenancy to provide services to many customers on shared hardware. Private cloud environments use hardware that is dedicated to a single customer. Hybrid cloud environments make use of both public and private cloud services. Community clouds are dedicated to a group of customers with a shared characteristic. Some organizations choose to combine cloud services from several providers in a multi-cloud deployment.

Identify important related technologies.   Cloud computing benefits from and serves several related technologies. These include data science, machine learning, artificial intelligence, blockchain, the Internet of Things, containers, quantum computing, edge computing, fog computing, confidential computing, and DevSecOps.

Explain the shared considerations in the cloud.   As organizations decide whether to use cloud services, they must analyze several important considerations. These include interoperability, portability, reversibility, availability, security, privacy, resiliency, performance, governance, maintenance and versioning, service levels and service-level agreements, auditability, regulatory concerns, and the impact of outsourcing.

Review Questions

You can find the answers to the review questions in Appendix A.

1. Which of the following is *not* a common cloud service model?

    A. Software as a service (SaaS)

    B. Programming as a service (PaaS)

    C. Infrastructure as a service (IaaS)

    D. Platform as a service (PaaS)

2. Which one of the following emerging technologies, if fully implemented, would jeopardize the security of current encryption technology?

    A. Quantum computing

    B. Blockchain

    C. Internet of Things

    D. Confidential computing

3. Cloud vendors are held to contractual obligations with specified metrics by _____.

    A. Service-level agreements (SLAs)

    B. Regulations

    C. Law

    D. Discipline

4. _____ drive security decisions.

    A. Customer service responses

    B. Surveys

    C. Business requirements

    D. Public opinion

5. If a cloud customer cannot get access to the cloud provider, this affects what portion of the CIA triad?

    A. Integrity

    B. Authentication

    C. Confidentiality

    D. Availability

6. You recently worked with a third-party vendor to help you implement a SaaS offering provided by a different company. Which one of the following cloud service roles is not represented here?

   A. Regulator

   B. Customer

   C. Provider

   D. Partner

7. Which of the following hypervisor types is most likely to be seen in a cloud provider's data center?

   A. Type 1

   B. Type 2

   C. Type 3

   D. Type 4

8. All of these are reasons an organization may want to consider cloud migration except _____.

   A. Reduced personnel costs

   B. Elimination of risks

   C. Reduced operational expenses

   D. Increased efficiency

9. The generally accepted definition of cloud computing includes all of the following characteristics except _____.

   A. On-demand self-service

   B. Negating the need for backups

   C. Resource pooling

   D. Measured or metered service

10. You are working on a governance project designed to make sure the different cloud services used in your organization work well together. What goal are you attempting to achieve?

    A. Performance

    B. Resiliency

    C. Reversibility

    D. Interoperability

11. The risk that a customer might not be able to switch cloud providers at a later date is known as _____.

    A. Vendor closure

    B. Vendor lock-out

    C. Vendor lock-in

    D. Vendor synchronization

12. All of these are characteristics of cloud computing except _____.

    A. Broad network access

    B. Diminished elasticity

    C. Rapid scaling

    D. On-demand self-service

13. When a cloud customer uploads personally identifiable information (PII) to a cloud provider, who is ultimately responsible for the security of that PII?

    A. Cloud provider

    B. Regulators

    C. Cloud customer

    D. The individuals who are the subjects of the PII

14. We use which of the following to determine the critical paths, processes, and assets of an organization?

    A. Business requirements

    B. Business impact analysis (BIA)

    C. Risk Management Framework (RMF)

    D. Confidentiality, integrity, availability (CIA) triad

15. If an organization owns all of the hardware and infrastructure of a cloud data center that is used only by members of that organization, which cloud deployment model would this be?

    A. Private

    B. Public

    C. Hybrid

    D. Motive

16. The cloud deployment model that features ownership by a cloud provider, with services offered to anyone who wants to subscribe, is known as _____.

    A. Private

    B. Public

    C. Hybrid

    D. Latent

17. The cloud deployment model that features joint ownership of assets among an affinity group is known as _____.

    A. Private

    B. Public

    C. Hybrid

    D. Community

18. You are concerned that an attacker might be able to use a guest virtual machine to gain access to the underlying hypervisor. What term describes this threat?

    A. VM escape

    B. SQL injection

    C. Man-in-the-middle

    D. VM sprawl

19. You are considering purchasing an e-commerce system where the cloud provider runs a hosted application on their own servers. What cloud service category is the provider offering?

    A. IaaS

    B. PaaS

    C. SaaS

    D. FaaS

20. If a cloud customer wants to build their own computing environment using storage, net-working, and compute resources offered by a cloud provider, which cloud service category would probably be best?

    A. IaaS

    B. PaaS

    C. SaaS

    D. FaaS

Chapter

2

Data Classification

THE OBJECTIVE OF THIS CHAPTER IS TO ACQUAINT THE READER WITH THE FOLLOWING CONCEPTS:

✓ **Domain 1: Cloud Concepts, Architecture, and Design**

- 1.3. Understand security concepts relevant to cloud computing
  - 1.3.3. Data and media sanitization

✓ **Domain 2: Cloud Data Security**

- 2.1. Describe cloud data concepts
  - 2.1.1. Cloud data lifecycle phases
  - 2.1.3. Data flows
- 2.2. Design and Implement Cloud Data Storage Architectures
  - 2.2.1. Storage Types (e.g., long-term, ephemeral, raw storage)
  - 2.2.2. Threats to storage types
- 2.3. Design and apply data security technologies and strategies
  - 2.3.1. Encryption and key management
  - 2.3.2. Hashing
  - 2.3.3. Data Obfuscation (e.g., masking, anonymization)
  - 2.3.4. Tokenization
  - 2.3.5. Data Loss Prevention (DLP)
  - 2.3.6. Keys, secrets, and certificates management
- 2.4. Implement data discovery
  - 2.4.1. Structured data
  - 2.4.2. Unstructured data
  - 2.4.3. Semi-Structured data
  - 2.4.4. Data location
- 2.5. Plan and implement data classification
  - 2.5.1. Data classification policies

Data is an asset. As with all other assets, knowing what data you have and where it is (logically and physically) as well as its relative value and need for protection is essential for properly leveraging security resources. In this chapter, you will see how data is categorized and classified, why the location of the data matters, how information rights management tools are used to protect data, data control, data retention, and deletion requirements.

Data Inventory and Discovery

In the previous chapter, we discussed the importance of creating an asset inventory; part of that effort will require identifying all the data owned by the organization. Knowing where your data is, who owns it, what can be done with it, and what its lifecycle looks like is important to managing data throughout an organization.

We will cover the full cloud data lifecycle in Chapter 3, "Cloud Data Security." For now, you'll want to keep in mind that data is created and used in an organization before eventually being disposed of and that life-cycle relies on data classification and rights management to succeed.

Data Ownership

In order to properly handle and control data, one of the most important steps is to assign responsibilities according to who has possession and legal ownership of it. Those responsibilities are commonly associated with named roles. While organizations may define these terms and names for themselves, they may also be defined in specific ways in laws, regulations, and contracts.

The following terms are commonly used to describe data ownership:

- The *data owner* is the organization that has collected or created the data, in general terms. Within the organization, we often assign a specific data owner as being the individual with rights and responsibilities for that data; this is usually the department head or business unit manager for the office that has created or collected a certain data-set. From a cloud perspective, the cloud customer is usually the data owner. Many international treaties and frameworks refer to the data owner as the *data controller*.

- The *data custodian* is any person or entity that is tasked with the daily maintenance and administration of the data. The custodian also has the role of applying the proper security controls and processes as directed by the data owner. Within an organization, the custodian might be a database administrator.

- *Data stewards* are tasked with ensuring that the data's context and meaning are understood, and they use that knowledge to make certain the data they are responsible for is used properly.

- The *data processor* is any organization or person who manipulates, stores, or moves the data on behalf of the data owner. *Processing* is anything that can be done to data: copying it, printing it, destroying it, utilizing it. From an international law perspective, the cloud provider is a data processor.

Here are essential points to remember about the rights and responsibilities of data ownership and custody:

- Data processors do not necessarily all have direct relationships with data owners; processors can be third parties, or even further removed down the supply chain.

- Data owners remain legally responsible for all data they own. This is true even if data is compromised by a data processor several times removed from the data owner.

- Ownership, custody, rights, responsibilities, and liability are all relative to the dataset in question and therefore are only specific to certain data in certain circumstances. For instance, a cloud provider is usually the data processor for a cloud customer's data, but the provider is the data owner for information that the provider collects and creates, such as the provider's own customer list, asset inventory, and billing information.

- System owners are not necessarily data owners. Cloud providers may be system owners for the underlying infrastructure, but may not be responsible for the data resident on those systems.

 The European Union's General Data Protection Regulation (GDPR) describes data controllers and data processors as well as specific roles like that of a data protection officer. If you're concerned about GDPR compliance, make sure you know the specific definitions it uses. (See www .gdpreu.org/the-regulation/key-concepts.)

Data Categorization

Data owners are in the best position to understand how data is going to be used by the organization. This allows the data owner to appropriately categorize the data. Organizations can have any number of categories or types of information; these might be clearly defined and reused throughout the organization, or they might be arbitrarily assigned by data owners when data is created. Categorization is commonly driven by one or more of the following:

Regulatory Compliance   Different business activities are governed by different regulations. The organization may want to create categories based on which regulations or requirements apply to a specific dataset. This might include the Graham–Leach–Bliley

Act (GLBA), the Payment Card Industry Data Security Standard (PCI DSS), Sarbanes–Oxley (SOX), Health Insurance Portability and Accountability Act (HIPAA), the EU's General Data Protection Regulation (GDPR), or other international, national, state, or local requirements.

Business Function   The organization might want to have specific categories for different uses of data. Perhaps the data is tagged based on its use in billing, marketing, or operations; by types of customers; or by some other functional requirement or descriptor.

Functional Unit   Each department or office might have its own category and keep all data it controls within its own category.

By Project   Some organizations might define datasets by the projects they are associated with as a means of creating discrete, compartmentalized projects.

Whatever categorization method the organization uses should be adopted and enforced uniformly throughout the organization. Ad hoc categorization can lead to gaps that result in security, compliance, or other issues for the organization and may lead to breaches or data loss.

Data Classification

Much like categorization, data classification is the responsibility of the data owner and is assigned according to an overall organizational policy based on a specific characteristic of a given dataset. The classification, like the categorization, can take any form defined by the organization and should be uniformly applied.

Types of classification might include the following:

Sensitivity   This is the classification model used by the U.S. military. Data is assigned a classification according to its sensitivity, based on the negative impact an unauthorized disclosure would cause. In models of this kind, classification must be assigned to all data, even in the negative, so material that is not deemed to be sensitive must be assigned the "unclassified" label. We will discuss labeling shortly.

Jurisdiction   The geophysical location of the source or storage point of the data might have significant bearing on how that data is treated and handled. For instance, personally identifiable information (PII) data gathered from citizens of the European Union (EU) is subject to the EU privacy laws, which are much stricter and more comprehensive than privacy laws in the United States.

Criticality   Data that is deemed critical to organizational survival might be classified in a manner distinct from trivial, basic operational data. As we know from the previous chapter, the business impact analysis (BIA) helps us determine which material would be classified this way.

There are no industry-defined, statutory-mandated definitions for *categorization* versus *classification* of data, except in those areas covered by specific regulations (for instance, the U.S. military uses classification constructs defined by federal law). The terms can often be used interchangeably. For the purpose of this book, data is categorized by its use and classified by a certain trait. It is worth noting that (ISC)² does not create a specific distinction between the terms.

Data Classification Policies

Data classification is often based on organizational policies. Policies will typically help to identify classification levels that the organization wishes to use, particularly those specified by regulations or contracts. They may assign responsibilities and define roles and are an important part of organizational data governance. They are also an important tool when organizations consider automated tools to support classification, since they provide the foundation for classification processes.

Data Mapping

Data that is shared organizations (or sometimes even between departments) must be normalized and translated so that it conforms in a way that's meaningful to both parties. This is typically referred to as *data mapping*. When used in the context of classification efforts, mapping is necessary so that data that is known as sensitive (and in need of protection) in one system/organization is recognized as such by the receiving system/organization so that those protections can continue. Without proper mapping efforts, data classified at a specific level might be exposed to undue risk or threats.

Data mapping can be manual, automated, or somewhere in between, but regardless of how you approach it, it is important to ensure that data classifications and labels are carried through the mapping to ensure that data that is used in another context does not lose its security controls and oversight.

An increasing number of privacy-based regulations now require data mapping. That means you may be legally required to identify data like PII to meet compliance requirements. Examples of laws that include data mapping requirements include the European Union's General Data Protection Regulation (GDPR) as well as California's Consumer Privacy Act of 2018.

Data Labeling

When the data owner creates, categorizes, and classifies the data, the data also needs to be labeled. The label should indicate who the data owner is, usually in terms of the office or role instead of an individual name or identity (because, of course, personnel can change roles within an organization or leave for other organizations). The label should take whatever form is necessary for it to be enduring, understandable, and consistent; for instance, while labels on data in hard copy might be printed headers and footers, labels on electronic files might be embedded in the filename or added as metadata.

The need to create persistent data labels can be a challenge when data is moved through different services and transformations. As you read the next section about data flow diagrams, consider how you might carry data labels forward through data usage patterns in your own organization, including between disparate services and cloud providers.

Labels should be evident and communicate the pertinent concepts without necessarily disclosing the data they describe.

Depending on the needs of the organization and the nature of its operations, labels might include the following kinds of information:

- Date of creation
- Date of scheduled destruction/disposal
- Confidentiality level
- Handling directions
- Dissemination/distribution instructions
- Access limitations
- Source
- Jurisdiction
- Applicable regulation

Labels are often used as part of data management tools to allow lifecycle controls as well as to support security controls like data loss prevention systems. While labels can be intentionally removed, using labels consistently, especially for sensitive data, can have a significant impact on your organization's ability to handle data appropriately.

That also means that automated labeling is a key technology component and capability in the data lifecycle—both at creation and in use when data may be modified or combined with other data, resulting in a need to update data labels on the resulting output.

 Real World Scenario

Labels Work Both Ways

Labels can aid in security efforts by readily indicating the nature of certain information and how it should be handled and protected. For instance, in the U.S. military and federal government, classified data in hard copy is labeled in a number of ways, including the use of cover sheets. Cover sheets convey only one characteristic of the data: the sensitivity of the material (in military taxonomy, this is called *classification*, with a somewhat different meaning than that used in this book). Sensitivity is indicated in at least two ways: the title of the class (e.g., Secret, Top Secret) in large, bold letters, and the color of the sheet and markings (blue for Confidential, red for Secret, and so forth). This reminds the user (the person carrying or reading the documents) in a very simple way how to secure the material when it is not in use or is unattended. It also informs anyone else how to react if they come across such material unattended; a manager leaving the office at the end of the workday might do one last walk-through of the workspace, and a red cover sheet left on a desk will immediately catch the eye.

Of course, this also has the same effect for malicious actors. The cover sheet lets someone with ill intent instantly know the potential value of specific material: the pages with the red cover sheet are more valuable than the ones with the blue cover sheet.

Data Flows

Figure 2.1 shows an example of the type of *data flow diagram* you might prepare for a cloud service environment. In this simplified model, an account is created and data is sent to an analytics platform where everything but the password is used to conduct data analysis and reporting for the organization. At the same time, key user information is sent to an account renewal system that sends notifications when subscriptions are expiring. If the account is not renewed, the organization will use the canceled account process that removes some data from the active accounts list but is likely to retain things like the UserID and other data in case the subscriber chooses to resubscribe in the future.

FIGURE 2.1   Simplified data flow diagram for a cloud service account lifecycle

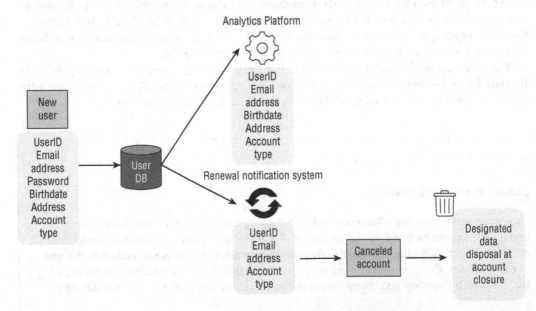

Data flow diagrams like this help organizations track where their data is flowing, what ports and protocols are in use, how data is secured, and what controls are in place. A more complex diagram would show how the data is transferred, such as via an HTTPS encrypted connection between web services or a native SQL query to the user database. It may also include details about security devices or services, key service accounts, and other information that will fully describe where and how data flows through the organization.

It is important to remember that data flow diagrams may include third-party services and systems and that you may need to document what data exits your organization or comes into it through those third-party services and systems. As you document data flows, you'll need to ensure they are complete and don't simply end at your organization's borders.

Data Discovery Methods

To determine and accurately inventory the data under its control, the organization can employ various tools and techniques. *Data discovery* is a term that can be used to refer to several kinds of tasks: it might mean that the organization is attempting to create that initial inventory of data it owns or that the organization is involved in electronic discovery (*e-discovery*, the legal term for how electronic evidence is collected as part of an investigation or lawsuit; we'll discuss this in more depth in Chapter 9, "Legal and Compliance Issues"), and it can also mean the modern use of data mining tools to discover trends and relations in the data already in the organization's inventory.

Label-Based Discovery

Obviously, the labels created by data owners will greatly aid any data discovery effort. With accurate and sufficient labels, the organization can readily determine what data it controls and what amounts of each kind. This is another reason the habit and process of labeling is so important.

Labels can be especially useful when the discovery effort is undertaken in response to a mandate with a specific purpose, such as a court order or a regulatory demand: if all data related to X is required, and all such data is readily labeled, it is easy to collect and disclose all the appropriate data, and only the appropriate data.

Metadata-Based Discovery

In addition to labels, metadata can be useful for discovery purposes. Colloquially referred to as "data about data," metadata is a listing of traits and characteristics about specific data elements or sets. Metadata is often automatically created at the same time as the data, often by the hardware or software used to create the parent data. For instance, most modern digital cameras create a vast amount of metadata every time a photograph is taken, such as date, time, and location where the photo was shot, make and model of the camera, and so forth; all that metadata is embedded in the picture file and is copied and transferred whenever the image itself is copied or moved.

Data discovery can therefore use metadata in the same way labels might be used; specific fields of the metadata might be scanned for particular terms and all matching data elements collected for a certain purpose.

 Labels are often a type of metadata, so it's important to remember that these discovery methods may overlap.

Content-Based Discovery

Even without labels or metadata, discovery tools can be used to locate and identify specific kinds of data by delving into the content of datasets. This technique can be as basic as term searches or can use sophisticated pattern-matching technology.

 Content analysis can also be used for more specific security controls as well as discovery; we will discuss egress monitoring solutions in Chapter 3.

Structured, Semi-Structured, and Unstructured Data

Data that is sorted according to meaningful, discrete types and attributes, such as data in a relational database, is said to be *structured data*. Unsorted data (such as the content of various emails in a user's Sent folder, which could include discussions of any topic or contain all types of content) is considered *unstructured data*. It is typically much easier to perform data discovery actions on structured data because that data is already situated and arranged.

Semi-structured data uses tags or other elements to create fields and records within data without requiring the rigid structure that structured data relies on. Examples of semi-structured data include XML (extensible markup language) and JSON (JavaScript object notation), both of which provide flexible structures that still allow data descriptions. An increasing number of databases rely on semi-structured data formats like JSON. MongoDB is one example of a commonly encountered database that uses JSON. Much like structured data, semi-structured data is easier to perform data discovery on, but it can be more challenging than structured data due to the flexibility of semi-structured data.

XML's structure will look familiar if you have worked with HTML before, as shown in the following brief code example. You can see that the XML has some structure but that it is not rigidly defined. Markup is used, but there is more flexibility than a database table might have.

```
<menu id="example" value="example">
  <popup>
    <menuitem value="action1" onclick="action1()" />
    <menuitem value="action2" onclick="action2()" />
    <menuitem value="action3" onclick="action3() />
  </popup>
</menu>
```

Since XML is very flexible, not all XML code you encounter will look exactly like the preceding example. In the context of the CCSP exam, you need to understand the difference between structured data, semi-structured data like XML, and unstructured data.

Data Locations and Data Discovery

Data locations can create a number of challenges when you're conducting data discovery. Laws and regulations may limit the types or methods of discovery you can engage in, or what you can do with the data, as well as where and how you can store it. The EU's General Data Protection Regulation (GDPR) has requirements that impact where and how you store data and thus may have an impact on discovery, and other regulations may also apply, depending on your organization's compliance requirements.

Data location can also create technical hurdles to discovery. If data is stored in unstructured form, or in a service that handles data in ways that make it challenging to conduct discovery, you may have to design around those constraints. Location can also have a bearing on costs because cloud ingress and egress costs can vary greatly, potentially impacting both where you process data and whether you transfer it or process it in place.

It will be far easier to conduct some types of discovery actions against traditional databases containing structured data. Unstructured data with data embedded inside of it, like freeform text from customers, can require far more complex queries, which is more likely to result in missed data. Semi-structured data like log files or JSON-based databases may be relatively simple or may have additional complexity depending on the data and how it is created and structured.

All of this means that you need to understand where data is located, what type of data you are dealing with, and what the goals of discovery are. Understanding the type of data usage and how it will be analyzed are key to both designing and securing data discovery and usage models.

Data Analytics and Data Discovery

Data analytic systems and tools can provide additional ways to perform data discovery. In many cases, these tools create new data feeds from sets of data that already exist within the environment, often in automated or semi-automated ways. That means you'll need to consider how to handle data labeling, classification, and all of the other tasks you'd normally undertake for other datasets with these datasets as well. Common types of data analytics methods include the following:

Data Mining The term for the family of activities from which the other options on this list derive. This kind of data analysis is an outgrowth of the possibilities offered by regular use of the cloud, also known as "big data." When the organization has collected various data streams and can run queries across these various feeds, it can detect and analyze previously unknown trends and patterns that can be extremely useful.

Real-Time Analytics In some cases, tools can provide data mining functionality concurrently with data creation and use. These tools rely on automation and require efficiency to perform properly.

Business Intelligence State-of-the-art data mining involves recursive, iterative tools and processes that can detect trends in trends and identify even more oblique patterns in both historical and recent data.

Information Rights Management

You've likely heard the term *DRM*, or digital rights management. DRM is used to control access to digital data, attempting to ensure that rights holders and owners can decide who modifies, shares, or accesses the files and media it is used to protect. *Information rights management (IRM)* is used to describe the application of digital rights management tools and techniques to files created by individuals and is typically focused on protecting the information contained in the documents rather than who can watch a movie or play a video game.

 Other terms used to describe rights management tools include *enterprise rights management (ERM)*, *document rights management* (confusingly also using *DRM* as an acronym), and *intelligent rights management* (another *IRM* acronym) as well as offshoots such as *E-DRM* for *electronic-digital rights management*. There is no conclusive international or industry standard defining these terms or how they might be applied in a given process or tool, so what organizations and vendors call them may vary based on their application, marketing, or purpose.

In broad terms, rights management tools rely on the use of specific controls that act either with or in addition to the organization's other access control mechanisms to protect certain types of assets, usually at the file level. For example, an organization might have an overall access control program that requires users to log in to the systems that they use for performing job functions. Beyond that basic access, specific files the users manipulate, such as sensitive financial documents, might have additional protections for "rights management" that prevent the users from deleting, modifying, or copying those files.

The CCSP exam focuses on three IRM objectives that you'll need to be prepared to consider from a design and implementation perspective:

Data Rights Rights describe the actions that authorized users can take on a given asset and how those rights are set, applied, modified, and removed. Typical rights match those for other file types you're already familiar with: creating, editing, copying, viewing or accessing, printing, forwarding, and deleting are all things that are commonly controlled by IRM tools. Forwarding may stand out because IRM tools may be applied to email and other communications tools, and you'll want to think about IRM as a tool to control data throughout its lifecycle.

Provisioning Provisioning rights for users in IRM systems is critical to ensuring that use of IRM does not disrupt the business while still being effective for rights management. Roles and groups need to be created and used in most cases to ensure IRM can be used broadly. Granular permissions and detailed control of rights adds complexity, so security administrators must consider the impact of the rights decisions they make and whether they can be managed on a broad scale via provisioning processes, particularly for new users.

Access Models   The access model your organization uses for IRM protected files is a critical part of the design and implementation. If files are provided via a web application, you may need to ensure that protections are in place to prevent copy and paste from the web application, or to prevent screenshots from being used to extract information. If you use file-based tools like SharePoint, encrypting the files and ensuring that they are paired with license files that describe what can and cannot be done with them and who can perform those actions will be the route you need to take. Thus, as a test taker, you should consider the access models in use for the data as part of IRM design.

Certificates and IRM

One common method of identifying both users and computers in an IRM system is to issue certificates and licenses. Licenses describe the rights the users have to the content they are attached to, and certificates are used to validate the identity of the user or computer. Using a central certificate management system to issue and revoke certificates, and then providing a way to check the certificate status for every certificate as needed, is a key part of this.

IRM in the Cloud

Information rights management capabilities exist natively in many cloud platforms. While there are many options, it can help to look at an example to understand what an IRM tool can provide inside of a vendor's platform In Azure, IRM can be found in tools like the SharePoint administration center, where Azure Rights Management allows you to control document libraries, lists, and a range of supported file types. The tool encrypts files, allowing only authorized users to view them, and each file uses licensing information included with it to determine what rights individuals have on the file.

   As you would expect, IRM attached to files requires local clients or web applications that can decrypt the file and that support the rights management capabilities and requirements that the IRM system provides.

IRM Tool Traits

IRM can be implemented in enterprises by manufacturers, vendors, or content creators. Material protected by IRM solutions typically requires labeling or metadata associated with the material in order for the IRM tool to function properly in an automated or semiautomatic fashion.

IRM implementations can vary in technological sophistication and technique. Here are some ways that IRM has been or could be applied:

Rudimentary Reference Checks   The content itself can automatically check for proper usage or ownership. For instance, in many vintage computer games, the game would pause in operation until the player entered some information that could only have been acquired with the purchase of a licensed copy of the game, like a word or a phrase from the manual that shipped with the game.

Online Reference Checks   Microsoft software packages, including Windows operating systems and Office programs, are often locked in the same manner, requiring users to enter a product key at installation; the program would then later check the product key against an online database when the system connected to the Internet.

Local Agent Checks   The user installs a reference tool that checks the protected content against the user's license. Again, gaming engines often work this way, with gamers having to download an agent of Steam or GOG.com when installing any games purchased from those distributors; the agents check the user's system against the online license database to ensure the games are not pirated.

Support-Based Licensing   Some IRM implementations are predicated on the need for continual support for content; this is particularly true of production software. Licensed software might be allowed ready access to updates and patches, while the vendor could prevent unlicensed versions from getting this type of support.

IRM implementations often include another layer of access control (beyond what the enterprise employs for its own operational purposes) on files and objects containing protected material. IRM can also be used to implement localized information security policies; specific users or groups of users might have all content they create specially tagged and marked with appropriate access restrictions, for instance.

Employing IRM in the cloud rather than in a locally hosted environment can introduce additional challenges:

- **Replication restrictions:** Because IRM often involves preventing unauthorized duplication, and the cloud necessitates creating, closing, and replicating virtualized host instances (including user-specific content stored locally on the virtual host), IRM might interfere with automatic resource allocation processes.

- **Jurisdictional conflicts:** The cloud extends across boundaries and borders, which can pose problems when intellectual property rights are restricted by locale.

- **Agent/enterprise conflicts:** IRM solutions that require local installation of software agents for enforcement purposes might not always function properly in the cloud environment, with virtualization engines, or with the various platforms used in a bring your own device (BYOD) enterprise.

- **Mapping Identity and Access Management (IAM) and IRM:** Because of the extra layer of access control (often involving content-specific access control lists, or ACLs), the IRM

IAM processes might conflict or not work properly with the enterprise/cloud IAM. A conflict is even more possible when cloud IAM functions are outsourced to a third party, such as a cloud access security broker (CASB).

- **API conflicts:** Because the IRM tool is often incorporated into the content, usage of the material might not offer the same level of performance across different applications, such as content readers or media players.

In general terms, IRM should provide the following functions, regardless of type of content or format:

Persistent Protection   The IRM should follow the content it protects, regardless of where that content is located, whether it is a duplicate copy or the original file, or how it is being utilized. This protection should not be easy to circumvent.

Dynamic Policy Control   The IRM tool should allow content creators and data owners to modify ACLs and permissions for the protected data under their control.

Automatic Expiration   Because of the nature of some legal protections of intellectual property (described earlier in this chapter), a significant amount of digital content will not be protected in perpetuity. The IRM protections should cease when the legal protections cease. Conversely, licenses also expire; access and permissions for protected content should likewise expire, no matter where that content exists at the end of the license period.

Continuous Auditing   The IRM should allow for comprehensive monitoring of the content's use and access history.

Replication Restrictions   Much of the purpose of IRM is to restrict illegal or unauthorized duplication of protected content. Therefore, IRM solutions should enforce these restrictions across the many forms of copying that exist, to include screen-scraping, printing, electronic duplication, email attachments, and so on.

Remote Rights Revocation   The owner of the rights to specific intellectual property should have the ability to revoke those rights at any time; this capability might be used as a result of litigation or infringement.

Data Control

Organizations need to control data throughout its lifecycle. The CCSP exam focuses on data retention, archiving, and deletion policies, as well as legal holds, as key knowledge you'll need to be ready to answer questions about.

While the CCSP exam outline focuses on policies in 2.7, it also mentions procedures and mechanisms. As you think about each of these topics, consider how policies impact the implementation in practice through technology and systems as well as how the policy itself may be used.

Data Retention

Data retention policies are a core part of organizational data handling. Data retention policies need to address the following key items:

Retention Periods   The retention period is the length of time the organization should keep data. This usually refers to data that is being archived for long-term storage—that is, data not currently being used in the production environment. The retention period is often expressed in a number of days for ephemeral data like logs and in years for business data or data that is required to be retained for legal or regulatory reasons. Data retention periods can also be mandated or modified by contractual agreements.

Regulations and Compliance   As just mentioned, the retention period can be mandated by statute or contract; the retention policy should refer to all applicable regulatory guidance. This is especially true in cases where there is conflicting regulation; the policy should reflect management's decision for how to approach and resolve this conflict with the policy as an appropriate mechanism. For instance, laws may impose different retention periods for specific kinds of data, and the organization might operate in states or countries with differing mandated retention periods.

Data Classification   Highly sensitive or regulated data may entail specific retention periods, by mandate or contract or best practice. The organization can use the classification level of data to determine how long specific datasets or types of data need to be retained.

Retention   The policy should specify requirements for how the data is actually archived if there are requirements that need to be met for specific types of data. For example, some types of data are required by regulation to be kept encrypted while in storage. In these cases, the policy should include a description of the encryption requirements.

Data Deletion   Once data hits the end of its retention period, it must be properly disposed of. While we'll dive into the specifics of data deletion in a few pages, the policy and mechanisms that policy drives are important here to ensure that data is properly disposed of. Policies for deletion should specify who will delete data and what the requirements for deletion are and typically point to procedure documentation that provides guidance on how to ensure secure deletion occurs and is validated.

In addition, data deletion policies and procedures need to take compliance and legal requirements into account. That may include requirements due to legal holds, industry compliance requirements that set a fixed retention or disposal period, or requirements that require customer data to be deleted when requested.

Archiving and Retrieval Procedures and Mechanisms   Having data in storage is useful; stored data can be used to correct production errors, can serve as disaster recovery and business continuity (DR/BC) backups, and can be data mined for business intelligence purposes. But stored data is only useful if it can be retrieved and put back into production in an efficient and cost-effective manner. The policy should mandate the creation of a detailed description of the processes both for sending data into storage and for recovering it, as well as periodic testing of both archiving and retrieval capabilities. The detailed processes might be included as an attachment to the policy or mentioned by reference to the actual documentation for the processes; the processes might require more frequent updates and editing than the policy and should be kept separate—in most organizations, procedures are far more easily updated than policies!

Backups are great, but backups you haven't tested aren't. All too often organizations don't practice recovery from backup and are unprepared for situations where recovery is necessary and recovery efforts are hampered or fail because the backups aren't working properly. Testing backups on a regular basis is a critical part of archiving and retrieval processes.

Monitoring, Maintenance, and Enforcement   As with all policies in the organization, the policy should list, in detail, how often it will be reviewed and amended, by whom, consequences for failure to adhere to the policy, and which entity within the organization is responsible for enforcement.

Addressing Retention, Deletion, and Archiving in the Cloud

Since there are many cloud models in place, ranging from software as a service tools (that will set their own underlying backup and retention practices) to infrastructure as a service offerings (that rely on you to build your own solution on top of underlying services that also have their own redundancy and resiliency capabilities), addressing these topics in the cloud is a complex problem.

Managing data retention in the cloud can be especially tricky. It can be difficult to ensure that the cloud provider is not retaining the organization's data beyond the retention period; this is because underlying cloud storage is often designed to replicate data automatically, and deleting data in a way that is visible to your organization may not actually delete it everywhere at once in the provider's infrastructure. Part of the appeal of the cloud for many organizations is how good cloud providers are at retaining data and not losing it—intentionally getting rid of data is a whole other matter! When considering cloud migration, and during negotiations with potential cloud providers, the organization should make a point of ensuring the provider can support the organization's retention policy and that it understands what is actually happening when it uses the cloud service.

Archiving data in cloud services may also introduce additional complexity due to the variety of services you can use as part of the archiving process. Organizations using

Amazon's S3 for storage may want to archive to a service like Glacier, which is much cheaper for long-term, low-access rate storage. Decisions like that involve both design practices that understand usage and access models and policy that determines how long data should be available and when it will be disposed of.

Finally, deletion can also create additional concerns in the cloud. You need to understand both how your cloud provider removes data that is deleted and what common activities like deprovisioning systems or services mean to your deletion process. While many cloud providers have technology in place that ensures that remnant data will not be accessible to the next user of the underlying infrastructure, remnant data has been recoverable in some cases in the past.

All of this means that your organization's policies may remain the same when you're operating in a cloud environment, but that your designs and implementation in practice need to take into account the specific capabilities and models that exist in the cloud environments in which you operate.

Legal Holds

Electronic discovery, or e-discovery, involves the identification, collection, and production of data related to a case, and legal holds (sometimes called litigation holds) are intended to ensure that the data required for the case is collected and preserved. In addition to organizational and regulatory needs for data retention, legal holds are also a driver for retention processes and may require deviation from the organization's normal practices for data retention and destruction.

e-discovery will be covered in more depth in Chapter 9.

A legal hold occurs when an organization is notified that either (a) a law enforcement or regulatory entity is commencing an investigation or (b) a private entity is commencing litigation against the organization. Once the organization receives proper notice, it must suspend all relevant data destruction activities until the investigation/lawsuit has been fully resolved. This means that processes and technical capabilities need to be able to be modified for legal holds. At the same time, the organization can continue to destroy data that is not associated with the particular case, based on its normal retention and destruction schedule.

Legal holds normally take precedence over other existing organizational policies and practices or contractual agreements. For instance, in the United States, this concept is dictated by the Federal Rules of Evidence, which mandates that a legal hold notice has primacy, even over federal laws (such as HIPAA) that would require data to be destroyed at the end of a retention period.

Many organizations consider the potential for legal holds in their retention policies. If you don't have the data, you can't produce it for a court case, and long-term retention of data may be seen as a driver of risk to the organization. Thus, retention periods are a careful balance of organizational need against legal risk.

Data Audit and Audit Mechanisms

As with other assets both in the cloud and outside of it, organizations need to regularly review, inventory, and inspect the usage and condition of the data it owns. Data audit is a powerful tool for these purposes. Organizations may choose to create a policy for conducting audits of its data that includes detailed descriptions of the following items:

- Audit periods
- Audit scope
- Audit responsibilities (internal and/or external)
- Audit processes and procedures
- Applicable regulations
- Monitoring, maintenance, and enforcement

 As with all types of audits, the organization should be particularly careful about ensuring that auditors do not report to anyone in the management structure that owns or is affected by the data being audited; conflicts of interest must be avoided for the audits to have validity and utility.

In most organizations and enterprises, audit is predicated on logging. Logging can happen in many forms: event logging, security logging, traffic logging, and so forth. Logs can be generated by applications, OSs, and devices and for general or specific purposes (e.g., devices that collect logs as a byproduct of operations, such as servers, or devices that do logging as their main purpose, such as IDSs [intrusion detection systems] and SIEMs [security information and event management systems]).

Log review and audit is a specialized task for personnel with specific training and experience, and log analysis for cloud services can require additional specific knowledge about the service's logging capabilities, formats, and syntax. Logging itself is fairly easy; most software and devices and services in modern enterprises provide logging functionality, allowing organizations to log most things they might want to capture. Reading and analyzing these logs, however, can prove challenging, with common issues for organizations:

Log review and analysis is not often a priority. Most organizations do not have the wherewithal to dedicate the personnel required to effectively analyze log data, especially in the volume that it can be generated. Usually, log review becomes an additional duty for someone tasked to another office (the security department, for instance). Automation helps, but it also requires configuration and maintenance itself.

Log review is mundane and repetitive. The volume of logs, particularly when they're not filtered or configured effectively to meet organizational goals, can result in a lack of attention by those tasked with monitoring them.

The reviewer needs to have an understanding of the operation. If the reviewer cannot distinguish between what is authorized activity and what is not, they are not adding security value to the process.

Logging can be expensive.   Logging can take up a lot of space and time and often comes with additional software costs to manage and oversee all of the information gathered. Thus, organizations often struggle to maintain all of the logs they want or may need to maintain.

Logs are like data backups, though: many organizations perform logging, and logs are easy to set, acquire, and store. The challenge, then, is to determine how often logs will be reviewed or audited, by whom, the processes for doing so, and so forth. Having the logs is one thing; reviewing the logs you have is something else.

Logging capabilities can vary greatly between cloud service providers—much like the data retention differences between SaaS and IaaS providers, logging may be very different depending on the cloud service you're using. The cloud provider may not want to (or, indeed, even be able to, for operational or contractual reasons) disclose underlying log data to the customer for security, liability, or competitive reasons. Therefore, the organization must consider, again, specific audit requirements when opting for cloud migration and include any such specifications in the contract with the cloud provider.

Audit Mechanisms

The CCSP Exam Outline (Candidate Information Bulletin) asks you to consider three specific areas for audit mechanism planning and implementation in cloud environments.

Log Collection   The first component of audit mechanism design you'll need to consider for the CCSP exam is log collection. Log collection in cloud environments for auditing purposes has both advantages and challenges. Many cloud service providers have native log collection tools that can be enabled or are automatically available that can make logging activities easier to tackle. At the same time, multi-cloud, SaaS, and hybrid cloud and on-premises environments can make log collection more difficult. As you plan for auditing, carefully consider the impact that your organization's cloud service selection and design may have on your ability to collect and access logs.

Log Correlation   Simply collecting logs isn't enough—you still need to do something with them. That's where correlation comes in, and where even more challenges start to pop up. Correlation may be easier in a single cloud environment with built-in or third-party tools, but organizations that need to correlate logs between multiple cloud vendors, or between on-premises and cloud environments, can face additional challenges. Fortunately, modern security information and event management (SIEM) tools and other security platforms have ingestion and correlation tools that can help.

While it may seem obvious, ensuring that the time stamps between your services are accurate and are properly interpreted is an important step in setting up a logging environment for auditing. Something as simple as having the wrong time zone or not having the accurate time can cause events to not be correlated or to be incorrectly correlated, sending security practitioners chasing ghosts!

Packet Capture   Auditing cloud and on-premises systems can require packet capture to validate traffic flows, but it may also be used for other purposes during assessments. Cloud environments can make packet capture far more difficult—or even impossible—and security practitioners need to consider the architectural, technical, and contractual limits that cloud service providers may have in place before assuming that packet capture will be feasible.

In general, packet capture is not available in most SaaS or PaaS environments without direct vendor involvement, and that level of involvement is rare because the underlying service layers aren't designed for customers to see the traffic between services. That means that cases where you would both want and potentially be able to perform packet capture are almost entirely limited to IaaS environments like AWS, Azure, and similar services.

Even in those services you may face limitations. Traditional packet capture using a tool like Wireshark and setting network interfaces to promiscuous mode to gather information may not be technically feasible or may not work as intended. Fortunately, IaaS vendors often offer packet capture or virtual network tap capabilities directly. That doesn't mean it will always be simple or easy, as cloud environments can have limitations even inside of a single vendor's products and solutions. For example, some vendors provide infrastructure as a service environments that integrate with abstracted solutions they provide, like databases where packet capture capabilities may not be available. As a security practitioner, you'll need to understand what your vendor allows, what capabilities they offer, and how those can be used to meet your auditing requirements for packet capture.

Data Destruction/Disposal

In an on-premises environment where the organization has ownership and control of all the infrastructure including the data, hardware, and software, data disposal options are relatively direct and straightforward. In the cloud, data disposal can require more planning and forethought in order to accomplish your goals.

In an on-premises environment, your options are as follows:

Physical Destruction of Media and Hardware   Any hardware or portable media containing the data in question can be destroyed by burning, melting, impact (beating, drilling, grinding, and so forth), or industrial shredding. This is often the preferred method of sanitization since the data is physically unrecoverable.

Degaussing   This involves applying strong magnetic fields to the hardware and media where the data resides, effectively making them blank. It does not work with solid-state drives like SSDs, flash media, and USB thumb drives.

Overwriting   When media needs to be reused, overwriting is one option to allow data to be destroyed while leaving the media intact. Overwriting uses multiple passes of random characters written to the location where data resides, or may simply write zeroes—a process called zeroization. This can be extremely time-consuming for large devices and is also not an effective technique for solid-state drives, which are resistant to overwriting, and may result in remnant data.

Crypto-Shredding (Cryptographic Erasure)   This involves encrypting the data with a strong encryption engine and then taking the keys generated in that process, encrypting them with a different encryption engine, and destroying the resulting keys of the second round of encryption. Crypto-shredding is considered a better solution than overwriting because data that is encrypted from the beginning of its lifecycle and then shredded cannot be recovered even if remnant data remains. The primary downfall of crypto-shredding is due to the CPU and performance overhead of encrypting and decrypting files.

WARNING   Hardware and media can never be sanitized by simply deleting the data. Deleting, as an operation, does not erase the data; it simply removes the logical pointers to the data for processing purposes.

In the cloud, many of these options are unavailable or not feasible. Because the cloud provider, not the data owner, owns the hardware, physical destruction is usually out of the question unless there is specific contractual coverage for dedicated hardware and disposal, which is quite costly. In addition, because of the difficulty of knowing the actual specific physical locations of the data at any given moment (or historically), it would be next to impossible to determine all the components and media that would need to be destroyed. For the same reason, overwriting is not a practical means of sanitizing data in the cloud. In a multitenant environment like a public cloud, a customer cannot physically destroy or overwrite storage space or media, as that would affect other customers' data. Each of these concerns is even more significant with a SaaS provider where the entire solution is hidden away from the customer. In SaaS and most PaaS environments, data destruction can be approached only through contractual requirements.

That leaves crypto-shredding as the sole pragmatic option for data disposal in the cloud. Crypto-shredding can require time to complete, with time varying based on the size of the volume and technology used. In general, since crypto-shredding is part of a data, device, or system lifecycle, the speed of the shredding process is not a significant obstacle to its use.

As with the other data management functions, the organization needs to create a policy for data disposal. This policy should include detailed descriptions of the following:

- The process for data disposal
- Applicable regulations
- Clear direction of when data should be destroyed

Of course, security practitioners are also concerned with data remanence—that is, any data left over after sanitization and disposal methods have been attempted. If crypto-shredding is performed correctly, there should be no remanence; however, material that is somehow not included in the original encryption (say, a virtual instance that was offline during the encryption process, then added to the cloud environment) might be considered remanence. As in all cryptographic practices, proper implementation is essential for success.

The data disposal policy addresses activities that take place in the Destroy phase of the data lifecycle, which you will learn about in Chapter 3.

Summary

This chapter discussed the data lifecycle and data management functions within the data lifecycle, including data retention, auditing, and disposal. The various roles, rights, and responsibilities associated with data ownership were described.

Data discovery allows organizations to identify data as structured, semi-structured, or unstructured data. Once data is identified, it is typically classified based on the organization's classification scheme. That classification is used to label the data, and it may be mapped through transformations and transfers to allow it to be used in other systems and services. This chapter also focused on data flows and the importance of understanding and documenting them, especially in complex and interconnected cloud systems.

As data is moved through an organization and accessed by systems, services, and individuals, information rights management (IRM) tools are used to ensure that data rights are enforced. IRM relies on access models to determine which subjects can take which actions, and those models drive provisioning processes that provide users and systems with the rights they need in an automated fashion.

Finally, we reviewed auditing as a security control for data, including log collection, correlation, and analysis in cloud and hybrid environments. Packet capture as an audit and security mechanism is also important, and it can be complex if not impossible in some cloud environments like software as a service and platform as a service providers.

Exam Essentials

Describe data flows and their use in a cloud environment. Data flows are used to describe where and how data moves throughout an environment. Details like ports, protocols, services, and what data fields or types are sent and received are important components of data flows, and this information is typically captured in data flow diagrams.

Understand the purpose and method of data categorization and classification. Know why and how data owners assign categories and classifications to specific datasets under their control. Explain the typical parts of data classification policies. Describe data mapping and data labeling. Know how and when data is labeled, and by whom. Understand content-based discovery and the use of metadata in discovery efforts.

Understand the various roles, rights, and responsibilities related to data ownership.   Know who the data subject, owner, controller, processor, and custodian are. Understand the rights and responsibilities associated with each.

Be familiar with data discovery methods.   Describe the differences between structured, semi-structured, and unstructured data and offer examples of each type of data. Understand why data location matters and what impact it may have on data discovery processes and capabilities.

Understand the objectives of and tools used to implement information rights management.   IRM tools are designed to protect data rights and require provisioning that gives appropriate users permission based on their roles and responsibilities. Access models are used to determine who will receive rights, and a combination of certificates for identification and licenses that list the permissions or rights of the users or systems are used to make IRM work.

Know what should be included in policies for data retention, deletion, and archiving.   Understand essential aspects like the terms *retention* and *disposal*. Know retention formats, how regulations dictate these things, and how every policy needs to include details for maintenance, monitoring, and enforcement.

Understand data and media sanitization.   Most traditional sanitization methods will not work in cloud environments. Cryptographic erasure is one of the few ways to ensure secure data disposal in environments where you cannot ensure physical destruction of data and devices. Overwriting and other techniques cannot provide assurance of data destruction in cloud environments.

Review Questions

You can find the answers to the review questions in the Appendix.

1. Which of the following is not a common method of data discovery?
    A. Content-based
    B. User-based
    C. Label-based
    D. Metadata-based

2. Sara is planning to implement data labeling for her organization. Which of the following is not a data label field that she should consider?
    A. Date data was created
    B. Data owner
    C. Data value
    D. Date of scheduled destruction

3. Sarah is continuing her data labeling efforts and has received suggestions for appropriate data labels for data that will be used in multiple countries in which her company operates as part of ongoing security and data lifecycle efforts. Which of the following is not a label that would help with that usage?
    A. Source
    B. Language
    C. Handling restrictions
    D. Jurisdiction

4. Asha wants to document the path that data takes from creation to storage in her institution's database. As part of that effort, she creates a data flow diagram. Which of the following is not a common element of a data flow diagram?
    A. Credentials used for each service listed
    B. Hostnames and IP addresses or address blocks for each system involved
    C. Ports and protocols used for data transfer
    D. Security controls used at each point in the diagram

5. Mei wants to conduct data discovery activities in her organization. Which of the following types of data discovery is best suited for identifying all photos that were taken using a specific model of camera based on the original files generated by the camera?
    A. Label-based
    B. Metadata-based
    C. Extension-based
    D. Content-based

6. Felix wants to monitor data transfers between two systems inside of his IaaS cloud–hosted data center. Which of the following audit mechanisms is unlikely to be available to him that is commonly available in on-premises environments?

    A. Log review

    B. Packet capture

    C. Data flow diagrams

    D. Log correlation

7. Megan is documenting roles as part of the implementation of her organization's data classification policy. Her organization uses a software as a service tool to accept applications from customers. What term best describes the SaaS vendor?

    A. A data custodian

    B. A data owner

    C. A data processor

    D. A data steward

8. Jaime has been informed of legal action against his company and must now ensure that data relevant to the case is kept. What term describes this?

    A. Legal retention

    B. Legal archiving

    C. Court hold

    D. Legal hold

9. All policies within the organization should include a section that includes all of the following except _____.

    A. Policy maintenance

    B. Policy monitoring

    C. Policy enforcement

    D. Policy transference

10. Melissa knows that many data destruction options are not available for data kept in the cloud due to how the services are architected using shared hardware and services. Which of the following is the best option for her organization to select for cloud-hosted data that must be disposed of in a secure manner?

    A. Melting

    B. Crypto-shredding

    C. Zeroization

    D. Overwriting

11. Which of the following is not a common data right controlled by an IRM system?

    A. Copyright

    B. Creating

    C. Editing

    D. Viewing

12. Jason wants to properly describe the type of data his organization is using. He knows that the data is stored in a MySQL database. What type of data is Jason's organization storing?

   A. Unstructured data

   B. Tabular data

   C. Structured data

   D. Warehoused data

13. Sensitivity, jurisdiction, and criticality might all be considered for what cloud data security activity?

   A. Crypto-shredding

   B. Data flow diagramming

   C. Classification

   D. Tokenization

14. Angela wants to provide users with access rights to files based on their roles. What capability of an IRM system most directly supports this requirement?

   A. Provisioning

   B. DRM

   C. CRM

   D. Data labeling

15. Nina's company has stored unstructured data in an S3 bucket in AWS. She wants to perform data discovery on the data, but the discovery tool that she has requires the data to be local. What concern should Nina express about retrieving large volumes of data from a cloud service?

   A. Performance may be low.

   B. Data ingress costs may be high.

   C. Data egress costs may be high.

   D. The data will need to be structured before discovery can run.

16. Tej wants to conduct data discovery across his organization's databases; however, he knows that data is stored in multiple countries. What concern should he raise before the discovery process is conducted?

   A. Structured data is harder to conduct discovery on.

   B. The discovery process may create a denial of service condition on the database servers.

   C. Jurisdiction and local laws may impact the ability to perform discovery.

   D. Unstructured data is harder to conduct discovery on.

17. Naomi has implemented a data archiving process as part of her organization's cloud design. What important part of her archiving plan should she prioritize to ensure its long-term success?

   A. Data classification

   B. Periodic testing

   C. Data mapping

   D. Hashing

18. Yasine's organization wants to enable systems to use data controlled by an IRM. What method is most commonly used to identify systems while allowing them to have their trust revoked if needed?

   A. LEAP authentication

   B. Multifactor authentication

   C. Certificate-based authentication and authorization

   D. TACACS

19. Meena is conducting data discovery with data encoded in JSON. What type of data is she working with?

   A. Structured

   B. Semi-structured

   C. Super-structured

   D. Unstructured

20. Isaac wants to describe common information rights management (IRM) functions to his team. Which of the following is not a common IRM function?

   A. Persistency

   B. Crypto-shredding

   C. Automatic expiration

   D. Dynamic policy control

Chapter

3

Cloud Data Security

THE OBJECTIVE OF THIS CHAPTER IS TO ACQUAINT THE READER WITH THE FOLLOWING CONCEPTS:

✓ **Domain 1: Cloud Concepts, Architecture, and Design**

- 1.3. Understand security concepts relevant to cloud computing

  - 1.3.1. Cryptography and key management

- 1.4. Understand design principles of secure cloud computing

  - 1.4.1. Cloud secure data lifecycle

✓ **Domain 2: Cloud Data Security**

- 2.1. Describe cloud data concepts

  - 2.1.1. Cloud data lifecycle phases

- 2.2. Design and Implement Cloud Data Storage Architectures

  - 2.2.1. Storage Types (e.g., long-term, ephemeral, raw storage)

  - 2.2.2. Threats to storage types

- 2.3. Design and apply data security technologies and strategies

  - 2.3.1. Encryption and key management

  - 2.3.2. Hashing

  - 2.3.3. Data Obfuscation (e.g., masking, anonymization)

  - 2.3.4. Tokenization

  - 2.3.5. Data Loss Prevention (DLP)

  - 2.3.6. Keys, secrets, and certificates management

- 2.8. Design and implement auditability, traceability, and accountability of data events

  - 2.8.1. Definition of event sources and requirement of event attributes (e.g., identity, Internet Protocol (IP) address, geolocation)

  - 2.8.2. Logging, storage, and analysis of data events

✓ **Domain 3: Cloud Platform and Infrastructure Security**

- 3.1. Comprehend cloud infrastructure and platform components
  - 3.1.5. Storage

✓ **Domain 5: Cloud Security Operations**

- 5.6 Manage security operations
  - 5.6.3 Log capture and analysis (e.g., security information and event management (SIEM), log management)

Securing data in the cloud relies on many of the same concepts you might use to secure data on premises. It also requires you to think about the concerns that are specific to the cloud, including threats, capabilities, and how cloud infrastructure designs vary from on-premises configurations and options.

Cloud Data Lifecycle

Data in the cloud has many of the same security requirements and threats as data in a legacy or on-premises environment. Data still follows a data lifecycle, but the implementation particulars will change. Figure 3.1 shows the common stages in the data lifecycle.

FIGURE 3.1 Stages of the data lifecycle

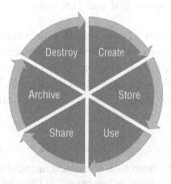

Data will still be created in the Create phase—both in the cloud itself and by remote users. It will be stored in the cloud, in both the short term as part of the Store phase and for the long term in the Archive phase. It will be manipulated and modified during the Use phase as part of the organization's business. It may be transmitted to other users and/or made available for collaboration in the Share phase within the cloud. In addition, we will still have a need to remove data from the production environment and sanitize the media afterward in the Destroy phase.

As you'd expect, the particulars of performing these activities, and doing them in a secure fashion, will evolve to match any new environmental challenges.

In the cloud, each phase of the data lifecycle will require particular protections. Let's review each of the phases in turn and examine some specific control mechanisms we may want to apply in each.

Create

Data creation may occur in a multitude of locations. Data may be created in the cloud environment, it can be created on premises or at a remote location, or it can be created in another cloud. The threats to data in the Create phase vary based on where it is created and how it will be transferred to the cloud for storage.

Data Created Remotely   Data created by the user should be encrypted before uploading to the cloud in order to protect against attacks like packet capture and on-path attacks as well as insider threats at the cloud data center. That means selecting strong encryption methods and implementing good key management practices, which we'll cover later in this chapter. Of course it's also desirable to ensure that the network traffic itself is secured—most often using Transport Layer Security (TLS) through an HTTPS connection.

TLS replaces the deprecated Secure Sockets Layer (SSL) standard, but the term SSL is still utilized in many IT environments, and the practitioner may see both terms, *SSL* and *TLS*, used.

Data Created within the Cloud   Data created within the cloud should also be encrypted upon creation. This helps to protect against both attackers who might gain access to the environment and the staff who work for the cloud service provider itself, gaining access to it in unencrypted form. As with data created remotely, key management remains a critical part of securing the data—if the keys can be obtained by malicious actors, encryption is not a useful protection!

Regardless of where data is created or resides, the Create phase should include the activities you reviewed in Chapter 2, "Data Classification," including categorization and classification, labeling, tagging, marking, and assigning metadata.

Store

As you review the data lifecycle diagram, you may be wondering why there is a Store phase and an Archive phase—they can sound pretty similar. The Store phase is what occurs immediately after creation and describes what happens to data when it is created. Here, critical security controls include provisioning access rights to the storage locations, ensuring that the storage locations are properly secured, and continuing to protect data through encryption at rest where it is needed or required.

Use

The Use phase becomes more complex for data stored in the cloud. Some cloud environments simply present an interface via a web application, while other provide programmatic access via application programming interfaces (APIs) or services. Hybrid cloud environments may transfer data via a multitude of means as part of its usage.

This means that securing the Use phase requires understanding the specific uses and data flows that occur in your organization. Each data transfer needs to be secured, and data needs to be protected in each location in which it is stored, while it is in transit, and wherever it may temporarily or permanently reside.

Data security in the Use phase requires considering other operational aspects as well. The platforms with which users connect to the cloud also have to be secured. That may be a matter of corporate security policy and implementation, or it may be a complex task in a bring your own device (BYOD) environment with diverse technology and configurations. In addition to the technical controls that many organizations use, user education and awareness become important, because users may be able to manipulate or extract data in use. They need to be trained to understand the new risks that go along with cloud computing and how they will be expected to use the technology and the data it contains.

Rights and role management remain important here as well. *Data owners*, the individuals responsible for classifying, protecting, and overseeing the use of data in organizations, should also be careful to restrict permissions for modifying and processing their data; users should be limited to those functions that they absolutely require in order to perform their assigned tasks. And, as in many circumstances in both the cloud and legacy environments, logging and audit trails are important when data is being manipulated in any fashion.

Cloud providers need to ensure that they provide secure environments for data use as well. That means strong protections in the implementation of virtualization or shared services. Providers must ensure that data on a virtualized host can't be read or detected by other virtual hosts on that same device. They also have to implement personnel and administrative controls so data center personnel can't access any raw customer data and so their actions are monitored in case of malicious activity. These controls are most often ensured via contractual language and third-party audits when working with cloud providers.

Share

Although global collaboration and massive scale to many locations are both powerful capabilities afforded by the cloud, they come with risks. If users, systems, and data can be anywhere on the planet, so can threats.

Many of the same security controls implemented in prior phases will be useful when defending the storage phase: encrypted files and communications, using information rights management (IRM) solutions, and the use of tagging and permissions models all remain key controls. We also have to craft sharing restrictions based on jurisdiction and legal requirements. Organizations may need to limit or prevent data being sent to certain locations in accordance with regulatory requirements or contractual obligations. These restrictions can take the form of either export controls or import controls, so the security professional must be familiar with both for all regions where the organization's data might be shared.

 Information rights management (IRM) tools include a number of different solutions, such as dedicated IRM solutions, data loss prevention (DLP) tools, and various other means to tackle classification, authentication and authorization, tagging, and similar data management capabilities, to name a few.

Cloud customers should also consider implementing some form of egress monitoring in the Share phase; this will be discussed in the section "Data Loss Prevention" later in this chapter.

Export and Import Restrictions

Here are export restrictions you should be familiar with:

- **International Traffic in Arms Regulations, or ITAR (United States):** State Department prohibitions on defense-related exports; can include cryptography systems.

- **Export Administration Regulations, or EAR (United States):** Department of Commerce prohibitions on dual-use items (technologies that could be used for both commercial and military purposes).

And here are import restrictions you should be familiar with:

- **Cryptography (Various):** Many countries have restrictions on importing cryptosystems or material that has been encrypted. When doing business in or with a nation that has crypto restrictions, it is the security professional's responsibility to know and understand these local mandates.

- **The Wassenaar Arrangement:** A group of 41 member countries have agreed to mutually inform each other about conventional military shipments to nonmember countries. Not a treaty, and therefore not legally binding, but may require your organization to notify your government in order to stay in compliance.

Archive

This is the phase for long-term storage, and thus you will have to consider data security over a longer time frame when planning security controls for the data.

Cryptography remains an essential consideration, but the strength of the cryptosystem and its resistance to long-term attacks and future attacks are both considerations. Key management is still extremely important since mismanaged keys can lead to exposure or to total loss of the data, no matter how strong your encryption is. If the keys are improperly stored (especially if they are stored alongside the data), there is an increased risk of loss, and modern attackers are aware of and look for keys as part of their attacks.

 One aspect of cryptography to be aware of is elliptical curve cryptography (ECC). ECC uses algebraic elliptical curves that result in much smaller keys that can provide the same level of security as the much larger ones used in traditional key cryptography.

The physical security of the data in cloud-based long-term storage is also important. In choosing a storage location, you need to carefully assess risks and benefits for each of these areas:

Location   You should consider the following common questions when you are choosing your long-term storage solutions in the cloud environment:

- Where is the data being stored by the cloud provider? Are multiple cloud providers involved?

- What environmental factors will pose risks in that location (natural disasters, climate, etc.)?

- What jurisdictional aspects might bear consideration (local and national laws)?

- Will it be feasible to access the data during contingency operations (for instance, during a natural disaster)?

- Is it far enough away to be safe from events that impact the production environment?

- Is it replicated in multiple locations or in multiple clouds? Does that replication create any additional concerns such as an inability to ensure deletion?

Format   Regardless of its location, whether the data is on premises or in the cloud, questions about formatting and long-term access are essentially the same:

- Is the data being stored on some physical medium such as tape backup or magnetic storage and in an offline mode, or it is online and replicated?

- Is the media highly portable and in need of additional security controls against theft?

- Will that medium be affected by environmental factors?
- How long do you expect to retain this data?
- Will it be in a format still accessible by production hardware when you need it?

It may seem strange to consider the media format for data, but understanding the underlying technology that your cloud provider is using can impact your security control planning and which services you choose to use. Of course, not all cloud providers disclose how they're building the services they sell, so you may not have all of this detail and will have to assess your risks based on the knowledge that you do have as well as contracts and their ongoing performance.

Staff   Staffing for cloud service providers may directly impact the data that you can store and process in their cloud. Some contractual, government, or other requirements may require that foreign national employees not have access to certain types of data, creating a hurdle you'll have to overcome before using a cloud provider. At the same time, it is important to ensure that providers are performing appropriate personnel security checks like background checks and ongoing monitoring.

Procedure   How is data recovered when needed? How is it ported to the archive on a regular basis? How often are you doing full backups (and incremental or differential backups)?

Archive phase activities in the cloud will largely be driven by whether you are doing backups in the cloud, and whether you are using the same cloud provider for backups and your production environment or using a different cloud provider for each. You will have to consider many of the same factors you would have in the traditional environment but then also determine whether those decisions are a concern in the cloud environment, if the cloud provider introduces new concerns, or whether you can handle them via contractual means, as well as how you'll monitor the solution and enforce requirements.

Destroy

We discussed destruction options for cloud environments in Chapter 2. Cryptographic erasure (crypto-shredding) is the only feasible and thorough means currently available for this purpose in the cloud environment. Destruction of encryption keys is also important when you consider the end of data lifecycles because strong encryption without a key makes data very difficult to access, even over extended time frames, and can provide a useful additional control—particularly if it is difficult to ensure that your provider has truly deleted data due to how they architect underlying storage or services.

In some cases, cloud providers manage the entire lifecycle of your data and how it is handled at the system and storage levels, particularly in SaaS and PaaS environments. That means that you'll need to consider data lifecycle requirements as part of your organization's contracts. You may also want to consider how you would recover your data if you switched vendors or if your vendor was acquired or went out of business.

All of this means that you have to design your cloud architecture and service use to include the eventual need for destruction, and that your contracts and service agreements need to address destruction when you adopt software as a service, platform as a service, and similar systems.

Cloud Storage Architectures

There are various ways to store data in the cloud, each with attendant benefits and costs. These ways apply both to larger organizational needs and to personal cloud storage of a single user's data.

Storage Types

The CCSP exam considers three specific types of storage: long-term, ephemeral, and raw storage.

Long-term storage is storage specifically designed to be used for extended periods of time. Amazon's Glacier, Azure's Archive Storage, and Google's Coldline and Archive tiers are all examples of long-term storage solutions. In fact, each of the major cloud vendors has multiple tiers of storage, ranging from frequent use storage to nearline storage, often used for short-term storage like logs and media content, as well as the longer-term storage provided for backups and to meet regulatory requirements.

Figure 3.2 shows Amazon's S3 storage classes and some of the data that differentiates the tiers. Note that long-term storage costs more for retrieval, whereas S3 standard doesn't, a key difference in their usage and pricing models. This chart doesn't show all of Amazon's S3 tiers and instead focuses on examples to describe the differences in storage types.

FIGURE 3.2   Storage class differentiation in AWS

	S3 Standard	S3 Glacier Instant Retrieval	S3 Glacier Flexible Retrieval	S3 Glacier Deep Archive
Minimum storage duration charge	N/A	90 days	90 days	180 days
Retrieval charge	N/A	Per GB retrieved	Per GB retrieved	Per GB retrieved
First byte latency	Milliseconds	Milliseconds	Minutes to hours	Hours
Durability	99.999999999%	99.999999999%	99.999999999%	99.999999999%

Ephemeral storage in the cloud is used for data that often exists only as long as an instance does. Consider the /tmp directory that AWS's Lambda provides. Data that is created and used can be stored there, but it's meant as an ephemeral scratch resource and shouldn't be used for durable storage because it will be deleted when a new execution environment is created.

Raw storage is storage that you have direct access to. You can think of this like access to a hard drive, SSD, or storage volume where you have direct access to the underlying storage rather than a storage service.

Volume Storage: File-Based Storage and Block Storage

In addition to the high-level types of storage that the CCSP exam considers, you'll need to be aware of common storage presentation models used in the cloud. With volume storage, the customer is allocated a storage space within the cloud; this storage space is represented as a drive attached to the user's virtual machine. From the customer's perspective, the virtual drive performs very much in the same manner as would a physical drive attached to a tangible device; actual locations and memory addresses are transparent to the user.

Volume storage architecture can take different forms and may be presented as either file storage or block storage.

File Storage (also File-Level Storage or File-Based Storage)   The data is stored and displayed just as with a file structure in the traditional environment, as files and folders, with all the same hierarchical and naming functions. File storage architectures have become popular with big data analytical tools and processes.

Block Storage   Block storage is a blank volume that the customer or user can put anything into. Block storage might allow more flexibility and higher performance, but it requires a greater amount of administration and might entail installation of an OS or other app to store, sort, and retrieve the data. Block storage might be better suited for a volume and purpose that includes data of multiple types and kinds, such as enterprise backup services or active volumes for online transaction processing (OLTP) databases.

Storage architecture for volumes can include underlying data protection solutions that replicate data to prevent loss. Volume storage can be offered in any of the cloud service models but is often associated with infrastructure as a service (IaaS).

Object-Based Storage

Object storage is just what it sounds like: data is stored as objects, not as files or blocks. Objects include not only the actual production content, but metadata describing the content and object and a unique address identifier for locating that specific object across an entire storage space.

Object storage architectures allow for a significant level of description, including marking, labels, classification, and categorization. This also enhances the opportunity for indexing capabilities, data policy enforcement (such as IRM, described in Chapter 2, and DLP, discussed later in this chapter in the section "Data Loss Prevention"), and centralization of some data management functions.

Any cloud service model can include object storage architectures, but object storage is usually associated with IaaS.

Databases

Like their traditional counterparts, databases in the cloud provide some sort of structure for stored data. Data will be arranged according to characteristics and elements in the data itself, including a specific trait required to file the data known as the primary key. In the cloud, the database is usually back-end storage in the data center, accessed by users utilizing online apps or APIs through a browser.

Cloud providers may provide multiple different types of databases—common examples include traditional relational databases, nonrelational (NoSQL databases) including key-value databases, and document-oriented databases, to name a few. Databases can be implemented in any cloud service model, but they are most often configured to work with PaaS and SaaS. Regardless of the database type you select or use, you may need to consider security practices like minimizing your datasets and anonymization or pseudonymization to ensure that breaches don't allow attackers to use the data successfully.

What's pseudo-anonymization? It's anonymization that could still allow individuals to be identified using other information that may also be in the database. Removing an individual's name but leaving their age and address doesn't fully anonymize a record, but it does create additional work for attackers who might want to identify who is in the records.

Threats to Cloud Storage

Since the CCSP looks at three major types of cloud storage, it helps to consider threats in those categories as well.

For long-term storage like Amazon's Glacier, threats include exposure and malicious access due to credential theft or compromise or privilege escalation, risks to the integrity of the data due to issues with the underlying service, and exposure of the data due to attacks against the encryption protecting it. They can also include denial of service and service outages and attacks that deny access to the data, like cryptographic malware–style attacks.

Ephemeral data shares the same risks and also presents risks to the incident response and forensics process, as ephemeral systems and storage devices may be automatically destroyed or removed when those systems are terminated. Since many environments automatically scale as needed, this means that forensic artifacts may be lost unless they are intentionally preserved.

Finally, raw storage may be allocated directly on devices. In some cloud systems, reallocation of raw storage has left fragments of data available to the next user of that block storage. While that has been remediated in major cloud providers' infrastructure, that type of risk is another reason to always encrypt data throughout cloud infrastructure so that inadvertent exposure of your storage does not result in a breach.

Finally, since cloud services typically run on shared infrastructure, you also need to consider side channel attacks that operate outside of your environment. Information may be available to attackers or insiders who can perform network traffic capture or even physical theft of the underlying servers or media.

 NIST Special Publication (SP) 800-209 provides specific guidance on storage security and is an excellent starting point if you're looking in depth at securing storage in the cloud or on premises. You can find it at https://nvlpubs.nist.gov/nistpubs/SpecialPublications/NIST.SP.800-209.pdf. Pages 17–23 list a range of threats that you may want to consider, including some that we don't list here.

Designing and Applying Security Strategies for Storage

Architecture and solution design are an important part of providing data security in the cloud. The CCSP Exam Outline (Candidate Information Bulletin) specifically considers a handful of technologies and concepts related to data security: encryption and key management; hashing; data obfuscation; tokenization; data loss prevention; and keys, secrets, and certificate management.

Encryption

It should come as no surprise that cloud computing has a massive dependency on encryption to provide security for data. Encryption is used to protect data at rest, in transit, and in use. Encryption is used between the remote user endpoint and the server or service to create the secure communication connection. It is used within the cloud customer's enterprise environment to protect their own data and within the data center by the cloud provider to ensure various cloud customers don't accidentally access each other's data.

The CCSP exam outline mentions the broad concept of cryptography and specifically mentions key management as an important topic related to cryptography in the cloud.

Key and Secrets Management

How and where encryption keys and other secrets are stored can affect the overall risk to the data significantly. Here are some things to remember and consider regarding key management for cloud computing:

Level of Protection   Encryption keys, which are the strings of bits that allow for encryption and decryption to occur, must be secured at the same level of control, or *higher*, as the data they protect. The sensitivity of the data dictates this level of protection, according to the organization's data security policies. It is important to remember that the strength of the cryptosystem is only valid if keys are not disclosed (except for public keys, as part of asymmetric encryption), and current, secure cryptosystems are used.

Sometimes databases use transparent encryption, in which the encryption key for the database is stored in the database itself. You can read about one real-world example that shows how this works and remains secure with a key stored with the database at `https://docs.micro-soft.com/en-us/sql/relational-databases/security/encryption/transparent-data-encryption?view=sql-server-ver16`. Transparent encryption can provide protection against attacks on data at rest, meaning it makes sense if your threat model includes compromise of the server or backups.

Key Recovery   For anyone other than a specific user, accessing that user's key should be difficult; however, there are situations in which an organization needs to acquire a user's key without the user's cooperation. This might be because the user was fired from the organization, died, or forgot their passphrase or lost their key. You need to have the technology and processes for getting that key to access that data. Usually, this entails a procedure that involves multiple people, each with access to only a portion of the key as well as an underlying key escrow system. Key recovery is more commonly used for keys that are used by systems or services and thus are managed by more than one person.

Key Distribution   Issuing keys for a cryptosystem can be difficult and fraught with risk. If the key management process requires a secure connection to initiate the key creation procedure, how do you establish that secure session without a key? Often, passing keys out of band (via a different means than that in which they will be used, like on paper or via the phone instead of via email or other electronic means) is a preferable, yet cumbersome and expensive, solution. Moreover, keys should never be passed in the clear.

A hardware security module (HSM) is a device that can safely create, store, and manage encryption keys and is used in servers, data transmission, and log files. If implemented properly, it is far more secure than saving and storing keys in software. Cloud providers frequently have a cloud HSM service, which you can use to securely store keys; however, you'll want to consider the HSM in the same threat modeling you would for other services in their cloud implementation.

Key distribution for cloud services often relies on their native capabilities. You may have to create keys locally and upload them, use a web service and save the private keys to a secure location, or use a cloud key management service. A key component of a secure cryptographic solution in the cloud is understanding the services provided and designing an appropriate set of practices and policies to ensure keys are managed securely.

Key Revocation   In situations where a user should no longer have access to sensitive material, or where a key has been inadvertently/illicitly disclosed, the organization needs a process for suspending the key or that user's ability to use it. Key revocation implementations vary, but the concept remains the same: keys are marked as revoked and no longer valid. Some implementations are centralized, while others may require more manual actions depending on how the keys are used, distributed, and managed.

Key Escrow   Key escrow is used to hold keys in a secure way so that they can be recovered by authorized parties. In many cases, having copies of keys held by a trusted third party in a secure environment is highly desirable; this can aid in many of the other key management efforts listed in this section. In an on-premises implementation, BitLocker keys for Windows workstations are often escrowed so that organizations can decrypt drives if they need to. In a cloud environment, similar uses for escrow are common, particularly when incident response or legal holds may require access to a system or data.

Key Lifetime   Keys shouldn't live forever. In fact determining how long key should be used before they are replaced is an important part of security design processes. You can read more about best practices for key lifespans are part of NIST's key management guidelines at https://csrc.nist.gov/projects/key-management/key-management-guidelines.

Outsourcing Key Management   Keys should not be stored with the data they're protecting, and we shouldn't make physical access to keys readily available to anyone who doesn't have authorization and need to know for that data; therefore, in cloud computing, it is preferable to have the keys stored somewhere other than the cloud provider's data center. One solution is for the cloud customer to retain the keys, but that requires an expensive and complicated set of infrastructure and skilled personnel. This would reduce some of the benefit in reduced costs we get from offloading our enterprise to the cloud provider. Another option is using a cloud access security broker (CASB). CASBs are third-party providers that handle IAM and key management services for cloud customers; the cost of using a CASB should be much lower than trying to maintain keys within the organization, and the CASB will have core competencies most cloud customers won't. Commonly used CASBs include Zscaler, Netskope, and McAfee's Enterprise CASB tool, but the market is constantly changing as companies enter and are acquired.

Whoops, I Lost the Keys to the Cloud

A common issue with keys in the cloud is inadvertent exposure of private keys in public repositories. Malicious actors and others commonly scan GitHub and other code repositories looking for private keys that may have been uploaded along with other materials when coding projects are submitted. With those keys in hand, attackers will then attempt to use them to access the accounts or services they are tied to. This can result in thousands or tens of thousands of dollars of service usage, creating both financial and security issues for the organization that owns the keys. While cloud service providers may offer some options if this happens to your organization, and they often monitor for it themselves using similar scanning tools, the cleanup from a breach can be time consuming and complex.

If you do end up in this situation, remember to check locations, services, and other service options that you don't normally use. Attackers often spin up services and systems in obscure locations hoping to preserve a foothold and continue using your accounts for as long as they can!

Certificate Management

Certificates are used to identify both individuals and systems, and much like key management, certificate management is critical to security for cloud solutions. Certificates rely on both a public and private key and may be self-generated or generated by a certificate authority (CA).

Certificate authorities will typically provide a certificate repository that allows for storage and distribution of certificates as well as supporting a certificate revocation list (CRL) that allows the status of certificates issued by the CA to be verified. In the event a certificate is compromised, or if it expires, it can be listed on the CRL to prevent those who might otherwise rely on it from trusting it. Certificates, much like data, have a lifecycle. They are created, managed, and discovered and may be revoked or expire.

As you consider your cloud environments, you will need to design your certificate management and security practices and policies much as you would plan ahead for your encryption keys. Private keys for certificates must be stored securely, and certificate revocation processes need to be understood in case they need to be revoked due to a breach or other issue. In addition, lifecycles, creation and distribution processes, and ownership or responsibility must all be planned for.

Hashing

Hashing uses an algorithm to transform a given string of characters into another value. Hash functions are intended to return unique values for any given input, and to do so quickly, and their output is typically far smaller than the input that is provided. That means that hashes are used for a variety of purposes, including checking if a file has changed, storing and retrieving data quickly, and a variety of other purposes. It's important to note that hashing is not encryption, although the two are often confused. Hashes are one-way functions that don't have keys like regular encryption. This means you can't decrypt a hash value.

You may already be familiar with tools like rainbow tables that allow you to determine what the input for a given hash was. That's not reversing a hash algorithm. Instead, it's a quick lookup in a database of a given hash, which is matched to the input that created it. That's only possible because the set of passwords that are possible as inputs is relatively small. Hashes of files of any reasonable size would be essentially impossible to generate rainbow tables for due to the number of different inputs that are possible.

Masking, Obfuscation, Anonymization, and Tokenization

In many cases, using the actual data instead of an alternative obfuscated version can create security risks. The term *obfuscation* refers to the application of any of these techniques in order to make the data less meaningful, detailed, or readable in order to protect the data or the subject of the data. That's where obfuscation practices like *masking*, *anonymization*, and *tokenization* can be useful, amongst other practices.

Randomization   The replacement of the data or part of the data with randomized information. Randomization is useful when you want to remove the real data but maintain its attributes, including things like the length of the string, its character set (whether it was alphabetic or numerical, whether it had special characters, whether there was upper-/lowercase, etc.), and so forth so that testing will be working with equivalent data, ensuring issues will still be caught.

Anonymization   Anonymization requires removing identifiable data like names, addresses, phone numbers, and other elements that can identify individuals. In some cases, you can use techniques like pseudo-anonymization, which removes some data but leaves elements that could be used to de-anonymize the data, like addresses or zip code and age in place.

Hashing   Hashing involves using a one-way cryptographic function to create a digest of the original data. Using a hash algorithm to obscure the data gives you the benefit of ensuring it is unrecoverable while retaining the ability to reference the data uniquely. That means that hashes are sometimes used to mask or anonymize data when the data content itself is not important for a field.

Shuffling   Using different entries from within the same dataset to represent the data. This has the obvious drawback of using actual production data but can help to create more realistic test data. A shuffled user field might have a randomized first name, last name, address, and other data from an existing dataset.

Masking   Hiding the data with useless characters; for example, showing only the last four digits of a Social Security number: XXX-XX-1234. This can be used where the customer service representative or the customer gets authorized access to the account but you want to obscure a portion of the data for additional security.

Nulls   Deleting the raw data from the display before it is represented, or displaying null sets. Obviously, some of the functionality of the dataset will be dramatically reduced with this method.

Tokenization   Tokenization involves replacing sensitive data with a replacement value called a token. Hashes are sometimes used to create tokens, although they're rarely direct hashes of the data, to avoid attacks against hashes using generated datasets.

Obscuring can be done in either static or dynamic configurations. With the static technique, a new (representational) dataset is created as a copy from the original data, and only the obscured copy is used. In the dynamic method, data is obscured as it is accessed.

It is important to remember that sensitive information may be obtained from otherwise mundane elements, even if one of these techniques was used. For instance, even if you're obscuring a person's name in a given dataset, if you allow other information, such as age, location, and employer, it may be possible to determine the name without having direct access to that field.

Removing the telltale nonspecific identifiers is called *anonymization* or sometimes *de-identification*. Anonymization can be difficult because sensitive data must be recognized and marked as sensitive when it is created; if the user inputs the data into open fields (free entry), determining sensitivity might not be simple. Moreover, the mark indicating sensitivity creates metadata that might be valuable to an attacker.

Tokenization is the practice of having two distinct databases: one with the live, actual sensitive data and one with nonrepresentational tokens mapped to each piece of that data. In this method, the user or program calling the data is authenticated by the token server, which pulls the appropriate token from the token database, then calls the actual data that maps to that token from the real database of production data, and finally presents it to the user or program. Tokenization adds significant overhead to the process but creates an extra degree of security and may relieve the organization's requirement or dependence on encryption (for instance, PCI DSS allows tokenization instead of encryption for sensitive cardholder data). For tokenization to function properly, the token server must have strong authentication protocols. To see how this works a little more clearly, review the following steps, also shown in Figure 3.3:

1. User A creates a piece of data.

2. The data is run through a DLP/discovery tool, as an aid to determine whether the data is sensitive according to the organization's rules (in this example, the data is PII). If the data is deemed sensitive, it is pushed to the tokenization database.

3. The data is tokenized; the raw data is sent to the PII server, while a token representing the data is stored in the tokenization database. The token represents the raw data as a kind of logical address.

4. User B requests the data. This user must be stringently authenticated so the systems can determine if the user should be granted access to the data.

5. If User B authenticates correctly, the request is put to the tokenization database.

6. The tokenization database looks up the token of the requested data, then presents that token to the PII database. The raw data is not stored in the tokenization database.

7. The PII database returns the raw data based on the token.

8. The raw data is delivered to User B.

FIGURE 3.3   Basic tokenization architecture

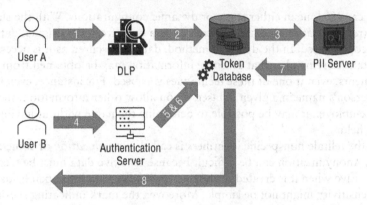

Situations including the following are common reasons to use these capabilities:

Test Environments   New software should be tested in sandboxed environments before being deployed to the production environment. When this type of testing is performed, actual production data should *never* be used within the sandbox. However, in order to determine the actual functionality and performance of the system, it will be necessary to use data that closely approximates the traits and characteristics of the production data.

Enforcing Least Privilege   We know that the concept of least privilege entails limiting users to permissions and access absolutely necessary to perform their duties. In some cases, that might mean allowing the user access to elements of a dataset without revealing its entirety, or for a limited period of time. For instance, a customer service representative might need to access a customer's account information and be shown a screen with that information, but that data might be an abridged version of the customer's total account specifics (such as not showing the customer's full credit card number).

Secure Remote Access   When a customer logs onto a web service, the customer's account might have some data abridged as it was in the least privilege example. The screen might display some of the customer's preferences, but you might not want to display certain elements of the customer's account data, such as payment or personal information, to avoid risks such as hijacked sessions, stolen credentials, or shoulder surfing.

Data Loss Prevention

Data loss prevention (DLP) tools, sometimes called egress monitoring tools, are used to prevent data from leaving organizational control, particularly during the Share phase of the data lifecycle. They can be used on premises, with mobile devices, and in cloud environments, making them flexible tools for data protection. DLP solutions generally have several major goals:

Security Control   DLP can be used as another control in a layered defense strategy designed to mitigate the possibility of inadvertent release or malicious disclosure.

Policy Enforcement   Users can be alerted by the DLP when they are attempting to perform an action that would violate the organization's policy (either accidentally or intentionally). Encrypting data as it leaves and requiring decryption and authentication to access it are common examples of policy enforcement actions.

Enhanced Monitoring   The DLP tool can be set to provide one more log stream to the organization's monitoring suite.

Regulatory Compliance   Specific types and kinds of data can be identified by the DLP solution, and dissemination of that data can be controlled accordingly in order to better adhere to regulatory mandates.

 NOTE   DLP solutions can often be linked to IRM tools, allowing extra functionality to the controls on intellectual property.

DLP tools identify controlled data, typically using tagging, pattern matching, and similar functionality. They then monitor activity involving data or files that match their rules and enforce policies set by the organization.

The identification task can be automated, manual, or a combination of both. The tool might search all of the organization's storage volumes and its production environment to match data against known templates; for instance, the DLP might search for numeric strings nine characters in length that use the right series of numbers based on a rule in order to detect Social Security numbers. The DLP also might use categorization and classification markings, labels, and metadata assigned by the data owner during the Create phase of the data lifecycle. Or the DLP might use keyword searches for particular information known by the organization to be sensitive for its purposes.

The monitoring task can be implemented at the points of network egress (in traditional systems at the demilitarized zone (DMZ), but in the cloud this would be on all public-facing devices) or on all hosts that process data within the production environment. In the latter case, the DLP solution usually includes local agents installed on user workstations/endpoint devices.

The enforcement mechanism can take many forms. The DLP might be set to alert management or security personnel when a user is conducting an activity that violates policy (say, sending an email attachment that contains data the organization has deemed sensitive). If what we're trying to prevent is more accidental disclosures (as opposed to malicious activity), the DLP might just warn users that the email they're sending contains sensitive data and ask them to confirm that they really intended to send it. Or the DLP might be a bit more draconian and prevent the user from sending the attachment, locking the user out of the account, and notifying management and security. The organization can tailor DLP action to its own needs.

DLP implementation in the cloud comes with related difficulties and costs. For one thing, the cloud provider may not allow the cloud customer sufficient access to the data center environment (in terms of both administrative permissions and installation of the requisite systems for implementation), complicating successful configuration and usage. DLP utilization also incurs significant processing overhead; all that monitoring and functionality comes with a processing cost.

Log Capture and Analysis

Security operations rely heavily on the ability to capture logs and analyze them. Infrastructure, applications, and services, both in the cloud and on premises, generate log data when events occur and as part of their ongoing function. Those logs can provide critical data both for day-to-day monitoring and for incident response and security-related monitoring activities.

Many cloud services provide log creation, monitoring, and analysis tools, but organizations may also want to use their own services as part of the capture or analysis process. When you consider log capture and analysis, you will need to take time to understand the capabilities, costs, and limitations of the tools available from the specific vendor or service your organization is using.

Amazon's monitoring service is called CloudWatch, and it provides extensive monitoring for Elastic Compute Cloud (EC2) instances and other services. You can read more about its functionality at https://docs.aws.amazon.com/AmazonCloudWatch/latest/logs/WhatIsCloudWatchLogs.html.

Azure's equivalent service is called Azure Monitor, and much like CloudWatch, it provides analysis, alerting, and visualization capabilities. You can read more about Monitor at https://docs.microsoft.com/en-us/azure/azure-monitor/logs/data-platform-logs.

Google's monitoring service is the GCP operations suite, with details available at https://cloud.google.com/products/operations.

Event Sources and Attributes

Understanding where your log entries are coming from and what the information in the logs means is critical to making sure your logs are useful. The CCSP Exam Outline (Candidate Information Bulletin) specifically mentions identity (the system, user, or service's identity), the Internet Protocol (IP) address (which should include the source and destination if they are relevant to the log), and the geolocation of events and IP addresses, but you should also consider time stamps as one of the basic elements of any log you capture.

Events typically also contain information about what occurred, whether that's a service log entry, an event ID, or simply the query or request that was processed. Security analysts and system administrators need to know what these are, which ones need to be actively monitored for, and how to identify unexpected or malicious events based on that information.

Cloud data storage specific events have their own specific log entries, event IDs, and related details like permissions usage and security groups. When you design cloud data security models and architecture, you will need to identify what you log, what events are most important, which should be alerted on, where logs are stored and analyzed, how long you will retain the logs, and how you will secure them. That may seem difficult, but cloud computing logs and events should use similar, if not the same, designs as your existing logging and analysis infrastructure.

Cloud vendors often have best practices for logging and analysis. Amazon provides its Well-Architected Tool at https://aws.amazon.com/well-architected-tool, which can help with your design efforts. Azure's equivalent is called the Well-Architected Framework and it can be found at https://docs.microsoft.com/en-us/azure/architecture/framework. Google's Cloud Architecture Framework can be found at https://cloud.google.com/architecture/framework.

Log Management

Organizations tend to generate a massive number of log events during normal operations, and sorting out important logs from the volume of incidental data can be a real challenge. The sheer volume of logs also takes up a lot of storage space and can consume other resources as well. All of that comes with a cost, particularly in a cloud environment where services are billed by usage.

That makes log management a critical part of your design and operations. Determining what logs you'll preserve, for how long, and how you will keep them secure so that an attacker cannot access or modify them must be part of your initial configuration and ongoing architecture maintenance.

Fortunately, tools like security information and event management (SIEM) systems can help.

Security Information and Event Management

To better collect, manage, analyze, and display log data, a set of tools specifically created for that purpose has become popular. These are known by a variety of terms, since there is no accepted standard. Nomenclature includes *security information management*, *security event management*, *security information and event management*, and permutations of these (including acronyms such as SIM, SEM, and SIEM, pronounced in various ways). The CCSP exam specifically refers to SIEM, so that's the term we'll use here.

SIEM implementation includes the following goals:

Centralize Collection of Log Data   Because logs can be drawn from so many sources (workstations, OSs, servers, network devices, Internet of Things devices, and services, to name a few), it can be useful to have a place to aggregate it all for additional processing. If nothing else, this simplifies the activity for the admins and analysts who will be tasked with monitoring the environment. This does create an additional risk, however: having all the log data in one location makes that location an attractive target for attackers, so any SIEM implementation will require additional layers of security controls.

Enhanced Analysis Capabilities   Log analysis is frequently a repetitive task that requires a special skill set and experience and is not suited for full-time tasking (an analyst who stares at the same dataset and data feeds all day, day after day, will be less likely to notice events and issues, whereas an analyst who doesn't see the data from the environment often enough won't be as familiar with the baselines and therefore won't recognize anomalous behavior). One way you can offset some of the problems with log analysis is to automate some of the process. SIEM tools provide this capability in addition to other functions such as advanced trend detection based on large datasets. One thing to remember, however, is that most automated tools may not recognize a particular set of attacks—the "low and slow" style of persistent threats, which may develop over weeks or months and don't have dramatic indicators, and therefore may be confused with background attack noise and go undetected by automated analysis.

Dashboarding   SIEMs often offer graphical output display that is more intuitive and simple, allowing staff to quickly grasp situations within the environment. Visualization via dashboarding makes it easy to see when something isn't right.

Automated Response   Some SIEMs include automated alert and response capabilities that can be programmed to suit your policies and environment.

WARNING   Like logging itself, SIEMs are only useful when someone is actually looking at what they produce; simply having the shiny box that performs security functions is nice, but unless the information it provides is being harvested by someone who knows what they're looking at, the SIEM can be just another bandage in a damaged environment and won't really offer any benefit to the organization.

Summary

This chapter addressed the data lifecycle within the cloud environment as well as specific security challenges in each phase. We reviewed the data lifecycle in the cloud as well as different data storage architectures that might be implemented in the cloud, the types of threats that those storage types and designs can face, and ways to protect storage. We reviewed encryption, including the importance of and difficulties with key and certificate management. We explored why we might want to obfuscate data and only display selected portions during operations, and you learned about various methods for performing this task. Next, we reviewed logging, log analysis, and SIEM solutions as well as how and why they're implemented and some risks associated with their use. Finally, we addressed the topic of egress monitoring, how DLP tools work, and specific problems that might be encountered when trying to deploy DLP solutions in the cloud.

Exam Essentials

Understand the risks and security controls associated with each phase of the cloud data lifecycle. Explain what the risks to data are in each phase and which controls you would select to address the risks.

Understand the various cloud data storage architectures. Be able to differentiate between long-term, ephemeral, and raw storage as well as file-based storage, block storage, and databases.

Understand how and why encryption is implemented in the cloud. Understand the role of cryptography and encryption in securing cloud data. Know the essential elements of key management, why keys must be kept securely, and the risks of key compromise or exposure. Apply key management and certificate management technologies like hardware security modules, key escrow, and certificate revocation lists.

Be familiar with the practice of obscuring data. Know the different techniques of data masking, hiding, anonymization, and tokenization. Explain hashing and its role in data obfuscation.

Be familiar with logging, storage, and analysis of data events and the use of SIEM technology. Understand the purposes of SIEM implementation and the challenges associated with using those solutions. Explain the challenges and importance of logging in cloud environments. Describe key data elements like identities, IP addresses, and geolocation for event data.

Understand the importance of egress monitoring. Be familiar with the goals of data loss prevention solutions; how they are implemented; how data is identified using tags, pattern matching, and labels; and what challenges a cloud customer might face trying to implement DLP within the cloud.

Review Questions

You can find the answers to the review questions in Appendix A.

1. Naomi is working on a list that will include data obfuscation options for her organization. Which of the following is not a type of data obfuscation technique?

    A. Tokenization

    B. Data hiding

    C. Anonymization

    D. Masking

2. The goals of SIEM solution implementations include all of the following except_____.

    A. Centralization of log streams

    B. Trend analysis

    C. Dashboarding

    D. Performance enhancement

3. Wei's organization uses Lambda functions as part of a serverless application inside of its Amazon-hosted environment. What storage type should Wei consider the storage associated with the instances to be?

    A. Long-term

    B. Medium term

    C. Ephemeral

    D. Instantaneous

4. Selah wants to securely store her organization's encryption keys. What solution should she ask her cloud service provider about?

    A. A PKI

    B. A DLP

    C. A cloud HSM

    D. A CRL

5. Jim's organization wants to ensure that it has the right information available in case of an attack against its web server. Which of the following data elements is not commonly used and thus shouldn't be expected to be logged?

    A. The version of the executable run

    B. The service name

    C. The source IP address of the traffic

    D. The destination IP address of the traffic

6. Susan wants to ensure that files containing credit card numbers are not stored in her organization's cloud-based file storage. If she deploys a DLP system, what method should she use to identify files with credit card numbers to have the best chance of finding them, even if she may encounter some false positives?

    A. Manually tag files with credit card numbers at creation.

    B. Require users to save files containing credit card numbers with specific file-naming conventions.

    C. Scan for credit card numbers based on a pattern match or algorithm.

    D. Tag files with credit card numbers at destruction.

7. Rhonda is outlining the threats to her cloud storage environment. Which of the following is not a common threat to cloud storage?

    A. Credential theft or compromise

    B. Infection with malware or ransomware

    C. Privilege reuse

    D. Human error

8. Ben wants to implement tokenization for his organization's data. What will he need to be able to implement it?

    A. Authentication factors

    B. Databases

    C. Encryption keys

    D. Personnel

9. Yasmine's organization has identified data masking as a key security control. Which of the following functions will it provide?

    A. Secure remote access

    B. Enforcing least privilege

    C. Testing data in sandboxed environments

    D. Authentication of privileged users

10. Megan wants to improve the controls provided by her organization's data loss prevention (DLP) tool. What additional tool can be combined with her DLP to most effectively enhance data controls?

    A. IRM

    B. SIEM

    C. Kerberos

    D. Hypervisors

11. What phase of the cloud data lifecycle involves data labeling?

    A. Create

    B. Store

    C. Use

    D. Archive

12. Charles wants to ensure that files in his cloud file system have not been changed. What technique can he use to compare files to determine if changes have been made?

    A. Obfuscation

    B. Masking

    C. Tokenization

    D. Hashing

13. Liam wants to store the private keys used to generate certificates for his organization. What security level should he apply to those keys?

    A. The highest level of security possible.

    B. The same or lower than the data the certificates protect.

    C. The same or greater than the data that the certificates protect.

    D. Private keys can be shared without issues.

14. Best practices for key management include all of the following except_____.

    A. Having key recovery processes

    B. Maintaining key security

    C. Passing keys out of band

    D. Ensuring multifactor authentication

15. Valerie wants to be able to refer to data contained in a database without having the actual values in use. What obfuscation technique should she select?

    A. Masking

    B. Tokenization

    C. Anonymization

    D. Randomization

16. Samuel wants to check what country a file was accessed from. What information can he use to make a guess as accurate as possible, given information typically available in log entries?

    A. The username

    B. The source IP address of the request

    C. The destination IP address of the request

    D. The hostname

17. What is the correct order of the phases of the data lifecycle?

    A. Create, Store, Use, Archive, Share, Destroy

    B. Create, Store, Use, Share, Archive, Destroy

    C. Create, Use, Store, Share, Archive, Destroy

    D. Create, Archive, Store, Share, Use, Destroy

18. Stanislaw wants to use log information to create accountability for data events. Which of the following data elements would be most useful for his purpose?

    A. Time stamps

    B. Host IP addresses

    C. UserIDs

    D. Certificate IDs

19. Nina replaces all but the last four digits of credit card numbers stored in a database with asterisks. What data obfuscation technique has she used?

    A. Masking

    B. Randomization

    C. Tokenization

    D. Anonymization

20. Greg has implemented logging for his company's worldwide web services implementation running in Azure. What concern should Greg address when he enables logging of all web requests?

    A. Data lifecycle planning

    B. Secrets management

    C. Log volume

    D. Geolocation of log events

Chapter 4

Security in the Cloud

THE OBJECTIVE OF THIS CHAPTER IS TO ACQUAINT THE READER WITH THE FOLLOWING CONCEPTS:

✓ **Domain 1: Cloud Concepts, Architecture, and Design**

- 1.4. Understand Design Principles of Secure Cloud Computing

  - 1.4.5. Security considerations and responsibilities for different cloud categories (e.g., Software as a Service (SaaS), Infrastructure as a Service (IaaS), Platform as a Service (PaaS))

  - 1.4.6 Cloud design patterns (e.g., SANS security principles, Well-Architected Framework, Cloud Security Alliance (CSA) Enterprise Architecture)

✓ **Domain 3: Cloud Platform and Infrastructure Security**

- 3.1. Comprehend Cloud Infrastructure Components

  - 3.1.4. Virtualization

- 3.3. Analyze Risks Associated with Cloud Infrastructure

  - 3.3.1 Risk assessment (e.g., identification, analysis)

  - 3.3.2. Cloud vulnerabilities, threats, and attacks

  - 3.3.3. Risk mitigation strategies

In this chapter, we will discuss the various rights and responsibilities involved in cloud computing, how those should be apportioned between the cloud provider and customer, specific risks posed by each cloud platform and service, and BC/DR strategies for use in the cloud.

Shared Cloud Platform Risks and Responsibilities

Because the cloud customer and provider will both be processing data that, at least in some part, belongs to the customer, they will share responsibilities and risks associated with that data. Simply put, these risks and responsibilities will be codified in the service contract between the parties. That contract, however, will be the result of a complex process of deliberation and negotiation.

Although the risks and responsibilities will be shared between the cloud provider and customer, the ultimate legal liability for unauthorized and illicit data disclosures remains with the customer as the data owner. The cloud provider may be financially responsible, in whole or in part, depending on the terms of the contract, but the legal responsibility is the customer's. This concept is repeated throughout the book, as it's repeated throughout the CCSP Common Body of Knowledge (CBK).

As an example of what this means and how it could affect the customer, let's say an unauthorized disclosure of *personally identifiable information (PII)* that belongs to the customer occurs because of some failure on the part of the cloud provider. For the sake of argument, we'll also assume that the contract stipulates that the provider is financially liable for damages resulting from this failure.

Depending on the jurisdiction where the breach occurred and the nationality or residence of the subjects of the PII, statutes could dictate specific monetary damages owed by the cloud customer to either the government or the subjects or both. It is possible for the customer to eventually recover those damages from the provider, but the government will not seek them from the provider; the government will seek damages from the customer. It is the customer that the government will serve injunctions and orders to, not the provider. In addition, depending on the jurisdiction and the breach itself, it is the customer's officers who could face imprisonment, not the provider.

Moreover, even if the customer is protected by the provider's acceptance of financial responsibility, the legal repercussions are not the only negative impact the customer faces.

The customer will likely be adversely affected by negative publicity, loss of faith among its clientele, perhaps decreased market share and a drop in company value, and an increase in insurance premiums. It is therefore important for the customer to realize that the cash involved in damage awards and assignment of liability is only one aspect of the risk.

Of paramount importance is to understand that the customer's ultimate legal liability for data it owns remains true *even if the provider's failure was the result of negligence or malice.* That is a very considerable burden of risk, especially because it's a much higher standard than what we usually face in the security profession.

That said, the provider and customer still must come to terms regarding their particular responsibilities and obligations under the contract. To some degree, this will be driven by the nature of the service in question and what service and model the customer is purchasing. A graphical depiction of the general gradations of the various arrangements is shown in Figure 4.1.

FIGURE 4.1 Responsibilities according to service model

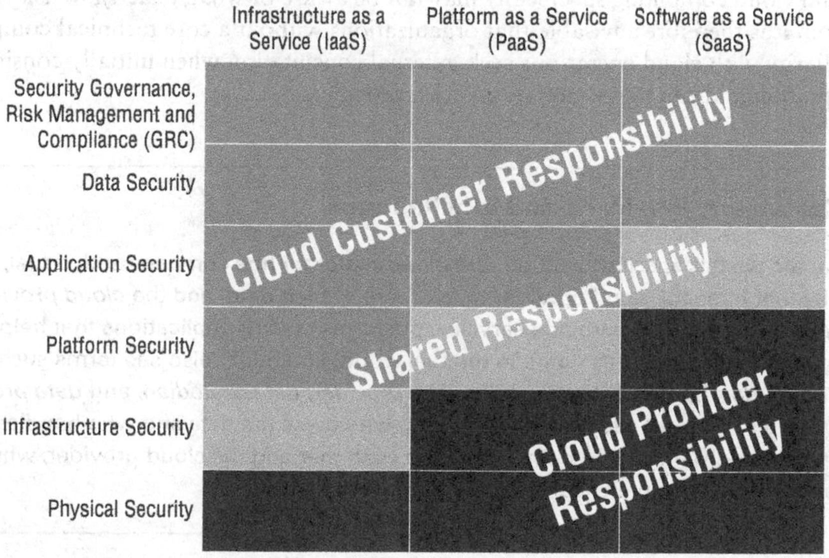

Again, this is not prescriptive, but a guide for possible contract negotiation.

There will be some dichotomy because of the two perspectives. The cloud provider and the customer are most concerned with two different things. The cloud customer is concerned about the data. The production environment being hosted on the cloud data center is the customer's lifeblood. Breaches, failures, and lack of availability are the things that most affect the customer. The provider, on the other hand, is mostly concerned with the security and operation of its data center, which is the provider's core competency and the way it survives and maintains profitability.

Therefore, the customer will be seeking maximal control over their data, with all the administrative power and insight into the data center operations it can acquire. The customer will want to impose policy, get logging data, and audit the performance and security of the data center.

The provider will be attempting to limit access to information as much as possible. The provider wants to refrain from disclosing any information that might be used for malicious purposes, which includes the list of security controls used for protecting the data center, procedures, and live monitoring equipment and data. In some cases, the provider might not even want to disclose the physical location of the data center, to protect it from physical attack and proprietary intellectual property.

This creates an adversarial dynamic in the negotiation. Both parties must have a clear awareness of what outcomes they're seeking and the best means to get them. In many cases, the provider has an advantage in this regard because the provider understands the function and design of the data center and therefore the known and expected outcomes of operation much better than most customers do. Organizations that are new to managed services in general and cloud computing specifically may not be aware of what, exactly, to ask for in the negotiation. It is therefore advisable that organizations without a core technical competency and familiarity with cloud operations seek external consultation when initially considering cloud migration and entering negotiations with providers.

Cloud Customers, Providers, and Similar Terms

In this chapter, we talk specifically about the *cloud customer* (the company, individual, or other entity that hires the cloud provider to take care of their data) and the *cloud provider* (the company that is hired to provide services, platforms, and/or applications that help with managing the cloud customer's data). In the real world, you might also see terms such as *data customer*, *data owner*, *data controller*, *data provider*, *data custodian*, and *data processor*. These terms are all attempts at describing who owns the data and who handles the data, which generally sifts out to being the cloud customer and the cloud provider, which are the terms we will use pretty consistently for our discussion.

Cloud Computing Risks by Deployment Model

To prepare for cloud migration and the requisite contract negotiation (and for familiarization with CCSP CBK content), it is useful to review the risks particular to each of the cloud deployment models. These include the private, community, public, and hybrid cloud models.

Private Cloud

A *private cloud* is a distributed computing environment with only one customer. A private cloud can be implemented by an organization running its own data center and supplying cloud services to itself, or it can be hosted by a provider.

In some situations, the provider owns the hardware that contains the private cloud, hosted in the provider's data center. The customer is granted exclusive access to that particular set of hardware, and no other customers will have their cloud hosted on those same devices. In some cases, the customer owns the hardware, which is hosted physically inside the provider's data center (often referred to as a *co-lo*, or colocation center).

A private cloud might be a more appropriate cloud option for customer organizations that exist in highly regulated industries or that process a significant amount/degree of sensitive information; the private cloud allows the customer to dictate and specify a much more detailed level of security controls and overall governance. This is, of course, more expensive (in terms of the amount paid to the provider) than the public cloud model and impedes the elasticity/scaling of the cloud (instead of having theoretically infinite capacity, the private cloud capacity will reach a natural maximum of whatever components are dedicated to the customer's environment).

All private cloud operators face the following risks:

Personnel Threats   This includes both inadvertent and malicious threats. If a managed provider/data center is used, the provider's administrators remain outside the customer's control.

Natural Disasters   All the deployment and service models are still susceptible to natural disasters.

External Attacks   These attacks can take many forms, such as unauthorized access, eavesdropping, denial of service (DoS)/distributed denial of service (DDoS), and so on.

Regulatory Noncompliance   While the customer has much more control over the configuration and controls in a private cloud model (compared to a public cloud), regulators will still enforce mandates.

Malware   This can be considered an external or internal threat, depending on the source of the infection.

None of these risks are unique to the private cloud, but having a greater degree of control and specificity may give the customer a greater level of assurance in combatting them.

Community Cloud

In a *community cloud* configuration, resources are shared and dispersed among an affinity group. Infrastructure can be owned and/or operated jointly, individually, centrally, across the community, or in any combination and mixture of these options.

The benefits of this deployment model each come with attendant risks:

Resiliency through Shared Ownership   Because the network ownership and operation is scattered among users, the environment is more likely to survive the loss of a significant number of nodes without affecting the others. However, this introduces additional risks because each node is its own point of entry and a vulnerability in any one node can result in an intrusion on the others. This, of course, means that unity of configuration management and baselines is almost impossible (and very difficult to enforce). With distributed ownership comes distributed decision-making in terms of policy and administration.

Shared Costs   Overhead and cost of the infrastructure is shared among the members of the community, but so are access and control.

No Need for Centralized Administration for Performance and Monitoring   Although this removes many burdens of centralized administration, it also removes the reliability of centralized and homogenized standards for performance and security monitoring.

 Real World Scenario

Online Gaming as a Community Cloud

Online gaming is an excellent example of the community cloud model. Each individual gamer owns their own device (a console or a computer). The individual gamer is responsible for the purchase price of the device, maintaining the device, and establishing/maintaining a connection to the internet. Each individual gamer can also disconnect their own device voluntarily, whenever they feel like it (or even destroy their own device, if they choose, because they own the device completely).

Then there is usually a centralized identity and access management (IAM) node involved in the gaming setup. Some entity (such as Microsoft or Sony) acts as the validator of identity/permission for each individual gamer; this entity has full control/ownership of the IAM function and must pay to create/maintain that node. Individual gamers log into the centralized IAM node in order to get access to the shared game environment.

Finally, there is often another, distinct entity that is the game host; they run the server that handles the online interactions between the verified players. These back-end game machines are wholly owned and maintained by the game host (often the game manufacturer or distributor).

Each entity is responsible for their own components and participation in the community; each takes part voluntarily and can leave at any time. Ownership, processing, and storage are shared among the participants, depending on their role in the interaction.

Public Cloud

This is the deployment model that has the most focus in the CCSP CBK and is most likely to provide the greatest benefit to the largest number of cloud customers. In the *public cloud*, a company offers cloud services to any entity that wants to become a cloud customer, be it an individual, company, government agency, or other organization.

Many of the same risks exist in the public cloud as in the private cloud: personnel threats (inadvertent and malicious), external threats, natural disasters, and so forth. Some of them are obviated by the public cloud's similarity to the community cloud, such as distributed infrastructure, shared costs, and reduced need for administrative capability. However, it is these same benefits that entail the additional risks of the public cloud. The organization will lose control, oversight, audit, and enforcement capabilities—basically, all the assurance of maintaining a private cloud internal to the organization.

There are some additional risks that are unique to the public cloud that also must be considered. We'll discuss those in some detail in the following sections.

Vendor Lock-In

In ceding control of the production environment and data to an external party, the organization creates a dependency on that provider. The expense and trouble of moving the data out of the provider's data center could be crippling to the customer, especially if the customer chose to do so before the end of the contract term. In a sense, this can make the customer a hostage of the provider and allow the provider to decrease service levels and/or increase prices as they see fit. It's important to stress that this is *not* a commonplace occurrence. We do not mean to suggest that cloud providers are maliciously luring customers into unfavorable arrangements. However, the possibility exists for that dependency, and dependency is a risk.

Vendor lock-in (also known as provider lock-in) can be caused by other circumstances as well. For instance, if the provider uses a proprietary data format or medium to store information, the customer may not be able to move their data to another provider. The contract itself can be considered a form of lock-in, too, if it is punitive and puts an undue onus on the customer if the customer chooses to go to another provider. Alternatively, vendor lock-in can be caused by some sort of regulatory constraint, where finding another provider that will meet the specific regulatory needs of the organization could be difficult.

To avoid lock-in, the organization has to think in terms of *portability* when considering migration. We use the term *portability* to describe the general level of ease or difficulty when transferring data out of a provider's data center (regardless of whether it's being moved to another provider or to a private cloud).

There are several things an organization can do to enhance the portability of its data:

> **Ensure favorable contract terms for portability.**   Make sure the organization considers an exit strategy, even while creating the initial agreement with the provider at the outset of cloud service acquisition. Is there a reduced-rate trial period in the provider environment? What is the penalty for early transfer (severing the contract)? At the end of the contract term, will there be any difficulty, contractually or in terms of performance, in moving the data to another provider? (See the real-world example "Ambiguity Is Scary.")

Avoid proprietary formats.   Don't sign with a provider unless the raw data can be recovered in a format that could be used at another provider's site. This might involve using some form of conversion before moving the data, and that conversion should be simple and inexpensive if the customer chooses to move. Some abstraction techniques make it easier to move workloads between cloud providers. For example, Terraform is an open-source infrastructure as code (IaC) tool that can be used in place of provider-proprietary formats.

Ensure there are no physical or technical limitations to moving.   Make sure that the bandwidth leaving the old provider is sufficient for the purposes of moving your organization's entire dataset and that the new provider can handle that size of importation. Also ensure that the cloud provider provides data exportability features that make it technically possible to extract data from the provider.

Check for regulatory constraints.   There should be more than one cloud provider that can handle your organization's specific compliance needs. If your needs are bizarrely unique and restrictive (for instance, if your organization is a medical school that takes credit card payments, thus requiring you to simultaneously comply with FERPA, PCI DSS, and HIPAA), that number of providers may be extremely limited.

 Real World Scenario

Ambiguity Is Scary

In the case of one public cloud provider, the contract stipulated a set of maximum monthly upload/download parameters, with additional fees assessed if these bounds were exceeded in any given month. This is commonplace and the usual way cloud providers establish rates and provide for the appropriate level of resources to meet their customers' regular needs and still allow for cloud bursting.

Elsewhere in the contract, the terms for leaving at the end of any contract period were detailed to include a duration in which the customer could move their data away from the provider (it was 30 days).

What the contract *didn't* state was whether the same monthly limits (and fees for exceeding those limits) would be in effect during the month-long movement of data out of the provider's space in the event the customer chose to leave.

You may think that the limits wouldn't be enforced during the transition period. Otherwise, how could a customer reasonably leave the provider? Assuming the customer was making maximal use of the service and uploading x bytes of data each month of a year-long contract term, there would be $12x$ bytes (12 times the established monthly limit) stored in the provider's data center at the end of the contract. If the limits were still in place, the customer would be facing considerable penalties in fees to move 12*x* bytes in that final month. Can the customer assume that this reasonable conclusion was the intention of the contract?

Of course not. We can never assume anything, especially when crafting contracts. Therefore, this is a question that would have to be resolved in writing and agreed to as an amendment or addition to the contract before both parties sign.

Vendor Lock-Out

Another problem associated with ceding control of the organization's data and production environment is referred to as *vendor lock-out* (also known as provider lock-out). Vendor lock-out can be caused when the cloud provider goes out of business, is acquired by another company, or ceases operation for any reason. In these circumstances, the concern is whether the customer can still readily access and recover their data.

We cannot really plan for all the possible reasons vendor lock-out might occur. We can, however, be aware that the possibility exists and make decisions accordingly. We may want to consider the following factors when selecting a cloud provider:

Provider Longevity   How long has the provider been in business? Does it seem to be a market leader? This aspect may be more difficult than others to assess, because IT is an extremely volatile field and new providers are constantly entering while stalwarts often leave with little warning. Cloud technology and services on a large scale, in particular, are a fairly recent development and may be more prone to significant and unexpected turbulence.

Core Competency   Can this provider offer your organization what it needs? Is it capable of meeting all your service requirements? Does it have the staff, resources, and infrastructure to handle your organization's demands as well as those of its other customers? One measure of the possible strength and suitability of a given provider is whether a cloud service is central to its offerings or is an additional function for its company.

Jurisdictional Suitability   What country is the provider in, and which state? This question must be asked in terms of both where it is chartered and where it operates. Where is the data center? Where is its long-term storage and backup capability? Will your organization's data be crossing boundaries and borders? Can your organization use this provider and remain compliant with all applicable regulations?

Supply Chain Dependencies   Does the provider rely on any other entities for its critical functions, both upstream and downstream? Are there essential suppliers, vendors, and utilities without which the provider could not perform? This aspect will be very difficult to investigate without considerable disclosure on the part of the provider.

Legislative Environment   What pending statutes might affect your organization's ability to use that provider? This facet might carry the most potential impact for cloud customers and also be the most challenging to predict. For instance, almost nobody foresaw that Great Britain would leave the European Union in 2016, and the Brexit referendum entailed significant political and regulatory modifications for companies operating in both jurisdictions.

Not If, But When

Some people might think that a provider's record of incidents should be used as a discriminator when considering vendor lock-out and that if a given vendor has proven susceptible to breaches or attacks or failures in the past, this should be a telling portent of its ability to survive in the future. This may not be the most useful method for measuring the suitability of a vendor. Instead, knowing that a vendor has suffered through incidents may indicate that this is a vendor you should strongly consider to handle your business. Simply put: everyone can and will be breached at some point, every system fails, and every organization experiences security issues. We should not be expecting a zero-fault environment. We should be looking for a fault-tolerant environment. How did the provider respond to the incidents? What did it do? What didn't it do? How did the market (and its customers) respond to the provider's handling of the matter? We can learn more from a provider that has dealt with past security issues (and how) than from a provider that claims to have never had any.

Multitenant Environments

Going into a public cloud means entering a multitenant environment. There will be no providers that will host your organization as their sole customer. Indeed, you should be wary of any provider that would *want* to be in that position. It doesn't scale and wouldn't be profitable. There are therefore specific risks in the public cloud configuration that do not exist in other models, including these:

Conflict of Interest   Provider personnel who administer your data and systems should not also be involved with any of your competitors who might also be that provider's customers. The provider should be careful to not create these situations or even the perception that they might exist.

Escalation of Privilege   Authorized users may try to acquire unauthorized permissions. This might include users from organizations other than your own. A user who gains illicit administrative access may be able to gain control of devices that process other customers' data.

Information Bleed   With multiple customers processing and storing data over the same infrastructure, there is the possibility that data belonging to one customer will be read or received by another. Moreover, even if this does not happen with raw data, it might be possible for one customer to detect telltale information about another customer's activity, such as when the customer is processing data, how long the procedure takes, and so on.

Legal Activity   Data and devices within a data center may be subpoenaed or seized as evidence in a criminal investigation or as part of discovery for litigation purposes. This is of concern to any cloud customer because of the possibility that a particular asset might contain not only data that is the specific target of the investigation/litigation but also data belonging to other customers. (In other words, your data might be seized because it's on the same box as the data of another customer who is a target of law enforcement or plaintiffs.)

The Brewer and Nash Model

Although the Brewer and Nash model is not part of the official material and you don't need to know it for the exam, it's useful to understand. Also known by the title of the paper in which it was proposed, "The Chinese Wall Security Policy" (www.cs.purdue.edu/ homes/ninghui/readings/AccessControl/brewer_nash_89.pdf), it is the concept of aligning separation of duties and least privilege with data flows to prevent conflicts of interest.

Brewer and Nash is perhaps the most relevant model for cloud computing because of the nature of cloud administrators—inside a cloud data center, administrators working for the cloud provider could have physical (and perhaps logical) access to every cloud customer served by that facility. This might include customers in direct competition in the same industry. This creates a conflict of interest for the cloud administrator as well as a potential avenue for corruption.

Proper use of the Brewer and Nash model might address these issues by reducing their likelihood and creating a policy that supports and enforces the model.

Hybrid Cloud

A *hybrid cloud* is simply a combination of two or more of the other models. Hybrid cloud configurations, of course, include all the risks of the various models they combine. An organization considering utilizing a hybrid cloud setup ought to be aware of all the risks discussed in each of the previous sections that are applicable to their particular choice of hybrid.

Cloud Computing Risks by Service Model

Another consideration in cloud migration and contract negotiation is the risks inherent in each of the cloud service models. The most common cloud service models include infrastructure as a service (IaaS), platform as a service (PaaS), and software as a service (SaaS). In addition to the concerns specific to each service model, the service models inherit the risks of whichever deployment model they are used with. This coverage is by no means exhaustive or prescriptive and should only be taken as a means to inform the reader and stimulate consideration of possible security activity.

Infrastructure as a Service (IaaS)

In the *infrastructure as a service (IaaS)* model, the customer will have the most control over their resources, which might alleviate some concerns about trusting the provider or lacking insight into the environment. However, there are still risks that exist in the IaaS motif, although they are not usually unique to that configuration:

Personnel Threats   Again, a malicious or negligent insider (working for the provider) may cause significant negative impact to the customer, in large part because they have physical access to the resources within the data center where the customer's data resides.

External Threats   These include malware, hacking, DoS/DDoS, on-path (also known as man-in-the-middle) attacks, and so forth.

Lack of Specific Skillsets   Because so much of the environment will be administered by the customer, and all access will be via remote connections, there will be a significant burden on the customer's administrators and staff to provide both operational and security functions in IaaS. An organization that does not have sufficient personnel with the training and experience necessary for conducting these tasks in a cloud environment is introducing a sizable risk to its operations.

Platform as a Service (PaaS)

The *platform as a service (PaaS)* model will have other risks in addition to those included in the IaaS model. These include the following:

Interoperability Issues   Because the OS will be administered and updated by the provider, the customer's software may or may not function properly with each new adjustment to the environment.

Persistent Backdoors   PaaS is often used for software development and development operations (DevOps) efforts because the customer can install any software (production or test bed) over the infrastructure (hardware and OS) within the cloud environment. This model lends itself well to serving as a test bed for new applications. It can mimic the production environment with a structured sampling of all the systems from the live enterprise, and it also tests the interface with various platforms through the remote access capability and opportunity to spread the test over multiple OSs. With all these benefits for DevOps, it is important to remember a significant risk that comes with that industry: backdoors left by developers after the final product ships. These are used for efficient editing and test cases so that the developer doesn't have to run the program all the way from the beginning to find the particular function that needs to be addressed. However, backdoors also serve as attack vectors if discovered and exploited by malicious parties. What was yesterday's development tool is tomorrow's zero-day exploit.

Virtualization   Because most PaaS offerings utilize virtualized OSs, the threats and risks associated with virtualization must be considered in this model. Please see the section "Virtualization" later in this chapter for more information about this.

Resource Sharing   Programs and instances run by the customer will operate on the same devices used by other customers, sometimes simultaneously. The possibility of information bleed and side-channel attacks exists and must be considered.

Software as a Service (SaaS)

All the risks inherent in the PaaS and IaaS models remain in the *software as a service (SaaS)* environment along with these additional risks:

Proprietary Formats   The provider may be collecting, storing, and displaying data in a format owned by and unique to that provider. This can lead to vendor lock-in and decrease portability.

Virtualization   The risks from virtualization are enhanced in the SaaS environment because even more resource sharing and simultaneous multitenancy is going to occur. For more information, refer to the next section, "Virtualization."

Web Application Security   Most SaaS offerings rely on access through a browser with some kind of application programming interface (API). Potential weaknesses within web apps pose a wide variety of risks and threats.

Virtualization

We have discussed the importance of *virtualization* throughout the book. We'll now discuss the risks related to the use of virtualization in the cloud. Many of these possibilities require attenuation through the use of controls that can only be implemented by the cloud provider, so the cloud customer must rely on contractual provisions for implementation and enforcement.

Attacks on the Hypervisor   Instead of attacking a virtualized instance, which might only result in successfully breaching the content of one (virtualized) workstation, malicious actors might attempt to penetrate the hypervisor, which is the system that acts as the interface and controller between the virtualized instances and the resources of the given host devices on which they reside.

There are two types of hypervisors, known as Type 1 and Type 2. *Type 1 hypervisors* are also called bare-metal or hardware hypervisors. They reside directly on the host machine, often as bootable software. *Type 2 hypervisors* are software hypervisors, and they run on top of the OS that runs on a host device.

Attackers prefer Type 2 hypervisors because of the larger surface area. They can attack the hypervisor itself, the underlying OS, and the machine directly, whereas Type 1 attacks are restricted to the hypervisor and the machine. OSs are also more complex than hypervisors, creating the increased potential for included vulnerabilities.

Guest Escape   An improperly designed or poorly configured virtualized machine or hypervisor might allow for a user to leave the confines of their own virtualized instance. This is referred to as *guest escape* or *virtual machine (VM) escape*. A user who has successfully performed guest escape might be able to access other virtualized instances on the same host and view, copy, or modify data stored there. Worse, the user might be able to access the host itself and therefore be able to affect all the instances on the machine. And the worst potential situation is known as *host escape*, where a user can not only leave their own virtualized instance, they can even leave the host machine, accessing other devices on the network. This may be unlikely, as it would only result from some rather egregious failures in hardware, software, policy, and personnel performance (or significant combinations thereof), but it is a risk and must be considered.

Information Bleed   This is another risk stemming from malfunctions or failures. The possibility exists that processing performed on one virtualized instance may be detected, in whole or in part, by other instances on the same host. In order for this risk to be detrimental, the loss does not even have to involve the raw data itself. It might instead be only indicative of the processing occurring on the affected instance. For example, it might be possible to detect that a certain operation is happening on the affected instance and that the operation lasts for a specific duration. This kind of process-specific information can tell a malicious actor about the types of security controls on the instance or what kind of operations are being conducted. This can provide the attacker with an advantage because they might be able to narrow down a list of possible attack vectors to only those that will function in that circumstance, or they might gain an insight into what types of material might be acquired from a successful attack. This tactic is often referred to as a *side channel attack* or *covert channel attack*.

Data Seizure   Legal activity might result in a host machine being confiscated or inspected by law enforcement or plaintiffs' attorneys, and the host machine might include virtualized instances belonging to your organization, even though your organization was not the target.

Cloud data centers can be perceived as similar to demilitarized zones (DMZs) in legacy enterprises. Because everything in the cloud can be accessed remotely, it can be considered exposed to the internet, to a greater or lesser extent. Instead of the discrete perimeter of a private network, cloud configurations may be more porous or might be considered to have no specific perimeter boundary at all.

In the following sections, we'll discuss threats to specific cloud platforms and countermeasures that may facilitate trust in cloud usage.

Threats

Although many of the threats to cloud computing are the same as those we faced in traditional IT operations, they might manifest in novel ways or pose a greater risk. In this section, we'll examine the threats to the private, community, public, and hybrid cloud models. This coverage is by no means exhaustive or prescriptive and should only be taken as a means to inform the reader and stimulate consideration of possible security activity.

Malware   Malicious software downloaded from the internet or uploaded to the internal network can cause a wide variety of problems, including data loss, loss of control of devices, interruption of operations, and so forth. This is less likely in a SaaS environment because the customer doesn't normally install software, but it is sometimes possible for customers to use browser extensions and add-ons that supplement SaaS products and may serve as an avenue for malicious code. For example, the FriarFox malicious extension to Firefox allowed attackers to take over user Gmail accounts.

Internal Threats   These can be the result of malicious or accidental activity on the part of employees or others who have been granted access (such as contractors and maintenance personnel). For example, a rogue employee might provision services from a cloud provider for their own personal use.

External Attackers   Entities outside the organization may want to attack the network for any number of reasons, including financial gain, hacktivism, political goals, perceived grievances, and so on. These attacks can take many forms and manifest a variety of effects, including DoS/DDoS, data breach, legal repercussions, syn flooding, brute force, and more.

Man-in-the-Middle Attacks   Man-in-the-middle attacks, also known as on-path attacks, occur when attackers insert themselves between the sender and receiver. This can take the form of simple eavesdropping to acquire data, or it can be a more advanced attack, such as the attacker posing as one of the participants in order to gain further control/access or modifying data traffic to introduce false or damaging information into the communication. The remote access capability of a private cloud enhances the exposure to this type of threat, compared to legacy configurations where all network access was limited to internal users.

Theft/Loss of Devices   Again, the convenience and enhanced operational capability of remote access also comes with additional threats. In a BYOD environment, especially, the loss or theft of a user's device can lead to unauthorized access and exploitation of the organization's cloud network.

Regulatory Violations   Regulations affect almost all IT operations, but a private cloud adds greater risk that the organization will not be able to maintain compliance. The increased opportunity and efficiency for disseminating information also increases the likelihood of violating applicable regulations. For example, a health clinic that falls out of compliance with HIPAA may find itself subject to significant fines.

Natural Disasters   All operations are prone to disruption from natural disasters, and no geographical region is free of risk from this threat. They only differ in location. (Location and climate dictate the types and frequencies of disasters, such as hurricanes, floods, wildfires, tornadoes, earthquakes, volcanoes, mudslides, and so on.)

Loss of Policy Control   Because ownership is distributed in the cloud, centralized policy promulgation and enforcement is not usually an option. This often moves organizations to adopt *cloud access security broker (CASB)* solutions that provide for centralized cloud policy enforcement.

Loss of Physical Control   Lack of physical control equates to a relative decrease in physical security. This threat can be accentuated in a community cloud if ownership is distributed among many participants.

Lack of Audit Access   Tied to the loss of physical control, it may be impractical or impossible to conduct audits in a distributed environment.

Rogue Administrator   This is an enhanced form of the insider threat. The public cloud incurs the possibility that an insider with more than just basic access may act in a malicious or irresponsible manner. Because public cloud providers will be managing your systems and data, a bad actor or careless employee could take the form of a network/system architect, engineer, or administrator, potentially causing far more damage than a user in the legacy environment could accomplish.

Escalation of Privilege   This is another extension of the insider threat category. This type of threat is what happens when authorized users try to increase their level of access/permissions for either malicious or operational reasons. (Not all attempts to escalate privilege are malicious in nature. Some users are willing to violate policy in order to increase their own ability to perform their tasks or to avoid annoying or cumbersome controls.) The likelihood of this type of threat increases in the cloud because users are faced with not one but at least two sets of governance—that of their own organization and that of the provider. This can cause delays in requests to modify or grant additional access/permission, which can in turn lead to user attempts to circumvent policy.

Contractual Failure   A poorly crafted contract can lead to vendor lock-in, unfavorable terms, lack of necessary services, and other risks, and it should be perceived as a threat.

Although natural disasters can still affect the public cloud architecture, the public cloud can actually provide some protection and insulation from natural disasters as well. In fact, one of the advantages of migrating to a public cloud configuration is the security offered by fast replication, regular backups, and distributed, remote processing and storage of data offered by cloud providers (assuming the provider has appropriately apportioned resources and the customer is utilizing the resources properly).

Risk Mitigation Strategies

The following is a discussion of some countermeasures that can be adopted in order to address the threats for each of the cloud models discussed in the preceding sections. This coverage is by no means exhaustive or prescriptive and should only be taken as a means to inform the reader and stimulate consideration of possible security activity.

Malware Host-based and network-based anti-malware applications and agents can be employed in actual host devices and virtualized instances. Specific training can be provided for all users regarding the methods used for introducing malware into a cloud environment and how to defeat them. Continual monitoring of network traffic and baseline configurations can be used to detect anomalous activity and performance degradation that may be indicative of infections. Regular updates and patches should be implemented, perhaps including automatic checks for virtual machines as they are instantiated at every boot.

Internal Threats Before hiring new personnel, the organization should conduct aggressive background checks, resume/reference confirmation, and skills and knowledge testing. For addressing the risks associated with existing employees, the organization should have appropriate personnel policies that might include comprehensive and recurring training, mandatory vacation and job rotation, and two-person integrity in those situations where it makes financial and operational sense. Solid workflow policies should include separation of duties and least privilege. Active surveillance and monitoring programs, both physical and electronic, can be used. Data should be masked, reducing the view of all personnel who don't need to work directly with raw data. Egress monitoring should be implemented as well (using DLP solutions).

External Attackers Countermeasures include hardened physical devices, hypervisors, and virtual machines, with a solid security baseline and thorough configuration and change management protocols as well as strong access controls, possibly even outsourced to a third party such as a cloud access security broker (CASB). It's also important for the organization to understand how it is perceived by adversaries; this kind of data can be used for threat assessment and identification as well as offering some predictive capability, which could provide a much more timely response than a reactive way of handling threats. Threat intelligence services offer this functionality.

⊕ **Real World Scenario**

Protection vs. Security

In 2011, Sony sued a man named George Hotz after Hotz published an exploit that allowed PlayStation 3 owners to subvert internal controls on the game console and take full control of the device. Sony's actions are understandable. The company intended to protect its brand by obviating opportunities for PlayStation users to breach IRM solutions and infringe on software copyrights. Hotz's position is likewise reasonable. Hotz asserted that the owner of a device should be allowed to utilize it in any manner they see fit and that preventing such capabilities on the pretense that this ability might be abused by malicious actors ought not restrict those who have no such intent.

Sony's legal right to defend its property notwithstanding, the action was seen by some as abusive. Sony, a multinational giant with vast resources, was pursuing what was obviously a punitive course against an individual with limited resources and supposedly no ill intent. The hacking group known as Anonymous considered Hotz a kindred spirit and took umbrage at Sony's actions. A hacker claiming to act on behalf of Anonymous launched a three-day attack against Sony's PlayStation Network (PSN), resulting in a breach that exposed account information of 77 million PSN users (arguably the largest known breach at that time) and an extended shutdown of the game service. The eventual cost of the attack, according to statements attributed to Sony in news reports, exceeded $171 million, including lost revenue, legal fees, and customer restitution.

It's difficult to imagine the loss of root control over PlayStation devices costing Sony more than the damages related to the hack. This in no way suggests that the illegal attack on PSN is justifiable or reasonable. However, Sony's failure to understand public perception of its position and action exposed Sony to a much greater threat than the one the company was trying to prevent. In handling security matters, even when your organization is legally and ethically in the right, an objective, holistic view can be useful to attenuate unintentional escalation of risk.

Sony and Hotz reached an out-of-court settlement, the full terms of which are not available.

Man-in-the-Middle (MITM)/On-Path Attacks   One way to mitigate these attacks is to encrypt data in transit, including authentication activity. You can also use secure session technology and enforcement.

Social Engineering   Training, training, training. Use incentive programs (perhaps including spot bonuses and accolades) to identify personnel who resist social engineering attempts and alert the security office.

Data Loss from Theft/Loss of Devices   Countermeasures include encryption of stored material to attenuate the efficacy of theft, strict physical access controls, limited or no USB functionality (up to and including physically destroying USB ports), detailed and comprehensive inventory control and monitoring, and remote wipe or remote kill switch capability for portable devices.

Regulatory Violations   Hire knowledgeable, trained personnel with applicable skillsets. Defer to general counsel in planning and managing your systems. Implement IRM solutions. Use encryption and obfuscation and masking as necessary.

Natural Disasters   The cloud provider should ensure multiple redundancies for all systems and services for the data center, including ISPs and utilities. The cloud customer can arrange for a disaster backup with the same cloud provider, with another cloud provider, or offline. For further discussion of this topic, see the section "Disaster Recovery (DR) and Business Continuity (BC)" later in this chapter.

Loss of Policy Control   Strong contractual terms should be employed that ensure the provider is adhering to a security program that is at least as effective and thorough as what the customer would institute in an enterprise the customer owned and controlled. Detailed and extensive audits should be conducted by the customer or a trusted third party.

Loss of Physical Control   You can use all of the protections listed in the internal threats, theft/loss of devices, and loss of policy control entries in this list.

Lack of Audit Access   If the provider refuses to allow the customer to directly audit the facility, the customer must rely on a trusted third party instead. If the provider limits access to full third-party reports, the customer must insist on contractual protections to transfer as much of the financial liability for security failures to the provider as possible, including additional punitive damages.

Rogue Administrator   Countermeasures include all the controls listed in the internal threats entry in this list, with additional physical, logical, and administrative controls for all privileged accounts and personnel, including thorough and secure logging of all administrative activities, locked racks, monitoring of physical access to devices in real time, implementation of video surveillance, and financial monitoring of privileged personnel (where legally allowed).

Escalation of Privilege   Extensive access control and authentication tools and techniques should be implemented. Countermeasures also include analysis and review of all log data by trained, skilled personnel on a frequent basis combined with automated tools such as SIEM/SIM/SEM solutions.

Contractual Failure   To protect against vendor lock-in/lock-out, the customer might consider full offsite backups, secured and kept by the customer or a trusted third-party vendor, for reconstitution with another cloud provider in the event of severe contractual disagreement.

Legal Seizure   Legal action (either for prosecutorial or litigatory purposes) might result in unannounced or unexpected loss or disclosure of the organization's data. The organization may consider using encryption of its data in the cloud or possibly employing data dispersion (spreading the data across multiple logical/physical locations). The revised BIA should take this possibility into account, and we need to consider the use of encryption for data in the cloud.

> Virtual machine introspection (VMI) is an agentless means of ensuring a VM's security baseline does not change over time by examining things such as physical address, network settings, and installed OS. These ensure that the baseline has not been inadvertently or maliciously tampered with.

Disaster Recovery (DR) and Business Continuity (BC)

In the following sections, we'll focus on those areas of disaster recovery (DR) and business continuity (BC) that are most directly applicable to cloud computing, specifically with the CCSP CBK and exam in mind. We'll go over BIA concerns specific to cloud platforms and the establishment of shared BC/DR planning and responsibilities between the cloud provider and customer.

Cloud-Specific BIA Concerns

In migrating to a cloud service architecture, your organization will want to review its existing business impact analysis (BIA) and consider a new BIA, or at least a partial assessment, for cloud-specific concerns and the new risks and opportunities offered by the cloud. Some of the potential impacts are things you should have already included in your original BIA, but these may be more significant and take new forms in the cloud. For instance, the loss of an internet service provider (ISP) might have affected your organization in its previous (non-cloud) configuration, but losing connectivity after migration might have a more detrimental effect. Unlike in a traditional IT environment, an organization conducting operations in the cloud will not be able to conduct scaled-back, local computing without connectivity to the provider.

Potential emergent BIA concerns include, but are not limited to, the following:

New Dependencies   Your data and operations will be reliant on external parties in whole new ways after migration. Not only will you have to depend on the cloud provider to meet your organization's needs, but all the downstream and upstream dependencies associated with the provider as well, including the provider's vendors, suppliers, utilities, personnel, and so on. The BIA should take into account possibilities involving the provider's inability to meet service requirements in addition to similar failings on the part of any of the provider's requisite entities.

Regulatory Failure   The efficiency and ease of data distribution in the cloud enhances potential violations of regulations as users and administrators alike promulgate and disseminate data in new ways. The cloud provider presents another potential point of failure for regulatory compliance as well. Even if your organization is fully compliant internally, the provider might be unable or unwilling to adhere to your policies. Regulatory failures could include insufficient protection for PII/ePHI data to comply with statutory requirements such as GDPR, GLBA, HIPAA, FERPA, or SOX, and they might also take the form of contractual inadequacies, such as copyright licensing violations. The BIA needs to include discussion of possible impacts from this situation.

Data Breach/Inadvertent Disclosure   Cloud computing magnifies the likelihood and impact of two existing risks: internal personnel and remote access. Moreover, because full legal liability for breaches of PII can't be transferred to the provider, the cloud customer must reassess the potential impact and effect of an unauthorized disclosure, especially in terms of costs resulting from data breach notification legislative mandates. Other potential adverse results from breaches that should be addressed in the revised BIA include, but aren't limited to, public disclosure of deleterious internal communication and reporting; loss of competitive advantage; negative effect on customer, supplier, and vendor goodwill; and contractual violations.

Vendor Lock-In/Lock-Out   The BIA should take these risks into account for any operations migrated to the cloud. Much of the data for this part of the report should be readily available and won't have to be re-created for the BIA, as it should have been performed as part of the cost-benefit analysis when the organization first considered migration.

Customer/Provider Shared BC/DR Responsibilities

The negotiation between the customer and the provider will be extensive, addressing service needs, policy enforcement, audit capabilities, and so forth. One of the elements that definitely should be included in this discussion is provisions for BC/DR, how and where it will be done, who is responsible for each part of the process, and so on. In the following sections, we'll describe aspects of cloud BC/DR that should be considered in these negotiations.

Logical Location of Backup Data/Systems

There are three general means of using cloud backups for BC/DR. For discussion purposes in this section, we'll be referring to both replicated data and systems as "backups." The basic ways of using cloud backups for BC/DR include the following:

Private Architecture, Cloud Service as Backup   If the organization maintains its own traditional IT data center for the primary production environment, BC/DR plans can include the use of a cloud provider as the backup. Negotiations with providers will have to include periodic upload bandwidth costs (which often include monthly caps as the limiting factor); frequency of backups; whether the organization will use a full, incremental, or differential backup schedule; the security of the data and systems at the backup data center; and ISP costs. In this methodology, the customer should determine when failover will occur—that is, the customer can decide what constitutes an emergency situation and when normal (internal) operations will cease and the backup will be utilized as the operational network. This may involve a formal declaration to include notifying the provider and will almost certainly require additional cost for the duration of the crisis event. Failover might take the form of using the cloud service as a remote network (in an IaaS, PaaS, or SaaS arrangement), or it might require downloading the backup data from the cloud to another physical production site for contingency operations. The negotiation between customer and provider should determine how and when that download occurs, how long it should take, and how and when data will be restored to the normal operations location at the end of the crisis event.

Cloud Operations, Cloud Provider as Backup   One of the attractive benefits of cloud operations is the resiliency and redundancy offered by cloud data centers, especially from market leaders. Cloud providers might offer a backup solution as a feature of their service—a backup located at another data center owned by the provider in case of disaster-level events. Preferably, these backups will be stored in a different geographic region than the primary systems to provide resiliency in the event of a major failure.

In this motif, the provider will have all the responsibility for determining the location and configuration of the backup and most of the responsibility for assessing and declaring disaster events. The customer may have some minimal participation in the failover process, but that's the exception rather than the rule. BC/DR activity, including failover, should usually be transparent to the customer in this case. Moreover, if this feature is offered as part of the normal cloud operation, it will usually be at no or little additional cost.

Cloud Operations, Third-Party Cloud Backup Provider   In this situation, regular operations are hosted by one cloud provider, but contingency operations require failover to another cloud provider. The customer may opt for this selection in order to distribute risk, enhance redundancy, or preemptively attenuate the possibility of vendor lock-out/ lock-in. This may be the most complicated BC/DR arrangement to negotiate because it will have to involve preparations and coordination between all three parties, and roles and responsibilities must be explicitly and thoroughly delineated. Under this arrangement, both the primary cloud provider and the cloud customer will take part in emergency assessment and declaration, and failover may require joint effort. This can impede the process, especially during crises, when cooperation and clear communication is most difficult. The cloud customer will also have to negotiate all the terms in the first model in this list (private architecture, cloud service as a backup) with both the primary and backup cloud providers. Usually, this will also be a relatively expensive methodology—the backup provider will not be a cost bundled with other features offered by the primary provider, and both failover and contingency operations will entail additional expenses. (However, some of the increased costs might be offset by payments from the primary provider if conditions of SLAs are not met because of the crisis event.) Also, data format/system interoperability may be a significant concern; the customer may need to perform additional activity when porting data from one cloud provider to another in order for the data to be used properly at the destination.

Declaration

The declaration of disaster events is a crucial step in the BC/DR process. The cloud customer and provider must decide, prior to the contingency, who specifically will be authorized to make this decision and the explicit process for communicating when it has been made.

Within the customer organization, this authority should be formally assigned to a specific office or person, and there should be a deputy or backup named in case the primary is unavailable. Both the primary and backup should receive detailed emergency operations training that should include extensive and thorough understanding of the organization's specific BC/DR plan. The persons selected for this authority should be empowered by senior management to have the full capability to declare the emergency and initiate failover procedures.

The organization should have a warning system in place to assess impending disaster situations. This is not always possible with certain kinds of contingencies, but some may be anticipated with at least slight notice. The organization should be prepared to fail over in advance of the actual crisis event in order to maintain continuity of operations. The customer and the provider must agree on what will constitute formal notice so that failover occurs, but they may set up a preliminary schedule of preparatory communications before formal declaration is finalized and announced.

If the cloud provider has to conduct some failover activity, the contract should stipulate the time within which this has to be done after notice has been received (for example, within 10 minutes of formal declaration). If failover is automated and fully controlled by the customer, that should also be expressly detailed in the contract.

Resumption of normal activities following a contingency event will likewise require formal notification. Early return to operations may cause an extension of the disaster or result in the loss of data or assets. As with emergency declaration, return to normal operations should be tasked to a specific entity within the customer's organization, and the person making that decision should be fully aware of the risks and implications inherent in it. The process for doing so should also be enumerated within the contract.

As in all things related to security practices, but especially in disaster situations, health and human safety are the paramount concern of any plan or process.

Testing

Having backups is an admirable practice, fulfills statutory requirements, and satisfies some legal due care obligations. However, merely creating a backup is not sufficient. If you never try to use your backups until an actual crisis event, you have no assurance that they will function as planned.

Failover testing must be performed in order to demonstrate the efficacy of the plan and procedures and the ability to return to normal operations. This testing also hones the skills of the personnel involved and allows for additional training opportunities. Of course, the testing itself constitutes an interruption in normal service and ought not to be taken lightly. There is risk and cost involved with performing the test.

Most industry guidance stipulates that such testing occur at least annually. This frequency might be increased depending on the nature of the organization and its operations.

BC/DR testing will have to be coordinated with the cloud provider. This coordination should take place well in advance of the scheduled testing. Care should be taken to determine and assign specific responsibilities to participants, and all liability for problems incurred during the failover or in returning to normal operations should be detailed in the contract.

Cloud Design Patterns

As you continue your journey in the world of cloud computing and cloud security, you'll find that new services and techniques appear pretty much constantly and it's very difficult to stay on top of the best way to design security for each of these new developments.

Fortunately, you're not on your own. You're part of a community of vendors and security professionals working together to help you create a safe and secure computing environment in the cloud. *Design patterns* are an excellent way to do this. Design patterns offer you blueprints for configuring and using cloud services in a secure manner, drawing upon the wisdom of the engineers who created those services and your peers who work with them every day. As you prepare for the CCSP exam, you should be familiar with a few commonly used industry resources.

The CCSP exam objectives specifically mention embracing the security principles published by the SANS Institute. You'll find more information on these principles at www .sans.org.

Another excellent source of information cited by the CCSP exam objectives is the enterprise architecture reference guide published by the Cloud Security Alliance. You'll find this reference guide at https://cloudsecurityalliance.org/artifacts/enterprise-architecture-reference-guide-v2.

You should also be familiar with vendor-specific design patterns. These are extremely useful sources of information because they provide you with the practical implementation details for using the resources provided by a specific vendor. The following are major examples:

- AWS Well-Architected Framework (`https://aws.amazon.com/architecture/well-architected`)

- Microsoft Azure Well-Architected Framework (`https://docs.microsoft.com/en-us/azure/architecture/framework`)

- Google Cloud Architecture Framework (`https://cloud.google.com/architecture/framework`)

Each of these documents provides practical, hands-on advice for using the services offered by those vendors.

Summary

In this chapter, we've discussed the shared and distinct responsibilities of the cloud customer and provider in terms of managing risk as well as BC/DR activities. We also explored the specific risks associated with each of the cloud computing platforms (private, community, public, hybrid, IaaS, PaaS, and SaaS) and detailed countermeasures for dealing with them. Finally, we discussed some of the potential threats and vulnerabilities that constitute the cloud attack surface.

Exam Essentials

Know how cloud security responsibilities are shared between the customer and provider. The shared responsibility model states that security is the responsibility of both the cloud provider and the customer. The division of this responsibility depends upon the type of service and the details of the contract. In general, providers bear more responsibility under a SaaS model and customers bear more responsibility under an IaaS model.

Know the design patterns available to assist you in developing secure cloud architectures. There are many resources that you can draw upon to help you in designing secure cloud environments. These include the well-architected frameworks available from major cloud vendors including AWS, Microsoft, and Google, as well as vendor-neutral design principles available from the SANS Institute and the Cloud Security Alliance.

Know the risks associated with each type of cloud platform. Understand that the more services provided by a vendor, the greater the degree of risk introduced by that vendor relationship. Risks also differ based upon the nature of the shared cloud environment, with private clouds offering a lower risk exposure than public and community clouds.

Understand BC/DR in the cloud. Be aware of the similarities to BC/DR plans and activities in the traditional environment, but pay particular attention to the increased complexity of arrangements necessary between cloud customer and provider and the significant importance of the contract in this regard.

Review Questions

You can find the answers to the review questions in Appendix A.

1. What is the term we use to describe the general ease and efficiency of moving data from one cloud provider to another cloud provider or down from the cloud?

   A. Mobility

   B. Elasticity

   C. Obfuscation

   D. Portability

2. The various models generally available for cloud BC/DR activities include all of the following except_____.

   A. Private architecture, cloud backup

   B. Cloud provider, backup from same provider

   C. Cloud provider, backup from another cloud provider

   D. Cloud provider, backup from private provider

3. Countermeasures for protecting cloud operations against external attackers include all of the following except_____.

   A. Continual monitoring for anomalous activity

   B. Detailed and extensive background checks

   C. Hardened devices and systems, including servers, hosts, hypervisors, and virtual machines

   D. Regular and detailed configuration/change management activities

4. All of the following are techniques to enhance the portability of cloud data in order to minimize the potential of vendor lock-in except_____.

   A. Avoiding proprietary data formats

   B. Using IRM and DLP solutions widely throughout the cloud operation

   C. Ensuring there are no physical limitations to moving

   D. Ensuring favorable contract terms to support portability

5. Which of the following is a technique used to attenuate risks to the cloud environment, resulting in loss or theft of a device used for remote access?

   A. Remote kill switch

   B. Dual control

   C. Muddling

   D. Safe harbor

6. Each of the following are dependencies that must be considered when reviewing the BIA after cloud migration except_____.

   A. The cloud provider's suppliers

   B. The cloud provider's vendors

   C. The cloud provider's utilities

   D. The cloud provider's resellers

7. When reviewing the BIA after a cloud migration, the organization should take into account new factors related to data breach impacts. One of these new factors is_____.

   A. Legal liability can't be transferred to the cloud provider.

   B. Many states have data breach notification laws.

   C. Breaches can cause the loss of proprietary data.

   D. Breaches can cause the loss of intellectual property.

8. The cloud customer will have the most control of their data and systems and the cloud provider will have the least amount of responsibility in which cloud computing arrangement?

   A. IaaS

   B. PaaS

   C. SaaS

   D. Community cloud

9. After a cloud migration, the BIA should be updated to include a review of the new risks and impacts associated with cloud operations; this review should include an analysis of the possibility of vendor lock-in/lock-out. Analysis of this risk may not have to be performed as a new effort because a lot of the material that would be included is already available from which of the following?

   A. NIST

   B. The cloud provider

   C. The cost-benefit analysis the organization conducted when deciding on cloud migration

   D. Open-source providers

10. A poorly negotiated cloud service contract could result in all the following detrimental effects except_____.

    A. Vendor lock-in

    B. Malware

    C. Unfavorable terms

    D. Lack of necessary services

11. All of the following are cloud computing risks in a multitenant environment except_____.

    A. Risk of loss/disclosure due to legal seizures

    B. Information bleed

    C. DDoS

    D. Escalation of privilege

12. Countermeasures for protecting cloud operations against internal threats include all of the following except_____.

    A. Aggressive background checks

    B. Hardened perimeter devices

    C. Skills and knowledge testing

    D. Extensive and comprehensive training programs, including initial, recurring, and refresher sessions

13. Countermeasures for protecting cloud operations against internal threats include all of the following except_____.

    A. Active physical surveillance and monitoring

    B. Active electronic surveillance and monitoring

    C. Redundant ISPs

    D. Masking and obfuscation of data for all personnel without need to know for raw data

14. Countermeasures for protecting cloud operations against internal threats at the provider's data center include all of the following except_____.

    A. Broad contractual protections to make sure the provider is ensuring an extreme level of trust in its own personnel

    B. Financial penalties for the cloud provider in the event of negligence or malice on the part of its own personnel

    C. DLP solutions

    D. Scalability

15. Countermeasures for protecting cloud operations against internal threats at the provider's data center include all of the following except_____.

    A. Separation of duties

    B. Least privilege

    C. Conflict of interest

    D. Mandatory vacation

16. Benefits for addressing BC/DR offered by cloud operations include all of the following except_____.

    A. One-time pads

    B. Distributed, remote processing and storage of data

    C. Fast replication

    D. Regular backups offered by cloud providers

17. All of the following methods can be used to attenuate the harm caused by escalation of privilege except_____.

    A. Extensive access control and authentication tools and techniques

    B. Analysis and review of all log data by trained, skilled personnel on a frequent basis

    C. Periodic and effective use of cryptographic sanitization tools

    D. The use of automated analysis tools such as SIM, SIEM, and SEM solutions

18. What is the hypervisor malicious attackers would prefer to attack?

    A. Type 1

    B. Type 2

    C. Type 3

    D. Type 4

19. What is the term used to describe loss of access to data because the cloud provider has ceased operation?

    A. Closing

    B. Vendor lock-out

    C. Vendor lock-in

    D. Masking

20. Because PaaS implementations are so often used for software development, what is one of the vulnerabilities that should always be kept in mind?

    A. Malware

    B. Loss/theft of portable devices

    C. Backdoors

    D. DoS/DDoS

Chapter 5

Cloud Platform, Infrastructure, and Operational Security

THE OBJECTIVE OF THIS CHAPTER IS TO ACQUAINT THE READER WITH THE FOLLOWING CONCEPTS:

✓ **Domain 1: Cloud Concepts, Architecture, and Design**

- 1.3. Understand security concepts relevant to cloud computing

    - 1.3.4. Network Security (e.g., network security groups, traffic inspection, geofencing, zero trust network)

✓ **Domain 3: Cloud Platform and Infrastructure Security**

- 3.1. Comprehend cloud infrastructure and platform components

    - 3.1.2. Network and communications

    - 3.1.3. Compute

    - 3.1.6. Management plane

- 3.4. Plan and implementation of security controls

    - 3.4.2. System, storage, and communication protection

✓ **Domain 4: Cloud Application Security**

- 4.5. Use verified secure software

    - 4.5.3. Third-party software management

    - 4.5.4. Validated open-source software

✓ **Domain 5: Cloud Security Operations**

- 5.1. Build and implement physical and logical infrastructure for cloud environment

- 5.1.1. Hardware specific security configuration requirements (e.g., hardware security module (HSM), Trusted Platform module (TPM))

- 5.1.2. Installation and configuration of management tools

- 5.1.3. Virtual hardware specific security configuration requirements (e.g., network, storage, memory, central processing unit (CPU), Hypervisor type 1 and 2)

- 5.1.4. Installation of guest operating system (OS) virtualization toolsets

- 5.2. Operate and maintain physical and logical infrastructure for cloud environment

  - 5.2.3. Network security controls (e.g., firewalls, intrusion detection systems (IDS), intrusion prevention systems (IPS), honeypots, vulnerability assessments, network security groups, bastion host)

  - 5.2.4. Operating system (OS) hardening through the application of baselines, monitoring, and remediation (e.g., Windows, Linux, VMware)

  - 5.2.11. Configuration of host and guest operating system (OS) backup and restore functions

  - 5.2.12. Management plane (e.g., scheduling, orchestration, maintenance)

- 5.6. Manage security operations

  - 5.6.5. Vulnerability assessments

✓ **Domain 6: Legal, Risk, and Compliance**

- 6.3. Understand audit process, methodologies, and required adaptations for a cloud environment

  - 6.3.1. Internal and external audit controls

  - 6.3.3. Identify assurance challenges of virtualization and cloud

  - 6.3.7. Audit planning

Securing cloud platforms requires a change in mindset from on-premises systems and practices. While many of the same basic capabilities exist at a conceptual or functional level, their implementation and the ways in which you can use them are often meaningfully different. As you consider securing a cloud environment, you need to take into account the infrastructure and systems or services you'll use, how they'll communicate and how to secure network traffic in a shared environment, how it will all be managed securely—and how to secure the management plane itself!

As you use this chapter to prepare for the CCSP exam, consider how you might apply traditional onsite controls in a cloud environment and what might be different or raise new concerns due to how the cloud provider presents systems, services, and capabilities to your organization. You'll need to think about ephemeral machines that are part of containerized environments, how to use baselines to harden systems and services, how to apply access controls using both host and cloud-native controls, and how to configure and manage network security controls, among many other tasks, to ensure a secure cloud operations and infrastructure environment.

Finally, the ability to audit and assess your environment needs to be a consideration throughout your design and implementation process. Unlike tradition environments, where auditors can simply walk into your data center and examine physical systems, cloud environments can have additional constraints—including the fact that auditing the underlying environment is typically prohibited.

Foundations of Managed Services

Cloud services are built to allow cloud service providers to sell access to their systems, services, and capabilities to a range of customers. That means that they're designed to allow providers to make access available to portions of their capabilities and that customers need to understand that most of their operations will be conducted in a shared environment.

Typically, they include some of the following components:

- *Network and communications capabilities* that allow customers to transfer data into and out of the cloud computing vendor's environment. Vendors have to design for large-scale use of their networks and connectivity and need to build redundancy and scalability into their underlying infrastructure. As a security professional, this means that you will need to think about both your organization's use of the infrastructure and capabilities and what else may be occurring that might impact the cloud provider. Do they have protections in place against denial-of-service attacks? Is their network connectivity connected to your internet service provider in a way that provides low latency or other desirable features?

- *Compute* is the focus of infrastructure as a service (IaaS) providers. While this may seem to be bound to virtual machines or central processing units (CPUs), interpreted broadly compute includes storage, serverless computing, and containers as well as other functions that providers sell. In essence, if it's not part of the network and communications capability, and it's not part of the management plane, it is likely to be compute. This means that a lot of what you, as a security practitioner, will be securing can fall into the compute category in the CCSP list of platform and infrastructure components. Compute is typically shared among customers, although cloud providers provide dedicated instances that only run a single customer's workload on a system for greater security when necessary, albeit at a higher cost!

- A *management plane* is the third component of a platform. Management planes allow you to control the network, communications, compute, and other service elements of a cloud environment. That means that securing your management plane is an absolutely critical component of your design and implementation.

 You'll notice a bias toward IaaS environments in the CCSP exam. That's because of a lot of the work that a security practitioner can do in the cloud occurs in those environments. In a SaaS or PaaS environment, most of the infrastructure and design security decisions are already made, and operational security is all that remains. That doesn't mean that security isn't important in those environments, but you'll spend your time assessing providers and their audit responses and ensuring operational security practices are in place instead of designing and architecting a secure environment in most scenarios other than an IaaS deployment.

It helps to consider roles and responsibilities for security for the cloud based on whether they belong to the cloud provider or the customer or are shared by both.

Cloud Provider Responsibilities

Cloud service providers design, build, and maintain the underlying hosting environments that they then use to sell services. That means everything from choosing data center locations and designs and selecting internet service providers (ISPs) to hiring and managing the staff who run facilities. It also involves designing, building, operating, and securing the underlying software platforms and tools that they use to make their services available.

To do this, the cloud provider needs one or more data centers or other facilities from which to provide services to its customers. They have to consider where the facilities are located, the physical components inside that facility, and the services that support and connect them. That means they need to perform key tasks like securing the hardware components; investing in power, connectivity, and environmental controls; ensuring that they have enough capacity to meet their commitments and customer demand; and securing both the facility and the systems that make up the cloud environment.

Shared Responsibilities by Service Type

The major cloud service providers have different responsibility models for providers and customers. Figure 5.1 shows a typical breakdown for the three most common service models.

FIGURE 5.1   Responsibilities by service model

	Infrastructure as a Service (IaaS)	Platform as a Service (PaaS)	Software as a Service (SaaS)
Security, risk, and compliance (GRC)			
Data Security			
Application Security			Shared
Platform Security		Shared	Provider
Infrastructure Security	Shared	Provider	Provider
Physical Security	Provider	Provider	Provider

Customer Responsibility (white)

Shared Responsibility (gray)

Provider Responsibility (black)

IaaS

In an infrastructure as a service provider model, the cloud provider is only hosting the hardware and utilities and thus is responsible for the physical security of the facility and systems. Both parties share the responsibility for securing the infrastructure. The customer bears responsibility for all other security aspects.

> Providers have a vested interest in their customers building and maintaining secure infrastructure and systems. That means that they also invest in guidelines for secure operations in their environments. Amazon's AWS Well-Architected framework (https://aws.amazon.com/architecture/well-architected) and Azure's Well-Architected Framework (https://docs.microsoft.com/en-us/azure/architecture/framework) are both useful examples of this type of design and implementation guidance. If you're not familiar with them, reviewing one or both will give you a good idea of what cloud IaaS providers think useful best practices are like today.

PaaS

In a platform as a service model, the service provider delivers a platform that the customer configures and uses. While the lines between SaaS and PaaS can be blurry, in a PaaS environment customers typically build more of the functionality and capabilities through configuration activities. That means that the customer shares responsibility for the platform's security and has full responsibility for the applications, data, and risk management involved in their use of the platform.

SaaS

Software as a service implementations give customers the least control over the environment, and thus the service provider has the greatest level of responsibility in this model. Customers merely have to worry about access and administration. Despite this, because the customer is the data owner, the customer will always have ultimate control of who has authorization to view and manipulate the data itself.

Securing Communications and Infrastructure

The CCSP exam expects test takers to consider four critical concepts related to network security from a design and architecture perspective:

- *Network security groups*, often simply called *security groups*, are virtual firewalls used in cloud environments. Security groups use rules to control traffic, using ports and protocols exactly like the firewalls you're likely used to, and you can typically control inbound and outbound traffic using separate rules. Much like traditional firewalls, security groups are typically stateful, meaning that they track requests and responses to allow responses to return to systems that make an allowed request.

- *Traffic inspection* in cloud and virtual environments can be more challenging or may require using tools that are designed for the environment. Since traffic is typically sent directly to the virtual resource, there often isn't a direct equivalent of promiscuous mode traffic capture that would allow you to see more of a network's traffic. Fortunately, cloud vendors know that you'll want to be able to see, capture, and analyze traffic and provide tools like AWS's VPC traffic mirroring capability (`https://aws.amazon.com/blogs/aws/new-vpc-traffic-mirroring`).

- *Geofencing* can be an important tool because security practitioners and organizations often want to restrict access to services or systems based on where that access is occurring from. While geofencing is built into many apps for other reasons, security tools are most likely to use geofencing to correlate logins and activity to the locations where they originate, to ensure credentials aren't being misused, and to identify unexpected traffic patterns based on geoIP information.

- Zero trust relies on identities and authorization to ensure that users and entities are validated before they access data. Implementing zero trust in cloud systems can sometimes be easier than in legacy environments due to greenfield builds and capabilities that are built into the environment. You can read about Azure's Zero trust support at `https://azure.microsoft.com/en-us/blog/enabling-zero-trust-with-azure-network-security-services`, Google's at `https://cloud.google.com/beyond-corp`, and Amazon's at `https://aws.amazon.com/security/zero-trust`.

Why is packet capture and traffic inspection harder in the cloud? Cloud environments operate at Layer 3 of the OSI model, while traditional networks can be accessed at Layers 1 and 2.

In addition, the CCSP specifically mentions a number of network security controls in this context that you'll need to be ready to explain and implement in the cloud. They are as follows:

Firewalls

Firewalls are tools that limit communications based on some criteria. In cloud environments, security groups (or network security groups) are often the first firewall capability that is deployed. Traditional firewall vendors also make virtual appliance or cloud service–enabled versions of their tools available, allowing you to use the same firewall technologies between on-premises and cloud sites or to leverage specific capabilities you may want that a simple security group doesn't provide, like those delivered by the combined security devices known as next-generation firewalls (NGFWs). Regardless of their delivery method, firewalls tend to work in a similar manner: the criteria for determining which traffic is allowed and which is not is handled by rules that are defined by administrators.

One of the key changes that occur in cloud and virtual environments is that systems are often ephemeral and may scale quickly. That means that firewalls and firewall rules need to account for those changes and be either adjusted by the same code that adds new systems or scaled inside of the rules themselves to handle the number of devices that could exist, or load balancers and other tools may be used to account for changes in infrastructure without requiring new rules.

While the CCSP exam calls out these specific technologies, all of the other security tools in a typical on-premises environment's arsenal exist in the cloud as well. As you tackle security designs, you should consider tools like web application firewalls to protect web apps as well as application gateways and the whole range of other network security devices available to today's security practitioners.

Firewall and firewall-like technologies include a broad range of solutions ranging from simple access control lists (ACLs) and network access control lists (NACLs) to firewall systems that can maintain session states and track attack patterns to adjust rules in response to unwanted traffic. More advanced tools like NGFWs integrate even more security services and capabilities, often serving as all-in-one security devices. All of this means that when you consider firewall-like technologies, you need to consider both your requirements and the full range of features and functions that your potential solutions can provide to see what type of solution best fits your organization's needs.

Intrusion Detection/Intrusion Prevention Systems

Intrusion detection systems (IDS) are designed to identify malicious traffic and alert on it. *Intrusion prevention systems (IPS)* can both detect and respond to malicious traffic by stopping it or taking other action beyond alerting. Each of the major cloud providers has third parties who provide IDS and IPS services, many of which are essentially the same as those in legacy environments, simply virtualized and cloud enabled.

Honeypots

A *honeypot* is a tool used to detect, identify, isolate, and analyze attacks by distracting attackers. This is usually a dummy machine, often with seemingly valuable but fake data, partially secured and configured as if it was a realistic portion of the production environment. When attackers penetrate it and attempt nefarious activity, the security team can monitor and record the attackers' behavior. This information can be used for defensive purposes in the actual production environment or as evidence in litigation and prosecution actions. Unlike on-premises networks, where large segments of "dark" or unused public network space are likely to exist, many cloud environments charge per public IP address, adding cost to running a honeypot or honeynet. Practitioners need to determine the cost and value of running a honeypot in a cloud environment as part of their design and evaluation.

Vulnerability Assessment Tools

Vulnerability assessment tools, or vulnerability scanners, are available in cloud environments as both native tools like Azure's Defender (https://docs.microsoft.com/en-us/ azure/defender-for-cloud) and Amazon's Inspector service (https://aws.amazon. com/inspector). Third-party vulnerability assessment tools are also available from their marketplaces, allowing you to select and use a familiar tool or one that best fits your organization's need. Much like in a traditional on-premises environment, you need to consider the network location and visibility of hosts to your vulnerability scanner as well as ensure the security of the scanner in your design efforts. It is also crucial to remember that many systems in cloud environments are ephemeral and may be run in an infrastructure as code environment. That means that your scans need to validate both the original system and any changes that may occur as code updates and component updates occur. A strong presence of vulnerability scanning in your system release pipeline can help!

Bastion Hosts

A bastion host is used to allow administrators to access a private network from a lower security zone. A bastion host will have network interfaces in both the lower and higher security zones and will receive additional security attention because of this.

Bastion hosts are sometimes called jump servers or jump boxes because they let you jump between zones.

Figure 5.2 shows a simple bastion host design with a bastion host in a lower trust public network used to access a protected private network. Security groups between the network segments and host security controls on the bastion host help to ensure the bastion host remains secure.

FIGURE 5.2 Bastion host in a simple cloud environment

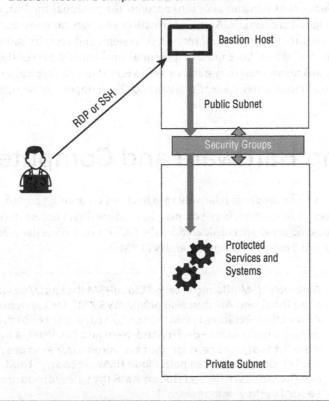

If you want to try setting up a Linux bastion host, AWS provides a quickstart guide for how to deploy them. You can give it a try by following the instructions at https://aws.amazon.com/quickstart/architecture/linux-bastion.

Identity Assurance in Cloud and Virtual Environments

The CCSP exam outline points to identity assurance in both virtual and cloud systems as a challenge for practitioners. There are a number of reasons that this can be the case.

The most common identity challenge in cloud environments is when organizations want to allow users to bring their own identities. Identity proofing, the process by which an identity is validated as belonging to a user, can be nearly impossible if you're allowing users to bring a Gmail account as their identity to your service. Even Facebook accounts, which can be somewhat easier to tie to an actual person, in some cases are problematic.

The problem of identity proofing is less likely to come up in an environment where an organization knows its own employees and other users and is handling identity proofing through normal onboarding processes. The next challenge is validating that users are legitimately the person who is supposed to use the credentials that are being used in a given circumstance or to access a system or service. Compromised credentials—particularly secrets, API keys, and similar artifacts—can provide attackers with entrances into services.

Identity assurance thus needs to take into account the potential for lost, compromised, or intentionally shared credentials. Audit information and logs must contain information that can help to identify the individual, service, or system, and security monitoring systems need to be able to find when those indicate potential problems. Whether that's a geographic location change, unknown remote system, or behaviors that are atypical or commonly associated with malicious activity, identity assurance is an important security layer—and an ongoing challenge.

Securing Hardware and Compute

While direct access to hardware is relatively rare in cloud computing environments, there are a small number of instances where you may have more direct access to or control of hardware. Two specific areas are considered by the CCSP exam objectives: hardware security modules (HSMs) and Trusted Platform Modules (TPMs).

Amazon's HSM offering is called CloudHSM (https://aws.amazon.com/cloudhsm), and Amazon also offers AWS KMS for key management. Azure offers Dedicated HSM (https://azure.microsoft.com/en-us/services/azure-dedicated-hsm) and Key Vault, a free secrets store (https://azure.microsoft.com/en-us/services/key-vault). Google provides both Cloud HSM (https://cloud.google.com/kms/docs/hsm) and Google KMS (https://cloud.google.com/security-key-management).

Hardware security modules (HSMs), are used to generate, store, and manage cryptographic keys as well as for other cryptographic uses in support of hashing and digital signatures and for encryption and decryption of data through TLS offloading and database transparent encryption purposes. That means that HSMs hold some of the most sensitive secrets organizations use in the cloud, making them both a target for knowledgeable attackers and a critical component to secure for cloud security practitioners.

Cloud providers may provide HSMs either as a service or as a hardware device. Organizations that have very high security or compliance requirements may opt for the dedicated hardware device rather than using the HSM service, but in both cases the device is in the physical control of the cloud service provider. Redundancy and backups remain critical because a HSM failure and data loss would potentially mean the loss of all of the keys stored in the HSM. Since cloud services rely heavily on keys for security, a HSM failure could stop an organization in its tracks.

Although the CCSP Exam Outline (Candidate Information Bulletin) only describes HSMs, you should also be aware of key management system (KMS) functions that provide HSM features as a service rather than as dedicated instances or hardware like the cloud HSM offerings discussed earlier. Understanding your organization's functional and security requirements can help you choose between a dedicated HSM and a key management service.

While HSMs may be the most common solution for cloud-based environments due to the large-scale use of secrets, the *Trusted Platform Module (TPM)* also has a role to play. Trusted Platform Module is a hardware device used to secure, store, and manage cryptographic keys for disk encryption, trusted boot, hardware validation, and password management for devices.

 Both Amazon and Azure provide guidance on IoT devices and TPM. Visit https://azure.microsoft.com/en-us/blog/device-provisioning-identity-attestation-with-tpm and https://aws.amazon.com/blogs/iot/using-a-trusted-platform-module-for-endpoint-device-security-in-aws-iot-greengrass for insight into the use of TPM for endpoint devices connected to both major cloud service providers.

Since cloud providers typically present virtualized hardware, hardware-based TPMs are not a common feature provided to cloud service customers. Software TPMs and TPMs integrated into Internet of Things devices are both more likely to be concerns for security practitioners.

Keeping Cloud Storage Secure

Securing cloud storage has its own set of design and implementation requirements, but a number of common best practices can serve you well.

- Leveraging built-in tools designed to ensure that environments are secure is a critical step. Amazon's Trusted Advisor and Azure's Advisor both provide configuration and usage analysis capabilities to help you.

- Least privilege remains a critical control, and identity and access management is needed to ensure least privilege is manageable.

- Encrypting data at rest and in transit helps to prevent misconfigurations and data leaks from becoming larger issues.

- Blocking public access by default is one of the best ways to ensure storage doesn't become a data leakage nightmare.

- Ensuring wildcard or broad access to storage buckets is not allowed helps to ensure that you can track who has access to data.

- Building secure default access control lists and checking them for overly broad access on a regular basis helps to prevent issues with overly broad permissions.

- Versioning and replication are critical for availability.

- Monitoring, auditing, and alerting are all important parts of a secure storage management program.

Securing Software

In infrastructure as a service environments, managing software ranging from applications to operating systems is an ongoing element in security operations. Third-party software requires updates, configuration, and monitoring to ensure that it is as secure as possible.

The use of code-defined infrastructure means that validating open-source and third-party software is an ongoing challenge. When libraries and software components are available from Git repositories, how can your organization ensure that the software has not been compromised?

Compromising Repositories

In 2021, the core PHP Git repository was compromised, allowing a malicious actor to push two commits. The commits included a code injection vulnerability with the intention being to make any organization that pulled PHP from the trusted repository potentially vulnerable to an injection attack. Fortunately, the issue was discovered before the code in the commits made it into any builds that were released.

You can read more about the incident at https://news-web.php.net/php
.internals/113838.

The CCSP Exam Outline (Candidate Information Bulletin) focuses on three areas related to securing software: third-party software management; validated open-source software; and OS hardening, baselines, monitoring, and remediation.

Third-Party Software Management

Managing third-party software can be a challenge, as releases, updates, and other changes can have broad-ranging impacts for your organization. Management processes start with software selection, where focusing on both fit-to-business need and the third-party provider's practices for updates and security patching, as well as their notification process, is useful for the selection processes.

Once software has been selected, organizations need to identify what the software's configuration requirements are. That means understanding security implications and capabilities as well as functional configuration items. Vendors often provide best practice configuration guidelines that can play an important role in successful and secure implementation.

With software in place, organizations need to ensure that they receive information about patches and updates that improve security and functionality. Software needs to be tested before deployment in many cases, requiring test environments and practices that may involve vulnerability scans or other automated testing and validation steps. It's also important to ensure that your organization is receiving customer update emails or other notifications and that you know how to reach out to the vendor for assistance.

In cases where the software is noncommercial, such as open-source software packages, these practices may not all be possible due to the difference in support models. Organizations may need to balance the cost of software support or commercial software against the benefits of open-source software in their environment. In many cases, there may not be a direct replacement for open-source software, and organizations must work to understand what the patching, security, and notification processes are for that software package.

 Automatic updates can be very useful, but they can also automatically introduce new issues into an organization. For that reason, organizations often turn off automatic updates for key infrastructure and software packages so that they can validate new updates in a test environment before deploying them to mission-critical systems. When you consider patching, you should also consider how patches will be tested and how long you might delay an update based on security criticality versus the potential to disrupt your business. That's often a tough risk equation!

Common code elements like libraries and other dependencies are a major concern for open-source software security, but they can also exist for commercial software packages. That means that package management is a concern for security professionals, developers, and system administrators who need to know if the components that make up their services and systems have vulnerabilities themselves. Software composition analysis tools, package management tools, and similar technologies all have a role to play in the complex mazes of dependencies that modern software relies on.

Validating Open-Source Software

Open-source software validation can be a challenge because you first need to identify a trusted source for the software and then ensure that the package or packages you're using are trusted. Some software packages provide cryptographic hashes for integrity checks to ensure the software was not tampered with, while others simply provide the software from their official site.

Some software is signed with a developer's certificate, or has a GPG or PGP signature. While checking these signatures can require extra time, validating software is likely to be necessary in high-security environments. Remember that you'll need the software provider's public key to validate signatures and that you'll need to ensure that the key that is provided is actually theirs, otherwise the validation process isn't trustworthy!

OS Hardening, Monitoring, and Remediation

The final third-party software objective for the CCSP exam is operating system hardening. You'll need to be aware of and know how to use baselines, monitoring, and remediation processes for Windows, Linux, and VMware as part of this objective.

Baselines are used as part of system hardening processes. A baseline is the organization's standard for how a system should be configured to meet functional and security goals. Baselines are available from, for example, the following organizations:

- The Center for Internet Security (`www.cisecurity.org/cis-benchmarks`)

- Microsoft's Security Compliance Toolkit (`https://docs.microsoft.com/en-us/ windows/security/threat-protection/windows-security-configuration- framework/security-compliance-toolkit-10`)

- Azure specific Linux security baselines (`https://docs.micro- soft.com/en-us/security/benchmark/azure/baselines/ virtual-machines-linux-security-baseline`)

- RedHat's security guides (`https://access.redhat.com/documentation/en-us/ red_hat_enterprise_linux/7/html/security_guide/index`)

- VMware's hardening guidelines (`www.vmware.com/security/hardening- guides.html`)

Figure 5.3 shows an example entry from the VMware NSX 3.2 security configuration guide's Data Plane recommendations found at `https://communities.vmware.com/t5/ VMware-NSX-Documents/NSX-T-3-2-Security-Configuration-Guide/ta-p/ 2885209`. Note that it identifies the action or objective, why the vulnerability is of concern, and how to assess the configuration. It offers cautionary information about the setting or changes and includes the desired setting or value and whether it is a default setting, and it references documentation.

FIGURE 5.3   Sample baseline documentation

ID	Component	Subcomponent	Title	Vulnerability Discussion	Assessment Procedure	Default Setting	Default Status	Is Exception Allowed	API	Reference
block-unused-ports	Various	PVTD	Block access to ports not used on data plane.	Blocking unneeded ports can prevent general attacks on these ports and thus reduce attack surface.	Verify that only ports listed in the "Reference" column in this sheet are open on data plane.	N/A	Only needed ports should be open.	No	N/A	https://docs.vmware.com/en/VM ware-NSX-T/index.html
disable-ssh-edge	NSX Edge	Edge	Disable Secure Shell (SSH) unless needed for diagnostics or troubleshooting purposes.	Secure Shell (SSH) is an interactive command line environment available for making remote connections to NSX edge node. Access via SSH requires the root/admin or higher privileged user account credentials. The activities performed from the SSH generally bypass NSX based RBAC and audit controls. Thus, SSH should only be turned on when needed to troubleshoot/re-solve problems that cannot be fixed via other procedures. It is also useful to block out site firewall rules on any interface that is not the internal one you want to use to access ssh. Doing so prevents brute force attacks from the actual internet if that is a gateway.	Try opening a connection via SSH to NSX edge . If the connection opens requesting for credentials, this means SSH is enabled and is available for making connections.	If you need to use SSH, set the thumbprint a single time at the client, and always reuse the same object to connect. If prompted for initial connection approval later from the same client, don't reapprove. Wherever possible, consider using vssh-console over SSH.	Turned off	Yes	Log in to the edge console with the admin user. On the command line, type the following: "start/stop ssmext-ssh", to enable/disable ssh.	https://docs.vmware.com/en/VM ware-NSX-T/index.html
isolate-storage-network	Storage	Network	Isolate storage network from other networks.	Current virtualized disk technologies rely on unencrypted and insecure transports such as iSCSI. Protect against rogue VM attacks by isolating these storage networks from data transport networks. If compromised, attackers may be able to mount VM disks and other sensitive information. Using VMware certified third party software such as pvscsi may be utilized to enhance data access security.	Do a thorough check on the infrastructure design and NSX deployment network diagram. Ensure that the storage network is isolated from any other networks.	Best practice guidance is to use dedicated vNIC and vLAN for storage and compute.	No	N/A	https://docs.vmware .com/products-infrastructure/vmwarevsphere/cloudnative/products/cloud-nativestorage/vmware-cloud-native-data.introduction/

If you've never reviewed a hardening baseline, it's worth some time to review at least one of the resources previously listed. The CIS benchmarks are widely used and are available for many operating systems and software packages. Understanding what a baseline includes and how you might apply one to your own organization is important knowledge both for the exam and for practitioners.

Regardless of which baseline your organization chooses to use, you'll need to review and adapt it to your needs. Baselines are a starting point and should not be applied without thought and consideration for business and security needs.

Monitoring is also a critical part of operating system hardening. In this context, monitoring involves ensuring that the operating system remains configured to meet the baseline and that changes are caught and restored to the desired configuration, accepted due to organizational needs, or alerted on as part of an incident response process. The Center for Internet Security Controls Self-Assessment Tool (CSAT) is a web application that tracks implementation of CIS controls. Tools like this can be used to help with monitoring efforts. You can find the CSAT tool at www.cisecurity.org/insights/blog/cis-csat-free-tool-assessing-implementation-of-cis-controls.

Finally, remediation efforts are conducted based on monitoring and baseline implementation processes. Remediation seeks to align systems and software to the baseline, whether it's done during system build and setup or after an incident or update.

Managing Virtual Systems

The CCSP Exam Outline (Candidate Information Bulletin) points to four major components you should be ready to address as part of the exam.

First is the installation and configuration of management tools. Virtualization management tools provide greater control of virtual systems and can help the virtualization management plane handle resource demands and other tasks more effectively. Of course, as with any additional software package, these create a new attack surface and could potentially impact either the virtual machine or the hypervisor.

Next, you'll need to be prepared to answer questions about security configuration requirements specific to virtual hardware:

- Network configurations may include use of virtual firewalls, switches, and other virtualized network devices as part of a secure design. It can also include configuring which virtual local area networks (VLANs) or network segment virtual systems will be on, network interface card (NIC) teaming for availability, and network path redundancy.

- Storage can be either allocated as needed or provisioned up front. In either case, encryption of storage spaces is an important control in any shared environment.

- Memory can be either allocated directly to a virtual machine or allocated as needed. Much like other resources, dedicated memory provides greater security but increases costs because the environment must be provisioned as needed rather than being allowed to resize and scale on demand.

- Central processing units (CPUs) are often shared in virtual environments, making them a potentially vulnerable component if malicious actors can gain access to processes being run in another virtual machine. Dedicating cores or entire physical CPUs can help to alleviate this risk but comes at a higher cost because the resource cannot be shared.

The Exam Outline (Candidate Information Bulletin) mentions Type 1 and Type 2 hypervisors. A Type 1 hypervisor runs directly on the underlying host's hardware, while a Type 2 hypervisor runs on an operating system as an application. If you're working to secure a Type 1 hypervisor, you need to focus on the hypervisor platform's security capabilities. With a Type 2 hypervisor, you must secure both the underlying operating system and the hypervisor. In most cloud environments, vendors use Type 1 hypervisors for efficiency and direct hardware control. Examples of Type 1 hypervisors include VMware ESXi and Microsoft's Hyper-V. VMware Workstation, VirtualBox, and Microsoft's Virtual PC are examples of Type 2 hypervisors.

Third, installation of guest operating system (OS) virtualization toolsets like VMware Tools or Amazon's paravirtual drivers for Windows instances, and similar drivers for other cloud environments, add functionality by connecting to the underlying virtualization host. They can help map storage and support improved networking, video output, sound, or input capabilities or otherwise improve the experience and functionality for virtualized operating systems.

Finally, configuration of host and guest operating system (OS) backup and restore functions allows virtual machines to be backed up via snapshots, which capture point-in-time configurations, memory state, disk images, and settings that can then be restored as needed. These are useful both for restoration after unforeseen events like issues during a patch or after an incident, but they can also be used to build baseline instances for later use.

Assessing Vulnerabilities

Scanning for vulnerabilities can require special consideration in cloud-hosted environments. While SaaS and PaaS vendors are unlikely to allow you to scan them at all, IaaS vendors may have restrictions on what can be scanned or may require notification or have an approval process if they allow scanning at all.

> While we're using AWS as an example here, the other major infrastructure as a service vendors have their own equivalent policies and procedures. The key thing to remember as a test taker is that you need to understand what your vendor allows and prohibits and ensure that your organization complies with them in order to avoid service disruptions or account issues.

Amazon's scanning policies describe both what can be scanned and what can't be scanned. As of March 2022, the permitted list for penetration testing without prior approval includes the following items:

- Amazon EC2 instances, NAT gateways, and Elastic Load Balancers
- Amazon RDS
- Amazon CloudFront
- Amazon Aurora
- Amazon API Gateway
- AWS Lambda and Lambda Edge functions
- Amazon Lightsail resources
- Amazon Elastic Beanstalk environments

Amazon prohibits a number of activities too. It's worth noting that most of these activities are more likely to result in denial-of-service conditions or resource exhaustion, thus interfering with other customers' use of the service.

- DNS zone walking via Amazon Route 53 hosted zones
- Denial of Service (DoS), Distributed Denial of Service (DDoS), Simulated DoS, Simulated DDoS (These are subject to the DDoS Simulation Testing policy.)
- Port flooding
- Protocol flooding
- Request flooding (login request flooding, API request flooding)

Amazon specifically prohibits testing of AWS infrastructure and underlying services and provides a request process to receive authorization to simulate other events. As you might expect, it requests dates, account information, and contact information as well as descriptions of what testers intend to do. Amazon also provides policies on stress testing and DDoS simulation.

Cloud services often provide their own vulnerability assessment tools. Amazon's tool is called Amazon Inspector, and it assesses both known vulnerabilities and gaps from common best practices. At the same time, vulnerability scanning tool providers make their own virtual appliances and services available via Amazon's marketplace, allowing organizations to pick the tools that they want or tools that match their existing on-premises deployments.

As you consider vulnerability scanning, you'll need to keep in mind the network architecture and security protections you have in place for your cloud environment. Much like in an on-premises data center, those protections may stop vulnerability scans from occurring between segments or security zones or may create additional complexity for your scan attempts. Designing your environment so that you can perform security assessments and making the tools available in each environment, segment, or zone that you need them in is part of a secure and complete cloud infrastructure design and operations plan.

Securing the Management Plane

Cloud services provide a management console or service that allows organizations to use their services. While each service provider's management console or service is different, they tend to have a similar set of features. Here we'll focus on what you'll typically find in an IaaS management plane, but bear in mind that SaaS and PaaS vendors will also have security capabilities and options built into their management consoles that are appropriate to the level of control the service provides to its users.

Figure 5.4 shows the web interface for Amazon's AWS management console. Access as a root or privileged user to the console or the command-line interface (CLI) for an AWS account provides control of the account and needs to be protected against compromise.

The CCSP Exam Outline (Candidate Information Bulletin) focuses on three specific areas as critical elements of a management plane, and we'll look at an AWS-centric example here:

- *Scheduling*, or the ability to start and stop resources at a planned time or due to events. In AWS, this can be done via the Instance Scheduler or via Lambda functions. Scheduling is a key element for cost control since it can allow you to run services only when they are needed.

  An AWS CLI command to create an example of an infrastructure called CCSP on a schedule might read as follows:

  ```
  scheduler-cli create-period --stack CCSPExample --name mon-7:30am-fri-
  5:30pm --periods mon-fri-start-7:30am,fri-stop-5:30pm --timezone
  America/New_York
  ```

- *Orchestration* means automating processes and workloads. Organizations will use orchestration capabilities to manage resources, workloads, and services. In an AWS environment, orchestration often uses a number of services to accomplish desired tasks:

- CloudFormation is used to manage and model infrastructure as code to control deployments.
- Service Catalog is used to control and manage what service and third-party software are in use.
- OpsWorks may be used to automate operations using tools like Puppet and Chef.
- AWS management tools like Control Tower, Organizations, and others play a role in governance and management.

You can read more about AWS orchestration at https://aws.amazon.com/products/management-and-governance/use-cases/provisioning-and-orchestration, and Azure's automation overview can be found at https://azure.microsoft.com/en-us/services/automation, and Google's advice on choosing the right orchestrator for its environment is at https://cloud.google.com/blog/topics/developers-practitioners/choosing-right-orchestrator-google-cloud.

FIGURE 5.4   The AWS management console

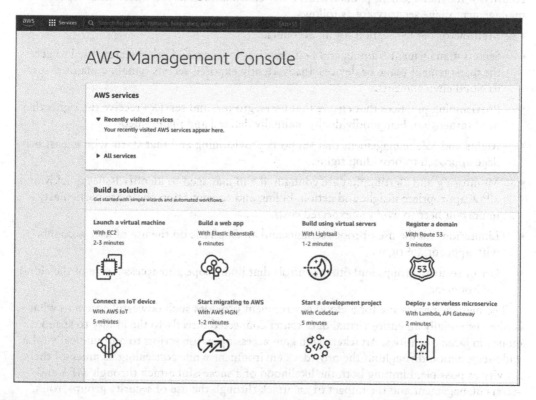

> Like many topics in this book, the topic of orchestration and management of a cloud environment could be a complete book by itself! For the purposes of the CCSP exam, you need to be aware of the concepts of scheduling, orchestration, and maintenance and to be able to understand how they work, how security requirements and best practices can be applied to them, and why they are necessary.

- *Maintenance* is often different in cloud infrastructure environments than it might be in traditional on-premises, dedicated hardware environments. Many cloud native designs emphasize ephemeral, code-defined machines that are deployed in pools and are destroyed rather than upgraded. Instead, upgraded systems are added to the pool and older systems are removed, allowing a seamless upgrade or patching process. That doesn't mean that it's impossible to patch or upgrade in the cloud, but it does mean that many environments will work differently than traditional systems management practices would.

While the exam outline emphasizes scheduling, orchestration, and maintenance, the security of the management plane itself is a key consideration as well. Best practices for management plane security are as follows:

- Multifactor authentication for all accounts.

- Secrets management training and best practices for keys and other secrets used to access the management plane or devices. Inadvertently exposed secrets remain a major threat to cloud environments.

- Provisioning practices that ensure that users, groups, and services receive the rights they need rather than being individually manually defined and maintained.

- Rights and role management that supports provisioning and that starts with a least privilege approach to providing rights.

- Monitoring and alerting that are configured and managed to identify issues quickly and allow appropriate insight and action. Billing and consumption alerts are particularly important here to avoid unexpected costs.

- Limitations on the use of root accounts and an emphasis on the use of user accounts with appropriate rights.

- Use of security groups and other controls that limit scope and access inside of the cloud environment.

The management plane for a cloud environment provides such powerful access to what is often essentially an entire virtual data center connected directly to the ability to spend money in large quantities. Attackers who gain access often use scripts to automatically take wide-scale action throughout the provider's environment while concealing as much of their activity as possible. Limiting both the likelihood of a successful attack through MFA and secrets management and the impact of an attack through the use of security groups, roles, and controls is incredibly important to all cloud service management planes.

Auditing Your Environment and Provider

Audits are typically broken into two major categories. The first is internal audits, which are conducted by organizational staff with the intent of ensuring ongoing operational integrity, identifying improvements, or validating against industry standards. The second is external audits. External audits are conducted by third parties and may rely on industry-standard practices or audit targets.

Audits often cover a variety of topics, including the organization and its administrative practices and procedures, how the organization assesses and addresses risks, its monitoring and alerting capabilities, the controls that handle both logical and physical access, and security and systems operations. In addition, management, patching, and similar topics are included as well as how the organization communicates and handles awareness, how change management is conducted, and if changes are properly documented.

Given this broad set of potential objectives, auditing in the cloud can be quite challenging. Since providers operate shared environments, they typically will not allow access to the underlying infrastructure and systems—something your organization is likely glad other organizations can't get either but that makes performing an audit much more difficult.

That means that many cloud providers engage external auditors and publicly publish their audit results. For example, Microsoft's Azure platform provides Service Organization Controls (SOC) 2, Type 2 audits on a recurring basis. You can find them at `https://docs` `.microsoft.com/en-us/azure/compliance/offerings/offering-soc-2`.

Google offers a wide range of compliance options at `https://cloud.google.com/` `security/compliance/offerings`.

Amazon provides a variety of reports as well at `https://docs.aws.amazon.com/` `audit-manager/latest/userguide/SOC2.html`.

Asking for audit information from any third-party vendor is a good security habit, and understanding the basics of SOC reports and what you'll get in each type is important for security practitioners.

Exploring SOC Audit Types

SOC reports are part of the SSAE reporting format created by the American Institute of Certified Public Accountants (AICPA). These are uniformly recognized as being acceptable for regulatory purposes in many industries, although they were specifically designed as mechanisms for ensuring compliance with the Sarbanes–Oxley Act (colloquially referred to as SOX), which governs publicly traded corporations.

There are three SOC report categories: SOC 1, SOC 2, and SOC 3. Each of them is meant for a specific purpose, and there are further subclasses of reports (called types) as well.

SOC 1 reports are strictly for auditing the financial reporting instruments of a corporation and therefore aren't a focus in most cloud provider audits. It's worth knowing they exist and that there are two subclasses of SOC 1 reports: Type 1 and Type 2.

SOC 2 reports are commonly used by security practitioners. They are specifically intended to report audits of any controls on an organization's security, availability, processing integrity, confidentiality, and privacy. Therefore, a cloud provider intending to prove its trustworthiness can help demonstrate it with a SOC 2 report.

SOC 2 reports also come in two types: Type 1 and Type 2. The SOC 2 Type 1 only reviews the design of controls, not how they are implemented and maintained or their function. Thus, the SOC 2 Type 1 is not extremely useful for determining the security and trust of an organization. The SOC 2 Type 2 report, however, does just that: it looks at the operating effectiveness of controls over time. This is why the SOC 2 Type 2 is the most commonly referenced by security practitioners, because it is a useful way of assessing an organization's security posture.

SOC 3 reports are designed to be shared with the public. They contain no actual data about the security controls of the audit target and are instead just an assertion that the audit was conducted and that the target organization passed.

This makes the SOC 3 report less useful for verifying the trustworthiness of an organization, but it may be all that some providers make available.

You'll learn more about audit types in Chapter 9, "Legal and Compliance Issues," so make sure you spend some time reading about SSAE, SOC, and ISAE there as well.

Adapting Processes for the Cloud

If your organization has existing audit policies and practices, or if you're using a third-party audit standard, you'll likely need to make some changes for cloud environments. Lack of direct access to hardware, shared services, and other limitations will mean that your process will need to either accept those restrictions or identify other ways to meet audit objectives.

The CCSP Exam Outline (Candidate Information Bulletin) specifically mentions a few assurance challenges that you need to bear in mind as you prepare for the exam, with a focus on virtualization.

 SOC reports don't have any specific requirements related to cloud compliance, meaning you'll have to read requirements in the context of your cloud implementation and vendor. Other programs do have cloud requirements or are specifically designed for the cloud, like the Cloud Security Alliance (CSA). FedRAMP, HITRUST, ISO 27017, and PCI DSS all have cloud components.

Assurance Challenges in Virtualized Environments and the Cloud

Assurance—or the ability to assert that a system, process, procedure, or data is as it is intended to be—can be particularly difficult to ensure in virtualized and cloud environments. The ephemeral nature of many virtualized, containerized, and cloud systems means that artifacts that would normally be auditable may not exist in a durable, verifiable way. Systems and services will be spun up, scaled, and then destroyed during the normal course of operations, potentially removing the auditable materials needed.

Those challenges mean that auditors and security practitioners need to adapt audit and validation processes to handle virtualized environments. Software or code-defined infrastructure can be audited at the code level by examining the code and related artifacts like system images, scripts, and shared data stores. Log information can be captured and used to document when an ephemeral system was created and used, what occurred on it, and when it was destroyed.

Containerization, virtualization, and similar concepts in cloud environments all need to be part of auditing and assessment plans, and as a security professional part of your role will be to ensure that the infrastructure design supports the creation of a verifiable audit trail.

Planning for Cloud Audits

The challenges we have discussed mean that preparing for a cloud audit starts in the infrastructure design phase, continues through operational phases, and ideally results in an organization that is well prepared for an audit.

In most cases the parameters of an audit engagement (duration, physical/logical locations, and so on) are negotiated prior to the start of the audit. Limitations are placed on which locations, artifacts, systems, and business processes will be examined as part of the audit. This is referred to as the *scope* of the audit. This is a crucial part of the overall audit process as crafting the scope can determine the impact, price, and usefulness of results of the audit.

Cloud audits require additional scoping care. Practices like port scanning that may have been possible in fully owned environments may be prohibited by the cloud service provider. At the same time, data that may be available in an on-premises audit may also not be available through the cloud provider. The ability to demonstrate that underlying hardware is properly disposed of at the end of its lifecycle, physical verification of servers and other hardware, and a multitude of other auditable items are no longer possible in most cloud service audits.

All of this means that cloud audits must be scoped to what can be accomplished in the environment and must also still meet the auditing needs of the organization. As you approach cloud audits, you will have to navigate what is possible, what is desired, and the level of understanding that the audit team has of cloud environments and providers. In addition, understanding remediation timelines as par of a corrective action plan, or CAP can be critical.

While they're not directly mentioned by the CCSP Exam Outline (Candidate Information Bulletin), there are other forms of certification available and widely used in the cloud computing industry, including HITRUST, which provides a framework for the healthcare industry; FedRAMP, which is the Federal Risk and Authorization Management Program for cloud service offerings (www.fedramp.gov); and the CSA Security, Trust, Assurance and Risk (STAR) program, which is available for free at https://cloudsecurityalliance.org/star.

If you do need to provide audit artifacts, there's some good news: Major cloud providers do have audit information available for standards like Payment Card Industry (PCI) reports and SOC audits. They also often have agreements available that may be required for the process or for compliance, like business associate agreements (BAAs) and nondisclosure agreements. You can find Google's audit artifacts for compliance at https://cloud.google.com/security/compliance.

Amazon provides both Artifact (https://aws.amazon.com/artifact), which provides exactly the audit artifacts you'd expect from the name, and Audit Manager, which automates audit evidence collection.

Azure's compliance-related documentation can be found at https://docs.microsoft.com/en-us/azure/compliance.

Summary

In this chapter, you've learned about the foundations of managed services, including mapping cloud provider and customer responsibilities in the three most common models of cloud computing. We explored how communications are secured, including through the use of encryption, and how infrastructure is protected using a variety of security techniques like network security groups, traffic inspection, geofencing, and zero trust. We also looked at common network security tools like firewalls, IDSs and IPSs, honeypots, vulnerability scanning, and bastion hosts, which can all be used to help secure your infrastructure. Hardware security devices like HSMs and TPMs also play a role by keeping secrets secure and helping with encryption throughout cloud environments.

Verifying that the software you use is secure and trustworthy is an important part of any environment, but code-defined systems like those found in cloud environments are often even more dynamic. That means that you need to know how to manage the software your organization uses and how to validate the packages and components that are in use.

The security of virtual environments, including virtual machines and containers, is critical to a cloud environment. We dug into how network, storage, memory, processors, hypervisors, operating systems, and virtualization toolsets all play a role in ensuring security in cloud services.

Cloud environments, much like on-premises systems, also require configuration management and hardening. Configuration techniques and practices for both host and guest operating systems, as well as considerations like backups and restoration capabilities, were all topics we reviewed in this chapter.

Identity assurance—making sure users are who they say they are and validating their usage of services and systems throughout a cloud environment—requires special attention in the cloud. Hosted services need to integrate with identity providers, and secrets and key management are important for organization and system security. In this chapter, you learned about the challenges that virtualization and the cloud add in addition to typical identity assurance hurdles.

Finally, organizations need to be able to ensure that what they believe is occurring actually is. That's where audits come into play. You should now be familiar with both internal and external audits, how to plan them, and the special considerations that you need to plan for in cloud and hybrid environments.

Exam Essentials

Understand how key network security concepts like security groups, traffic inspection, geofencing, and zero trust work in the cloud. Security in the cloud relies on many of the same concepts and technologies as on-premises infrastructure. Be able to describe security groups and their role as virtual firewalls. Explain why inspection remains useful but often requires use of provider-specific tools or is limited due to limitations on network visibility in the virtualized environment. Describe the role of geofencing and limitations on where in a provider's infrastructure activities can take place or which regional connections can provide an additional security layer. Explain why zero trust is sometimes easily built in new cloud environments where tooling exists natively to enable it.

Explain cloud infrastructure elements and how they can be secured. Cloud infrastructure design requires you to understand its capabilities, risks, and limitations. Explain why network communication should be encrypted end to end to prevent potential issues in shared environments. Explain why storage should also be encrypted by default in most environments to prevent attacks on data at rest as well as in transit. Understand that compute is typically a shared resource on underlying hardware, which could present risks if the provider does not effectively isolate customers or a vulnerability is found. Be able to outline how cloud management planes provide control over entire infrastructures and require strong practices and policies like universal multifactor authentication, secrets management, and security policies that are rooted in least privilege with effective monitoring and alerting. Describe key management plane functionality like scheduling, the ability to orchestrate complex systems, and features that make it easier to manage ephemeral and scalable systems.

Explain virtualization security in a cloud environment. Explain the role of VM management tools as well as security requirements for hardware components in a virtualized environment. Detail how to secure virtual networks, storage, and CPUs. Describe the differences between Type 1 and Type 2 hypervisors. Explain the role and purpose of virtualization toolsets and plug-ins. Explain the common challenges to identity assurance in cloud environments.

Apply best practices to cloud security operations. Describe hardware security modules (HSMs) and how they are used in cloud environments, including dedicated and shared modes of use. Explain what a TPM is and its role in securing systems. Explain the role of firewalls, intrusion detection, and prevention systems. Know how to use vulnerability scanning and assessment tools in segmenting traffic, detecting attacks, and finding potential attack vectors and how their deployment may be different in the cloud. Describe the role of bastion hosts in cloud infrastructure.

Use security baselines to protect systems in the cloud. Describe SOC 1 and SOC 2 Type 1 and Type 2 audits. Explain how to support audit objectives and processes in the cloud as well as how a security practitioner's role may differ in internal and external audits. Detail the basic concepts of audit planning in the cloud.

Review Questions

You can find the answers to the review questions in Appendix A.

1. Charles is working with internal auditors to review his organization's cloud infrastructure. Which of the following is not a common goal of internal audits?

   A. Testing operational integrity

   B. Improving practices

   C. Providing attestation of compliance to a standard to a third party

   D. Validating practices against an industry standard

2. Maria's organization wants to ensure that logins by most malicious actors would be prohibited if a system administrator's credentials were compromised. What technology is commonly used to check for potential malicious logins from international attacks?

   A. Geofencing

   B. IPOrigin

   C. Multifactor

   D. Biometric authentication

3. Alaina wants to ensure that her system instances for a web application hosted in her cloud data center have proper security for data at rest. What solution should she select to help ensure this?

   A. Disk or volume hashing

   B. Use only ephemeral disks or volumes

   C. Use read-only disks or volumes

   D. Disk or volume encryption

4. Jason wants to validate that the open-source software package he has downloaded matches the official release. What technique is commonly used to validate packages?

   A. Encryption

   B. Rainbow tables

   C. Decryption

   D. Hashing

5. Naomi's organization has adopted the CIS security controls for Windows. What type of solution have they adopted?

   A. A SOC template

   B. An ISO standard

   C. A security baseline

   D. A NIST standard

6. Yarif's organization wants to process sensitive information in a cloud environment. The organization is concerned about data throughout its lifecycle. What protection should it select for its compute elements if security is a priority and cost is less important?

    A. Memory encryption

    B. Dedicated hardware instances

    C. Shared hardware instances

    D. Avoiding installing virtualization tools

7. Valerie's organization uses a security baseline as part of its systems configuration process. Which of the following is not a typical part of a baselining process?

    A. Limiting administrator access

    B. Removing anti-malware agents

    C. Closing unused ports

    D. Removing unnecessary services and libraries

8. Hrant wants to ensure that traffic inside of his organization's Azure Virtual Network (VNet), Azure's basic building block for customer IaaS instances, is secure. What should he do to protect it?

    A. VNet traffic is already secure; he does not need to do anything.

    B. Set up VPN tunnels between each system.

    C. Set up and use a bastion host for all secure traffic.

    D. Use end-to-end encryption for all communications.

9. Asha is configuring a virtualized environment and wants to back up a virtualized server, including its memory state. What type of backup should she perform?

    A. A full backup

    B. A snapshot

    C. An incremental backup

    D. A differential backup

10. Felix is planning for his organization's third-party audit process after recently switching to a cloud SaaS provider. What information will Felix most likely be unable to provide?

    A. Access logs

    B. Operating system logs

    C. Activity logs

    D. User and account privilege information

11. Mark has set up a series of tasks that make up a workflow to ensure that his cloud-hosted web application environment scales, updates, and maintains itself. What cloud management plane feature is he leveraging?

    A. Maintenance

    B. Scheduling

    C. Orchestration

    D. Virtualization

12. Amanda downloads VeraCrypt, a free, open-source disk encryption software package. When she downloads the software, she sees the following information on the downloads page:

- Linux:
  - Generic Installers: veracrypt-1.25.9-setup.tar.bz2 (41.5 MB) (PGP Signature)
  - Linux Legacy installer for 32-bit CPU with no SSE2: veracrypt-1.25.9-x86-legacy-setup.tar.bz2 (13.8 MB) (PGP Signature)
  - Debian/Ubuntu packages:
    - Debian 11:
      - GUI: veracrypt-1.25.9-Debian-11-amd64.deb (PGP Signature)
      - Console: veracrypt-console-1.25.9-Debian-11-amd64.deb (PGP Signature)

What will she need to validate the signature and ensure that the software is legitimate?

A. VeraCrypt's private key

B. Her private key

C. VeraCrypt's public key

D. Her public key

13. Ting sets a system up in her Amazon VPC that exists in a low-security, public internet–facing zone and also has an interface connected to a high-security subnet that is used to house application servers so that she can administer those systems. What type of security solution has she configured?

A. A firewall hopper

B. A bastion host

C. A bridge

D. A bailey system

14. Lisa's organization installs virtualization tools on each virtual machine it sets up. Which of the following is not a common function of virtualization tools?

A. Access to sound and video cards

B. Mapping storage

C. Improved networking

D. Control of the underlying host operating system

15. Susan's organization is a cloud service provider that runs its hypervisor directly on the underlying hardware for its systems. What type of hypervisor is Susan running?

A. Type 1

B. Type 2

C. Type 3

D. Type 4

16. The CIO of Gurvinder's company wants him to have its audit company perform an audit of its cloud infrastructure provider. Why are cloud infrastructure vendors unlikely to allow audits of their systems and infrastructure by customer-sponsored third parties?

    A. They do not want to have problems with their service identified.

    B. Audits may disrupt their other customers or lead to risks of data exposure for those customers.

    C. It is required for compliance with industry standard best practices.

    D. It would have to be reported as a potential data breach.

17. Michelle wants to securely store her organization's secrets using a cloud service. What tool should she select?

    A. TPM as a service

    B. GPG as a service

    C. HSM as a service

    D. SSD as a service

18. Helen wants to apply rules to traffic in her cloud-hosted environment. What cloud tool allows rules permitting traffic to pass or be blocked to be set based on information like the destination or source host or IP address, port, and protocol?

    A. Security groups

    B. Stateless IDS

    C. VPC boundaries

    D. Stateful IPS

19. Jaime wants to set up a tool that will allow him to capture and analyze attacker behavior, including command-line activity and uploaded toolkits targeted at systems in his environment. What type of tool should he deploy?

    A. A dark web

    B. A honeypot

    C. A network IPS

    D. A network IDS

20. Chris is using a third-party vulnerability scanning application in his cloud-hosted environment. Which of the following issues is he unlikely to be able to detect with a vulnerability scanner?

    A. Malware

    B. Defined vulnerabilities

    C. Zero-day exploits

    D. Programming flaws

Chapter

6

Cloud Application Security

THE OBJECTIVE OF THIS CHAPTER IS TO ACQUAINT THE READER WITH THE FOLLOWING CONCEPTS:

✓ **Domain 1: Cloud Concepts, Architecture, and Design**

- 1.3. Understand Security Concepts Relevant to Cloud Computing

    - 1.3.2. Identity and access control (e.g., user access, privilege access, service access)

    - 1.3.6. Common Threats

✓ **Domain 3: Cloud Platform and Infrastructure Security**

- 3.4. Plan and implementation of security controls

    - 3.4.3. Identification, authentication, and authorization in cloud environments

✓ **Domain 4: Cloud Application Security**

- 4.1. Advocate Training and Awareness for Application Security

    - 4.1.1. Cloud development basics

    - 4.1.2. Common pitfalls

    - 4.1.3. Common cloud vulnerabilities (e.g., Open Web Application Security Project (OWASP) Top-10, SANS Top-25)

- 4.2. Describe the Secure Software Development Lifecycle (SDLC) Process

    - 4.2.1. Business requirements

    - 4.2.2. Phases and methodologies (e.g., design, code, test, maintain, waterfall vs. agile)

- 4.3. Apply the Software Development Lifecycle (SDLC)

    - 4.3.1. Cloud-specific risks

- 4.3.2. Threat modeling (e.g., Spoofing, Tampering, Repudiation, Information Disclosure, Denial of Service, and Elevation of Privilege (STRIDE), Disaster, Reproducibility, Exploitability, Affected Users, and Discoverability (DREAD), Architecture, Threats, Attack Surfaces, and Mitigations (ATASM), Process for Attack Simulation and Threat Analysis (PASTA))
- 4.3.3. Avoid common vulnerabilities during development
- 4.3.4. Secure coding (e.g., Open Web Application Security Project (OWASP), Application Security Verification Standard (ASVS), Software Assurance Forum for Excellence in Code (SAFECode))
- 4.3.5. Software configuration management and versioning

- 4.4. Apply Cloud Software Assurance and Validation
  - 4.4.1. Functional and non-functional testing
  - 4.4.2. Security testing methodologies (e.g., blackbox, whitebox, static, dynamic, Software Composition Analysis (SCA), interactive application security testing (IAST))
  - 4.4.3 Quality assurance (QA)
  - 4.4.4 Abuse case testing

- 4.5. Use verified secure software
  - 4.5.1 Securing application programming interfaces (API)
  - 4.5.2. Supply-chain management (e.g., vendor assessment)

- 4.6. Comprehend the specifics of cloud application architecture
  - 4.6.1. Supplemental security components (e.g., web application firewall (WAF), Database Activity Monitoring (DAM), Extensible Markup Language (XML) firewalls, application programming interface (API) gateway)

In this chapter, you will explore application design and architecture for the cloud as well as application testing and validation to ensure your cloud applications are secure. In addition to application design and architecture, you will review validation, threat modeling, software acquisition, testing, and the software supply chain. Along the way, you'll learn about the software development lifecycle and various models in use today, as well as the tools used to build, deploy, and secure successful cloud applications like cloud application security brokers.

It takes more than just software to keep applications secure, and identity and access management, including authentication and authorization, are critical parts of building a secure application environment. You'll also learn about single sign-on, multifactor authentication, and federation, and how they interact with identity providers.

Developing Software for the Cloud

Developing software for the cloud has many similarities to traditional software development models. In fact, the main differences are typically in the underlying infrastructure and capabilities, particularly in areas where scalability and performance are involved. Since cloud infrastructure is typically billed on a usage basis and can be easily scaled as needed, cloud application design normally focuses on the ability to horizontally scale across inexpensive instances and the ability to handle sessions and other transactional data, regardless of the instance or infrastructure component that initially handled connections or queries.

Many modern software development practices are commonly used for cloud applications, ranging from *continuous integration/continuous delivery (CI/CD)* practices, *DevOps* (development/operations), and DevSecOps (development, security, and operations) staffing and responsibility models.

If you're not familiar with CI/CD, IBM explains it clearly here: www.ibm .com/cloud/blog/ci-cd-pipeline. Atlassian explains DevOps and the DevOps lifecycle well at www.atlassian.com/devops.

Regardless of whether your organization uses CI/CD practices, DevOps teams, or a traditional software development lifecycle, training on secure development practices and awareness of the security implications and requirements for cloud applications are key to ensuring your organization remains secure.

Common Cloud Application Deployment Pitfalls

Any training and awareness program needs to ensure that developers and other staff working in an organization's cloud environment understand the most common places that problems occur in cloud applications. While there are many potential issues, ranging from cloud lock-in to a lack of cloud vendor support for zones that cross regions, some of the most common are described in the following sections.

Performance

Cloud software development often relies on loosely coupled services. That means that designing for performance and ensuring performance goals are met can be complex, as multiple components may interact in unexpected ways, even in relatively simple designs.

At the same time, cloud designs can offer massive scalability if the solution is well architected. The same complexity that can lead to performance issues can also allow developers to operate at almost any scale without maintaining infrastructure for the highest use cases, even when the solution is not being heavily used.

Scalability

One of the key features of cloud environments is the ability to scale, allowing applications and services to grow and shrink as need and demands fluctuate. The ability to scale also requires developers to think differently about how their application should work. It needs to be able to run across many instances at once, to retain state regardless of which instance or server is handling requests, and to handle faults with individual servers cleanly. At the same time, developers need to ensure that data remains secure in transit and at rest in an environment that is scaling as needed.

 A cloud instance is a virtual server running in a cloud environment. We'll reference instances throughout the book, but in many cases the same statements are true for a hosted server or virtual machine in a third-party data center or a private cloud.

Interoperability

Interoperability, or the ability to work across platforms, services, or systems, can be very important for cloud environments. If you're providing a service, being able to interoperate with the systems that customers rely on can be a business advantage. If you're running your own services, being able to work on multiple platforms or in different cloud provider environments can help control costs and increase your options for hosting and service provider choice.

Portability

Designing software that can move between on-premises and cloud environments, or between cloud providers, requires that the software be portable. Portability concerns in cloud software development typically center around avoidance of components specific to certain cloud vendors, like APIs or internal tools. At the same time, avoiding use of those APIs and tools can require additional work or may make it harder to leverage the advantages that the cloud environment can offer to applications and services that leverage their native tools.

If you're not familiar with application programming interfaces (APIs), they're described in more detail in the section "Cloud Application Architecture" later in this chapter.

Availability and Reliability

In most cases, you'll likely presume that cloud-hosted services and software are more reliable than services that are self-hosted. That's often true, with cloud providers providing many nines of uptime for their service.

We talk more about uptime in Chapter 7, "Operations Elements." If you're not familiar with uptime concepts like data center tiers, you can flip ahead to learn more.

At the same time, cloud providers do experience outages, and those outages can have a widespread impact. Even an outage that impacts a different cloud service provider than your own, or one that is centered in a different region or availability zone, can cause issues for your infrastructure or applications. If GitHub is down and your tools rely on components that are pulled from GitHub when applications are built, deployed, or run, you may experience an outage even if your entire infrastructure is otherwise online. The interwoven and complex nature of cloud services means that understanding dependencies and how they may impact the reliability and availability of your own services can be challenging. In fact, they may be close to impossible to fully document in many organizations.

API Security

Application programming interfaces, or APIs, are relied on throughout cloud application design. Of course, that means that API security and designing APIs to work well with cloud architectures are both common challenges for developers and architects.

API security is also part of the design process, so we'll talk about how to design secure APIs in the discussion of cloud application architecture, in the section "Application Programming Interfaces."

Cloud Application Architecture

Cloud application architecture can vary greatly from solution to solution, but a number of common components are found in many cloud application designs. The CCSP exam objectives point to a number of common elements that you'll need to be aware of for the exam, including cryptography, sandboxing, application virtualization and orchestration, and supplemental security components used to add an additional layer of security.

Cryptography

Cryptography is a key element of data security in the cloud, and application designs and architecture need to take into account where cryptography will be used throughout the data lifecycle.

Encryption of Data at Rest

Data at rest, whether it be short-term or long-term storage, should be protected from potential issues created by the use of shared infrastructure (multitenancy) in cloud environments. Encrypting data at rest is a great way to prevent unauthorized access to data and to prevent breaches if inadvertent access occurs or if remnant data is accessible to future users of the shared infrastructure.

Customers or users can also add another layer of protection by encrypting specific files or folders. This way, the customer holds the keys to unencrypt the data should the disk or volume be breached in some manner.

Keep in mind that the primary requirement for securing any encryption scheme is the safe storage and management of the keys used to encrypt and decrypt.

Whole-Instance Encryption and Full Disk Encryption

Also known as *full-disk encryption (FDE),* whole-instance encryption involves encrypting a complete system's disk or storage. Full-disk encryption protects data on the device in the event the device itself is lost or stolen, including if a shutdown instance or snapshot is stolen or breached.

Volume Encryption

Much like encrypting an entire device, volume encryption refers to encrypting only a partition on a hard drive or cloud storage that is presented as a volume, as opposed to an entire disk. This is useful when the entire disk does not need to be encrypted because only the protected sections have data of any value, such as underlying operating system files that do not contain sensitive data.

Encryption of Data in Transit

Encryption of data in transit helps prevent attacks on the network path between systems or users. The most common means of protecting data in transit is via Transport Layer Security (TLS), a protocol designed to ensure privacy when communicating between applications.

You may hear TLS referred to as SSL (Secure Sockets Layer), the protocol that was used before TLS. In almost all modern cases, references to SSL actually mean TLS, but as a security practitioner you'll have to make sure you check. SSL is outmoded and shouldn't be in actual use!

What about protocols that don't support encryption, or unencrypted protocols? That's where opportunistic encryption schemes come into play. The term *unencrypted protocols* describes systems that attempt to encrypt traffic whenever they can, only falling back to unencrypted when they don't succeed. This often means wrapping communications using TLS.

Sandboxing

Sandboxing places systems or code into an isolated, secured environment where testing can be performed. Cloud sandboxing architectures often take advantage of the ability to quickly create independent, short-lived environments with built-in instrumentation and code-based infrastructure to allow sandbox testing. Cloud service providers like Zscaler also provide dedicated sandboxing capabilities designed to contain and analyze malware, while others provide sandboxes to perform application development or other tasks where isolation can help prevent security issues.

Application Virtualization and Orchestration

Application virtualization allows applications to be run without being directly linked to the underlying operating system. Unlike hypervisors for system virtualization, application virtualization does not virtualize the entire system. Instead, application virtualization tools insert themselves between applications and the operating system and virtualize that interface. This allows for greater portability and segmentation while consuming fewer resources than a full virtual machine. Common examples of application virtualization include Amazon's App-Stream, Citrix's XenApp, Microsoft's App-V, and VMware's ThinApp.

The CCSP exam objective list doesn't specifically mention containerization, including technologies like Kubernetes and Docker, but you're likely to encounter them in many cloud environments. Containers bundle applications with the OS components, like libraries and other dependencies, that they need to run. Application and OS components are then bundled together into a container, which is highly portable and consumes fewer resources than a virtual machine. Containerization is a common part of software development environments that use continuous integration and continuous deployment processes because containers can be easily deployed using automated processes. Containers, much like other virtualization technologies, help to isolate problems, ensuring that problems are limited to the container, not the underlying system. Figure 6.1 shows a high-level view of the differences between each type of virtualization. Note that there are other models, including Type I and Type II hypervisors for OS virtualization, meaning that in some models there may be an operating system that the hypervisor runs on.

FIGURE 6.1 Components for virtualization and containerization

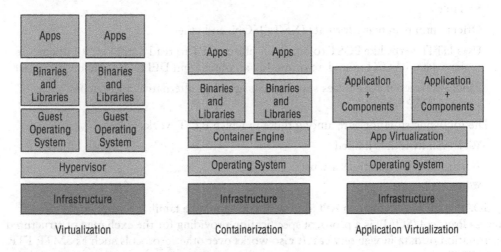

Containers and Container Orchestration

Many organizations have implemented containerization as part of their strategy, particularly cloud-native organizations. That means it's helpful to understand the difference between containerization tools like Docker that package containerized applications and run them on a single node and Kubernetes, which is used to control clusters of containers.

If Kubernetes and Docker aren't familiar to you, you can learn a lot through the official Kubernetes site: https://kubernetes.io/docs/tutorials/kubernetes-basics.

Application Programming Interfaces

The Exam objecitves focus on securing *application programming interfaces, or APIs,* but to properly secure an API, you need to understand what an API is and how they are commonly used.

There are two common types of APIs in use with cloud-based applications. The first is RESTful APIs. REST stands for Representational State Transfer. It is a software approach designed to scale the capabilities of web-based applications and is based on guidelines and best practices for creating scalable web applications. Other characteristics of the REST approach include the following:

- Low processing/traffic overhead ("lightweight")
- Uses simple URLs/URIs
- Not reliant on any single programming language
- Scalable
- Offers outputs in many formats (XML, JSON, and others)
- Uses HTTP verbs like POST to create an object, GET to read data, PUT to update or replace data, PATCH to update or modify an object, and DELETE to delete an object
- Efficient, which means it uses smaller messages than alternative approaches, such as SOAP

The following situations are among those in which REST works well:

- When bandwidth is limited
- When stateless operations are used
- When caching is needed

SOAP is the other common API approach you should be familiar with. Simple Object Access Protocol (SOAP) is a protocol specification providing for the exchange of structured information or data in web services. It also works over other protocols such as SMTP, FTP, and HTTP.

SOAP also has the following characteristics:

- Standards based
- Reliant on XML
- Highly intolerant of errors
- Slower
- Built-in error handling

SOAP is well suited to asynchronous processing, format contracts, and stateful operations.

Neither API format is necessarily better or more secure than the other. What is important is to understand that regardless of what type of API you use to offer web services, you are granting another application access to the primary application and any data it may have access to. This can present many security challenges for end users unable to evaluate the security of any specific API, or even which API (or APIs) they are using. This can lead to data leakage or other problems if the APIs in question have not been sufficiently vetted and validated to ensure they provide adequate security.

API security is called out separately in the CCSP Exam Outline (Candidate Information Bulletin) as part of 4.5, "Use Verified Secure Software," but understanding APIs is a critical part of application architecture and design, so we have included it here. As you review this section, remember that the exam outline also emphasizes the need to validate the security of APIs.

APIs tend to be offered in one of a few models:

- **Public APIs,** which are provided to those outside the organization, allowing for integration by third parties. These are often licensed or have a pay-per-use model and need to be secured against misuse and overuse.

- **Partner APIs** are provided to business partners or other organizations that your organization has an established relationship with. They're often used as part of shared business processes. Since they're exposed outside the organization, they often require additional security and monitoring.

- **Private, or Internal, APIs** which are used for internal uses and are not made available to third parties. Private APIs are often exposed via an internal API directory and can leverage internal authentication and authorization capabilities more easily than a public or partner API.

Threats to APIs and API Security Best Practices

While threats can vary somewhat based on the API model in use, the most common attacks against APIs should be considered for any API that is created or used. The following API threats are common:

- Injection attacks
- Denial-of-service attacks
- Poorly secured API servers or services
- On-path attacks
- Credential attacks, including stolen credentials, accidental API key exposures, and brute force attacks
- Poor API key generation techniques

API keys are unique identifiers used for authentication and authorization to an API. API keys may be associated with privileges or resource restrictions, and API key breaches can allow third parties to gain unauthorized access to an API, so keeping API keys secure is a critical security task. Common practices include avoiding API keys in code or in code repositories, restricting their use, deleting unneeded API keys, and regenerating keys so that long-lived keys aren't useful to malicious actors who acquire them. If you're not familiar with them, details of how to protect RESTful APIs can be found at https://cheatsheetseries.owasp.org/cheatsheets/REST_Security_Cheat_Sheet.html as a good starting point.

Regardless of the API models in use in an organization, a few API security best practices are common. They include implementing authentication and authorization (often using API keys), validating all requests, encrypting both requests and responses, using logging and throttling to document use and prevent overuse or misuse, conducting regular security tests, maintaining an API inventory or catalog, and of course, only sending the information that is required in an API request.

Organizations often leverage third-party APIs as well. That means they're reliant on the third parties whose APIs they consume to maintain those APIs, and they may be impacted if the API changes or is retired, or the underlying service is degraded or fails. Since organizations can't ensure the security of third-party APIs as they can their own, audit trails and proper handling of API keys are both common practices to help with third-party API security.

Multitenancy

Multitenancy refers to the concept that multiple cloud customers may share the same services, systems, networks, and other underlying resources. It is important that configurations be made in such a way as to ensure logical isolation of the various tenants, otherwise data leakage and corruption could occur. Organizations should design with the understanding that breaches, outages, and exposure due to the underlying infrastructure may occur.

The CCSP exam objectives don't specifically call out multitenancy, but it is a key concept for cloud providers—in fact, it's one of the key reasons that the cloud is an effective solution. As you consider the other elements of cloud application architecture, it is important to remember that you're one of many individuals and organizations using the same underlying platforms, systems, and services and that while the provider will attempt to limit the impact others can have on you, it's still likely shared among many others.

Supplemental Security Components

The CCSP exam objectives list a number of supplemental security components. These include security devices, appliances, and tools that are frequently used in application security architectures. As you prepare for the exam, you should consider how you would use each of them, what capabilities and limitations they have, and how they might fit into various architectures you're familiar with.

Web Application Firewalls

Web application firewalls, or *WAFs,* are used to protect web applications from attacks by monitoring both HTTP and HTTPS traffic. Much like other firewall devices, WAFs rely on policies to analyze traffic. They also typically act as a reverse proxy, protecting the application server from systems sending requests. WAFs are typically able to filter based on users, session information and data, and application-specific context and content, allowing them to provide nuanced controls over web traffic. Most WAFs are provided with a default set of rules intended to stop common attacks like SQL injection, denial-of-service attempts, and other similar malicious activity.

Cloud service providers often have some form of WAF capability, and third-party WAF virtual appliances are also available in the marketplaces for each of the major IaaS providers. WAFs aren't just available from IaaS providers, however, they're available in both SaaS and PaaS environments as well.

Database Activity Monitoring

Database activity monitoring (DAM) tools combine network data and database audit information in real time to analyze database activity for unwanted, anomalous, or unexpected behavior. It is used to monitor application activity and privileged uses and to detect attacks using behavioral analysis techniques. Much like the other services described here, cloud database services typically have some form of DAM tool or service available to support them.

XML Firewalls

Extensible Markup Language (XML) firewalls are used to protect services that rely on XML-based interfaces, including many forms of web applications. They provide both validation and filtering capabilities and add an ability to rate-limit and manage traffic flow to services they protect.

API Gateways

Application programming interface (API) gateways are used to manage, monitor, and aggregate APIs to produce results for requesting systems. API gateways can be used for authorization and access control, traffic flow control, and throttling, and they also typically provide filtering capabilities, creating an additional security layer for APIs. You can read more about an example of a cloud IaaS API gateway at `https://aws.amazon.com/api-gateway`.

Cloud Application Security Brokers

Cloud application security brokers, or *CASBs,* are used as enforcement points between consumer and service providers to ensure that use of cloud services matches organizational intentions and policies. They combine the ability to control use of service with data protection capabilities and threat management and monitoring features. CASBs can be deployed in on-premises, hybrid, or cloud-hosted models and are more heavily used in organizations that require high levels of control and assurance regarding cloud usage.

Cloud-Secure Software Development Lifecycle (SDLC)

While architecture is important, the development process for software has an even greater impact on the security and functionality of applications. The *software development lifecycle*, or *SDLC*, describes the steps in a model for software development throughout its life. As shown in Figure 6.2, it maps software creation from an idea to requirements gathering and analysis to design, coding, testing, and rollout. Once software is in production, it also includes user training, maintenance, and decommissioning at the end of the software package's useful life.

Software development does not always follow a formal model, but most enterprise development for major applications does follow most, if not all, of these phases. In some cases, developers may even use elements of an SLDC without realizing it!

FIGURE 6.2   High-level SDLC view

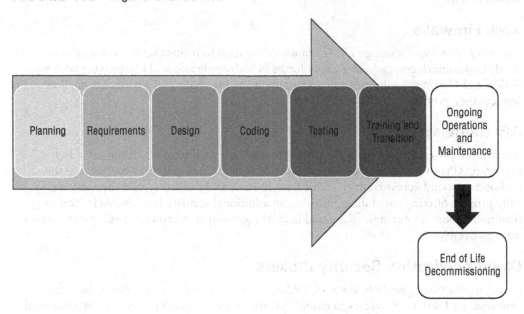

The SDLC is useful for organizations and for developers because it provides a consistent framework to structure workflow and provide planning for the development process. Despite these advantages, simply picking an SDLC model to implement may not always be the best choice. Each SDLC model has certain types of work and projects that it fits better than others, making choosing an SDLC model that fits the work an important part of the process.

Software Development Phases

Regardless of which SDLC or process is chosen by your organization, a few phases appear in most SDLC models:

1. The *planning* phase is where the effort is considered as a potential for the organization. Planning phases often also consider feasibility and costs.

2. Once an effort has been deemed feasible, it will typically go through a *requirements definition* phase. In this phase, customer input is sought to determine what the desired functionality is, what the current system or application currently does and what it doesn't do, and what improvements are desired. Business requirements may be ranked to determine which are most critical to the success of the project.

3. The *design* phase includes design for functionality, architecture, integration points and techniques, data flows, business processes, and any other elements that require design consideration.

4. The actual coding of the application occurs during the *coding* phase. This phase may involve testing of parts of the software, including *unit testing* (testing of small components individually to ensure they function properly) and code analysis or source code review.

The CCSP Exam Outline (Candidate Information Bulletin) only mentions a few phases: design, code test, and maintain. There are more steps in common SDLC models, so you'll want to make sure you remember those four steps for the exam while remaining aware of the longer list of steps for actual use.

5. While some testing is likely to occur in the *development* phase, formal testing with customers or others outside of the development team occurs in the testing phase. Individual units or software components are integrated and then tested to ensure proper functionality. In addition, connections to outside services, data sources, and other integration may occur during this phase. During this phase, user acceptance testing (UAT) occurs to ensure that the users of the software are satisfied with its functionality.

6. The important task of ensuring that the end users are trained on the software and that the software has entered general use occurs in the *training and transition* phase. This phase is sometimes called the acceptance, installation, and deployment phase.

7. Once a project reaches completion, the application or service will enter what is usually the longest phase: *ongoing operations and maintenance*. This phase includes patching, updating, minor modifications, and other work that goes into daily support.

8. The *end of life* or *decommissioning* phase occurs when a product or system reaches the end of its life. Although disposition is often ignored in the excitement of developing new products, it is an important phase for a number of reasons: shutting down old products can produce cost savings, replacing existing tools may require specific knowledge or additional effort, and data and systems may need to be preserved or properly disposed of.

The order of the phases may vary, with some progressing in a simple linear fashion and others taking an iterative or parallel approach. You will still see some form of each of these phases in successful software lifecycles.

Software Development Models

The SDLC can be approached in many ways, and over time a number of formal models have been created to help provide a common framework for development. While formal SDLC models can be very detailed, with specific practices, procedures, and documentation, many organizations choose the elements of one or more models that best fit their organizational style, workflow, and requirements.

Waterfall

The *Waterfall* methodology is a sequential model in which each phase is followed by the next phase. Phases do not overlap, and each logically leads to the next. A typical six-phase Waterfall process is shown in Figure 6.3. In Phase 1, requirements are gathered and documented. Phase 2 involves software architecture and design work. Implementation occurs next in Phase 3, then testing and validation in Phase 4. Once the software is complete, the software is deployed in Phase 5. Finally the software enters Phase 6, which is an operational phase, with support, maintenance, and other operational activities happening on an ongoing basis.

FIGURE 6.3   The Waterfall SDLC model

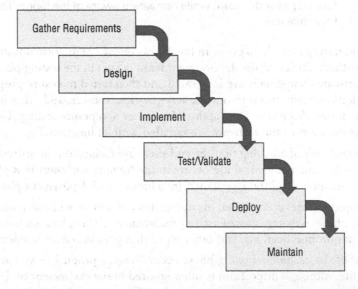

Waterfall has been replaced in many organizations because it is seen as relatively inflexible, but it remains in use for complex systems. Since Waterfall is not highly responsive to changes and does not account for internal iterative work, it is typically recommended for development efforts that involve a fixed scope and a known time frame for delivery and that are using a stable, well-understood technology platform. Examples of development processes that involve Waterfall methodologies include software for spacecraft and for utility plants, but even in those areas other development methodologies are gaining ground.

Agile

Agile software development is an iterative and incremental process rather than the linear processes that other models, including Waterfall, use. Agile is rooted in the *Manifesto for Agile Software Development*, a document that has four basic premises:

- Individuals and interactions are more important than processes and tools.
- Working software is preferable to comprehensive documentation.
- Customer collaboration replaces contract negotiation.
- Responding to change is key, rather than following a plan.

If you are used to a Waterfall or Spiral development process, Agile is a significant departure from the planning, design, and documentation-centric approaches that Agile's predecessors use. Agile methods tend to break work up into smaller units, allowing work to be done more quickly and with less up-front planning. It focuses on adapting to needs rather than predicting them, with major milestones identified early in the process but subject to change as the project continues to develop.

Work is typically broken up into short working sessions, called *sprints*, that can last days to a few weeks. Figure 6.4 shows a simplified view of an Agile project methodology with multiple sprints conducted. When the developers and customer agree that the task is done or when the time allocated for the sprints is complete, the development effort is completed.

FIGURE 6.4   Agile sprints

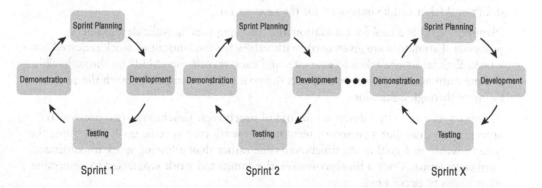

The Agile methodology is based on 12 principles:

- Ensure customer satisfaction via early and continuous delivery of the software.
- Welcome changing requirements, even late in the development process.
- Deliver working software frequently (in weeks rather than months).
- Ensure daily cooperation between developers and businesspeople.
- Projects should be built around motivated individuals who get the support, trust, and environment they need to succeed.
- Face-to-face conversations are the most efficient way to convey information inside the development team.
- Progress is measured by having working software.
- Development should be done at a sustainable pace that can be maintained on an ongoing basis.
- Pay continuous attention to technical excellence and good design.
- Simplicity—the art of maximizing the amount of work not done—is essential.
- The best architectures, requirements, and designs emerge from self-organizing teams.
- Teams should reflect on how to become more effective and then implement that behavior at regular intervals.

These principles drive an SDLC process that is less formally structured than Spiral or Waterfall but that has many opportunities for customer feedback and revision. It can react more nimbly to problems and will typically allow faster customer feedback—an advantage when security issues are discovered.

Agile development uses a number of specialized terms:

- *Backlogs* are lists of features or tasks that are required to complete a project.
- *Sprint retrospectives* are held at the end of sprints to discuss what went well and what didn't and what can be improved for the next sprint.
- *Planning poker* is a tool for estimation and planning used in Agile development processes. Estimators are given cards with values for the amount of work required for a task. Estimators are asked to estimate, and each reveals their "bid" on the task. This is done until agreement is reached, with the goal to have estimators reach the same estimate through discussion.
- *Timeboxing*, a term that describes the use of timeboxes. Timeboxes are a previously agreed-upon time that a person or team uses to work on a specific goal. This limits the time to work on a goal to the timeboxed time rather than allowing work to continue until completion. Once a timebox is over, the completed work is assessed to determine what needs to occur next.
- *User stories* are collected to describe high-level user requirements. A user story might be "Users can change their password via the mobile app," which would provide direction for estimation and planning for an Agile work session.

- *Velocity tracking* is conducted by adding up the estimates for the current sprint's effort and then comparing that to what was completed. This tells the team whether they are on track, faster, or slower than expected.

Looking Past Agile and Waterfall

The CCSP exam objectives only cover Waterfall and Agile models, but there are quite a few other models in use. Among those are the following models:

- The Spiral model uses the linear development concepts from the Waterfall model and adds an iterative process that revisits four phases multiple times during the development lifecycle to gather more detailed requirements, design functionality guided by the requirements, and build based on the design. In addition, the Spiral model puts significant emphasis on risk assessment as part of the SDLC, reviewing risks multiple times during the development process.

- The Rapid Application Development (RAD) model is an iterative process that relies on building prototypes. Unlike many other methods, it has no planning phase; instead, planning is done as the software is written. RAD relies on functional components of the code being developed in parallel and then integrated to produce the finished product. Much like Agile, RAD can provide a highly responsive development environment.

- The V model, which is an extension of the Waterfall model, pairs a testing phase with each development stage. Each phase starts only after the testing for the previous phase is done. Thus, at the requirements phase, the requirements are reviewed (or tested), and at the design phase, a test phase for the system design is completed before coding is started.

- The Big Bang SDLC model relies on no planning or process. Instead, it focuses on making resources available and simply starting coding based on requirements as they are revealed. Obviously, the Big Bang model doesn't scale, but it is a common model for individual developers working on their own code.

Secure Coding and the SDLC

There are a variety of resources available to help organizations and individual developers avoid common vulnerabilities during development of software and applications. One of the best known is the Top 10 lists from the *Open Web Application Security Project* (*OWASP*). There two major Top 10 lists relevant to cloud secure coding:

- The Cloud Native Application Security Top 10 (`https://owasp.org/www-project-cloud-native-application-security-top-10`)
- The Top 10 Web Application Security Risks (`https://owasp.org/www-project-top-ten`)

As of the writing of this book, the Cloud Native Application Security Top 10 is in draft but includes the following items:

- Insecure cloud, container, or orchestration configuration
- Injection flaws (app layer, cloud events, cloud services)
- Improper authentication and authorization
- CI/CD pipeline and software supply chain flaws
- Insecure secrets storage
- Over-permissive or insecure network policies
- Using components with known vulnerabilities
- Improper asset management
- Inadequate compute resource quota limits
- Ineffective logging and monitoring (e.g., runtime activity)

The other major resource used for developer awareness is the SANS Top 25 most dangerous software errors, which are listed at www.sans.org/top25-software-errors. These errors are not specific to cloud native environments like the OWASP draft list is, but they're common to many application and development environments. They include items like improper input validation, improper authentication, missing authorization, out of bounds reads and writes, and incorrect default permissions, among many other common issues.

CWE Scores

The SANS Top 25 uses the Common Weakness Scoring System, or CWSS. It relies on three scores: the base finding score, which includes items like technical impact and the level of acquired privilege; the environmental score, which accounts for business impact and related items; and the attack surface score, which identifies items like the deployment scope and required privilege for the exploit or attack. You can read more about how CWSS works at https://cwe.mitre.org/cwss/cwss_v1.0.1.html.

Additional resources include *Application Security Verification Standard (ASVS)* and *Software Assurance Forum for Excellence in Code (SAFECode)*. ASVS sets a community standard for testing application security controls, allowing organizations to rely on the quality and types of testing done for an application. It consists of three levels of security verification, from Level 1's low assurance level that can be done entirely through penetration testing to Level 3's critical applications security validation that requires in-depth validation and testing.

Each ASVS category includes numbered requirements, whether each requirement is required for each of the three levels, and a CWE number if the issue is identified in the CWE listings.

You can read about the ASVS at https://owasp.org/www-project-application-security-verification-standard.

SAFECode (https://safecode.org) is an industry group that is composed of many large industry vendors and focuses on secure software development. SAFECode provides what it calls the "SAFECode Fundamental Practices for Secure Software Development." It includes sections on design, secure coding practices, third-party component risks, testing and validation, managing findings, and handling vulnerabilities and disclosure processes. You can download the entire document at https://safecode.org/uncategorized/fundamental-practices-secure-software-development.

 The SAFECode standards were last updated to version 3 in 2018. Industry practices have continued to change since then. As you look for resources as a practitioner, remember to check how current they are. The CCSP exam may require you to know both SAFECode and OWASP standards, but OWASP's materials are more up to date as of the publication of this book.

Configuration Management and Versioning for the SDLC

Managing software versions, the software bill of materials (SBOM) that lists all of the components in an application or service, and ensuring that the proper configurations are in place are all important parts of the software development lifecycle.

Organizations may adopt different versioning processes, but a common approach is to use a format that lists the major version, the minor version, and the patch version, if any. For example, a software package might be 11.3.1, the 11th major release, 3rd update, 1st patch. As this book is being written, Chrome version 99.0.4844.82 is the current version available; Chrome uses a slightly different version, which is MAJOR.MINOR.BUILD.PATCH, adding the build number into the version.

Versioning helps you to know if you're using the current version, and if issues are identified, it can be used to track which versions are impacted by the flaw. In addition, version control tools rely on versioning to help ensure that proper patches are installed and to determine if the proper version of software is installed.

Configuration management is also critical, because knowing what configuration is in place, being able to change it centrally in cloud environments where systems and services are managed through code, and being able to revert to an old configuration or deploy a new one while tracking changes helps make DevOps and CI/CD pipelines work smoothly. As a security practitioner, you need to know about configuration management and consider your organization's tools, processes, and needs in your security architecture designs and security testing.

Cloud Application Assurance and Validation

Applications are tested during their coding process, before they're deployed, and during their operational lifecycle. To effectively test web applications, you need to be familiar with a number of application security testing methods and tools, starting with threat modeling.

Threat Modeling

The CCSP exam objectives cover a number of threat modeling processes, including STRIDE, DREAD, ATASM, and PASTA. We'll look briefly at each of these models and their uses as part of the SDLC process.

The *STRIDE* model was created by Microsoft and provides a standardized way of describing threats by their attributes. Developers can use this model to attempt to discover flaws and vulnerabilities in the software they're creating.

The STRIDE acronym stands for the following:

Spoofing   Can the identity of the entity using the application be obscured in some way? Does the user have the capability to appear as a different user?

Tampering   Does the application allow a user to make unauthorized modifications to actual data, affecting the integrity of information or communications?

Repudiation   Is the user capable of denying they took part in a transaction, or does the application track and log the user's actions?

Information Disclosure   Does the application reveal information while the data is being processed or information about the application's function while it runs?

Denial of Service   Is there a way to shut down the application through unauthorized means? This might include crashing, overloading, or restarting the application.

Elevation of Privilege   Can a user change their level of permissions in order to perform unauthorized actions, such as gaining administrative control of the application?

The "user" in each of these categories may be a legitimate employee who is granted access to the application or someone who has gained unauthorized access. The various threats may be the result of accidental input by a user or intentional effort to misuse the application.

STRIDE is particularly useful as part of the SDLC in attempting to identify vulnerabilities throughout the build process, allowing developers and security professionals to focus on where threats may occur and whether they need to be addressed.

STRIDE Resources

Microsoft has made the STRIDE model and suggestions for its implementation freely available on its website: `https://msdn.microsoft.com/en-us/library/ee823878(v=cs.20).aspx`

An example of how STRIDE might be used to evaluate the potential attacks on a web commerce server is provided as well: `https://msdn.microsoft.com/en-us/library/ee798544(v=cs.20).aspx`

Microsoft also offers an automated tool designed to aid in applying the STRIDE model to any software. It is available, free of charge, from Microsoft's website: `https://docs.microsoft.com/en-us/azure/security/azure-security-threat-modeling-tool`

A second model for assessing security threats is *DREAD*. Like STRIDE, DREAD was created at Microsoft, but unlike STRIDE it has largely been abandoned. DREAD's categories of risk are as follows:

Damage   If the attack occurred, how bad would it be?

Reproducibility   Is the attack one that can be easily reproduced?

Exploitability   Can it be easily exploited?

Affected Users   How many users would be impacted if an exploit occurred?

Discoverability   How easily can the threat be discovered?

DREAD analysis rates each risk category on a 1–10 scale, and the scores are totaled to provide an overall score.

The next model you'll need to be aware of is *ATASM*, or Architecture, Threats, Attack Surfaces, and Mitigations. This model includes the following steps:

1. Seek to understand the architecture.
2. List all threat agents, their goals, methods, and objectives.

3. Look at your architecture's potential attack surfaces and look at how the attack methods and objectives already identified would interact with the attack surfaces being assessed.

4. Review security controls and the attack surfaces, removing any attack surfaces that are sufficiently secured by existing controls.

The remaining list is then secured using new controls, with a focus on defense in depth as part of the implementation.

 You can read about ATASM in more detail at `https://brookschoenfield` `.com/?page_id=341`.

Finally, *PASTA*, the Process for Attack Simulation and Threat Analysis, is a seven-stage framework. The seven stages are as follows:

1. Defining business objectives

2. Defining the technical scope of assets and components

3. Factoring applications and identifying application controls

4. Performing threat analysis based on threat intelligence

5. Vulnerability detection

6. Analyzing and modeling attacks

7. Performing risk and impact analysis and developing countermeasures

PASTA focuses on how attackers would view infrastructure and applications.

Common Threats to Applications

Threat modeling helps prepare for some of the more common application vulnerabilities that developers will encounter when working with cloud applications, which include the following:

Injection   Injection occurs when a malicious user attempts to inject a string or code of some type into a field or other target in order to manipulate the application's actions or reveal unauthorized data. Examples include such things as SQL, LDAP, and OS injections. If the injection is successful, data may be exposed or unwanted system or application behaviors may occur.

Broken Authentication   Authentication issues can have a wide range of impacts based on the user, account, or privileges that can be exploited.

Cross-Site Scripting (XSS)   XSS occurs when an application allows untrusted data to be sent to a web browser without proper validation or escaping. This then allows the malicious user to execute code or hijack sessions in the user's browser.

Insecure Direct Object Access   Direct object access issues occur when an attacker is able to reference to an internal object, like a file, without access control checks or other controls in place to ensure attackers cannot manipulate data.

Security Misconfigurations   Security misconfigurations are often unintentional, caused by authorized entities and a result of basic human error.

Sensitive Data Exposure   The disclosure of information such as PII, medical data, credit card material, and so on. Without proper controls in place (such as encryption, data masking, tokenization, and so on), sensitive data can be leaked by an application or system.

Missing Access Control   An application should always verify access privileges before granting access to functionality. If access control is not implemented properly, malicious users may be able to forge requests that will allow them functionality without authorization.

Cross-Site Request Forgery (CSRF)   A CSRF manipulates a logged-on user's browser to send a forged HTTP request, along with cookies and other authentication information, in an effort to force the victim's browser to generate a request that a vulnerable application thinks is a legitimate request from the user.

Using Components with Known Vulnerabilities   This can occur when developers use application/programming libraries of known components but do not heed security comments or fail to understand the context in which the component will eventually be used in production.

Quality Assurance and Testing Techniques

The *quality assurance (QA)* testing process is frequently a combination of automated and manual validation testing techniques. The overall goal of quality assurance is to ensure that software meets standards or requirements. It typically involves reviews, testing, reporting, and other activities to complete the QA process.

QA processes can involve a number of different roles in an organization. Dedicated quality assurance staff may handle functional or nonfunctional testing. Developers may do code reviews as part of nonfunctional testing, or they may oversee unit testing as they complete segments of their code. End users will be involved in user acceptance testing and may be involved in functional testing in areas where they are experts. While there aren't set rules around who can do testing, these are some of the most common assignments in many organizations.

Functional and Nonfunctional Testing

Functional testing tests software to determine if it meets the specifications for the software. Functional testing can be conducted in a number of ways, ranging from integration testing that validates whether components work together to regression testing that validates whether bugs were reintroduced between versions. User acceptance testing, which tests how users interact with and operate software, is also a form of functional testing. The key thing to remember is that if the function of the software is being tested, it is likely functional testing.

Nonfunctional testing focuses on testing the quality of the software, looking for things like stability of the software or its performance. Load testing, stress testing, and similar testing techniques are all examples of nonfunctional testing.

Software Testing Methodologies and Techniques

Static application testing involves reviewing the source code. This requires a testing team with two kinds of skills and knowledge: how to read the code the program was written with and a deep understanding of security and other topics that are important to the quality and function of the code to determine if it will behave appropriately and is well designed and written.

Dynamic application testing uses actual running code or applications as part of the test. It can involve both automated and manual processes designed to validate the functionality of the code and how it performs in the real world.

Interactive application security testing (IAST) analyzes code for vulnerabilities while it is being used and focuses on real-time reporting to optimize the testing and analysis process. IAST is often associated with CI/CD processes, where it can be built into the SDLC process as part of automated release testing. Unlike static and dynamic testing, IAST analyzes the internal functions of the application while it is running instead of testing what the application is presenting to users, as a dynamic test would, or testing the source code as a static test would.

Software Composition Analysis (SCA) is used to track the components of a software package or application. It is most frequently used with open-source components but could be used for commercial packages as well. SCA can help to identify vulnerabilities in components and dependencies.

White box testing, increasingly called "full knowledge" testing, is conducted with full access to and knowledge about the systems, code, and environment. Static testing is thus one type of white box testing, as you need the source code to conduct static testing.

Black box testing, often called "zero knowledge" testing, is conducted as an external attacker would access the code, systems, or environment, without knowledge of the outset of a test.

The CCSP exam outline doesn't mention partial knowledge, or gray box, testing. As you'd expect from the name, that's a form of testing where you may have some but not all knowledge about the application, system, or environment you're testing.

Abuse case testing focuses on using features in ways that weren't intended by the developer. It can involve exploiting weaknesses or coding flaws and can help organizations to consider the security functionality, features, and controls they need for an application.

You can find a great cheat sheet on abuse case testing from OWASP at https://cheatsheetseries.owasp.org/cheatsheets/Abuse_Case_Cheat_Sheet.html.

Supply Chain Management and Licensing

A significant portion of software that any organization runs is typically provided by third parties. That means that organizations need to manage both their software supply chain and third-party software itself, including licensing it properly for the organization's use.

Supply chain management requires assessing vendors' ability to provide software and updates, their ability to respond to issues and remediate them in a reasonable amount of time, their long-term stability and viability as vendors, and their business practices that might impact your organization. In addition, you may need to understand additional components that your primary vendor relies on, including both open-source and closed-source tools.

Licensing also requires attention, including ensuring that you understand the licenses for the software your organization uses, that you are properly licensed and have enough licenses of the right type, and that you are using software in accordance with the licenses.

Organizations can create risks to their own operations if they do not invest time and thought into validating their software supply chain, maintaining relationships with their vendors, and ensuring license compliance.

Identity and Access Management

IAM is about the people, processes, and procedures used to handle the full lifecycle of identities. IAM systems typically consist of several components, including identification creation mechanisms; authentication and authorization methods; rights and privilege management; monitoring, logging, and alerting tools; and lifecycle management capabilities.

NOTE   While identity and access management (IAM) is a broad topic, the CCSP Exam Outline (Candidate Information Bulletin) groups it in cloud application security. As you review these sections of the chapter, remember that IAM concepts and technologies are used in many areas outside of application security.

Identity Management   Identity management is the process whereby individuals are given access to system resources by associating user rights with a given identity. Provisioning is the first phase of identity management, where each subject is issued a unique identity assertion (something that serves as an identification, such as a user ID). During this process, the user is usually also issued a password for use in authenticating the identity assertion. The entity issuing the password and identity assertion will retain a record of each for use in recognizing the user later (when the user logs in to resources with that user ID/password combination).

Access Management   Access management is the part of the process that deals with controlling access to resources once they have been granted. Access management identifies who a user is and what they are allowed to access each time they attempt to access a resource. This is accomplished through a combination of means:

> **Authentication**   Establishes identity by asking who you are and determining whether you are a legitimate user (often by combining the use of an identity assertion and an authentication factor; for example, a user ID and password).
>
> **Authorization**   Evaluates what you have access to after authentication occurs. In many cases, this means comparing the identity assertion against an access control list (ACL).
>
> **Policy Management**   Serves as the enforcement arm of authentication and authorization and is established based on business needs and senior management decisions.
>
> **Federation**   An association of organizations that facilitate the exchange of information, as appropriate, about users and access to resources, allowing them to share resources across multiple organizations using identities and authentication supported by their home organization rather than requiring unique credential sets for each service offered by other parts of the federation.
>
> **Identity Repositories**   The directory services for the administration of user accounts and their associated attributes.

Cloud Identity and Access Control

Identity and access management in the cloud is a key feature of most cloud environments. While you may encounter many different IAM features and capabilities depending on what type of cloud service you're using, a few core concepts are detailed in the CCSP exam objectives. You should make sure you understand the following identity and access control concepts, not only how they apply in infrastructure as a service environments but how they may differ in platform as a service and software as a service settings as well.

> **User Access**   User access in cloud environments may either rely on the cloud provider's own authentication and authorization capabilities or leverage the customer's own infrastructure and systems. Regardless of which of these is chosen, at least one top-level account is typically maintained that is native to the cloud provider, which allows the configuration and maintenance of the environment.
>
> A key feature of many cloud environments is fine-grained access controls that allow detailed configuration and control of which accounts and entities can access services, systems, or other components of the cloud environment.

It is also important to remember that many cloud environments rely heavily on secrets (keys and certificates) in addition to traditional usernames and passwords. This means that paying attention to how and where secrets are used, stored, and secured is critical to securing user access in the cloud.

Privilege Access   You're likely already familiar with the concepts needed to protect privileged access for systems that are found in a data center or desktop and mobile devices throughout your organization. The cloud carries the same need to protect privileged access to ensure the security of your cloud environment. The fine-grained access controls available via cloud providers are a first step in that direction, but additional controls, like requiring multifactor authentication for all privileged access, logging, and alerting, as well as using behavior-based detection systems, and of course auditing and assessing privileged access, are all needed as well.

The CCSP exam objectives use the term *privilege access*, but you'll more frequently encounter the term *privileged access*, meaning a super user, root, administrative, or other account with higher levels of access than typical users.

Service Access   Many cloud services are built out of *microservice*, which is a service-oriented architecture that splits applications into collections of loosely coupled services using lightweight protocols. Others rely on more traditional services as critical components in their architecture. That means that controlling service access using IAM is both necessary for security and often a somewhat complex issue in large environments or those with multiple use cases.

Key concepts when considering service access in cloud environments include the need to implement appropriate access controls, the need to maintain identities or service credentials in secure ways, and the importance of monitoring and managing access so that individual service accounts or entities who use services do not disrupt them.

Single Sign-On

When an organization has a variety of resources that each require authentication, usage and utilization can become cumbersome for users. *Single sign-on (SSO)* is a way to address this and simplify the operational experience for the user.

While there are several ways to implement SSO, the term generally refers to a situation where the user signs in once, usually to an authentication server, and then, when the user wants to access the organization's resources, each resource queries the authentication server to determine if the user is logged in and properly authenticated; the authentication server then approves the request and the resource server grants the user access. All of this should be transparent to the user, streamlining their use of the resources on the network.

SSO is very common in modern organizations but does come with risks. Removing requirements to reauthenticate and using the same credentials throughout an environment mean that a single compromised credential set or a compromised SSO server or service can result in much broader access than a credential or server that is only useful in one place. Despite that risk, most organizations opt to allow SSO because of the significant improvements in usability and user acceptance that it provides.

Identity Providers

Identity providers (IdPs) are services or systems that store and manage identities. IdPs receive authentication requests, validate the requests and information provided, and then provide information to services that let them know that the identity is valid and that the user can access the service if they're authorized to do so.

You're likely already familiar with using common IdPs like Google and Facebook, although organizations may use their own IdP or leverage another organization's capabilities as well.

Federated Identity Management

Federated identity (or *federation*, in general) is much the same as normal identity management except it is used to manage identities across disparate organizations. You can think of it as single sign-on (SSO) that works across systems or services from multiple organizations.

Let's look at an example. A group of research universities want to share their research data. They can create a federation so that a scientist signing in at their own university, on their own system, can then access all the research resources of the other universities in the federation without having to present other, new identity and authentication credentials.

Figure 6.5 shows the basic flow for this type of federation model. A user who wants to use services at another institution logs in and is directed to the identity provider. The provider authenticates them and provides them with a token to pass to the service provider, which allows the user to access their services based on rules and authorization that the service provider maintains.

In the web of trust, each member of the federation (that is, each organization that wants to share resources and users) has to review and approve each other member for inclusion in the federation. While it's a good method to be sure that everyone else in the federation reaches your particular level of trust, this can become costly and unwieldy once the federation reaches a significant number of member organizations—it just doesn't scale well.

By using a third-party identifier, on the other hand, the member organizations outsource their responsibilities to review and approve each other to some external party who will take on this responsibility on behalf of all the members. This is a popular model in the cloud environment, where many organizations use Google, Facebook, LinkedIn, or other identity providers for their own services.

FIGURE 6.5 There are two general types of federation: the web-of-trust model and use of a third-party identifier.

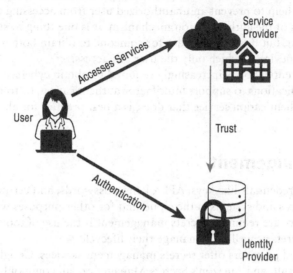

When discussing federation, we apply the terms *identity provider (IdP)* and *relying parties*. The identity provider is the entity that provisions and authenticates identity assertions, including validating users and provisioning user IDs and passwords, as well as all of the other components of the identity lifecycle. The relying party is any member of the federation that shares resources based on authenticated identities. Relying parties then handle authorization based on their own policies. This allows a relying party to determine their level of trust in third-party IdPs and to map permissions on their own rather than relying on the IdP to provide both authentication and authorization.

In the web-of-trust model, the identity provider is each member of the federation, meaning that they provision identities for each of their users, and they are also often the relying parties who provide services.

In the trusted third-party model of federation, the identity provider is the trusted third party, and the relying parties are each member organization within the federation.

Multifactor Authentication

Multifactor authentication (MFA) is composed of, at a minimum, two of the following aspects: something you know, something you are, and something you have. Something you know can be a password, passphrase, and so on. Something you have can be something like a number-generating key fob, a smartphone capable of receiving text messages or using an application, or even a phone and phone number unique to an individual that can receive a number or key. Something you are is a biometric trait of yourself, as a living creature. This could be as unique and specific as your DNA fingerprint or as cursorily general as a photograph.

The authentication solutions featuring the "know" and "have" aspects are especially useful with remote access security where presenting a biometric factor would be awkward, because they help to prevent an unauthorized user from accessing an account or data without both pieces of the authentication mechanism. It is one thing to steal or guess a password for an account, but it is much harder for someone to obtain both a password and a key generated by a device to which only the user has access.

Multifactor authentication is increasingly required to obtain cybersecurity insurance, and designing your applications to support multifactor authentication, or to rely on an identity provider or authentication service that does, is a best practice for almost any modern application.

Secrets Management

Secrets are digital credentials like keys, API tokens, passwords, and certificates used to provide access to services and systems in the cloud and for other purposes where encryption or validation of identity are required. Secrets management is the use of tools and techniques to create and store secrets as well as to manage their lifecycle.

Fortunately, cloud providers offer secrets management services. Google's Secret Manager, Azure's Key Vault, and Amazon's Secrets Manager are all commonly used for secrets management, and other vendors often offer a way to handle secrets management as well as to detect the potential exposure of secrets in their environments as well.

That's not the only way that secrets are managed; in fact, secrets management is often built into the development process, regardless of whether an application is built for the cloud or to run locally. OWASP provides an in-depth secrets management cheat sheet at `https://cheatsheetseries.owasp.org/cheatsheets/Secrets_Management_CheatSheet.html`. It includes ways to ensure availability, comments about the importance of centralization and standardization, best practices for automation of secrets management and why access control is important, auditing guidelines, and an outline of the typical lifecycle for secrets (creation, rotation, revocation, and expiration). It also tackles policies, metadata, and how to work with secrets in a CI/CD pipeline.

If you're not familiar with secrets management services from IaaS vendors, you can find an overview of the services of each of the three major vendors at the following sites:

`https://cloud.google.com/secret-manager/docs/overview`

`https://azure.microsoft.com/en-us/services/key-vault/#product-overview`

`https://aws.amazon.com/secrets-manager`

Common Threats to Identity and Access Management in the Cloud

Threats to cloud identity are growing, as attackers have learned that gaining access to identities is one of the best ways to gain access to cloud environments. The following are common threats to IAM in the cloud:

- Lost or inadvertently exposed credentials and secrets
- Improperly configured or lax permissions
- Excessive permissions
- Lack of appropriate monitoring and alerting
- Misconfigurations of cloud environments, including security policies
- IAM misconfiguration

As you consider the role of IAM in application development and application architecture, you should keep these common threats in mind to guide your design approach.

Zero Trust

An ever-increasing number of organizations are moving toward a zero trust architecture. Zero trust designs emphasize the need to verify that each user, device, or service must be validated whenever it wants to perform an action. Validation is continuous, ongoing, and mutual, meaning both sides in a transaction need to trust the other side's identity and integrity to allow actions to occur.

A complete zero trust design can be complex, if not almost impossible to implement in a legacy environment, but clean implementations in the cloud as well as partial implementations based on risk models are becoming more common. As you consider IAM architecture, you'll want to consider if zero trust is part of your design and what requirements it might place on your IAM design. If you'd like to read more about Zero Trust, NIST provides details in at https://csrc.nist.gov/publications/detail/sp/800-207/final.

Summary

Developing software and applications for the cloud requires attention to security throughout the development process. That often starts with awareness and training, and then progresses through the rest of the software development lifecycle. Developers and security professionals need to be aware of common pitfalls as well as the most common cloud vulnerabilities, like those described by the OWASP Top 10 and SANS Top 25 lists. You'll also need to understand the SDLC, common models, and what each phase of the SDLC involves.

Along the way, you'll apply technologies like cryptography, sandboxing, and application containerization, as well as security components like web application firewalls and API gateways. Threat modeling using models like STRIDE and ATASM, as well as secure coding, are part of the planning, design, and coding processes. Testing also plays a role; analysts need to be familiar with functional and nonfunctional testing, static and dynamic testing, and a variety of other parts of the testing and QA process.

Finally, in addition to software development concepts, identity and access management is an important part of application architectures and implementation. While it plays a broad role in the cloud, the CCSP exam objectives pair it with application development, focusing on federated identity, identity providers, SSO, and MFA as well as secrets management. Since each of those is part of a secure design, familiarity with threats to IAM is also important for this domain.

Exam Essentials

Explain cloud development basics, including common pitfalls and vulnerabilities to avoid. Understand common pitfalls in application development like ensuring performance, scalability, portability, and interoperability. Be familiar with the OWASP Top 10 and SANS Top 25, including examples of the vulnerabilities from both lists.

Describe the software development lifecycle and how it can be applied. Explain common software development models like Agile and Waterfall. Describe threat models including DREAD, STRIDE, PASTA, and ATASM. Be familiar with secure coding practices and standards like OWASP, ASVS, and SAFECode.

Apply testing methodologies to application software. Describe functional and nonfunctional testing. Explain methodologies like full knowledge, zero knowledge, static and dynamic testing, and interactive application security testing. Understand QA processes and the role of QA in the SDLC.

Manage the software supply chain and use verified secure software. Explain API security best practices and security concerns. Describe supply chain security practices and why supply chain security is important. Understand the importance of assessing vendors, particularly for open-source and third-party software components.

Explain common application security technologies and supplemental security controls. Be familiar with design elements like when and where to use cryptography to protect data in motion and data at rest. Explain the use of and differences between sandboxing, application virtualization, microservices, and containers. Describe the role of orchestration in application environments. Be familiar with the uses for and roles of web application firewalls, database activity monitoring, XML firewalls, API gateways, and cloud application security brokers.

Understand IAM solutions as well as common threats to identity and access management. Explain federated identity and the role of identity providers in federated environments. Describe the differences between SSO and MFA. Understand the basics of secrets management and why secrets need to be protected in application environments. Explain the differences between user, privileged, and service access. Be ready to explain threats like lost or exposed credentials, improper configurations, excessive permissions, and a lack of monitoring and alerting in the context of identity and access management for applications in the cloud.

Review Questions

You can find the answers to the review questions in Appendix A.

1. Which of the following is not a component of the STRIDE model?
   A. Spoofing
   B. Repudiation
   C. Information disclosure
   D. Exploitation

2. In a federated identity arrangement, which organization authorizes users to perform actions on systems or services?
   A. The identity provider
   B. The service provider
   C. The token provider
   D. All of the above

3. Henry knows that multifactor authentication consists of at least two items and that they have to be of different types. Which of the following is a valid multifactor authentication option?
   A. A complex password and a secret code
   B. Complex passwords and an HSM
   C. A hardware token and a magnetic strip card
   D. A password and an application generated PIN on a smartphone

4. Amanda has been told that the organization she is joining uses a sandbox as part of its CI/CD pipeline. With what SDLC phase is the sandbox most likely associated?
   A. The design phase
   B. The coding phase
   C. The testing phase
   D. The operations phase

5. Yarif's organization uses a secrets management tool to handle its secrets lifecycle. Yarif wants to explain a typical secret's lifecycle to one of his staff. What order is typical for a secret?
   A. Creation, revocation, rotation, expiration
   B. Expiration, creation, rotation, revocation
   C. Creation, rotation, revocation, expiration
   D. Creation, rotation, expiration, revocation

6. Heikka has deployed a web application firewall and is preparing to write policies to analyze traffic. Which of the following is not a typical filtering capability for WAFs?

   A. Users

   B. Privileged database use

   C. Session information

   D. Application-specific context

7. Lin wants to conduct nonfunctional testing of her organization's new application. Which of the following items is not tested by nonfunctional testing?

   A. User acceptance

   B. Stability

   C. Performance

   D. Quality

8. Software composition analysis tools are used to help protect against which of the following OWASP Top-10 Cloud Native Application Security issues?

   A. CI/CD pipeline and software supply chain flaws

   B. Injection flaws

   C. Improper asset management

   D. Insecure orchestration configurations

9. Joanna's team of developers is reviewing source code to identify potential issues. What type of testing is Joanna's team conducting?

   A. Dynamic

   B. Interactive

   C. Black box

   D. Static

10. Geoff's organization has designed its application to rely on Docker. What type of application virtualization model has Geoff's organization adopted?

    A. Sandboxing

    B. Containers

    C. Microservices

    D. Multitenancy

11. Jim's organization uses the Waterfall SDLC model. What occurs after testing and debugging has been finished in the Waterfall model?

    A. Quality assurance testing

    B. Interactive software testing

    C. Operational activities

    D. Business rule validation

12. OWASP identifies cloud native application security risks. Which of the following should Jean identify as the most critical issue to address to ensure the security of her organization's SSH keys?

   A. Injection flaws

   B. Insecure secrets storage

   C. Using components with known vulnerabilities

   D. Ineffective logging and monitoring

13. The broad use of many small instances to allow applications to increase or decrease performance as needed is part of what cloud application development pitfall?

   A. Scalability

   B. Interoperability

   C. Portability

   D. API security

14. Which of the following is not a common threat to cloud applications that should be considered during threat modeling?

   A. Firmware vulnerabilities

   B. Broken authentication

   C. Sensitive data exposure

   D. Using components with known vulnerabilities

15. Murali is using the Process for Attack Simulation and Threat Analysis (PASTA) framework as part of his organization's security processes. He has just completed Stage 3, factoring applications and identifying application controls. What will he do next in Stage 4?

   A. He will analyze and model attacks.

   B. He will define business objectives.

   C. He will perform threat analysis based on threat intelligence.

   D. He will run vulnerability scans.

16. Selah wants to assess her organization's application security using the Application Security Verification Standard, and wants to perform a penetration test as the validation method for security. What ASVS level does she want to use?

   A. Level 0

   B. Level 1

   C. Level 2

   D. Level 3

17. The auditor that Ian's company works with has inquired about whether his organization uses a software composition analysis tool as part of its risk management efforts. What capability is the auditor asking Ian about?

A. The ability to identify the language in which source code is written

B. The ability to identify software version numbers in a codebase

C. The ability to identify the language in which compiled code is written

D. The ability to identify open-source software in a codebase

18. Mike's organization has determined that it wants to use interactive application security testing (IAST) as part of its SDLC. In which stage in a typical SDLC is IAST typically performed?

A. Design

B. Code

C. Test

D. Maintain

19. Susan wants to monitor privileged use in her database system as part of an effort to detect attacks using behavioral analysis. What tool should she recommend to her database team?

A. A CASB

B. A WAF

C. A DAM

D. A SDLC

20. Jason wants to add traffic flow control and access control to his organization's APIs. What security tool can he use to add this additional security layer most effectively?

A. An API gateway

B. An IPS

C. An API firewall

D. An IDS

Chapter 7

Operations Elements

THE OBJECTIVE OF THIS CHAPTER IS TO ACQUAINT THE READER WITH THE FOLLOWING CONCEPTS:

✓ **Domain 1: Cloud Concepts, Architecture, and Design**

- 1.3. Understand Security Concepts Relevant to Cloud Computing

    - 1.3.5. Virtualization security (e.g., hypervisor security, container security, ephemeral computing, serverless technology)

✓ **Domain 2: Cloud Data Security**

- 2.1. Describe cloud data concepts

    - 2.1.2. Data dispersion

✓ **Domain 3: Cloud Platform and Infrastructure Security**

- 3.1. Comprehend cloud infrastructure and platform Components

    - 3.1.1. Physical environment

- 3.2. Design a secure data center

    - 3.2.1. Logical design (e.g., tenant partitioning, access control)

    - 3.2.2. Physical design (e.g., location, buy or build)

    - 3.2.3. Environmental design (e.g., Heating, Ventilation, and Air Conditioning (HVAC), multi-vendor pathway connectivity)

    - 3.2.4 Design resilient

✓ **Domain 5: Cloud Security Operations**

- 5.2. Operate and maintain physical and logical infrastructure for cloud environment

    - 5.2.1. Access controls for local and remote access (e.g., Remote Desktop Protocol (RDP), secure terminal access,

Secure Shell (SSH), console-based access mechanisms, jumpboxes, virtual client)

- 5.2.2 Secure network configuration (e.g., virtual local area networks (VLAN), Transport Layer Security (TLS), Dynamic Host Configuration Protocol (DHCP), Domain Name Security Extensions (DNSSEC), virtual private network (VPN))

- 5.2.7 Availability of clustered hosts (e.g., distributed resource scheduling, dynamic optimization, storage clusters, maintenance mode, high availability (HA))

- 5.2.8 Availability of guest operating system (OS)

- 5.6 Manage security operations

- 5.6.1 Security operations center (SOC)

- 5.6.2 Intelligent monitoring of security controls (e.g., firewalls, intrusion detection systems (IDS), intrusion prevention systems (IPS), honeypots, network security groups, artificial intelligence (AI))

- 5.6.4 Incident management

The cloud relies on physical data centers to exist. CCSP candidates are required to understand how the data centers and facilities where the cloud is hosted are designed, built, and operated in secure and reliable ways. In this chapter you will learn about what makes a secure, resilient data center. Along the way, you'll explore concepts like heating and cooling, power and connectivity resilience, and logical design for security. You'll also delve into access controls for local and remote access, network security elements commonly used in data centers, and how virtualization is built for availability and security. Finally, you'll explore how organizations monitor for and respond to security issues and incidents using security operations centers (SOCs) and incident response processes.

Designing a Secure Data Center

Cloud data centers have to be robust and resilient to all types of threats, from natural disasters and hacking attacks to underlying infrastructure and utilities failures. They are designed to provide close to continuous system operation and data access (referred to as *uptime*) for multiple customers with a wide spectrum of service needs.

While there's no set standard for uptime, organizations often describe what percentage of time in a given year they're fully functioning without an outage. You may read about providers who promise five nines of uptime, which means 99.999% uptime. If you do the math, five nines over a calendar year equals fewer than six downtime minutes per year. That means that cloud data center designs need to be resilient in a multitude of ways. In the following sections, we'll review design elements that involve logical, physical, and environmental best practices that cloud service providers and other organizations rely on to build highly reliable data centers.

Build vs. Buy

Building your own data center facility is an expensive undertaking, but larger organizations and cloud providers often build their own. Designing and building your own facility allows you to choose location, services, and design elements that fit your organizational needs. Justifying the cost of one or more complete facilities does require appropriate scale to make the cost make sense!

The alternative option is to buy or lease space in a preexisting data center or colocation facility. Buying space allows organizations to leverage services and facilities that are shared with other organizations, reducing costs and providing additional flexibility and efficiency they might not otherwise be able to access on their own. Data center facilities often also provide staffing that smaller organizations may not be able to afford, like 24/7 operations and onsite staff.

When organizations consider build versus buy decisions for data center space, they will often consider the following items:

- The cost of the facility or the cost to lease space over time.

- If the organization may scale up or down in terms of requirements over a reasonable period of time, and if that means that the facility needs to be bigger or able to change in scale during that time frame.

- Whether they can be more efficient in terms of power, heating and cooling, and staffing over time in their own facility or one they rent.

- Whether there are specific security controls or requirements that fit a build or buy model better.

- Whether they have the ability to staff a data center or if having third-party expertise and skills would be preferable. Organizations may not want to invest in staffing or IT overhead because it's not aligned to their business, or it may make sense as a direction to grow into.

- Organizations must consider that their strategy may result in changes in hosting, particularly if the organization might move services to a cloud service provider from self-hosting or might grow to a point where managing its own cloud makes sense.

Location

One of the first parts of data center design is selecting a location. Cloud service providers pick data center locations for a number of reasons, including the availability of inexpensive (or at least lower cost) electricity, the ability to get high-speed connectivity for the facility, the likelihood of natural disasters, how challenging it will be to provide temperature control inside of the facility, and how close the location is to other data centers they may operate in the area. In some cases, they may also consider whether other vendors have facilities in the same region if interconnection is important to their operations too.

With so many factors in play, cloud service providers need to carefully balance each factor. As more data centers are brought online, they can increase the resilience of the provider's services, allowing less-ideal choices to be made for some factors. Cloud providers also take advantage of vertical integration for their data centers, sometimes going so far as to generate their own power and designing their own hardware to take advantage of custom design elements throughout their facilities.

Figure 7.1 shows Amazon Web Services's North American regions (the large circles), and edge locations where end users access services located at AWS (the smaller circles). There are seven regions, or major geographic locations, in North America, with each region having multiple availability zones. Availability zones are the distinct locations within a data center region. The US East region, which is the oldest of Amazon's regions, has six availability zones as of mid-2022. Amazon's regions take advantage of proximity to large population centers, recognize power and cooling needs, and offer geographic diversity to prevent natural disasters from significantly disrupting operations.

FIGURE 7.1 AWS's North American region map

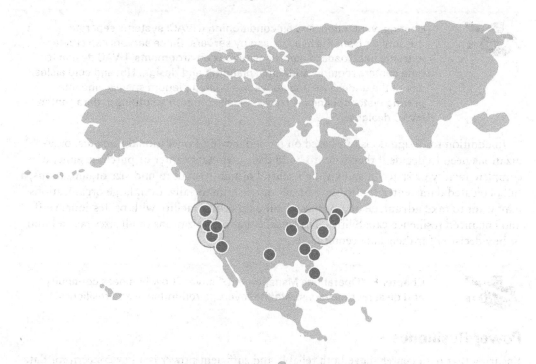

Amazon Web Services, Inc., Regions and Availability Zones. Last accessed by July 18, 2022. https://aws .amazon.com/about-aws/global-infrastructure/regions_az

> If you're designing international facilities, or even facilities in another region, the differences in laws and regulations may impact your facility design and placement decisions.

Data center customers also need to consider locations for a variety of reasons. They may want to have physical access if they're working with a hosting provider, or they may want to select a data center that is closer to reduce latency between their locations and where their systems and services are located. While cloud and hosting providers are responsible for assessing risk to their facilities, customers also bear responsibility for thinking through whether the decisions of their providers fit their own risk tolerance.

Facilities and Redundancy

Data center resilience focuses on a broad range of infrastructure and systems components, including utilities like electrical, water, connectivity, and heating and cooling. Resilience also includes staffing and elements designed to help handle failures, like generators, fuel storage, and fire suppression systems.

Heating, ventilation, and air conditioning (HVAC) systems separate the cool air from the heat caused by servers. Since servers can create extreme heat loads in high-density rack environments, HVAC design for data centers requires additional planning and design. Hot and cold aisles, use of the underfloor and above-the-ceiling plenum spaces, and integrating water cooling into racks are all common solutions in data center HVAC designs.

In addition to design decisions based on redundancy and operational elements, organizations need to decide if they want to build their own data center or purchase either a complete facility or space in an existing facility. For many small to mid-size organizations, a full dedicated data center facility may be out of reach financially. Even large organizations may want to take advantage of a purpose-built data center facility with professional staff and enhanced resilience capabilities. That means that organizations of all sizes face a build or buy decision for their data center facilities.

Chapter 8, "Operations Management," covers how business continuity and disaster recovery strategies leverage redundancy and resiliency.

Power Resilience

Ensuring that data centers have both reliable and sufficient power is a key concern for data center design. That means that ensuring power resilience involves a handful of critical items at the provider and external infrastructure levels:

- Can the data center be connected to multiple grids? The ability to acquire power from different grids or providers can ensure that a provider outage or severed connection does not disable the data center.

- Are there distinct physical paths for power? Any utility that the data center relies on should be designed to ensure that there isn't a single point of failure where multiple connections could be disrupted by a single event that cuts a power line or causes a power outage.

- Is there enough power for the expected load that the data center will create? Data centers can have significant power draws, and providers may not have the infrastructure in the area to provide the needed power without appropriate planning and communications. Adding additional capacity may create significant costs, creating challenges for data center owners.

Power infrastructure for the data center itself is also important. Uninterruptible power supplies that provide battery-based or flywheel-based power are commonly used in data center designs to cover brief power outages. Generators are typically used to provide power during longer outages, and they need to be powerful enough to keep the data center running. Generators themselves are typically deployed in redundant designs to ensure that a single generator not working doesn't stop the data center from functioning. Multiple-generator designs also allow generators to be removed from service for maintenance cycles during longer emergencies.

Generators need fuel, and getting fuel during disasters can be a challenge. That means that data center operators need to sign contracts with fuel providers that ensure that they will receive fuel as a priority during disasters or other events that may disrupt normal fuel deliveries. While hospitals and other lifesaving services typically receive preference, data center facilities often have contracts that place them next in line for fuel deliveries and may have multiple contracts in place to avoid a single provider's failure to deliver fuel from disrupting the data center.

Communications Redundancy

Cloud data centers—and data centers in general—are only useful if the systems and services they host can be accessed. That means ensuring communications and connectivity are redundant and resilient is a must. Much as with power, organizations should perform the following tasks to ensure communications redundancy:

- Identify their current and likely future bandwidth needs.

- Ensure connectivity to their potential data center locations from more than one internet service provider (ISP), a concept the CCSP Exam Outline (Candidate Information Bulletin) calls *multi-vendor pathway connectivity*.

- Ensure that those ISPs do not have shared upstream dependencies.

- Assess connectivity paths for environmental dangers and single points of failure.

- Design internal systems and networks to support redundant connectivity and resilience.

Wait, I Thought That Was Redundant.

The authors of this book experienced an unforeseen connectivity problem. The organization that they worked for had redundant connectivity through two separate internet service providers and thus felt like it was well prepared in the case of a failure by either of its providers. Unfortunately, both providers turned out to have hosted their points of presence in the same data center facility. When that facility had a power issue that wasn't handled properly by the facility's redundant power systems, both connectivity providers went dark, dropping the authors' organization off the internet completely.

The after-action review showed that what was thought to be proper due diligence didn't result in the right question being asked: Where do you host your point of presence for the region? The answer to that question would have immediately showed the issue. The organization opted to build out connectivity to a third provider, and both internet service providers recognized the issue and worked to ensure that they remediated their own infrastructure designs as well. The data center where they were renting space learned lessons about its own power infrastructure and also made changes.

While validating designs is important, learning from outages and mistakes is also key to improving resilient design.

Other Utilities

In addition to power and connectivity, other utilities are important. Water is a common concern, as many facilities use chilled water loops as their primary means to cool data center spaces. The backup system for chilled water loops is often water directly from the utility provider, which can be circulated to provide less-effective cooling if the chiller fails. Of course, water is also needed for other data center support needs and for fire suppression, so ensuring that there is a ready and sufficient supply of water is important.

Other utilities and resources can also be important, depending on design choices. Natural gas may be part of backup power generation systems, although on-site diesel tanks are more common since gas distribution can fail in a disaster. Natural gas can also be important for human-habitable service and support areas in colder regions. Even though data centers generate significant amounts of waste heat, HVAC systems are usually put in place to handle those areas independently if needed.

Physical Security

Much as in network and system security, defense in depth is a critical part of data center physical security as well. Defense in depth (or "layered defense") entails multiple differing security controls protecting the same assets, often with a variety of technological levels and an assortment of the three categories of controls: physical, administrative, and logical/technical.

A typical data center might employ layered physical defenses like a strong fence, a guard patrol who monitors the fence line, a video surveillance capability, and electronic monitoring of tampering attempts on the fence. This offers redundancy as well as resiliency.

In addition to the perimeter, the focus is on the following physical security design areas:

- Vehicular approach/access, including driveways that wind and curve and/or include speed bumps or bollards designed to prevent a vehicle from achieving sufficient speed to ram the building

- Guest and visitor access through a controlled entry point, involving formal reception with security measures such as a sign-in log, video surveillance, and specific staff tasked with that duty

- Camera and other monitoring systems with appropriate monitoring, alerting, and retention capabilities

- Protected placement of hazardous or vital resources such as electrical supply, storage, and distribution components, particularly generators and fuel, such that they are not directly located near personnel or in the path of vehicles

- Interior physical access controls such as badging, keys, access codes, and secured doors

- Specific physical protections for highly sensitive assets, such as safes and inventory tracking mechanisms

- Fire detection and suppression systems

- And of course, design elements that ensure that security controls keep working even during interruptions of power or network connectivity

The CCSP Exam Outline (Candidate Information Bulletin) doesn't cover much content regarding physical security; it focuses on logical design items like tenant partitioning and access control as well as traditional environmental and physical design concepts. Despite that focus, you should be aware that providing appropriate physical security is a key element in both cloud and traditional data center design. Physical access to a system remains one of the most effective ways to obtain data from it or to take it offline, so providers focus on effective security measures and are audited on them.

Restricted Physical Access to Devices

In addition to traditional physical security elements, data center–specific requirements are important to implement. Access to racks in the data center should be limited to administrators and maintenance staff who absolutely need to reach the devices in order to perform their job functions. Entry and egress should be controlled, monitored, and logged. Racks should be locked, and keys for each respective rack should be checked out only for the duration of use.

Specific technologies can help when limiting access is important. Power-Shell provides Just Enough Administration, or JEA. It enables delegation for anything controlled by PowerShell, allowing granular limits to often powerful controls. You can read more about JEA at https://docs
.microsoft.com/en-us/powershell/scripting/learn/remoting/
jea/overview?view=powershell-7.2.

Just in Time (JIT) management is a privileged access management method that focuses on least privilege by providing rights only when needed. Privileges are assigned on the fly and in context, rather than accounts having the privileges by default.

SLAs and Resilience

Each of these elements of resilience may be covered by service-level agreements, or SLAs. Guarantees from hosting providers and cloud service providers may include financial penalties if issues last beyond a certain time frame, or there may be other guarantees. Since these SLAs are tied to organizational control schemes, it is common to have them validated as part of audits, so requesting a SOC 2 Type 1 or Type 2 audit may provide information that can help you assess an organization's SLA compliance.

Data Center Tiers

One common measure of data centers is through the Uptime Institute's Tier Classification System. The system describes four tiers from Tier 1 to Tier 4, each with increasing requirements for maintenance, power, cooling, and fault tolerance. The tiers are intended to map to business needs, not to imply that a Tier 4 data center is better than a Tier 2 data center.

Tier 1

A Tier 1 data center is the basic infrastructure required to support an organization that wants to conduct IT operations. Tier 1 has the following requirements:

- An uninterruptible power supply (UPS) system for line conditioning and backup purposes
- An area to house IT systems
- Dedicated cooling systems
- A power generator for extended electrical outages

Tier 1 data centers are expected to help protect against human error, not outages or disasters. They're also expected to have redundancy for chillers, pumps, UPS devices, and generators but are likely to have to shut down for maintenance activities.

Tier 2

Tier 2 facilities provide more redundancy than Tier 1 facilities, including the following:

- Generators and UPS devices
- Chillers and cooling units
- Pumps
- Fuel tanks and other fuel storage

Unlike Tier 1 facilities, Tier 2 facilities are intended to ensure that critical operations are not interrupted due to planned maintenance.

Tier 3

The Tier 3 design is known as a "concurrently maintainable site infrastructure." As the name indicates, the facility features both the redundant capacity components of a Tier 2 build and the added benefit of multiple distribution paths where only a sole path is needed to serve critical operations at any given time.

Tier 4

Tier 4 data centers are the highest level described by the Uptime Institute. They have independent and physically isolated systems providing redundancy and resiliency at both the component and distribution path levels, ensuring that events that compromised one system would not take out the redundant system. Tier 4 data centers are not disrupted if there is a planned or unplanned event, although the Uptime Institute notes that planned maintenance may increase the risk of an outage if the remaining redundant systems are compromised while the maintenance is in progress. In addition, Tier 4 data centers are designed around fault tolerance for components, so a system that fails will not result in a failure of a service.

Uptime is also considered in tiers. Figure 7.2 shows the uptime percentage for each of the Uptime Institute's data center tiers. Tier 1 allows up to 28.8 hours a year of downtime, which might be startling for some organizations! Tier 4 should experience less than a half an hour of downtime a year, a huge difference in both time and cost.

FIGURE 7.2 Uptime Institute tiers

Data Center Tier	Uptime Percentage
Tier 1	99.671
Tier 2	99.741
Tier 3	99.982
Tier 4	99.995

Logical Design

A final component of data center design is found at the logical layer. The CCSP Exam Outline (Candidate Information Bulletin) specifically considers two elements of logical design that you'll need to be aware of.

The first is *tenant partitioning*. Commercial data centers and hosting providers often have multiple tenants in the same physical space, requiring methods to partition tenants. Partitioning may occur at the rack or cage level, where a locked rack or cage is used to separate tenants and provide physical security. It may also happen at the bay (room) or even the facility level for very large-scale tenant usage. While locked doors, cages, or racks can be helpful, additional controls are typically put in place as well. Cameras and other monitoring systems, security guards or data center staff to escort customers or control access, or other security controls may be employed.

 Tenant partitioning is frequently used to describe how tenants are logically separated in virtual and shared service environments as well as in data center design. Outside of the CCSP exam, you're more likely to run into the term describing ways to allow multiple users or organizations to share the same infrastructure without overlapping or causing resource conflicts.

Access control is also important when considering data center logical control. Access control at the physical level can leverage the tenant partitioning options we just explored. In addition, tools that allow console access; keyboard, mouse, and video (KVM) access; or other means to access server hardware or systems directly need access controls, logging, and monitoring to ensure that attacks against those means of access are prevented. This means that data center operators need to pay particular attention to how access is provisioned, managed, monitored, and maintained.

Virtualization Operations

From a cloud provider perspective, virtualization is an absolute necessity. It's the only way to properly manage the cost of hosting multiple customers in a scalable manner and still provide them with near-constant uptime.

Virtualization poses specific risks, many of which have been described in previous chapters. In the next few sections, we'll discuss what a cloud provider should be considering when planning virtualization operations.

Virtualization Concepts

The CCSP Exam Outline (Candidate Information Bulletin) highlights a handful of specific virtualization concepts you'll want to be familiar with for the exam:

- *Distributed resource scheduling*, which focuses on providing resources to virtual machines to ensure they can meet performance service-level requirements. It also allows migrations of systems to other underlying infrastructure during maintenance and includes monitoring and management capabilities. In short, distributed resource scheduling is the ability to manage resources across a cluster or environment in a way that optimizes reliable and consistent service delivery.

- *Dynamic optimization* is a term used to describe an optimization process that assesses performance or other factors and takes action to meet desired targets. Dynamic optimization relies on real-time data and defined goals or objectives to determine configuration and resource changes required to meet those goals.

- *Maintenance mode* in virtualization environments allows hosts to be removed from a cluster in a safe way to allow for system or hardware maintenance. Maintenance mode transfers running guest operating systems to other nodes in a cluster, then marks the system as being in maintenance mode, allowing needed work to be performed.

- *High availability,* or *HA,* is a major driver in the adoption of both virtualized and cloud-hosted systems and services. As part of that, the *availability of guest operating systems* is a key feature of virtualization environments. Guest operating systems can be moved to other hardware if a failure occurs, allowing systems to continue to operate in a scenario that would cause an outage for a hardware-based system. At the same time, virtualization environments allow hardware abstraction, meaning that a failed device can simply be remapped to a working system component with the same function in either the same underlying physical host or another virtualization server in the same cluster or environment.

- *Containerization* places an application or service, along with all of the libraries and components it needs, together in a form that can be run on an underlying environment. Unlike virtualization, it does not virtualize an entire OS, just the application environment. Container security has quite a few similarities to virtualization security, however. Keeping containers secure requires the images to be secured, much as VM and instance images are kept secure. The environment, orchestration platform, and runtimes must also be kept secure through patching and configuration, and appropriate monitoring and management must be in place. In addition, paying attention to the security of container registries, including signing containers, managing secrets, and validating signatures is important.

- *Ephemeral computing* is a key concept in many environments. It leverages the ability to quickly stand up virtual systems, then to shut them down when they are no longer needed to meet demand. Cloud computing environments leverage this, often using many smaller systems rather than fewer larger systems to allow for horizontal scaling.

- *Serverless* technology replaces constantly running servers with code that runs when needed. Cloud services that provide serverless functionality charge on an as-used basis, allowing for efficient use of resources.

Securing containers and containerization environments is another very broad and deep topic. It can help to take a tour through common security practices like those described in Aquasec's Docker security best practices blog post here: https://blog.aquasec.com/docker-security-best-practices

Virtualization is a broad topic, and you'll want to consider a number of other major concepts when thinking about secure and resilient cloud data centers.

Hypervisor and Management Plane Hardening

Hypervisor and cloud management planes are prime targets for attackers. They can allow access to the data for every instance, breaching barriers between customers and giving attackers unfettered access. This means that hypervisor and cloud management plane security is a prime focus for security efforts.

In order to provide appropriate levels of hypervisor security, you should make sure hypervisors are configured, updated, and patched to vendor standards and use industry best practices. Common elements of this type of effort include restricting use of superuser accounts, requiring multifactor authentication, using logging and alerting capabilities to monitor for improper or malicious use, and designing access to hypervisor and management planes to limit access to authorized users. In addition, controls like encrypting virtual machines, using secure boot for the underlying hardware, and performing regular audits of configurations and systems are all important.

Cloud vendors provide design patterns that can help when you're thinking about how to ensure that your control planes and management consoles are secure. Amazon's Well-Architected Framework is an example of this type of vendor documentation and can help you think through design concepts you might want to include in your organization's cloud environment:

https://aws.amazon.com/architecture/well-architected

Google's Cloud Architecture Framework provides similar recommendations for Google:

https://cloud.google.com/architecture/framework

Azure provides its framework as well:

https://docs.microsoft.com/en-us/azure/architecture/framework

Instance Isolation

Each virtual machine, whether it's a cloud instance or a VM guest operating system, should be logically isolated from the others with appropriate logical controls. That means limitations on access to other systems as well as the internet, firewalls or security group–based controls, security at the hypervisor layer to ensure that virtual machines can't access resources assigned to others, and similar protections.

Host Isolation

All underlying hosts must also be both physically and logically isolated from one another as much as possible. They will obviously still be connected to the network and so will potentially be able to be connected, so those connections should be minimized and secured as much as possible. Moreover, network monitoring should be thorough and detailed, such that any host escape activity would be immediately recognized and a response would result.

Storage Operations

In addition to hosts used to run virtualized instances for customer operations, the cloud data centers and virtualization environments also include devices and services used for near-term and long-term storage of data and instance images.

Storage Clusters

Most often, storage devices are clustered in groups, providing increased performance, flexibility, and reliability. Clustered storage architectures can be one of two types: tightly coupled or loosely coupled.

In the tightly coupled architecture, all the storage devices are directly connected to a shared physical backplane, thus connecting all of them directly. Each component of the cluster is aware of the others and subscribes to the same policies and rulesets. A tightly coupled cluster is usually confined to more restrictive design parameters, often because the devices might need to be from the same vendor in order to function properly. Although this may be a limiting factor, a tightly coupled architecture also enhances performance as it scales: the performance of each element is added to the overall performance of the cluster, allowing greater and greater power as it increases in size.

A loosely coupled cluster, on the other hand, allows for greater flexibility. Each node of the cluster is independent of the others, and new nodes can be added for any purpose or use as needed. They are only logically connected and don't share the same proximate physical framework, so they are only distantly physically connected through communication media. Performance does not necessarily scale, however, because the nodes don't build on one another. But this might not be an important facet of the storage architecture, since storage commands and performance requirements are fairly simple.

Regardless of the cluster type, clustering storage is an important design element when organizations consider resilient and highly available storage. Ensuring that failures do not result in storage outages and that data can be preserved despite loss or corruption is a critical need.

Data Resiliency

There are two general ways for creating data protection in a cloud storage cluster: RAID (redundant array of independent disks, although originally termed as redundant array of inexpensive disks) and *data dispersion*. Both options provide a level of resiliency—that is, a reasonable amount of assurance that although the physical and/or logical environment might be partially affected by detrimental occurrences (outages, attacks, and so on), the overall bulk of data will not be lost permanently.

In most RAID configurations, all data is stored across the various disks in a method known as *striping*. This allows data to be recovered in a more efficient manner because if one of the drives fails, the missing data can be filled in by the other drives. In some RAID schemes, parity bits are added to the raw data to aid in recovery after a drive failure.

Data dispersion focuses on distributing data among multiple data centers or locations. This broader-scale data distribution helps to ensure that a disruption in a single location cannot result in data loss or an availability issue. Some organizations take this a step further and use data dispersion techniques across multiple vendors or storage solutions to add even greater protections for their data.

Access Controls for Local and Remote Access

An important part of operations for cloud and virtualized data centers is providing remote access. There are a number of common methods that you are likely to already be familiar with from traditional data center environments:

Remote Desktop Protocol (RDP), the Windows native remote desktop tool. RDP provides remote access over an encrypted channel. Common RDP controls include requiring strong passwords and multifactor authentication, restricting which users can use RDP, and enabling account lockout policies. In addition, it is important to ensure updates are installed and that firewalls are in place.

Secure Shell, or *SSH*, is commonly used for command-line access to Linux and Unix systems. Much like RDP, requiring multifactor authentication and using SSH certificates is a common practice to protect authentication. In addition, providing appropriate network security through firewalls and using a bastion host or jumpbox are common security best practices for SSH.

Secure terminal access and *console-based access mechanisms* are both concepts that focus on physical access to terminals. Access control mechanisms in shared data center spaces are particularly important, and ensuring that your console access does not simply allow an individual to plug into the system and gain access without authentication and authorization is key.

Jumpboxes and bastion hosts are systems or devices placed at the boundary between a lower-security zone and a higher-security zone. They are used as control points, allowing access from the lower-security zone to the higher security zone while focusing on security for the device and allowing a single entry point to be instrumented and monitored. Figure 7.3 shows an example of a jumpbox in place in a secured network with an administrator in a lower-security zone accessing a higher-security zone containing databases via SSH on TCP port 22.

Virtual clients are the final option included in the CCSP Exam Outline (Candidate Information Bulletin). Virtual clients are software tools that allow you to remotely connect to a virtual machine and use it as though it is your local system. This allows additional layers of security to be put in place with management, monitoring, and data storage all occurring in a trusted data center or cloud environment while the remote PC merely provides a display, keyboard, and mouse for the virtual system. Virtual clients are increasingly used to provide processing, software, and security for organizations that may not be able to, or may not want to, provide endpoint security, particularly in bring your own device (BYOD) environments. Simply using a virtual client isn't enough to ensure security, however; practices like preventing clipboard access between security zones or systems, securing persistent data, using endpoint security solutions, and limiting what applications can be launched are all common.

FIGURE 7.3   Jumpbox access to protected systems

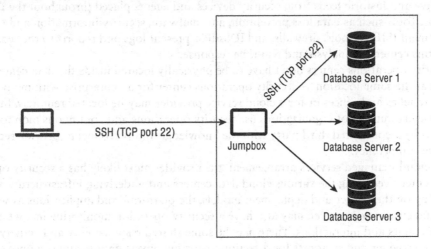

While we discussed the Just in Time and Just Enough Administration models earlier, additional local controls can be leveraged for local and remote access. In addition to the technologies the CCSP Exam Outline (Candidate Information Bulletin) lists, you should consider the following:

- Encryption, both in transit and at rest, to ensure that access and administration is protected
- Key access controls for cryptographic keys to ensure that attackers cannot acquire them
- Multifactor authentication
- Monitoring, logging, and alerting

Managing Security Operations

Even the most secure design needs ongoing monitoring and operational oversight. Larger organizations may have dedicated operations staff or teams, while smaller organizations may need to rely on outsourced services, monitoring tools, or other means to handle operations if they don't operate a 24/7 management and operations team or center.

Security Operations Center (SOC)

Most data centers have a centralized facility for continuous monitoring of network performance and security controls. This is commonly known as the security operations center. Typically, physical access is limited to security personnel and administrators overseeing live and historic feeds from security devices and agents placed throughout the IT environment. Tools such as data loss prevention, anti-malware, security information and event management (SIEM) tools, firewalls, and IDSs/IPSs present logs and reports to the security operations center for analysis and real-time response.

Security operations centers don't have to be physically located inside the data center itself or even at the same location. A security operations center for an enterprise with many different branches and offices or for a cloud service provider may be located remotely. In fact, an increasing number of organizations use security operations and continuous monitoring provided by a contracted third party with the knowledge and personnel to provide security as a core competency.

In a cloud-managed services arrangement, the provider most likely has a security operations center overseeing the various cloud data centers and underlying infrastructure and, depending on the service and deployment models, the platforms and applications as well. The cloud customer, however, may also have a security operation monitoring its own users/cloud accounts and interactions. There may be some shared responsibility and activity between the provider and customer for detection, reporting, investigation, and response actions. All of these need to be established in the contract.

Continuous Monitoring

Managing security operations also involves monitoring security devices, systems, and tools. Controls must be continually monitored to ensure that they are effective, operating as intended, and addressing the risks or vulnerabilities that they were supposed to mitigate. It's common to monitor the following controls:

- *Firewalls* and *network security groups*. Logging blocked connections and potential attacks can be useful both for troubleshooting and to determine if there are new threats that should be addressed.

- *Intrusion detection system (IDS)* and *intrusion prevention system (IPS)* logging is commonly used to identify attacks and to alert if an attack may have been successful based on traffic patterns or behaviors.

- *Honeypots* are sometimes used to capture attack techniques and tools.

- *Artificial intelligence (AI)* and machine learning capabilities are increasingly common, both as built-in tools for each of these devices and tools and as part of central security monitoring and log analysis tools. Understanding your organization's normal traffic patterns and behaviors and applying AI or machine learning–based detection techniques (looking for events like unexpected authentication from an unfamiliar location or large file transfers to new locations) can help with monitoring throughout your environment.

Incident Management

When the security operations center detects or receives a report of anomalous or illicit activity, an incident response action might be initiated. Incident response might include the following purposes:

- Minimizing the loss of value/assets
- Continuing service provision (availability)
- Halting increase of the damage

The intended outcome significantly impacts the course of action taken in the response, and it is different for every industry or organization. For example, a large online retailer that conducts thousands of commercial transactions per hour might be most concerned about availability—continuing the transactions. If the retailer discovers that a piece of malware is skimming money from the retailer so that the retailer is losing hundreds of dollars per hour, but the retailer's revenues are hundreds of thousands of dollars per hour, the retailer probably won't want to shut down operations in order to address the malware issue. The retailer may allow the loss to continue for an extended period of time because the impact of shutting down the environment would be much more damaging than the effect of the malware.

The organization should have an incident response policy and plan. Both the cloud provider and customer have their own approaches, goals, and methods for incident management. The two parties should coordinate and share these responsibilities and codify this arrangement in the contract.

Moreover, incident response in a managed services arrangement creates additional challenges and risks. For instance, which party can declare an incident unilaterally? Do both parties have to concur that an incident has occurred? If the provider declares an incident, is the provider relieved of the requirement to meet certain SLA performance targets (say, availability) for the duration of the incident? If there are additional costs associated with incident response, such as downtime, personnel tasking, or reporting actions, which party is responsible for absorbing these costs?

The customer should consider all these questions pertinent to incident management when planning cloud migration and selecting a provider.

Summary

In this chapter, we've discussed the core concepts required to design and build a secure data center. That process includes deciding whether to build a data center or to lease space in a preexisting data center. It also includes deciding where it should be located as well as ensuring redundancy and resilience are part of the design. Along the way we explored power, communications, and utility resilience as well as physical security design elements. You learned about data center tiers ranging from Tier 1 self-hosting facilities to Tier 4 highly available environments.

Logical design is also a critical part of data center design. Understanding how access control and tenant partitioning help to ensure that shared facilities are secure for each tenant is necessary to manage a secure data center. Virtualization operations, including hypervisor management and security, resource scheduling, optimization, maintenance, and high availability are all part of modern data centers. Clustering and ensuring storage resilience is another element that data center operators and customers need to pay attention to.

Finally, security operations, including security operations centers, that provide continuous monitoring and management of data center environments are needed. Tools like firewalls, security groups, IDS and IPS systems, honeypots, and a wide range of other technologies are combined to build a secure data center environment. With tools in place, organizations need to focus on incident management and incident response capabilities for when something goes wrong.

Exam Essentials

Design and describe a secure data center.   Understand the buy versus build decision for data centers. Describe physical design considerations including location, utilities redundancy, and facilities redundancy elements. Explain environmental design components related to HVAC, multivendor pathways, and other redundant components necessary to data center operations. Outline the logical design elements of tenant partitioning and access controls.

Understand how redundancy is implemented in the design of the cloud data center.   Explain how each critical infrastructure element can be implemented in a redundant and resilient way, including utilities like power, water, and connectivity; processing capabilities; and data storage. Consider how emergency services and business continuity capabilities can be built into data center design.

Ensure the availability of clustered hosts and guest operating systems.   Describe methods of ensuring high availability for virtualized systems. Understand technologies like containerization and serverless functionality and how they relate to virtualization and cloud environments. Explain distributed resource scheduling and dynamic optimization and how they differ. Know when to use maintenance mode and what it means in a virtualization cluster. Understand storage clusters and their impact on availability and resilience. Explain data dispersion for data resilience.

Describe access controls for both local and remote access methods.   Explain the most common remote access methods for systems in a data center, including RDP, SSH, and virtual clients. Describe jumpboxes and bastion hosts. Understand the role and application of secure terminals and console-based security mechanisms for physical access.

Explain network security controls as part of a cloud environment.   Explain common network security controls including firewalls and network security groups, IDSs/IPSs, honeypots, and bastion hosts. Describe the role of a SOC and how incident response occurs in a cloud data center environment.

Review Questions

You can find the answers to the review questions in Appendix A.

1. Megan has downloaded a container from a public repository. What should her next step be to use the container?

   A. Run the container using her containerization service.

   B. Scan the container for malicious software.

   C. Validate the container by decrypting it.

   D. Check the container into her organization's container repository.

2. Chris is considering whether his organization should build a data center or buy a preexisting data center. His organization needs a large amount of space and uses a significant amount of power. Which of the following is a common reason to build a new data center rather than pay for data center space in a scenario like the one Chris is facing?

   A. Cost

   B. Resilience

   C. Efficiency

   D. Flexibility

3. Stacey wants to detect attacks against her hosted systems and would like to be able to analyze the techniques and tools used in those attacks. What security tool could she use to accomplish both of these goals?

   A. A network security group

   B. A firewall

   C. A honeypot

   D. A beartrap

4. Olivia wants to ensure that her new data center cannot lose its internet connectivity due to a single event that damages the fiber optic cable run to her internet service providers. What term describes the solution Olivia is looking for?

   A. Linear continuity

   B. Multivendor pathway connectivity

   C. Separation of networks

   D. Redundant fiber assessment

5. Pete wants to configure network security defenses for his cloud-hosted instances. What cloud security tool is best compared to a firewall?

   A. Cloud watchers

   B. Cloud IDS

   C. Cloud IPS

   D. Network security groups

6. Daniel wants to provide SSH access to hosts in a protected subnet in his cloud-hosted data center environment. He deploys a system dedicated for this type of access with rules allowing lower security zones to connect through the system to higher security devices in the subnet. What type of device has Daniel deployed?

   A. A bastion host

   B. A security gateway

   C. A VPC span

   D. A span port

7. Charles wants to detect abnormal traffic in his organization's cloud environment. The vendor who provides his SIEM tool has advanced analytical tools that baseline normal traffic and then analyze logs and traffic to identify potential attacks based on learning models. Which of the following options best describes this type of technology?

   A. Behavior-based analysis

   B. Artificial intelligence

   C. Rules-based analysis

   D. Pattern matching

8. Geeta wants to connect to a Windows server using a full graphical user interface. What secure connection option should she use?

   A. Telnet

   B. SSH

   C. RDP

   D. Screen

9. The organization that Jules works for wants to ensure that a loss of chilled water does not cause an outage for her data center. What option should Jules ensure is in place in case of a failure of the chilled water system?

   A. The ability to switch to utility water

   B. A complete fire suppression system

   C. The ability to switch to external temperature air

   D. A complete generator system to provide backup power to the chiller

10. Amanda has joined a new company, and part of her orientation notes that staff use virtual clients to access secure data used by the company as part of their data center operations. What type of solution should Amanda expect to see?

    A. Virtual clients hosted on her laptop

    B. A cloud-based server environment

    C. Virtual clients hosted in the cloud or on servers

    D. A third-party managed data center

11. Jack wants to design a redundant power system for his data center. Which of the following is not a common element in a fully redundant power system?

    A. Power from two or more utility providers

    B. UPS devices in each rack

    C. Multiple generators

    D. Solar power arrays

12. Jim wants to harden his virtualization environment. Which of the following is not a common hypervisor hardening technique?

    A. Restricting the use of superuser accounts

    B. Requiring multifactor authentication

    C. Logging and alerting on improper usage

    D. Enabling secure boot for guest systems

13. Naomi wants to provide secure SSH connectivity to systems in a protected VLAN. Which of the following describes the best security method for doing so?

    A. Use SSH to a jumpbox, require multifactor authentication, and use SSH certificates.

    B. Use SSH directly to the host, require multifactor authentication, and use SSH certificates.

    C. Use SSH directly to the host, require multifactor authentication, and do not allow SSH certificates.

    D. Use SSH to a jumpbox, do not require multifactor authentication, and use SSH certificates.

14. Selah's cloud environment analyzes traffic patterns and load and adjusts the number of systems in a web server pool to meet the current and expected future load as needed. Which of the following terms best describes what her organization is doing?

    A. Distributed resource scheduling

    B. Dynamic optimization

    C. Maintenance mode

    D. High availability

15. Frank's organization wants to institute a 24/7 monitoring and response capability focused on security. What type of operations capability will Frank establish?

    A. A SIEM

    B. A NOC

    C. A SOC

    D. An IDS

16. Gary wants to drain currently running virtual machines from a VM server host so that he can replace failing hardware in the system. What should he enable to allow this to occur?

A. Distributed resource scheduling

B. Dynamic optimization

C. Storage clustering

D. Maintenance mode

17. Dana wants to ensure the availability of her guest operating systems. Which of the following techniques is not a common technique to help improve the availability of guest operating systems?

A. Clustering of VM hosts

B. Storage clustering

C. Distributed resource scheduling

D. Enabling a load balancer

18. Valerie has deployed an IDS to help protect her cloud-based systems. Which of the following actions isn't an option that she can use the IDS for if it detects an attack?

A. Log the attack

B. Block the attack

C. Send a notification about the attack

D. Display information about the attack on a dashboard

19. Which of the following is not a common type of facility-based tenant partitioning?

A. Separate racks

B. Separate facilities

C. Separate cages

D. Separate bays

20. Hu has placed copies of his data in multiple data centers. What data resiliency technique has he employed?

A. Mirroring

B. RAID

C. Data cloning

D. Data dispersion

Chapter 8

Operations Management

THE OBJECTIVE OF THIS CHAPTER IS TO ACQUAINT THE READER WITH THE FOLLOWING CONCEPTS:

✓ **Domain 1: Cloud Concepts, Architecture, and Design**

- 1.3. Understand security concepts related to cloud computing
  - 1.3.7. Security hygiene (e.g., patching, baselining)
- 1.4. Understand design principles of secure cloud computing
  - 1.4.2. Cloud-based business continuity (BC) and disaster recovery (DR) plan
  - 1.4.7. DevOps security

✓ **Domain 3: Cloud Platform and Infrastructure Security**

- 3.4. Plan and implementation of security controls
  - 3.4.1. Physical and environmental protection (e.g. on-premises)
- 3.5. Plan business continuity (BC) and disaster recovery (DR)
  - 3.5.1. Business continuity (BC)/disaster recovery (DR) strategy
  - 3.5.2. Business requirements (e.g., Recovery Time Objective (RTO), Recovery Point Objective (RPO), recovery service level)
  - 3.5.3. Creation, implementation, and testing of plan

✓ **Domain 5: Cloud Security Operations**

- 5.2. Operate and maintain physical and logical infrastructure for cloud environment
  - 5.2.5. Patch management
  - 5.2.6. Infrastructure as Code (IaC) strategy

- 5.2.9. Performance and capacity monitoring (e.g., network, compute, storage, response time)
- 5.2.10. Hardware monitoring (e.g., disk, central processing unit (CPU), fan speed, temperature)
- 5.3. Implement operational controls and standards (e.g., Information Technology Infrastructure Library (ITIL), International Organization for Standardization/International Electrotechncial Commission (ISO/IEC) 20000-1)
  - 5.3.1. Change management
  - 5.3.2. Continuity management
  - 5.3.3. Information security management
  - 5.3.4. Continual service improvement management
  - 5.3.5. Incident management
  - 5.3.6. Problem management
  - 5.3.7. Release management
  - 5.3.8. Deployment management
  - 5.3.9. Configuration management
  - 5.3.10. Service level management
  - 5.3.11. Availability management
  - 5.3.12. Capacity Management

This chapter covers the essential aspects of operations monitoring, capacity, maintenance, change and configuration management, and BC/DR for cloud data centers.

In other chapters, we often referred to the cloud customer as "your organization" or made other related associations (using *your* or *we* to indicate the cloud customer's perspective in many matters). In this chapter, the focus is almost exclusively on the cloud provider, specifically the provider's data center. We may refer to actions associated with the provider with the same pronouns used for the customer elsewhere (*you*, *your*, or *we*); hopefully, context will prevent any misunderstanding.

In this chapter, we'll discuss the various practices cloud data center operators should use to optimize performance and enhance durability of their infrastructure and systems. This will include coverage of systems monitoring, the configuration and change management program, and BC/DR from a vendor perspective.

Monitoring, Capacity, and Maintenance

It's important for data center operators to know how their hardware, software, and network are being utilized and what demand is being placed on all the relevant resources. This information helps data center operators know how to better apportion and allocate all those items in order to fulfill customer needs (and maintain compliance with service-level agreements, or SLAs). This fulfills three important IT service management functions:

- *Service-level management* ensures that the IT organization is fulfilling its obligations to internal and external customers.

- *Availability management* improves the resiliency of IT services to ensure their ability to meet customer needs.

- *Capacity management* ensures that IT resources are sufficient to meet current and future business demands.

Monitoring

Software, hardware, and network components need to be evaluated in real time to understand which systems may be nearing capacity and so the organization can respond as quickly as possible when problems arise. This can and should be done with several of the tools at the operator's disposal:

OS Logging   Most operating systems have integral toolsets for monitoring performance and events. Aside from the security uses mentioned elsewhere in the book, the cloud vendor can set OS logs to alert administrators when usage approaches a level of capacity utilization or performance degradation that may affect SLA parameters. These can include CPU usage, memory usage, disk space (virtual or tangible), and disk I/O timing (an indicator of slow writing to and reading from the disk).

Cloud Application Telemetry   As organizations integrate new cloud services into their operating environments, it is important to integrate the logs generated by those services into monitor efforts. *Cloud application telemetry* is a term that collectively describes the rich information sources provided by some cloud services that organizations may include in their security monitoring efforts. The use of cloud application telemetry also introduces new challenges because it may be difficult to import or export log sources from the cloud and these log entries may be delayed from real time.

Hardware Monitoring   As with the OS, many vendors include performance-monitoring tools in common device builds. These can be used to measure such performance indicators as CPU temperature, fan speed, voltages (consumption and throughput), CPU load and clock speed, and drive temperature. Commercial products are also available to collect and supply this data and provide alerts if this functionality is not integral to the devices from the manufacturer.

Network Monitoring   In addition to the OS and the devices themselves, the various network elements need to be monitored. These include not only the hardware and the software, but the distribution facets such as cabling and software-defined networking (SDN) control planes. The provider should ensure that current capacity meets customer needs and increased customer demand to assure that the flexibility and scalability traits of cloud computing are still provided. The provider should also ensure that the network is not overburdened or subjected to unacceptable latency.

As with all log data, the performance monitoring information can be fed into a centralized system, such as a security information and event management (SIEM) platform for centralized analysis and review. Operations teams should use these tools to monitor the performance and capacity of network, compute, and storage resources as well as the response time of business-critical services.

Physical and Environmental Protection

In addition to the hardware and software, it is important to monitor ambient conditions within the data center. In particular, temperature and humidity are essential data points for optimizing operations and performance. It's important to capture a realistic portrayal of the temperature within the data center, perhaps by averaging measurements across several thermometric devices located throughout the airflow process. For performance monitoring purposes, our target metrics will be the standards created by Technical Committee 9.9 of the American Society of Heating, Refrigerating and Air-Conditioning Engineers (ASHRAE), published in 2016. ASHRAE offers extremely detailed recommendations for a wide variety of aspects of the data center, including the IT equipment, power supply, and battery backups, all of which can be quite useful to a data center operator or security practitioner. These are available free of charge from the ASHRAE website: `https://tpc.ashrae.org/ FileDownload?idx=c81e88e4-998d-426d-ad24-bdedfb746178`. It's also a generally good read and worth investing some of your time reviewing.

While there are many specific and detailed recommendations, the general ASHRAE recommended ranges for a data center are as follows:

- **Temperature:** 64° to 81° F (18° to 27° C)

- **Humidity:** Dew point of 15° to 59° F (–9° to 15° C), relative humidity of 60%

While these ranges give a general notion of the condition of the ambient environment within a data center, the ASHRAE guidance is a lot more detailed regarding specific ranges, based on the type, age, and location of the equipment. The operator should determine which guidance is most applicable to their facility. Moreover, ASHRAE offers this advice solely from a platform-agnostic perspective. Data center operators must also take into account any guidance and recommendations from device manufacturers regarding ambient ranges affecting performance parameters for their specific products.

Effects of Ambient Temperature and Ambient Humidity

What roles do temperature and humidity play, in terms of affecting equipment performance?

An ambient temperature that is too high may allow equipment to overheat. We all routinely see this when our smartphones or laptops become hot to the touch. High-capacity electrical components generate a great deal of waste heat, and the devices can be sensitive to conditions that exceed their operating parameters. An ambient temperature that is too low can be a risk to health and human safety; touching bare metal at the freezing point can burn or remove skin; moreover, people working in such conditions would simply be uncomfortable and unhappy, conditions that lead to dissatisfaction, which in turn lead to security risks.

An ambient humidity that is too high can promote corrosion of metallic components as well as mold and other organisms. An ambient humidity that is too low can enhance the possibility of static discharge, which might affect both personnel and equipment as well as increase the potential for fires.

Maintenance

Continual uptime requires maintaining the overall environment constantly. This also includes maintaining individual components both on a scheduled basis and at unscheduled times as necessary. In the following sections, we'll discuss general maintenance matters, updates, upgrades, and patch management.

General Maintenance Concepts

Devices in a data center can be described as being in normal production mode or maintenance mode. When a system or device is put into maintenance mode, the data center operator must ensure the following tasks are successful:

All operational instances are removed from the system/device before it enters maintenance mode.   We don't want to affect any transactions in a customer's production environment. We therefore must migrate any virtualized instances off the specific systems and devices where they are hosted before we begin maintenance activities.

Prevent all new logins.   For the same reason as the previous task, we don't want customers logging in to the affected systems and devices.

Ensure logging is continued, and begin enhanced logging.   Administrator activities are much more powerful, and therefore rife with risk, than the actions of common users. It is therefore recommended that you log administrator actions at a greater rate and level of detail than those of users. Maintenance mode is an administrative function, so the increased logging is necessary.

Before moving a system or device from maintenance mode back to normal operation, it is important to test that it has all the original functionality necessary for customer purposes, that the maintenance was successful, and that proper documentation of all activity is complete.

Updates

Industry best practice includes ensuring we comply with all vendor guidance regarding specific products. In fact, failing to adhere to vendor specifications can be a sign that the operator has failed in providing necessary due care, whereas documented adherence to vendor instructions can demonstrate due diligence.

In addition to configuration prior to deployment (discussed as part of the section "Change and Configuration Management" later in this chapter), vendors will issue ongoing maintenance instructions, often as updates. These can be in the form of both application packages for software and firmware installs for hardware. The former can also be in the form of patches, which we'll discuss specifically in a later section.

The update process should be formalized in the operator's governance (as should *all* processes, and they should all spawn from policy). It should include the following elements, at a minimum:

Document how, when, and why the update was initiated.   If promulgated by the vendor, annotate the details of the communication, including date, update code or number, explanation, and justification; some of this may be included by reference, such as with a URL to the vendor's page announcing the update instructions.

Move the update through the change management (CM) process. All modifications to the facility should be through the CM methodology and documented as such. Details on the CM process are included later in this chapter, but it should be stressed that sandbox testing be included as part of CM before the update is applied.

1. Put the systems and devices into maintenance mode. Observe the recommendations in the previous section of this chapter.
2. Apply the update to the necessary systems and devices. Annotate the asset inventory to reflect the changes.
3. Verify the update. Run tests on the production environment to ensure all necessary systems and devices have received the update. If any were missed, repeat the installation until it is complete.
4. Validate the modifications. Ensure that the intended results of the update have taken effect and that the updated systems and devices interact appropriately with the rest of the production environment.
5. Return to normal operations. Resume regular business.

Upgrades

In this context, we distinguish updates from upgrades with this purpose: updates are applied to existing systems and components, whereas upgrades are the replacement of older elements with newer ones. The upgrade process should largely map to the one for updates, including formalization in governance, CM methodology, testing, and so forth. Particular attention in upgrading needs to be placed on documenting the changes in the asset inventory, not only adding the new elements but annotating the removal and secure disposal of the old ones. This, of course, means that secure disposal is one element of the upgrade process that is not included in updates.

Patch Management

Patches are a variety of update most commonly associated with software. We distinguish them here by their frequency: software vendors commonly issue patches both for immediate response to a given need (such as a newfound vulnerability) and for routine purposes (fixing, adding, or enhancing functionality) on a regular basis.

The *patch management* process must be formalized in much the same manner as updates and upgrades, with its inclusion in policy and so forth. However, patches incur additional risks and challenges, so this discussion is set aside to deal with those specifically. The following sections relate suggestions and considerations to take into account when managing patches for a cloud data center.

Timing

When a vendor issues a patch, there is a binary risk faced by all those affected: if they fail to apply the patch, they may be seen to be failing in providing due care for those customers utilizing the unpatched products; if the patch is applied in haste, it may adversely affect the production environment, harming the customer's ability to operate. The latter case is especially true when patches are issued in response to a newfound vulnerability and the vendor was rushed to identify the flaw, find and create a solution, publish the fix, and issue the patch. In the rush to deal with the problem (even more especially when the vulnerability is well publicized and garners public attention), the patch may cause other vulnerabilities or affect other systems by reducing some interoperability or interface capability.

It is therefore difficult to know exactly how soon after it was issued a patch should be applied. It is contingent upon the operator to make this decision after weighing the merits of the different choices.

In some environments (and with some vendors), it may be desirable to schedule a set patching day/time (per week or per month, for instance) so that it is a regular, anticipated occurrence. In this way, the various participants can coordinate the activity, the change control process can accommodate the required modifications, and specific types of patches can be prioritized and applied in a defined manner.

Of course, sometimes the customer has little to no control of when some patches might be applied, particularly with some platform or vendor updates. If the customer knows this might be an issue with a particular vendor or software, they can try to plan ahead about how they might deal with such situations.

WARNING A data center operator may be tempted to allow others in the field to apply the patch first in order to determine its effect and outcome based on the experiences of competitors. The risk in that option is that in the meantime, loss or harm might be caused by or occur via the vulnerability the patch was meant to remediate. This might lend strong support in a lawsuit to recover damages because those customers harmed by the loss can rightly claim that the provider knew of the risk, did not take the steps of due diligence made by others in the field, and allowed harm to come through negligence. This might even support claims for additional or punitive damages. Again, while the tactic may be sound, it carries this additional risk.

Implementation: Automated or Manual

Patches can be applied with automated tools or by personnel. There are obvious benefits and risks for both methods. The operator will have to decide which to use on both a general basis (by policy) and for each case when a patch is issued, if the circumstances demand. Each includes the following risks and benefits:

Automated   A mechanized approach will allow for much faster delivery to far more targets than a manual approach. Patch tools might also include a reporting function that annotates which targets have received the patch, cross-referenced against the asset inventory, and have an alerting function to inform administrators which targets have been missed. Without a capable human observer, however, the tool might not function thoroughly or properly, the patches might be misapplied, or the reports might be inaccurate or portray an inaccurate picture of completeness.

Manual   Trained and experienced personnel may be more trustworthy than a mechanized tool and might understand when anomalous activity occurs. However, with the vast number of elements that will need to be patched in a cloud data center, the repetitiveness and boredom of the patch process may lead even a seasoned administrator to miss a number of targets. Moreover, the process will be much, much slower than the automated option and may not be as thorough.

Dates

As the patch is pushed throughout the environment, the actual date/time stamp may become an important—and misleading—matter in acquiring and acknowledging receipt. For example, say that an automated tool requires an agent that is installed locally on each target. If certain targets are not running when the patch happens and won't be operating until the next calendar day (according to the internal clock on the target), the local agent may not receive the patch because it may check against the central controller for patches *for the current day*.

This problem can be compounded when patch agents are set to check for patches according to a time specified by the internal clock and different targets have internal clocks set to differing time zones (in the case, say, of customers who are geographically dispersed).

This problem is not limited to automated tools, either. If a manual method is used, the administrators may be applying a patch at a given time/date when not all customers and users have their targets operating, so those targets might not receive the patch, and the administrators might not realize that targets that don't currently appear in scans may need to be patched at some later time/date. Moreover, if patches are being applied manually, the process will necessarily be extended so that administrators can be sure to reach all potential targets as they come online.

All these possibilities are escalated in a cloud arrangement because of the wide use of virtualization. All virtualized instances saved as images and not currently instantiated during patch delivery will be receiving the patch only after they are next booted. This means that the process will endure until all virtual machines have been made live, which could represent a significant amount of time after the decision to implement the patch. The result is a relatively long delay between the time the operator decides to implement the patch and the time of 100 percent completion. This reflects poorly on the process and the operator, especially in the eyes of regulators and courts.

Perhaps the optimum technique is to combine the benefits of each method, using both manual and automated approaches. Manual oversight is valuable in determining applicability of patches and testing patches for suitability in the environment, while automated tools can be used to propagate patches and ensure uniform application.

Regardless of the approach taken, patching (like all forms of maintenance) should be mentioned in the SLA, and an agreed-upon schedule and threshold of patches is an important contractual consideration.

Change and Configuration Management

Data center operators, like anyone who owns an IT network, need to develop and maintain a realistic concept of what assets they control, the state of those assets, and explicit information about each asset. This goes beyond (but includes) the asset inventory—the hardware, software, and media they own. It also includes documented records of configuration for all these elements including versioning, deviations, exceptions, and the rationale for each, as well as a formal process for determining how, when, and why modifications need to be made.

There are two foundational and interrelated processes used to accomplish this effort: change management and configuration management. *Change management* is the process used to review, approve, and document any modifications to the environment. *Configuration management* entails documenting the approved settings for systems and software, which helps establish baselines within the organization.

Realistically, in many organizations both sets of functions are accomplished by a single process and body. For the purposes of our discussion of operational functions, we're going to aggregate them and put them under one label: change and configuration management (CM). We'll do this to simplify the information, even though a cloud vendor should probably have the wherewithal and functional and personnel specialization sufficient to provide both as separate activities. The purposes of both are so similar in intent and procedure as to be understood as one concept.

Baselines

CM, regardless of the flavor, begins with *baselining*, which is a way of taking an accurate account of the desired standard state. For change management, that's a depiction of the network and systems based on a comprehensive, detailed asset inventory. For configuration management, it's a standard build for all systems, from the settings in the OS to the setup of each application.

The baseline is a general-purpose map of the network and systems, based on the required functionality as well as security. Security controls should be incorporated in the baseline, with a thorough description of each one's purpose, dependencies, and supporting rationale (that is, a statement explaining what we hope to accomplish with each control). It is absolutely essential to include the controls so that we are fully informed about risk management as we consider modifications to the environment through the CM process. If we're changing the control set in any way or adding new systems and functionality to the environment, we need to know if there will be any resultant increased risk and, therefore, if we need to add any compensatory controls to manage the new risk levels.

While creating the baseline, it's helpful to get input from all stakeholders: the IT department, the security office, management, and even users. The baseline should be an excellent reflection of the risk appetite of the organization and provide the optimum balance of security and operational functionality.

Preferably, the baseline should suit the largest population of systems in the organization. If it's going to be used as a template (particularly in configuration management), we'll get the most value from it if it applies to the greatest number of covered systems. However, it may be useful or pragmatic to have a number of baselines that are based on each department's, office's, or project's needs, but it is still essential to ensure that each distinct baseline supports necessary mandates and requirements. It would be inopportune to have an entire department fail a regulatory compliance audit because that department's baseline lost a category of security coverage.

Deviations and Exceptions from Baselines

It is important to continually test the baselines to determine that all assets are accounted for and to detect anything that differs from the baseline. Any such deviations, intentional or unintentional, authorized or unauthorized, must be documented and reviewed because deviations pose additional risks/vulnerabilities to the organization. These deviations might be the result of faulty patch management processes, a rogue device set up by a particular office or user, an intrusion by external attackers, or poor versioning and administrative practices. It is the duty of those personnel who are assigned CM roles to determine the cause and any necessary follow-up activity. (CM roles are discussed in the next section.)

While the baseline serves as the standard against which to compare and validate all systems in the organization, it is best not to use it as an absolute. There will be a significant number of requests for exceptions for particular users, offices, and projects that need functionality not accorded by the general baseline.

Make sure that the baseline is flexible and practical and that the exception request process is timely and responsive to the needs of the organization and its users. A cumbersome, slow exception process will lead to frustrated users and managers, which can, in turn, lead to unauthorized workarounds implemented without the permission of the CM authority.

An adversarial, unresponsive exception process will undermine security efforts of the organization. Everyone will find a way to perform their job functions, regardless of whether their workarounds are approved or are the most secure means of performing those functions. Uninformed personnel, acting out of desperation, are more likely to make rogue modifications that lack the proper security countermeasures than would the trained, skilled professionals whose job it is to secure the environment. It is much better to compromise the sanctity of the baseline with full cooperation than to mandate that no exceptions will be allowed or to make the process burdensome and complicated for users and offices. Remember: It is the job of security practitioners to support operations, not to hinder those engaged in productivity.

Tracking exceptions and deviations is useful for another essential purpose in addition to ensuring regulatory compliance and security control coverage: if enough exception requests ask for the same or similar functionality that deviates from the baseline, *change the baseline*. The baseline is not serving the purpose if it continually needs routine modification for repeated, equivalent requests. Moreover, addressing exception requests takes more time and effort than modifying the baseline to incorporate new, additional security controls to allow for the excepted functionality.

Roles and Process

The CM process (like all processes) should be formalized in the organization's governance. This policy should include provisions for creating processes and procedures that provide the following:

- Composition of the *CM board (CMB)*, or sometimes CCB, for Change Control Board
- The process, in detail
- Documentation requirements
- Instructions for requesting exceptions
- Assignment of CM tasks, such as validation scanning, analysis, and deviation notification
- Procedures for addressing deviations, upon detection
- Enforcement measures and responsibility

The CMB should be composed of representatives of all stakeholders within the organization. Recommended representatives include personnel from the IT, security, legal, management, finance and acquisition, and HR departments/offices, in addition to general users. Any other participants that the organization deems useful can certainly be included in the CMB.

The CMB will be responsible for reviewing change and exception requests. The board will determine if the change will enhance functionality and productivity, whether the change is funded, what potential security impacts the change will incur, and what additional measures (in terms of funding, training, security controls, or staffing) might be necessary to make the change successful and reasonable.

The CMB should meet often enough that changes and exception requests are not delayed unduly so that users and departments are not frustrated by the process. However, it should not meet so often that the time set aside for the CMB becomes work; the personnel involved in the CMB all have other primary duties, and participation in the CMB will impact their productivity. In some cases, depending on the organization, the CMB meets on an ad hoc basis, responding only when change and exception requests meet a certain threshold. This can entail some risk, however, as CMB members might lose some familiarity with the process in the interim and scheduling a meeting of the CMB with so many disparate offices might be awkward if a meeting of the CMB is not a regular, prioritized occurrence. As with much of the material addressed in this book, this is a trade-off of risk and benefit, and the organization should decide accordingly.

The process has two forms: one that will occur once and one that is repetitious. The former is the initial baseline effort; the latter is the normal operational mode. A baseline will be created for each type of system in the environment.

The initial process should look something like this (amended as necessary for each organization's individual circumstances):

1. **Full asset inventory:** In order to know what is being managed, it's crucial to know what you have. This effort need not be independent of all other similar efforts and may in fact be aided by information pulled from other sources, such as the *business impact analysis (BIA)*. The systems affected by each baseline need to be determined.

2. **Codification of the baseline:** This should be a formal action, including all members of the CMB (and perhaps more, for the initial effort; each department and project may want to contribute and participate because the baseline will affect all their future work). The baseline should be negotiated in terms of cost-benefit and risk analyses. Again, it is quite reasonable to use existing sources to inform this negotiation, including the organization's risk management framework, enterprise and security architecture, and so on.

3. **Secure baseline build:** A version of the baseline, as codified by the CMB, is constructed and stored for later use.

4. **Deployment of new assets:** When a new asset is acquired (for instance, a new host purchased for use by a new employee), the relevant baseline configuration needs to be installed on that asset, in accordance with CM policy and procedures and CMB guidance.

In the normal operational mode of the organization, the CM process is slightly different:

1. **CMB meetings:** The CMB meets to review and analyze change and exception requests. The CMB can authorize or disallow requests, and it can require additional effort before authorization. For instance, the CMB can task the security office to perform additional detailed security analysis of the potential impact resulting if the request were authorized, or the CMB might require the requestor to budget additional funding for the request if the CMB determines the request would require supplemental training, administration, and security controls compared to what the requestor initially expected.

2. **CM testing:** If the CMB authorizes a request, the new modification must be tested before deployment. Usually, such testing should take place in an isolated sandbox network that mimics all the systems, components, infrastructure, traffic, and processing of the production network, without ever touching the production network. Testing should determine whether any undue impact on security, interoperability, or functionality is expected as a result of the modification.

3. **Deployment:** The modification is made in accordance with appropriate guidance and is reported to the CMB upon completion.

4. **Documentation:** All modifications to the environment are documented and reflected in the asset inventory (and, as necessary, in the baseline).

Secure disposal of an asset is also a modification to the IT environment and therefore needs to be reflected in the asset inventory and reported to the CMB.

Release and Deployment Management

As a supporting process to change management, *release management (RM)* is a software engineering process concerned with arranging all required elements to successfully, repeatably, and verifiably deploy new software versions. The scope of RM includes planning, scheduling, and deploying new software, and it encompasses all environments that code may pass through, including development, QA/testing, and staging—everything up to the production environment, at which point the software enters active maintenance. The progression of code and related activities from requirements (often called user stories) to coding, testing, and then to production is known as the pipeline.

> Each time a change is released into production, the team should have a rollback process in place that allows them to reverse the impact of the change if something goes wrong. These rollback procedures are a crucial part of the change management process.

RM has grown along with the rise in popularity of agile software development practices, which aim to deliver functional software more quickly using short development cycles. Waterfall, an older software development methodology, focused heavily on gathering all requirements and delivering them all at once, while agile focuses on small units of work that can be achieved in a short amount of time, then iterated to deliver additional functionality.

DevOps Security

DevOps has also grown as organizations adopt agile. DevOps aims to create cross-functional teams to ensure smoother, more predictable software delivery by encouraging tighter collaboration and more feedback. DevOps asks development and operations teams to work together to streamline the software development and release process, enabling more frequent software releases. These more frequent software releases have driven the need for tighter coordination between engineers developing software, operations staff responsible for maintaining the software, and users who drive the requirements for software.

While the increased speed of agile software development has made users happy (no more waiting a year for a new system module to go live), it has created some headaches for security practitioners. There simply isn't time to do many traditional activities like pen testing when new software is going live on a daily or sometimes even hourly basis. To compensate, security practitioners must make use of automation to decrease the time it takes to perform security functions.

Continuous integration/continuous delivery (CI/CD) incorporates heavy use of automation to dramatically shorten the software delivery pipeline. The ultimate goal is to get newly developed software live and running as quickly as possible after an engineer completes their work, sometimes within minutes of code being written. To achieve this, automated testing is used extensively to ensure the newly written code will not introduce bugs into the production environment. Security testing needs to be reevaluated to identify how needed security checks can be integrated with the CI/CD pipeline.

Security automation in CI/CD must include both administrative and technical controls. Examples of administrative controls include checking that new software has a verifiable set of requirements and approvals (i.e., a developer is delivering code that meets a defined user need rather than unwanted functionality) and that all processes have been followed (e.g., a peer review must be conducted). Automated technical controls can include checks such as passing a static code analysis or successful completion of a vulnerability scan run against a live version of the new code in a staging environment.

 The use of DevOps approaches is not limited to software development. Many organizations now seek to apply these agile approaches to the creation, deployment, and management of their technology infrastructure by adopting infrastructure as code (IaC) strategies.

Problem and Incident Management

Unfortunately, disruptions happen in the world of information technology, and mature IT organizations have processes in place to handle those disruptions. IT service management programs typically define an *incident* as an unplanned event that causes a service disruption and a *problem* as a potential cause of an incident. Every incident is the result of a problem, but not every problem results in an incident.

IT service management teams use two processes to address these potential and actual disruptions. Problem management provides the organization with the technologies, processes, and procedures required to reduce the likelihood or impact of incidents. Incident management provides a framework for addressing actual disruptions that occur.

IT Service Management and Continual Service Improvement

ITIL (formerly the Information Technology Infrastructure Library) comprises a set of practices businesses can use in designing, maintaining, and improving their IT services. This is known as IT service management (ITSM), and the practices can be implemented for any IT function, such as delivering email collaboration capabilities to employees, designing new customer-facing applications, or even the process of migrating from on-premises to cloud infrastructure.

ISO/IEC 20000-1, Information technology — Service management also defines a set of operational controls and standards that organizations can use to manage IT services. The ISO standard defines a service management system designed to support the practice of ITSM, as well as suggested processes, procedures, and organizational capabilities required.

Note that this is very similar to the approach in ISO 27001, which describes an *information security management system (ISMS)* and needed support for enabling security. ISO 20000-1 can be used to manage ITSM using a variety of approaches, including ITIL and the ISACA COBIT framework.

The goal of ITSM is to identify user needs, design an IT service that meets those needs, successfully deploy it, then enter a cycle of continuous improvements. *Continual service improvement management* aims to ensure that IT services provide ongoing business value and that the services are updated as needed to respond to changing business requirements. Obviously, the shift to cloud computing is a major example of business requirements driving changes to IT services.

Although ITIL was designed in an era when most infrastructure was maintained and used exclusively on premises, the general principles are quite useful when choosing new or evaluating existing cloud services. Both ITIL and ISO 20000-1 place a heavy emphasis on ensuring that IT services always deliver business value, so these are some key areas/questions to consider for continual service improvement in cloud environments:

- Which type of cloud service model best meets your organization's needs? Has a vendor developed a SaaS platform that can reduce the resources your organization must expend to keep systems up and running?

- Are your users on the move? A more mobile workforce makes secure network design more challenging. Rather than a VPN from your main office to the cloud environment, you may need to provide secure cloud access to users anywhere in the world.

- Do the selected services meet your organization's compliance needs? Expansion into new markets might bring new privacy or security requirements, which will drive changes in the cloud services your organization is using.

- Are your SLA goals being met? SLA metrics should be tied to requirements for the system, and a cloud provider's inability to meet those requirements might necessitate a change of providers.

- Do new cloud services provide cost, time, or resource savings? For example, many cloud PaaS database offerings include automatic data replication and high availability, which removes the need for separate backup/recovery procedures and equipment. Rather than conduct BC/DR exercises yourself, your organization may rely on a provider's SOC 2 Type 2 audit report for assurance of resiliency.

Continual service improvement relies heavily on metrics to identify needed improvements and to measure the effectiveness of any changes implemented. For example, page load time for a web app might be a key metric. Choosing a new distributed cloud web hosting service that significantly reduces page loads delivers an improvement in the user experience for that web app.

Business Continuity and Disaster Recovery

Business continuity and disaster recovery (BC/DR) has been addressed in other chapters of this book, relative to specific topics. Here, we cover some of the general aspects and approaches, with some additional focus on facility continuity.

There is no total agreement within our industry on the exact definitions of the terms *business continuity*, *disaster recovery*, *event*, or even simply *disaster* for that matter. For the purposes of this discussion and to create awareness of the (ISC)² perspective on the matter, we'll use the following explanations:

- *Business continuity* efforts are concerned with maintaining critical operations during any interruption in service, whereas *disaster recovery* efforts are focused on the resumption of operations after an interruption due to disaster. The two are related and in many organizations are rolled into one effort, often named *continuity management*.

- An *event* is any unscheduled adverse impact to the operating environment. An event is distinguished from a *disaster* by the duration of impact. We consider an event's impact to last three days or less; a disaster's impact lasts longer. An event can become a disaster. Causes of either/both can be anthropogenic (caused by humans), natural forces, internal or external, malicious or accidental.

Because they can be so similar, we'll discuss BC/DR efforts together for most of the coverage of the topic and only make distinctions when needed.

Prioritizing Safety

The paramount importance in BC/DR planning and efforts should be health and human safety, as in all security matters. There is almost no justification for prioritizing any asset to any degree higher than personnel.

Exam Tip

Any BC/DR efforts should prioritize the protection of human life over any other concerns.

Notification should take several redundant and differing forms to ensure the widest and most thorough dissemination. Suggestions for possible notification avenues include telephone call tree rosters, website postings, and SMS blasts. Notification should include the organization's personnel, the public, and regulatory and response agencies, depending on who might be affected by the circumstance.

Evacuation, protection, and egress methods will depend on the particular physical layout of the campus and facility. The following aspects are among those that are generally included in addressing these needs:

Getting the People Out   There should be no obstruction or delay of personnel leaving the facility. All doors along the emergency path should fail safe (that is, they can be opened from the inside, allowing egress, even if they are still secure from the outside, preventing ingress). Sufficient lighting should be considered.

Getting the People Out Safely   Sprinkler systems along the egress route should be set to inundate the area and not be restricted due to other considerations (such as property damage). Non-water fire-suppression systems (such as gas) cannot risk human life and must have additional controls (for instance, a last-out switch, which prevents the gas from being released until the final person triggers it on the way out of the affected area). Communicate the emergency plans to all personnel, and train them in execution of the plan.

Designing for Protection   Other architectural, engineering, and local construction code concerns must meet local needs, such as facilities that are built to withstand and resist environmental hazards (tornadoes in the midwestern United States, flooding along the coasts, and so on).

Continuity of Operations

After we've seen to health and human safety concerns, our primary business focus should be continuity of critical operations.

To begin with, we have to identify the organization's critical operations. In a cloud data center, that will usually be dictated by the customer contracts and SLAs. This simplifies delineation of those elements necessary to support critical needs. Other extant sources can be extremely useful in this portion of the effort, most particularly the BIA, which informs us which assets would cause the greatest adverse impact if lost or interrupted. For instance, in a cloud data center, our main focus should be on the critical operations of connectivity, utilities, and processing capacity. Other ancillary business functions, such as marketing, sales, finance, HR, and so on, might be wholly dismissed or greatly reduced without lasting impact to the organization and can be considered noncritical.

In formulating this inventory of critical assets, it is important to consider all elements that support critical functions, not limited to the hardware and tangible assets, but also specific personnel, software libraries, documentation, fundamental data, and so forth, without which we could not continue critical operations.

BC/DR Planning

Like all plans, the *business continuity plan* and *disaster recovery plan* should be formalized in and derive from the organization's governance. Policy should dictate roles, terms of the plan, enforcement, and execution.

The plan should include both an exhaustive, detailed description of all aspects of BC/DR efforts and also limited, simple, straightforward procedures for enacting the plan and all response activities. In places where the team would like to include additional detail, this might be done using an appendix or attachment that doesn't distract from the main procedures.

The plan should include the following items:

Critical Asset Inventory   This should include necessary hardware, software, and media, including versioning data and applicable patches.

Disaster Criteria   Response comes with a cost. It is important to distinguish normal administrative functions from event or disaster response because the formal response will obligate resources and affect productivity. Careful attention should be paid to balancing the risks and benefits of overreaction and underreaction in terms of response: too frequently and productivity will needlessly be adversely affected; too rarely and response activities may be hindered by delays for the sake of caution.

Disaster Declaration Process   An authority needs to be named (an individual, role, or office) for the purpose of formal declaration of an event or disaster. We want to avoid the possibility of overreaction by allowing just anyone to initiate a formal response (like an emergency brake line in public transit), and we want to ensure that initiation is instigated by someone who is informed, qualified, trained, and responsible for making such a determination.

An authorized party must also formally declare a cessation of BC/DR activity and resumption of normal operations. This should only be done when there is a high degree of assurance that all safety and health hazards have been abated and operating conditions and risks have returned to normal. Resuming standard operations too soon can exacerbate the existing event or disaster or cause a new one.

Essential Points of Contact   This should include the contact information of offices responsible for BC/DR activity and tasks as well as any external entities that may be involved (regulators, law enforcement, corporate authorities, press, vendors, customers, and so on). These should be as specific as possible to reduce difficulty in locating appropriate contacts during an actual response.

Detailed Actions, Tasks, and Activities   Checklists can be quite helpful for BC/DR procedures. Checklists serve several purposes. They describe the specific actions necessary, they can be aligned in order of execution, and they can constitute a record, after the activity is complete, of actions taken, by whom, and when (if each checklist step is annotated with the time and initials of the person completing the action as it occurs). Checklists also serve another fundamental requirement of BC/DR plans used during a response action: they allow for someone to conduct the appropriate actions, even if that person has not had specific training or experience with that plan in that organization.

Of course, it is always preferable to have the personnel assigned to BC/DR roles trained and practiced in the specific plan, but, especially during disasters or events, the assigned personnel are not always available.

All these elements can be included by reference. That is, each piece can be split out as an attachment or appendix to the BC/DR policy proper. The basic elements of all policies (explanation and rationale for the policy, enforcement activities, relevant regulations, and so on) can make up the body of the policy, as it will be less subject to continual changing and updating.

Updating the BC/DR policy is a continual process. Many of the listed elements, as you can see, will be in almost constant flux (the points of contact information, specific personnel assigned particular tasks, the list of the current state of critical assets), so the relevant parts of the plan (the specific appendices and attachments) need to receive updates from the offices that have the pertinent data. For instance, the current state of critical assets might be updated by the CMB as part of the CM process. The CMB is in the best position to know all the current versions of systems and components. Often, required CM updates can be detected during regular tests of the plan (see "Testing" later in this chapter).

The BC/DR Toolkit

There should be a container that holds all the necessary documentation and tools to conduct a proper BC/DR response action. This kit should be secure, durable, and compact. The container may be physical and/or virtual. The contents might contain hard-copy versions of the appropriate documentation or electronic copies.

We recommend that the BC/DR kit exist in both hard-copy and electronic versions, because while electronic forms are more convenient for team members to access, a disaster may render the digital version inaccessible.

The kit should have a duplicate in at least one other location, depending on the plan. If the plan calls for reconstitution of critical operations at an offsite location, there should be a mirrored kit in that location. Otherwise, having at least two identical kits on site, in different locations, aids in reducing the consequences of one being unreachable or destroyed.

The kit should contain the following:

- A current copy of the plan, with all appendices and addenda.
- Emergency and backup communication equipment. These can take whatever form suits the purpose, location, and nature of the organization: cell phones, handheld radios, laptop with satellite modem, and so on.

- Copies of all appropriate network and infrastructure diagrams and architecture.

- Copies of all requisite software for creating a clean build of the critical systems, if necessary, with media containing appropriate updates and patches for current versioning.

- Emergency contact information (not already included in the plan). This might include a full notification list.

- Documentation tools and equipment. Again, these can take many forms: pens and paper, laptop and portable printer, voice recorder, and so on.

- A small number of emergency essentials (flashlight, water, rations, and so on).

- Fresh batteries sufficient for operating all powered equipment in the kit for at least 24 hours.

Obviously, keeping the kit stocked and current requires a level of effort similar to that of maintaining the plan itself (and includes the plan itself, as it is updated).

Relocation

Depending on the nature of the event and disaster and the specifics of the plan, the organization may choose to evacuate and relocate those personnel involved in critical operations to a specified alternate operating location. Prior to the existence of cloud capabilities for the purpose of backing up and restoring data at a secure offsite location, hot and warm and cold sites were used for this purpose, and a skeleton crew of critical personnel were assigned to travel to the recovery site for the duration of the contingency operations and recovery.

With the advent of ubiquitous availability of cloud backup resources, the relocation site can be anywhere not affected by the event and disaster, as long as it has sufficient facilities for housing the personnel involved and bandwidth sufficient for the purpose. For instance, a hotel outside the area of effect could serve the purpose if it offers broadband capabilities and is additionally useful in that it also fulfills the function of safe lodging for the critical personnel.

If the organization considers relocation for BC/DR purposes, the plan might include these aspects:

- Tasking and activities should include representatives from the HR and finance departments, because travel arrangements and payments will be necessary for all personnel involved in the relocation.

- Sufficient support should be provided for relocating dependents and family members of the personnel involved in critical operations for the duration of the response. When a disaster affects a locality, everyone involved will rightfully be concerned about their loved ones first and foremost. If this concern is not alleviated, their morale and focus on the tasks at hand will be diminished. It is better to assume the additional costs related to this option so as to gain the full attention of the personnel involved in the response.

- The distance of the relocation is, like all things related to the practice of security, a balance. You want the relocation site to be far enough away that it is not affected by whatever caused the interruption to standard operations but not so far that the hazard, risk, delay, and expense of travel makes its utility unappealing or infeasible.

- Joint operating agreements and memoranda of understanding can be used to establish cost-effective relocation sites at facilities belonging to other operations in the local area if the event or disaster only affects your organization's campus (in the event of highly localized events and disasters, such as a building fire).

BC/DR Terminology

There are several BC/DR concepts that you need to understand:

MTD (Maximum Tolerable Downtime)   The longest amount of time that a business function is able to continue without access to a particular service. For example, if the HR department must be able to access the payroll system at least once a month to schedule the next month's payroll run, the maximum tolerable downtime for that system might be one month. On the other hand, if customers expect a website to be available 24/7, business leaders responsible for that website might set a much shorter MTD, such as 30 minutes.

RTO (Recovery Time Objective)   The BC/DR goal for recovery of operational capability after an interruption in service, measured in time. This does not have to include full operations (recovery); the capability can be limited to critical functions for the duration of the contingency event. The RTO should be less than the MTD. For example, a service might have an MTD of one week, while the company's BC/DR plan includes and supports an RTO of six days for that service.

RPO (Recovery Point Objective)   The BC/DR goal for limiting the loss of data from an unplanned event. Confusingly, this is often measured in time. For instance, if an organization is doing full backups every day and is affected by some sort of disaster, that organization's BC/DR plan might include a goal of resuming critical operations at an alternate operating site with the last full backup, which would be an RPO of 24 hours. The recovery point objective for that organization would be the loss of no more than one day's worth of data.

RSL (Recovery Service Level)   The proportion of a service, expressed as a percentage, that is necessary for continued operations during a disaster. For example, if a batch image processing service normally processes 10 images per second, business leaders may decide that it is only necessary to process 5 images per second during a disaster. This would be an RSL of 5/10, or 50%, for this service.

> **ALE (Annualized Loss Expectancy)**   Annualized loss expectancy (ALE) describes the amount an organization should expect to lose on an annual basis due to any one type of incident. ALE is calculated by multiplying the annualized rate of occurrence (ARO) by the single loss expectancy (SLE). The ARO is the rate of occurrence of a specific event or security incident one could expect in any given 12-month period. A single loss expectancy (SLE) is the amount of expected damage or loss from any single specific security incident.

Power

Interruptions to the normal power supply often result from events or disasters (or are themselves a reason to declare an event or disaster), so BC/DR plans and activities must take emergency power supply into account.

Near-term emergency power usually takes the form of battery backups, often as *uninterruptible power supply (UPS)* systems. These can be small units, feeding only particular individual devices or racks, or they can be large, supplying power to entire systems. Failover for these should be close to immediate, with appropriate line conditioning so that transitioning from utility power to UPS does not adversely affect the powered devices in any way. The line conditioner function in UPS often serves as an additional component of normal operations, dampening surges and dips in utility power automatically.

> If you ever see an exam question about the expected duration of UPS power, the answer will be, "UPS should last long enough for the activation of generator power or the graceful shutdown of affected systems." Battery backup should only be relied on to provide short-term power supply. Any power interruption for a longer period should be provided by other systems, such as generators.

Longer-term contingency power can be provided by *generators*. For the cloud data center, sufficient generator power is necessary for all critical systems and infrastructure, including HVAC and emergency lighting as well as fire suppression systems. For the higher-tier centers, redundant power is necessary, duplicating the minimum power required to ensure uninterrupted critical operations.

Generators that supply close to immediate power when utility electricity is interrupted have automatic transfer switches. Transfer switches sense when the utility provision fails, break the connection to the utility, start the generator, and provide generator power to the facility. An automatic transfer switch is *not* a viable replacement for a UPS, and the two should be used in conjunction with, not in lieu of, each other. Ideally, the generator and transfer switch should be rated to successfully provide sufficient power well within the duration of the expected battery life of the UPS. Realistically, generators with transfer switches can be expected to provide power in less than a minute after loss of utility power.

Generators need fuel; this is usually gasoline, diesel, natural gas, or propane. Appropriate storage, supply, and maintenance of fuel should also be described and included in the BC/DR plan. As fuel is flammable, health and human safety concerns must be addressed in the storage and supply designs. For all data centers, the Uptime Institute recommends that a minimum of 12 hours' worth of fuel for all generators powering all critical functions be available. Resupply of additional fuel should be scheduled and performed within those 12 hours. Supply contracts and appropriate notification information for the supplier should be included in the BC/DR plan and procedure checklists. For BC/DR purposes, the plan should anticipate at least 72 hours of generator operation before other alternatives are available.

Gasoline and diesel spoil, even with conditioning treatments that extend useful fuel life. If your generators use these types of fuel, the plan must also include tasking and contracts for regular resupply and refresh within the spoilage period. Some fuels, such as propane, do not spoil; you may want to consider this when choosing backup power alternatives.

All fuel storage should be in secure containers and locations. Fuel and generators should be far removed from the path of vehicles, ideally outside normal traffic areas (with a provision made for secure vehicle access for resupply purposes).

Testing

Much like having backups without trying to restore, or having logs without doing log review and analysis, having a BC/DR plan is close to useless unless it is tested on a regular basis. Because testing the BC/DR will necessarily cause interruption of production, different forms of testing can be utilized for different purposes, adjusting the operational impact while achieving specific goals. You should be familiar with the following testing methods:

Tabletop Testing   The essential participants (those who will take part in actual BC/DR activities and are formally tasked with such responsibilities) work together at a scheduled time (either together in a single room or remotely via some communication capability) to describe how they would perform their tasks in a given BC/DR scenario. This is the InfoSec equivalent of role-playing games, and it has the least impact on production of the testing alternatives.

Dry Run   The organization as a whole takes part in a scenario at a scheduled time, describing their responses during the test and performing some minimal actions (for instance, perhaps running the notification call tree to ensure all contact information is current) but without performing all the actual tasks. This has more impact on productivity than tabletop testing.

Full Test   The entire organization takes part in an unscheduled, unannounced practice scenario, performing the full BC/DR activities. As this could include system failover and facility evacuation, this test is the most useful for detecting shortcomings in the plan, but it has the greatest impact on productivity (to the extent that it can cause a full, genuine interruption of service).

> In all forms of testing, it behooves the organization to use moderators. These personnel will act as guides and monitors of the response activity, provide scenario inputs to heighten realism and introduce some element of chaos (to simulate unplanned deviations from the procedures due to potential effects of the event and disaster), and document performance and any plan shortcomings. The moderators should not be tasked with BC/DR response activities for actual situations. Anyone with formal tasking should be a participant in the test. It might be useful to employ external consultants to serve as moderators so that all organizational personnel can take part in the exercise.

Summary

In this chapter, we've reviewed several essential elements of operations management for cloud data centers. We discussed the importance of monitoring system and component performance and performing routine maintenance (to include patching) as well as certain risks and benefits associated with each. Issues related to environmental conditions such as temperature, humidity, and backup power supply were included. We also detailed specific approaches and methods for BC/DR planning and testing.

Exam Essentials

Understand the role of business continuity and disaster recovery programs in the cloud.   Business continuity efforts are concerned with maintaining critical operations during any interruption in service, whereas disaster recovery efforts are focused on the resumption of operations after an interruption due to disaster. The two are related and in many organizations are rolled into one effort, often named continuity management.

Explain key business continuity terms, including RTO, RPO, and RSL.   The recovery time objective (RTO) is the goal for recovery of operational capability after an interruption in service, measured in time. The recovery point objective (RPO) is the goal for limiting the loss of data from an unplanned event, and it is also measured in time. The recovery service level (RSL) is the proportion of a service, expressed as a percentage, that is necessary for continued operations during a disaster.

Explain the importance of security hygiene practices, including patching and baselining. Applying security patches, either manually or automatically, protects the organization from newly emerging security vulnerabilities. Baselining provides a standard, secure configuration from which systems may be built. Organizations should monitor systems and applications for deviations from security baselines that should be investigated and documented.

Explain the standard processes used for IT service management in an organization. Organizations often adopt standards for IT service management, including ITIL and ISO/IEC 20000-1. The processes covered in service management programs include change management, continuity management, information security management, continual service improvement management, incident management, problem management, release management, deployment management, configuration management, service-level management, availability management, and continuity management.

Understand the role of change and configuration management.   Change management is the process used to review, approve, and document any modifications to the environment. Configuration management entails documenting the approved settings for systems and software, which helps establish baselines within the organization.

Review Questions

You can find the answers in Appendix B.

1. Which form of BC/DR testing has the *most* impact on operations?
   A. Tabletop
   B. Dry run
   C. Full test
   D. Structured walk-through

2. Which form of BC/DR testing has the *least* impact on operations?
   A. Tabletop
   B. Dry run
   C. Full test
   D. Structured test

3. Which characteristic of liquid propane increases its desirability as a fuel for backup generators?
   A. Burn rate
   B. Price
   C. Does not spoil
   D. Flavor

4. How often should the CMB meet?
   A. Whenever regulations dictate
   B. Often enough to address organizational needs and reduce frustration with delay
   C. Every week
   D. Annually

5. Adhering to ASHRAE standards for humidity can reduce the possibility of _____.
   A. Breach
   B. Static discharge
   C. Theft
   D. Inversion

6. A UPS should have enough power to last how long?
   A. 12 hours
   B. 10 minutes
   C. One day
   D. Long enough for graceful shutdown

7. A generator transfer switch should bring backup power online within what time frame?
   A. 10 seconds
   B. Before the recovery point objective is reached
   C. Before the UPS duration is exceeded
   D. Three days

8. Which characteristic of automated patching makes it attractive?
   A. Cost
   B. Speed
   C. Noise reduction
   D. Capability to recognize problems quickly

9. Which tool can reduce confusion and misunderstanding during a BC/DR response?
   A. Flashlight
   B. Controls matrix
   C. Checklist
   D. Call tree

10. When deciding whether to apply specific updates, it is best to follow _____ in order to demonstrate due care.
    A. Regulations
    B. Vendor guidance
    C. Internal policy
    D. Competitors' actions

11. The CMB should include representations from all of the following offices except
    _____.
    A. Regulators
    B. IT department
    C. Security office
    D. Management

12. For performance purposes, OS monitoring should include all of the following except
    _____.
    A. Disk space
    B. Disk I/O usage
    C. CPU usage
    D. Print spooling

13. Maintenance mode requires all of these actions except_____.

   A. Remove all active production instances

   B. Initiate enhanced security controls

   C. Prevent new logins

   D. Ensure logging continues

14. What is one of the reasons a baseline might be changed?

   A. Numerous change requests

   B. Power fluctuation

   C. To reduce redundancy

   D. Natural disaster

15. In addition to battery backup, a UPS can offer which capability?

   A. Communication redundancy

   B. Line conditioning

   C. Breach alert

   D. Confidentiality

16. Deviations from security baselines should be investigated and _____.

   A. Documented

   B. Enforced

   C. Revealed

   D. Encouraged

17. The baseline should cover which of the following?

   A. As many systems throughout the organization as possible

   B. Data breach alerting and reporting

   C. A process for version control

   D. All regulatory compliance requirements

18. A localized incident or disaster can be addressed in a cost-effective manner by using which of the following?

   A. UPS

   B. Generators

   C. Joint operating agreements

   D. Strict adherence to applicable regulations

19. Generator fuel storage for a cloud data center should last for how long, at a minimum?

    A. 10 minutes

    B. Three days

    C. Indefinitely

    D. 12 hours

20. The BC/DR kit should include all of the following except_____.

    A. Flashlight

    B. Documentation equipment

    C. Fuel for the backup generators

    D. Annotated asset inventory

Chapter 9

Legal and Compliance Issues

THE OBJECTIVE OF THIS CHAPTER IS TO ACQUAINT THE READER WITH THE FOLLOWING CONCEPTS:

✓ **Domain 2: Cloud Data Security**

- 2.8. Design and Implement Auditability, Traceability and Accountability of Data Events

  - 2.8.3. Chain of Custody and Nonrepudiation

✓ **Domain 5: Cloud Security Operations**

- 5.4. Support Digital Forensics

  - 5.4.1. Forensic Data Collection Methodologies

  - 5.4.2. Evidence Management

  - 5.4.3. Collect, Acquire, and Preserve Digital Evidence

✓ **Domain 6: Legal, Risk and Compliance**

- 6.1. Articulate Legal Requirements and Unique Risks within the Cloud Environment

  - 6.1.1. Conflicting International Legislation

  - 6.1.2. Evaluation of Legal Risks Specific to Cloud Computing

  - 6.1.3 Legal Framework and Guidelines

  - 6.1.4. eDiscovery (e.g., International Organization for Standardization/International Electrotechnical Commission (ISO/IEC) 27050, Cloud Security Alliance (CSA) Guidance

  - 6.1.5. Forensics Requirements

- 6.2. Understand Privacy Issues

  - 6.2.1. Difference between Contractual and Regulated Private Data (e.g., Protected Health Information (PHI), Personally Identifiable Information (PII))

  - 6.2.2. Country-Specific Legislation Related to Private Data (e.g., Protected Health Information (PHI), Personally Identifiable Information (PII))

Operating in the cloud raises a significant number of legal and compliance issues, and cybersecurity professionals must be aware of these concerns. International courts and tribunals weigh in on laws and regulations concerning global networking. There is also no shortage of laws, regulations, and standards that require compliance. The combination of all these factors provides a rich arena for discussion.

It is important to remember that the nature of cloud computing lends itself to resource sharing based on demand as opposed to location. Therefore, data centers located around the world store cloud data and run applications from multiple sources simultaneously. This presents challenges with security and privacy issues due to the complexity of local and international laws, regulations, and guidelines. In this chapter, we will provide a background and review of the important concepts, laws, regulations, and standards so that the CCSP candidate can provide sound advice and guidance when navigating these complex waters.

Legal Requirements and Unique Risks in the Cloud Environment

Laws in the United States and around the world come from a variety of sources. Many people are already familiar with the laws contained in the Constitution itself, as well as the laws passed through the federal and state legislative processes. Other sources of law include the administrative rules and regulations promulgated by government agencies, case law, common law, and contract law.

Constitutional Law

The *U.S. Constitution* is the highest possible source of law in the United States, and no laws from other sources may conflict with the provisions in the Constitution and its amendments. The main text of the Constitution contains seven articles with the following purposes:

- Article I establishes the legislative branch.
- Article II establishes the executive branch.
- Article III establishes the judicial branch.
- Article IV defines the relationship between the federal government and the governments of the states.
- Article V creates a process for amending the Constitution itself.

- Article VI contains the supremacy clause, establishing that the Constitution is the supreme law of the land.

- Article VII sets forth the process for the initial establishment of the federal government.

Exam Tip

Under the U.S. legal system, the U.S. Constitution is the highest law of the land. No law may conflict with any constitutional requirements, and the only way to modify a constitutional requirement is through the amendment process.

Article V describes the process used to modify the Constitution through the use of amendments. This process is, by design, difficult, as the founders set the bar quite high for altering the terms of this important governing document. The amendment process requires that both houses of Congress pass the amendment by a two-thirds majority. After that approval by Congress, the amendment is sent to the states, who have the opportunity to ratify it. Amendments are only added to the Constitution after ratification by three-quarters (38) of the 50 states.

The U.S. Constitution currently contains 27 amendments, covering a range of topics from establishing individual rights to defining the terms of presidential succession. The first 10 of these amendments, known as the *Bill of Rights*, enumerate individual civil liberties protections, including freedom of speech, freedom of assembly, and freedom of religion.

Notably, the word *privacy* does not appear anywhere in the text of the Constitution, although there are established constitutional protections of individual privacy. These come from two sources: the Fourth Amendment and Supreme Court precedent.

The Fourth Amendment to the Constitution reads as follows:

> The right of the people to be secure in their persons, houses, papers, and effects, against unreasonable searches and seizures, shall not be violated, and no Warrants shall issue, but upon probable cause, supported by Oath or affirmation, and particularly describing the place to be searched, and the persons or things to be seized.

This amendment establishes the right of individuals to be protected against some government interference in their private lives. Supreme Court precedent further establishes the right of an individual "to be let alone."

While the U.S. Constitution does not explicitly grant a right to privacy, language in several state constitutions does explicitly grant this right. For example, Article 1, Section 23 of the California Constitution reads:

> Every natural person has the right to be let alone and free from governmental intrusion into the person's private life except as otherwise

provided herein. This section shall not be construed to limit the public's right of access to public records and meetings as provided by law.

The state of Florida includes the following language in Section 6 of its constitution:

The right of the people to privacy is recognized and shall not be infringed without the showing of a compelling state interest. The legislature shall take affirmative steps to implement this right.

Similar provisions protect the right to privacy in the constitutions of Alaska, Arizona, Hawaii, Illinois, Louisiana, Montana, New Hampshire, South Carolina, and Washington.

Legislation

Most of the privacy and security laws that apply within the United States today come not from the Constitution but from the standard legislative process, mentioned earlier in this chapter. Proposed bills are passed by both houses of Congress and then signed into law by the president. These laws are, of course, only enforceable if they are compatible with the terms of the Constitution.

Laws passed by the U.S. Congress become effective and binding in all states and territories of the United States. State legislatures may also pass laws through a similar process, with the laws that they pass applying only within their own states. Most state law–making processes follow a process that mirrors the federal process, with a requirement that laws pass both houses of the state legislature and be signed into law by the state's governor.

Administrative Law

Agencies of the executive branch promulgate sets of rules and regulations that implement many of the laws passed by Congress. These rules make up the body of *administrative law* that is commonly documented in the *Code of Federal Regulations (CFR)*.

For example, in 1996 President Clinton signed the Health Insurance Portability and Accountability Act (HIPAA) into law. This law, in part, imposed new security and privacy obligations on healthcare providers and other covered entities. It did not, however, go into great detail on the specific privacy and security requirements that applied to those entities. Instead, it charged the Department of Health and Human Services (HHS) with creating administrative law containing those implementation details.

Responding to this mandate, HHS published the HIPAA Privacy Rule and the HIPAA Security Rule, which contained detailed requirements for organizations subject to the law's provisions. These rules were created under legislative authority, but they were not passed through the legislative process, so they qualify as examples of administrative law.

Agencies may not create administrative law on a whim. They must go through a formal rule-making process that allows for public comment, and the provisions of administrative law remain subject to judicial review and may also be overridden by a legislative act.

Case Law

The main role of the judicial branch is to interpret the laws and apply them to resolve civil and criminal disputes. The interpretations made by courts over time establish a body of *case law* that other courts may refer to when making their own decisions.

In many cases, the case law decisions made by courts are binding on both that court and any subordinate courts. Courts generally follow the legal principle of *stare decisis* (Latin for "let the decision stand") that states that previous decisions on questions of law serve as precedent guiding the future decisions made by that court and its subordinates. For this reason, even the Supreme Court is reluctant to revisit decisions made by past courts, even if the justices believe that they might reach a conclusion that is different from that of their predecessors.

There is quite a bit of case law on the subject of privacy. For example, the 1996 *Smyth v. Pillsbury Corporation* decision in the U.S. District Court for the Eastern District of Pennsylvania established that employees generally do not have a right to privacy in their use of company-provided email accounts. Although this case was not appealed to higher courts, many other jurisdictions have cited it as relevant case law in their own decisions.

Common Law

The United States is among a large group of nations that observe *common law*, a set of judicial precedents passed down as case law through many generations. This subset of common law includes many long-standing legal principles that have never been codified in legislation but, nonetheless, guide many judicial decisions. The body of common law may be traced back to the English court systems and, therefore, is typically found in modern-day countries that were historically British colonies. Each of those nations gradually adapted common law principles to its own cultural and judicial philosophy over the years.

The body of common law in the United States includes protections of an individual's right to privacy. Later in this chapter, you will learn about the torts of negligence and invasion of privacy. Both of these concepts have their foundation in common law.

There is a delicate relationship between common law and laws with constitutional or legislative sources. Constitutional law and legislative law may override aspects of the common law. Common law also arises from other laws when those laws leave room for interpretation, and common law principles guide courts in making case law that fills those gaps. For this reason, many states have codified portions of the common law in their own statutes.

Later in this chapter, we discuss the invasion of privacy tort. This is an example of a privacy-related common law.

Contract Law

Contracts are legally binding agreements between parties that they will exchange things of value with each other. When two parties have agreed to enter into a contract, they become legally liable to uphold their obligations. As long as the terms of the contract do not violate the law, it is enforceable in court. Contracts should spell out the specific liability that each party has for violations of the contract.

Several conditions must be met for a contract to be valid:

- Each party to the contract must have the capacity to agree to the contract.

- There must be an offer made by one party. This offer may be verbal or in writing, but written terms always take precedence over verbal terms and many types of transactions, such as those involving real estate, must be conducted in writing.

- The other party must accept the offer.

- Consideration must be given, meaning that both parties must exchange something of value. For example, if I enter into a contract to sell you my car, I am giving you the car, something of value, and in return, you are paying me in cash, something of value.

- Finally, there must be mutual intent to be bound. Both parties must enter into a contract with the intention that they are agreeing to the terms.

Violations of a contract generally do not involve law enforcement agencies, so they are treated as private disputes between parties and handled in civil court. These cases are known as *breaches of contract* and courts may take action to enforce the terms of a contract, cancel a contract, or award damages to compensate one party for harm caused by the other party's breach of contract.

From a privacy perspective, organizations often include language in contracts with vendors obligating them to protect the privacy of personally identifiable information. For example, healthcare organizations governed by HIPAA use formal business associate agreements (BAAs) to document the privacy obligations of their service providers.

Analyzing a Law

Jurisdictions around the nation and the world are now frequently passing new privacy laws. These laws might cover new industries, new elements of information, or new jurisdictions. As security professionals, we are often called upon to read and interpret these privacy laws, determining how they apply to our organizations.

Determining Jurisdiction

When analyzing a new law, one of the first things that a privacy professional should do is determine the *jurisdiction* of the law. The jurisdiction is the geographic area to which the law applies. Determining jurisdiction is done by reading the law itself and also assessing the power of the body that created the law. Although this might seem straightforward, interpreting privacy laws is fairly complex.

For example, when the European Union first passed the General Data Protection Regulation (GDPR), the law stated that it applied to the personal information of EU residents worldwide. If a resident of the EU did business with a U.S. company and that information was physically stored in the United States, the EU claimed jurisdiction over that information. Privacy professionals at U.S. companies weren't sure that the EU actually had the jurisdiction to make this declaration.

The applicability of the GDPR is continuing to evolve, but a 2019 ruling by the European Court of Justice limited that applicability. In the ruling (*Google LLC v. Commission nationale de l'informatique et des libertés [CNIL]*), the court said that the right to be forgotten applies only within the EU. They made this decision in the context of a person requesting that their search results be removed from Google. The decision said that, although Google must remove the results shown to visitors from within the EU, the law does not require them to implement the right to be forgotten worldwide.

State data breach notification laws also create significant issues of jurisdiction, similar to those discussed in the Google case. We discuss those more later in this chapter.

Just as laws have jurisdictions, courts also have jurisdictions defined by the power that a court has to render legal judgments in both their subject matter and their geographic applicability. For example, federal courts have jurisdiction only over federal law, whereas state courts have jurisdiction only over state law. Federal circuit courts have geographic authority only over specific states. For example, the Seventh Circuit Court of Appeals has authority over Indiana, Illinois, and Wisconsin. Decisions made by that court apply only within that circuit. The Supreme Court, on the other hand, has nationwide jurisdiction.

Scope and Application

Once you establish the jurisdiction of a law, you should then determine the scope and applicability of the law to your own organization's operations. In many cases, this is obvious. For example, the Family Educational Rights and Privacy Act (FERPA) regulates the ways that most educational institutions handle student records. FERPA clearly applies to the student educational records maintained by colleges and universities. HIPAA clearly applies to medical records maintained by hospitals. But you might be surprised to learn that FERPA would not apply to employee professional education records maintained by hospitals and that HIPAA might not apply to medical records maintained by student health centers.

 The scope of FERPA is actually a bit more nuanced. The law applies only to educational institutions that receive federal funds under certain programs of the U.S. Department of Education. This includes virtually all institutions of higher education but excludes many private schools at the elementary and secondary levels.

It's incumbent upon privacy professionals to carefully read laws, consult with attorneys, and determine what business activities fall under the scope of each law.

Legal Liability

Liability is a term of art in the law. *Black's Law Dictionary* defines liability as "responsible or answerable in law; legally obligated." Simply put, liability is what allows a party to take action against another in court.

Liability comes in two general forms:

- *Criminal liability* occurs when a person violates a criminal law. If a person is found guilty of a criminal law violation, they may be deprived of their liberty through imprisonment, fined, and/or forced to pay restitution to their victims. Charges of criminal liability are normally brought by the government, acting through a state or federal prosecutor.

- *Civil liability* occurs when one person claims that another person has failed to carry out a legal duty that they were responsible for. Cases claiming civil liability are normally brought to court by one party, the *claimant*, who is accusing another party, the *respondent*, of the violation. The claimant may be an individual, a corporation, or the government bringing a civil enforcement action.

One element required to provide a criminal violation is *mens rea*. Latin for "guilty mind," *mens rea* requires that the person had criminal intent, meaning that they either intended to commit a crime or knew that their action or lack of action would result in a crime. The standard of proof in criminal cases is that the prosecution must present evidence that demonstrates the defendant committed the crime, *beyond a reasonable doubt*. This means that the prosecution must convince the jury that, after considering the evidence offered, there is no other plausible conclusion than that the defendant is guilty.

Civil penalties often use a different standard. Most commonly this is the *preponderance of the evidence* standard, which means that the prevailing party must present evidence demonstrating that there is a greater than 50 percent chance that their claim is correct. Some civil cases proceed under a different standard known as *strict liability*. The strict liability standard says that a person is responsible for the consequences of their actions, even if they could not reasonably anticipate the adverse outcome.

Some laws have both criminal and civil components. For example, HIPAA contains provisions that may impose both civil and criminal penalties. On the civil side, HIPAA fines can range from as little as $100 for a first-time offense by an individual who did not know that they were violating HIPAA to $50,000 if a violation was due to willful neglect and was not corrected. On the criminal side, HIPAA-covered entities and individuals who knowingly obtain health information in violation of HIPAA may be fined $50,000 and imprisoned for up to a year. Those penalties increase to a maximum $250,000 fine and 10 years in prison if there was an intent to use the information for commercial advantage, personal gain, or malicious harm.

Theories of liability describe the conditions that must be met for someone to be found liable of a criminal or civil violation of the law. These theories differ for civil and criminal violations and also vary based on the standard written into the law, decided in case law, and appropriate for the circumstances.

Torts and Negligence

Torts are another form of civil violation. Torts do not involve a contract but, instead, involve harm to one party caused by the actions of another party. The party who caused the harm is said to have committed a *tortious act*.

Negligence is a commonly occurring tort that occurs when one party causes harm to another party by their action or lack of action. The theory of liability for negligence involves four elements:

- There must be a *duty of care*. The person accused of negligence must have an established responsibility to the accuser. This may come from the nature of the relationship between the parties. For example, physicians have a duty of care to their patients that they will exercise good medical judgment.

- There must be a breach of that duty of care. The accused person must have either taken action or failed to take an action that violated the duty of care.

- There must be *damages* involved. The accuser must have suffered some type of harm, be it financial, physical, emotional, or reputational.

- There must be *causation*. A reasonable person must be able to conclude that the injury caused to the accuser must be a result of the breach of duty by the accused.

Invasion of privacy is another tort that is established in common law. Invasion of privacy occurs when there is a violation of an individual's reasonable expectation to be left alone. There are four legal torts that may result in a successful claim of invasion of privacy:

- The *invasion of solitude* is a physical or electronic intrusion into the private affairs of a person. Breaking into someone's home or accessing their email account may both be considered invasions of solitude.

- The public disclosure of private facts involves the disclosure of truthful information when the release of that information would offend a reasonable person. This only applies when the information is not newsworthy or of public interest.

- *False light* is a legal term that applies when someone discloses information that causes another person to be falsely perceived by others.

- *Appropriation* is the unauthorized use of someone's name or likeness.

The invasion of privacy torts are a common basis for class action lawsuits against companies that have experienced data breaches.

U.S. Privacy and Security Laws

As you prepare for the CCSP exam, there is a set of U.S. laws governing security and privacy that you'll need to understand. These laws apply to many cloud computing environments based upon the location of individuals, the types of data processed, and the industry involved. While there are emerging state laws that are more stringent and restrictive than federal laws within their jurisdictions, we will focus on U.S. federal laws as they apply to cloud computing. You may not have to have a detailed knowledge of each of these laws and regulations, but you should be able to easily identify them and give a brief explanation of what they are about and where they fit into the realm of cloud computing.

FedRAMP

Although it isn't a law, it is helpful for you to know about Federal Risk and Authorization Management Program (FedRAMP). FedRAMP is a U.S. federal program that mandates a standardized approach to security assessments, authorization, and continuous monitoring of cloud products and services. FedRAMP certification can be quite costly and difficult to achieve but is required for cloud hosting services provided to a U.S. government agency or contractor. Earning this certification can streamline the process of acquiring new government customers and expanding existing business.

For more information on the FedRAMP certification process, see www.fedramp.gov.

Health Insurance Portability and Accountability Act

In 1996, Congress passed the *Health Insurance Portability and Accountability Act (HIPAA)*. HIPAA was enacted to improve several aspects of the healthcare system, including the sharing of data among providers and insurers, the process of switching health plans, and more. HIPAA also set important standards for privacy and security of medical information.

HIPAA privacy and security rules apply to *protected health information (PHI)*. PHI includes medical information pertaining to patient health that is collected by healthcare providers for medical records, conversations with healthcare providers, individual medical information stored by health insurance companies, information used in healthcare billing or payment, and more. HIPAA also protects electronic protected health information (ePHI). ePHI includes any PHI stored or transmitted electronically.

HIPAA Scope

HIPAA is complex piece of legislation that regulates privacy across a wide range of healthcare-related activities. As mentioned earlier, not all medical information is protected by HIPAA under all circumstances. HIPAA applies to certain *covered entities* and to certain healthcare *transactions*. When a covered entity conducts a covered transaction, that entity and the transaction itself are both regulated under HIPAA. HIPAA-covered entities fall into three broad categories:

Health Insurance Plans   This category includes health insurance companies, HMOs, employer health plans, and government health programs, such as Medicare, that cover healthcare costs.

Healthcare Clearinghouses   These organizations help to manage the sharing of health-care information by converting healthcare data into formats that can be read by differing health information systems.

Healthcare Providers   Providers include doctors, hospitals, mental health professionals, dentists, long-term care facilities, pharmacies, and more.

HIPAA also extends to third-party *business associates* of covered entities if they meet certain conditions. A business associate is any third-party individual or organization that works with a covered entity to fulfill healthcare-related functions and that has access to PHI or ePHI. HIPAA requires covered entities to have written agreements with any third parties, called *business associate agreements (BAAs)*, that require the business associate to conform with HIPAA.

HIPAA Privacy Requirements

The HHS Centers for Medicare & Medicaid Services (CMS) provides the rules and standards for organizations subject to HIPAA. In the year 2000, HHS established the HIPAA *Privacy Rule* that lays out guidelines for protecting the privacy of PHI. The Privacy Rule does the following:

- Requires the implementation of information privacy practices
- Limits use and disclosure of data without patient authorization
- Gives patients additional rights with respect to their medical information, including the right to view and correct their medical records

All HIPAA-covered entities and business associates are subject to the Privacy Rule. The HHS Office for Civil Rights (OCR) is responsible for implementing and enforcing the Privacy Rule and may impose monetary penalties for violations. Let's take a closer look at the specific provisions of the rule and its enforcement.

Information Privacy Practices

The Privacy Rule requires covered entities to implement standards and practices to safeguard PHI. These standards and practices must be contained in written *privacy policy and procedures* documentation. These must be consistent with the Privacy Rule. Covered entities are required to retain any records related to their privacy policies and related activities, such as complaints or public notices, for six years.

 A privacy *policy* differs from a privacy *notice*. A privacy policy generally refers to an organization's internal practices for protecting information privacy. A privacy notice is published by an organization to inform the consumers about how it collects, uses, retains, and shares personal data.

Other privacy safeguards include the requirement to designate a privacy official responsible for the privacy policy, implementing a process for addressing privacy complaints, training employees on privacy practices, and implementing reasonable privacy safeguards. Safeguards may be physical, administrative, or technical. For example, safeguards may include ensuring all filing cabinets are appropriately locked (physical), only allowing need-to-know personnel to possess a key to the filing cabinets (administrative), or providing an electronic checkout system for accessing files (technical). Covered entities cannot retaliate against anyone for filing a privacy complaint or ask patients to waive any rights under the Privacy Rule as a condition of care or coverage.

Use and Disclosure

The Privacy Rule aims to protect patient privacy to the greatest extent possible while allowing for information sharing as necessary for the provision of healthcare services and to maintain public health and safety. The Privacy Rule is therefore intended to block entities covered under HIPAA from using PHI for practices such as selling PHI to advertisers or sharing PHI with prospective employers.

The Privacy Rule regulates both *use* and *disclosure* of PHI. According to HIPAA, the Privacy Rule regulates how PHI is handled within an organization. Regulations relating to use help ensure that PHI is only used for intended purposes and that access to PHI is not intentionally or inadvertently abused. HIPAA defines use of PHI as

> . . .the sharing, employment, application, utilization, examination,
> or analysis of such information within an entity that maintains such
> information.

Rules that regulate disclosure are intended to prevent organizations from sharing PHI with third parties. If PHI is shared with third parties by any means, it is considered a disclosure. It is important to remember that not all disclosures are illegal under HIPAA. The Privacy Rule, rather, regulates when and how disclosures may be made. HIPAA defines disclosure as follows:

> Disclosure means the release, transfer, provision of access to, or divulging
> in any manner of information outside the entity holding the information.

The Privacy Rule has specific requirements detailing how covered entities may use and disclose PHI. These requirements are intended to ensure that patients know how their

PHI is used and shared, that PHI is only used to provide healthcare services (with limited exceptions), and that patients must provide authorization before their PHI can be used for anything else.

HIPAA Security Requirements

The HIPAA *Security Rule* is similar to the Privacy Rule in that it was established by HHS to provide an information security framework for the implementation of HIPAA. The Security Rule applies to covered entities and business associates in the same way as the Privacy Rule, and it is also enforced by the OCR. However, the Security Rule applies only to ePHI, whereas the Privacy Rule applies to all PHI. The Security Rule is intended to apply the protections of the Privacy Rule to ePHI by providing standards for data security.

The HIPAA Security Rule states that it is intended to safeguard the "confidentiality, integrity, and availability" of PHI. To accomplish this, covered entities must attempt to foresee cybersecurity threats as well as risks of any other unauthorized PHI disclosure to a reasonable degree. Organizations must protect information, put controls in key places to address those threats, and include employee training in information security practices.

The Security Rule's requirements for confidentiality are intended to protect against unauthorized access as described by the Privacy Rule. This is a good example of a way in which the Security Rule supports the application of the Privacy Rule to ePHI. Similarly, the other terms in the four general rules detailed earlier are designed to support the Privacy Rule by making sure data isn't improperly destroyed, is available for authorized access, and isn't inadvertently disclosed to the wrong parties.

The Security Rule also requires that covered entities implement appropriate data controls. However, the specific information security controls may vary from organization to organization, depending on the scale, function, resources, and capabilities of the organization. The Security Rule handles the wide variety of data security strategies by requiring all covered entities to complete a regular risk analysis that identifies information risks and the probability and severity of each of those risks. Organizations are then allowed to implement security controls that respond appropriately to the unique risks they face. These controls must include an information security management program that identifies personnel responsible for the program, appropriate employee training, controlled access to ePHI, ongoing program evaluation, physical security of facilities and workstations, and technological controls to monitor and protect data.

The Health Information Technology for Economic and Clinical Health Act

The Health Information Technology for Economic and Clinical Health (HITECH) Act was passed in 2009 in order to improve healthcare by bringing health systems up to date with modern technology. For this reason, the HITECH Act provides incentives for healthcare organizations to use *electronic health records (EHRs)* and penalties that serve as disincentives for organizations that don't adopt EHR. The scope of the HITECH is aligned with

HIPAA, and HITECH applies to covered entities and transactions. Although the main purpose of the HITECH was to speed up innovation in healthcare, the act included important updates to HIPAA related to privacy.

Along with encouragement to adopt EHR, the HITECH Act provides additional privacy and security requirements for PHI, including requirements to notify victims about data breaches involving their information. *The Breach Notification Rule* is usually triggered when any unsecured PHI is used or disclosed in any way not authorized by the law. HHS uses four primary factors to determine whether an authorized use or disclosure constitutes a breach. To determine whether a breach has occurred, an organization must evaluate the following:

- The type of information involved and whether individual patients may be identified. If, for example, the data is fully anonymized and the information can't be assigned to any individual, then the information may not be PHI in the first place.

- The parties who used or accessed the information. Malicious actors, such as cybercriminals, may present far more risk to patients than an accidental disclosure to the wrong doctor.

- The likelihood that PHI was actually acquired or viewed by an unauthorized party. For example, if an organization was able to show that an email containing PHI was deleted before being read, then there is a lower risk of breach.

- How well PHI is secured. Organizations may mitigate risk through technological, physical, and administrative controls. For example, a breach is unlikely if the data is appropriately encrypted and therefore unviewable.

Covered entities must notify victims within 60 days of knowing about a data breach to explain the breach and any steps victims should take to protect themselves. If the breach affects more than 500 individuals in a given state, then the covered entity is also required to notify media outlets, usually in the form of a press release.

Covered entities are also required to notify HHS of any breaches. If the breach affects more than 500 people total, then HHS must be notified within 60 days. Breaches that affect fewer people may be reported annually. Finally, business associates must notify the covered entity of any breaches within 60 days. Once the covered entity has been notified of a breach by a business associate, the covered entity is responsible for the rest of the notification requirements. Importantly, covered entities can't merely claim they made all appropriate notifications after a breach—they have to prove it. Covered entities must therefore maintain documentation or other evidence to demonstrate that they fulfilled the notification requirements outlined by HITECH.

Gramm–Leach–Bliley Act

The Gramm–Leach–Bliley Act (GLBA), also known as the Financial Services Modernization Act of 1999, establishes broad federal regulation to improve information privacy and security for the financial services industry.

GLBA Scope

If a business is *significantly engaged* in offering financial services, then it is considered a *financial institution* and is regulated under GLBA. The standard of significant engagement hinges principally on two factors: the formality of offering financial services and the frequency of offering financial services. For example, if a barber occasionally allows a good customer to come back and pay later, then the barber probably does not meet the standard. However, if the barber starts a formal credit program as a regular service, then the barber would be significantly engaged in offering financial services.

Financial services and products may include obvious products like credit cards and bank loans. Less obvious activities include collecting debts, loan servicing, check cashing services, tax services, and higher education institutions that offer student loans. Firms that manage investments for others are also included.

GLBA Privacy Requirements

The *GLBA Privacy Rule* is intended to protect consumer privacy both by better informing consumers about how their financial information is used and by regulating the use of consumer information by financial institutions. Financial institutions must share their privacy notices with customers when they first begin a business relationship and provide updated privacy notices every year thereafter.

As with privacy notice requirements under other legislation, the notice must describe privacy policies and disclose how customer information is collected, used, and shared. The notice must also inform customers about any third parties who may access their data. It is significant to note that customers are merely *informed* about third-party information sharing and not given the right to explicitly *consent* to third-party sharing. The privacy notice must also reference the information security practices in place to protect customer data as described in the GLBA Safeguards Rule (see the next section).

GLBA also recognizes a legal difference between *customers* and *consumers*. Customers have an ongoing regular relationship with a financial institution. For example, an account holder at a bank would be a customer. Consumers, however, may only conduct isolated transactions with a financial institution, such as cashing a check at a bank or visiting a bank's website. For *customers*, financial institutions must provide their full privacy notices with all the details listed in GLBA when the customer relationship begins and then annually thereafter. For *consumers,* the financial institution only needs to provide a summary privacy notice that includes instructions for finding the full notice.

GLBA Safeguards Requirements

The *GLBA Safeguards Rule* provides a framework for financial institutions' obligations for protecting information security. The rule requires financial institutions to implement organized information security programs with the goals of safeguarding customer information security and confidentiality. The requirements for safeguards echo those of other similar laws discussed in this chapter. Financial institutions are required to attempt to anticipate threats as well as risks of any unauthorized information access or disclosure. These organizations must implement appropriate measures to protect against these threats and risks. When considering the risk of unauthorized access, the Safeguards Rule emphasizes protecting against scenarios where the consumer may be harmed as a result.

Under GLBA, information security programs must include designated personnel to manage information security, ongoing assessment of risks and the controls in place to minimize those risks, and assessment of any third-party partners to make sure those partners can meet the standards of the financial institution's information security program.

GLBA also offers guidance on the types of controls financial institutions should consider for lowering their risk. GLBA emphasizes three categories of information security controls: workforce training, securing of information systems, and ongoing monitoring of information systems for problems. As companies consider information risk, GLBA is not only concerned with safeguards that reduce the risk of cyberattacks but is also concerned with the risk of data loss or exposure due to failures in information systems or procedures, or human mistakes.

Sarbanes–Oxley Act

At the latter part of the last century, a number of large companies experienced total and unexpected financial collapse because of fraudulent accounting practices, poor audit practices, inadequate financial controls, and poor oversight by governing boards of directors. Some of the companies involved are now a distant memory (Enron, WorldCom, and Adelphia, for example). As a result, in 2002 the Sarbanes–Oxley Act (SOX) was enacted as an attempt to prevent these kinds of poor practices and fraudulent activities from occurring in the future. It applies to all publicly traded corporations in the United States and creates an environment of regulatory transparency where companies are required to disclose information about their financial status and implement controls to ensure the accuracy of that information.

The Securities and Exchange Commission (SEC) is the organization responsible for establishing SOX standards and guidelines and conducting audits and imposing subsequent fines, should any be required.

If you are interested in learning more about the Sarbanes–Oxley Act, visit www.sec.gov/about/laws/soa2002.pdf.

State Data Breach Notification Laws

When an organization suffers any sort of breach, or unauthorized disclosure of private information, they must manage the problem at several levels. They must respond defensively to stop the breach and recover lost and damaged systems and data. They must also manage any interruption to their business processes or company operations. Organizations must also meet all of their legal and ethical obligations to their customers and regulatory authorities when a breach occurs. Privacy professionals and legal counsel are most often called upon to help manage these compliance requirements.

State breach notification laws are an important pillar of data privacy protection in the United States. State breach notification laws help ensure that individuals have the opportunity to protect themselves if their information is compromised. Without such laws, individuals may be at risk for identity theft and never know it. Perhaps just as important, however, is the role state breach notification laws play in holding the U.S. private sector accountable. These laws serve as a powerful incentive for industry to protect against breaches. Responding to the various requirements in all of these laws is costly. These laws also increase corporate transparency and encourage organizations to protect their reputations by using personal information responsibly.

Some federal statutes have breach notification requirements. HIPAA, for example, requires notifications to the government, any affected individuals, and possibly even media outlets, depending on the breach. To further complicate this jurisdictional picture, all U.S. states have their own data breach notification laws. These laws may contain different definitions of what constitutes a data breach and different requirements for notification. In addition to federal and international rules, organizations suffering from a breach are faced with 54 additional legal regimes in the United States. These include the laws of 50 U.S. states, the District of Columbia, and the U.S. territories of Guam, Puerto Rico, and the U.S. Virgin Islands.

Defining Data Breaches

To comply with data breach notification laws, an organization must be able to determine whether an incident is considered a *breach*. Organizations must also determine whether the information exposed in a breach is considered to be *personal information* and therefore subject to breach notification rules. Since these definitions vary from state to state, a breach in one state may not always constitute a breach in another state.

Breach   Most states consider a breach to have occurred when an organization discovers that a third party has obtained unauthorized access to information. Many state laws specify that if the data in question was encrypted or sufficiently redacted, then the unauthorized access does not constitute a breach.

Personal Information   Most states trigger breach notification rules if a breach includes personal information on state residents. The definitions of personal information have broad similarities across most state laws. Typically, personal information must include a person's full name, or first initial and last name, linked with another piece of identifying information, such as a Social Security number (SSN).

Conditions for Notification

If an organization determines that a breach has occurred that involves personal information, as defined in a given state, it must comply with breach notification rules. These rules may contain several key parameters that vary by state. States have rules that specify who to notify, when an organization must deliver those notifications, and how those notifications must be transmitted. In many states, these rules will vary depending on the scale of the breach (how many people are affected) and the level of risk posed to those affected.

- **Who to notify:** States may require notification to individuals affected, state regulatory bodies, or even local media outlets. Most states require organizations to notify the major national credit reporting agencies of breaches as well.

- **When to notify:** Most state laws give an organization a deadline for delivering breach notifications. The clock typically starts when an organization is made aware of a breach, but states vary in how much time an organization has to provide notification. All states prefer speedy notification, but some specify a 30-, 45-, or 60-day deadline and some merely require notification "without unreasonable delay."

- **How to notify:** Some states have specific requirements that detail how notifications must be composed and/or transmitted. Some states require a notification to be sent by postal mail, while others allow electronic notifications, for example.

Data Subject Rights

State laws often further protect their residents by levying penalties or imposing other obligations against organizations either for violating the state's breach notification laws or, sometimes, for allowing the breach to happen in the first place. State laws may vary most widely in this area. Some states require organizations to offer free credit monitoring for affected individuals, some levy fines, and some (like California) afford state residents a private right of action to pursue damages on their own.

International Laws

Sovereign countries also have their own laws, applicable to their own jurisdictions. The *jurisdiction* is the land and people subject to a specific court or courts. The effects of a country's laws do not cease at its borders, though. If a citizen from another country, or even one of the country's citizens operating outside that country, breaks that country's law, they can still be subject to prosecution and punishment by that country. For instance, a hacker that uses the internet to attack a target in another country could be subject to that country's computer security laws. The hacker might be extradited (forcibly apprehended in their own country and transported to the country where the law was broken) to face trial. Because there is no global uniformity in how these laws are written and applied, the practitioner is strongly advised to consult with counsel whenever legal matters arise.

It's important to understand the distinctions of laws and principles of various nations because cloud providers and customers might be operating in many different jurisdictions. The cloud is not limited to the borders of any given country.

European Union General Data Protection Regulation

The General Data Protection Regulation (GDPR) took legal effect in 2018 and set a new standard for privacy protection. Even though the GDPR is promulgated by the EU, the law has sweeping implications for any U.S.-based corporations with operations in Europe or who transfer personal information to or from Europe. The GDPR is celebrated as a win by privacy advocates and a model for progressive privacy legislation in the United States.

Compared with existing U.S. law, the GDPR grants individuals far more rights to access and control how and by whom their data is accessed and used. In general, ensuring more rights for individuals means more restrictions for businesses that rely on customer data. For this reason, the GDPR may present challenges for some non-EU businesses. At a minimum, businesses may have to implement costly compliance programs and manage increased legal risks. Some businesses in the United States, such as data brokers of large datasets for digital advertising, may generate revenue through the relatively unfettered use and disclosure of customer data.

GDPR Scope

The scope of GDPR is notable for its breadth. The GDPR aims to protect all personal data for everyone in the EU by regulating any entity that handles the data. The GDPR defines several key concepts critical to understanding the full scope of the law:

Personal Data   *Personal data* includes any information that identifies an individual. Examples include names, IP addresses, and geolocation information as well as any characteristics of a person that might be used individually or in combination to identify that person. The GDPR refers to individuals protected by the law as *natural persons* or *data subjects*. Importantly, the GDPR does not restrict its scope to citizens of EU member states.

U.S.-based privacy professionals should note that U.S. corporations may collect data that is not protected by U.S. law as personal information but that is considered personal information in the EU.

Data Controllers and Processors   The GDPR applies to both *controllers* and *processors* of data. A data controller is usually the entity that ultimately is in charge of data. The GDPR says that a controller "… determines the purposes and means of the processing of personal data…." A data processor is any other entity that handles personal data for the controller. For example, a retailer may hire a digital marketing firm to help it increase online sales with better website analytics. In this case, the retailer would be the controller and the marketing firm would be the processor. Under GDPR, both controllers and processors have obligations and liabilities. With this framework, the GDPR aims to protect data even as it changes hands.

Territorial Jurisdiction   The jurisdiction of the GDPR is still somewhat unsettled. According to the text of the GDPR, it applies to all organizations established in the EU as well as any organizations that control or process data on EU data subjects for "the offering of goods or services" or for "the monitoring of their behavior" within EU territory. This may be interpreted to mean that GDPR regulates any e-commerce website that a person in the EU happens to click on.

Boundaries of GDPR

A body of case law is slowly taking shape to further define the GDPR's applicability beyond the geographic boundaries of the EU. Many of these issues are considered by the Court of Justice of the European Union (CJEU). The issue is difficult for the CJEU because their authority exists only within the EU, while data on the internet isn't constrained by geographic borders. In a series of prominent cases, EU data subjects have attempted to enforce GDPR provisions such as the right to be forgotten (discussed below) against Google's search engine.

An internet search engine does not explicitly host web pages that contain personal information, but search results may make reference to websites that do. For this reason, EU data subjects have asked the CJEU to order Google to remove references to certain websites from search results. This process, called dereferencing, only meaningfully protects privacy if Google dereferences websites globally, not only in the EU.

The CJEU, however, has ruled that it can only order Google to dereference search results for EU versions of its web pages and to discourage anyone in the EU from finding the dereferenced results. Without further restrictions, it remains relatively simple for a person in the EU to navigate to a U.S.-based Google website and search for any dereferenced information.

This area of law is by no means settled. Since the GDPR claims to apply to any monitoring of EU data subjects' behavior, it is difficult to enforce unless it applies to every website in the world. However, the GDPR is not settled international law and the CJEU does not claim extraterritorial jurisdiction over non-EU countries.

Despite the ongoing controversy, many U.S. companies consider it to be in their best interest to move towards compliance with the GDPR. Many large U.S. companies have substantial operations in the EU and have an interest in compliance with EU law. For many companies, it may be far simpler and more cost-effective to apply GDPR-style compliance across all of their operations rather than to create and maintain separate compliance programs for EU and non-EU operations. In addition, U.S. states are beginning to consider and adopt GDPR-style regulations.

Even though GDPR may not be directly enforceable across the globe in every case, the law limits how personal data can be shared outside the EU. GDPR prohibits the transfer of data to non-EU countries unless the recipient offers the same privacy protections as the EU. GDPR offers a few avenues for approving data transfers outside the EU. For example, EU authorities decide in advance that a non-EU country has adequate data privacy protections in place to allow data transfers to take place. This is known as an *adequacy decision*. Mechanisms to facilitate data transfer between the United States and the EU are in flux, but they include the EU-U.S. Privacy Shield program, Binding Corporate Rules, and Standard Contractual Clauses. These are discussed later in this chapter.

Data Subject Rights

The GDPR provides comprehensive rights to data subjects. Not unlike many U.S. laws, the GDPR requires that all data processors and controllers provide transparent notice to customers explaining what data is collected and how data is used and information about any third-parties with whom data may be shared.

The GDPR goes far beyond most U.S. regulations by requiring companies to obtain consent from data subjects before collecting personal data in most circumstances. Consent must be meaningful, and controllers must be able to show that they have obtained consent. GDPR requires that written consent must be "clearly distinguishable from other matters," easy to understand, and accessible. This means that a consent clause may not be buried in some long and obtuse end user agreement. Data subjects may also retract their consent whenever they like.

There are a few exceptions that include data processing required for legal obligations and for certain business operations, but the GDPR treats exceptions in a very limited way and errs on the side of requiring consent. Most U.S. privacy laws, in contrast, require (at most) that data subjects are given the chance to opt out of data collection and use, whereas GDPR generally requires an opt-in by default.

The GDPR provides a notable list of additional *data subject rights*. These are contained in Articles 15 through 22 of the GDPR and include the well-known *right to erasure*, also known as the *right to be forgotten*. The right to be forgotten means, quite simply, that EU data subjects have the right to ask data controllers to erase all of their personal data. A request for erasure may be made in a number of circumstances, including when a data subject withdraws consent. In such cases, controllers are required to erase the personal data in question "without undue delay." Other data subject rights are as follows:

- *Right of access*: Data subjects have the right to know what data is collected and why, know how their data will be processed, know with whom their data may be shared, obtain a copy of their personal data, and have access to information about how to request erasure under GDPR.

- *Right to rectification*: Data subjects have the right to request corrections to the information collected about them.

- *Right to restriction of processing*: Data subjects have the right to request that controllers halt processing activities, without requesting full erasure, in some circumstances.

- *Notification obligations*: Controllers have to notify data subjects when they fulfill requests for erasure, rectification, or restriction of processing.

- *Right to data portability*: Data subjects have the right to get a copy of their data in "machine-readable format" so that it can be ingested by other information systems. This right, for example, helps to prevent companies from locking customers into their products by keeping their data in a proprietary format that can't be moved to a competitor.

- *Right to object*: Data subjects have the right to object to any processing of their personal data they believe to be out of compliance with GDPR or to opt out of certain processing activities, such as direct marketing. The burden is on the data controller to demonstrate that data processing activities are authorized under GDPR in order to resume.

- *Automated individual decision-making, including profiling*: This right means that AI, or any "automated processing," alone can't make any decisions that have a significant or legal impact on a person.

Penalties for violating the GDPR can be very steep. Depending on which provision of GDPR is violated and whether the violation was intentional or negligent, administrative penalties for infringements may reach up to €20,000,000 or 4% of a company's annual revenue, whichever is greater. Data subjects may also pursue damages for any harm caused by a violation of GDPR.

Adequacy Decisions

Probably the smoothest and simplest mechanism to allow international data transfers to and from the EU is via an *adequacy decision*. An adequacy decision occurs when the EU reviews the privacy laws of another nation and decides those laws are adequate to protect EU data subjects' privacy at a level commensurate with the provisions of the GDPR.

The European Commission is empowered to make adequacy decisions under the GDPR. Once such a decision is made, international data transfers may occur to and from the EU and the other country without the need of any further legal approval. An adequacy decision allows the EU to treat a company from another country virtually just like a European Country. The EU has only made adequacy decisions in favor of a handful of nations so far, including Japan, New Zealand, Argentina, and Canada. Notably, the EU has not made an adequacy decision in favor of the United States.

U.S.-EU Safe Harbor and Privacy Shield

Safe harbor programs, for example, establish a common set of privacy regulations, and member nations commit to enforcing those privacy standards. Such arrangements allow companies established in nations with strict privacy regulations to transfer data to and from countries with less-strict laws. Typically, safe harbor frameworks are aligned with the strictest domestic laws of all members in order to function. Once a nation becomes a member of a safe harbor program, individual companies may join by seeking third-party certification to verify that their privacy practices meet the safe harbor standards.

Designed by the U.S. Department of Commerce in conjunction with EU authorities in 2016, the Privacy Shield program was designed to provide a framework to allow U.S. companies to transfer data to and from the EU without running afoul of the GDPR. The Privacy Shield program attempted to accomplish this by creating a privacy framework with provisions that matched the requirements of GDPR. U.S. companies could earn Privacy Shield status by demonstrating compliance with the framework and would be free to transact data to and from the EU. With the Privacy Shield program in place, the EU was able to make an *adequacy decision* to authorize data transfers with U.S. companies in the program.

This program underwent a legal challenge as a result of a case brought by an Austrian privacy advocate known as *Schrems II*. In July 2020, the EU courts struck down the Privacy Shield program and reversed the earlier adequacy decision.

In the *Schrems II* ruling, the CJEU left two other avenues in place for U.S. companies to engage in data transfer with the EU. These include Binding Corporate Rules (BCRs) and Standard Contractual Clauses (SCCs). Both of these are discussed in more detail in the following sections. The Schrems II decision, however, did suggested that the use of both BCRs and SCCs may be more limited than previously thought. For example, BCRs and SCCs must address concerns about U.S. government surveillance by putting safeguards in place, and EU authorities may abruptly order data processing by U.S. companies to cease if concerns arise.

> It is possible that the Privacy Shield program may be approved for use again in the future if U.S. laws or the program itself are modified sufficiently to address the concerns raised in the CJEU decision.

Binding Corporate Rules

The GDPR allows data transfer outside the EU to take place when all parties in a given corporate group agree to adopt specific rules for data privacy. BCRs are complex agreements wherein each party agrees to adhere to GDPR standards for data protection. The agreements must be legally binding in all jurisdictions concerned. In addition, an EU organization that acts as either a controller or a processor must assume liability for any damages caused as a result of violations by non-EU partners unless they can prove they weren't at fault.

BCRs require approval by an EU member state supervisory authority and must undergo rigorous review. Once established, however, BCRs provide a common framework for privacy compliance to which many organizations may agree. Despite the complexity of the arrangement, BCRs may be a good way to facilitate ongoing data transfer arrangements among multiple large multinational corporations.

In some cases, BCRs may obligate an organization to follow GDPR rules that conflict with laws in a non-EU country. For example, the U.S. government may require disclosure of personal data that would be prohibited by the GDPR. In such cases, BCRs generally require that the organizations must notify the appropriate EU authority. This is one of the areas of controversy surrounding BCRs that arose from the Schrems II case. It remains unclear how organizations that enter into a BCR arrangement can provide adequate safeguards to reconcile conflicting laws.

Standard Contractual Clauses

For smaller companies or more limited business relationships, setting up a full BCR framework may be overkill. In these cases, two parties entering into a contract may opt instead to include contract language that obligates the non-EU company to follow GDPR practices.

The European Commission issues prescribed and standardized contractual clauses that must be used for such arrangements.

To use SCCs, the company in the EU that plans to share data is designated as the *data exporter*. The non-EU company planning to receive the data is designated as a *data importer*. The European Commission's approved contractual clauses specify the contractual obligations for each party. The European Commission provides a couple of sets of SCCs that vary depending on whether the parties involved are controllers or processors and the level of legal liability assumed by each party. The SCCs must be used exactly as provided by the European Commission and may not be altered for specific contracts.

Other Approved Transfer Mechanisms

The GDPR allows for a limited number of circumstances in which data may be transferred to non-EU entities. These are known as *derogations* and describe specific and limited exemptions when an isolated data transfer may take place. Derogations that permit the transfer of personal data outside the EU without the protections of an adequacy decision, BCRs, or SCCs may occur only in the following circumstances:

- With the informed consent of the data subject
- To fulfill contractual obligations with the data subject
- For "important reasons of the public interest"
- To fulfill legal obligations
- To safeguard the "vital interests" of the data subject, and only if the data subject is unable to provide consent
- If the information is open to the public already

The only other exemptions permitted outside of these very limited derogations apply to one-time transfers that affect only a small number of data subjects when the data controller has a "compelling legitimate interest" in making the transfer that doesn't conflict with any of the rights of the data subject. In this case, a data controller has to notify their local EU supervisory authority of the transfer and the supervisory authority will inform the affected data subjects. Under GDPR, exercising such an exemption likely represents elevated legal risk to an organization and should be used only sparingly in cases of dire need.

Laws, Regulations, and Standards

So what is the difference between all of these laws, regulations, standards, and frameworks? Laws are legal rules that are created by government entities such as legislatures. Regulations are rules that are created by governmental agencies. Failure to properly follow laws and regulations can result in punitive procedures that can include fines and imprisonment.

Standards dictate a reasonable level of performance; they can be created by an organization for its own purposes (internal) or come from industry bodies/trade groups (external).

An organization can choose to adhere to a standard that it selects; in some cases, for some industries and jurisdictions, compliance with standards is imposed by law. Following a standard can reduce liability; demonstrating that compliance represents due care.

Laws, regulations, and standards can all impact the information security industry, often in similar or overlapping ways. For example, there are laws, regulations, and standards that all dictate and describe what sorts of data should be considered sensitive and personal information.

Rules related to the handling of sensitive data might come from another source, as well: contractual agreements between private parties. Two common examples of this are the Payment Card Industry Data Security Standard (PCI DSS) and the North American Electric Reliability Corporation Critical Infrastructure Protection (NERC CIP) program.

Regardless of whether you're dealing with laws, regulations, or standards, everyone expects a reasonable degree of transparency—in other words, making things clear for all types of regulators and interested parties, at least to the degree that is expected and possible.

Payment Card Industry Data Security Standard

PCI DSS compliance is wholly voluntary, but it is a requirement for those who choose to participate in credit card processing (namely, merchants who accept credit card payments). Those participants agree to submit to PCI oversight, including audits and review of the participants' adoption and implementation of standards and applicable controls. It's not a law, but it is a framework, complete with enforcers. For more information about PCI DSS, visit www.pcisecuritystandards.org.

Critical Infrastructure Protection Program

Similarly, utilities and others involved in energy production and transmission may be subject to a set of industry regulations set forth in the Critical Infrastructure Protection program set forth by the North American Electric Reliability Corporation (NERC CIP).

For more information on NERC CIP, see the website at www.nerc.com/ pa/Stand/Pages/CIPStandards.aspx.

Conflicting International Legislation

The internet and cloud facilitate international commerce, allowing individuals and businesses to trade goods and services worldwide. This can lead to legal difficulties because jurisdictions might have conflicting laws for similar activity. For instance, online gambling is against the law in the United States but is perfectly legal in many other parts of the world; providers offering services to American players may be subject to prosecution in the United States (see the case study "Online Gambling").

Cloud service providers may also have to comply with local requirements that differ greatly from the laws within the country where the service is headquartered or be forced to deviate from their own internal policies as well; for example, in order for Google to provide service in China, Google is required to disclose user behavior to the Chinese government, even though it is readily apparent that this reporting might be used to prosecute and persecute users for behavior that is normalized in Google's home country (the United States) but illegal in China.

As a security professional, you must be aware of the various laws affecting your organization's activities and users in the jurisdictions in which you do business, including the location of cloud data centers, providers, and end users. Contracts with cloud providers must be reviewed in detail for legal impacts in both the provider's and customer's jurisdictions.

Finally, as practitioners in the field of information security, we should all be aware of legal developments that might cause conflicts to arise in our international operations, such as laws that might dictate behavior that is legal in one jurisdiction but illegal in another. For example, the Clarifying Lawful Overseas Use of Data (CLOUD) Act requires companies in the United States to disclose data to federal law enforcement, even if that data is located outside the United States and the disclosure might be against the law in the jurisdiction where the data is located.

 Real World Scenario

Online Gambling

Sometimes, what is against the law in one jurisdiction is not against the law in another. In those circumstances, extradition can be difficult. If a person's actions are not illegal in their home nation and another nation wants to arrest them and bring them to trial, the home nation might refuse any such requests.

This was the case for David Carruthers, the CEO of a British-based online gambling company. In 2006, Carruthers was arrested by federal agents in the United States while he was changing planes in Dallas, between a flight from the UK and a flight to Costa Rica. The U.S. government charged Carruthers with "racketeering," stemming from the use of his company's services by U.S. citizens engaging in online gambling.

Online gambling, while illegal in the United States, is not illegal in the UK or Costa Rica, nor in many other parts of the world. It would have been difficult for the United States to extradite Carruthers from either the UK or Costa Rica because of this difference in the laws of the various countries, so federal agents waited until he was in the jurisdiction of the United States—the moment his plane touched down.

Carruthers served 33 months in prison.

Information Security Management Systems

ISO created the concept of an information security management system (ISMS), a holistic overview of the entire security program within an organization. The ISMS is detailed in ISO 27001.

The ISMS is intended to provide a standardized international model for the development and implementation of policies, procedures, and standards that take into account stakeholder identification and involvement in a top-down approach to addressing and managing risk in an organization. It is built on the premise that information should be adequately secured with practices accepted and recognized by the industry as a whole; it is platform/product agnostic and can be customized for any organization.

ISO 27001 is probably the most well-recognized security program standard globally and will be accepted by many regulators/jurisdictions as meeting due care requirements for reducing liability. However, applying the standard, and being certified as having applied it, is not inexpensive; ISO compliance is a very costly prospect, which may make it unattractive or impossible for small and medium-sized organizations.

For more information, see www.iso.org/iso/iso27001.

The management and oversight of security practices, devices, and tools, as well as business processes such as audit and security functions, constitute what the (ISC)² CCSP Exam Outline (Candidate Information Bulletin) describes as an "internal information security controls system," which is a holistic program for security controls within an organization. Under the ISO perspective, the ISMS fulfills this purpose.

ISO documents are not free! They can range in price from around $100 to several hundred, depending on the specific document, size, age, and so on. And there are literally hundreds of them. This is one of the ways in which the ISO generates revenue to continue developing its standards. They are developed primarily by subject matter experts from around the world, who are all volunteers with the exception of the ISO staff. For more information, go to www.iso.org/home.html.

ISO/IEC 27017:2015

The International Organization for Standardization (ISO) and the International Electrotechnical Commission (IEC) created ISO/IEC 27017:2015, a set of standards regarding the guidelines for information security controls applicable to the provision and use of cloud services and cloud service customers. In other words, it provides a set of standards not only for providing cloud services but also for how cloud customer information and privacy should be controlled. Although ISO standards are recognized internationally, they are not law, and they do not reflect regulation by governmental bodies such as the EU. However, in some jurisdictions, some industries are required by law to comply with ISO standards.

Privacy in the Cloud

As organizations move to the cloud, they must also consider the impact of their efforts on the privacy of personal information entrusted to their care. There are several important frameworks that help with this work, including the Generally Accepted Privacy Principles (GAPP) and ISO 27018.

Generally Accepted Privacy Principles

The *Generally Accepted Privacy Principles (GAPP)* is an attempt to establish a global framework for privacy management. GAPP includes 10 principles that were developed as a joint effort between two national accounting organizations: the American Institute of Certified Public Accountants (AICPA) and the Canadian Institute of Chartered Accountants (CICA). These two organizations sought expert input to develop a set of commonly accepted privacy principles.

The 10 GAPP principles are as follows:

1. Management
2. Notice
3. Choice and Consent
4. Collection
5. Use, Retention, and Disposal
6. Access
7. Disclosure to Third Parties
8. Security for Privacy
9. Quality
10. Monitoring and Enforcement

The following sections explore each of these principles in more detail.

Exam Tip

Pay careful attention to acronyms here! The AICPA and CICA publish both the Generally Accepted Privacy Practices (GAPP) and the Generally Accepted Accounting Practices (GAAP)!

Management

Management is the first of the 10 privacy principles, and GAPP defines it as follows: "The entity defines, documents, communicates, and assigns accountability for its privacy policies and procedures." The GAPP standard then goes on to list a set of criteria that organizations should follow to establish control over the management of their privacy programs.

These criteria are included:

- Creating written privacy policies and communicating those policies to personnel
- Assigning responsibility and accountability for those policies to a person or team
- Establishing procedures for the review and approval of privacy policies and changes to those policies
- Ensuring that privacy policies are consistent with applicable laws and regulations
- Performing privacy risk assessments on at least an annual basis
- Ensuring that contractual obligations to customers, vendors, and partners are consistent with privacy policies
- Assessing privacy risks when implementing or changing technology infrastructure
- Creating and maintaining a privacy incident management process
- Conducting privacy awareness and training and establishing qualifications for employees with privacy responsibilities

Notice

The second GAPP principle, *notice*, requires that organizations inform individuals about their privacy practices. GAPP defines notice as follows: "The entity provides notice about its privacy policies and procedures and identifies the purposes for which personal information is collected, used, retained, and disclosed."

The notice principle incorporates the following criteria:

- Including notice practices in the organization's privacy policies
- Notifying individuals about the purpose of collecting personal information and the organization's policies surrounding the other GAPP principles
- Providing notice to individuals at the time of data collection, when policies and procedures change, and when the organization intends to use information for new purposes not disclosed in earlier notices
- Writing privacy notices in plain and simple language and posting them conspicuously

Choice and Consent

Choice and consent is the third GAPP principle, allowing individuals to retain control over the use of their personal information. GAPP defines choice and consent as follows: "The entity describes the choices available to the individual and obtains implicit or explicit consent with respect to the collection, use, and disclosure of personal information."

The criteria associated with the principle of choice and consent are as follows:

- Including choice and consent practices in the organization's privacy policies

- Informing individuals about the choice and consent options available to them and the consequences of refusing to provide personal information or withdrawing consent to use personal information

- Obtaining implicit or explicit consent at or before the time that personal information is collected

- Notifying individuals of proposed new uses for previously collected information and obtaining additional consent for those new uses

- Obtaining direct explicit consent from individuals when the organization collects, uses, or discloses sensitive personal information

- Obtaining consent before transferring personal information to or from an individual's computer or device

Collection

The principle of *collection* governs the ways organizations come into the possession of personal information. GAPP defines this principle as follows: "The entity collects personal information only for the purposes identified in the notice."

The criteria associated with the collection principle are as follows:

- Including collection practices in the organization's privacy policies

- Informing individuals that their personal information will only be collected for identified purposes

- Including details on the methods used to collect data and the types of data collected in the organization's privacy notice

- Collecting information using fair and lawful means and only for the purposes identified in the privacy notice

- Confirming that any third parties who provide the organization with personal information have collected it fairly and lawfully and that the information is reliable

- Informing individuals if the organization obtains additional information about them

Use, Retention, and Disposal

Organizations must maintain the privacy of personal information throughout its lifecycle. That's where the principle of *use, retention, and disposal* plays an important role. GAPP defines this principle as follows: "The entity limits the use of personal information to the purposes identified in the notice and for which the individual has provided implicit or explicit consent. The entity retains personal information for only as long as necessary to fulfill the stated purposes or as required by law or regulations and thereafter appropriately disposes of such information."

The criteria associated with the use, retention, and disposal principle are as follows:

- Including collection practices in the organization's privacy policies
- Informing individuals that their personal information will only be used for disclosed purposes for which the organization has obtained consent and then abiding by that statement
- Informing individuals that their data will be retained for no longer than necessary and then abiding by that statement
- Informing individuals that information that is no longer needed will be disposed of securely and then abiding by that statement

Access

One of the core elements of individual privacy is the belief that individuals should have the right to access information that an organization holds about them and, when necessary, to correct that information. The GAPP definition of the *access* principle is as follows: "The entity provides individuals with access to their personal information for review and update."

The criteria associated with the access principle are as follows:

- Including practices around access to personal information in the organization's privacy policies
- Informing individuals about the procedures for reviewing, updating, and correcting their personal information
- Providing individuals with a mechanism to determine whether the organization maintains personal information about them and to review any such information
- Authenticating an individual's identity before providing them with access to personal information
- Providing access to information in an understandable format within a reasonable period of time and either for a reasonable charge that is based on the organization's actual cost or at no cost.
- Informing individuals in writing why any requests to access or update personal information were denied and informing them of any appeal rights they may have
- Providing a mechanism for individuals to update or correct personal information and providing that updated information to third parties who received it from the organization

Disclosure to Third Parties

Some challenging privacy issues arise when organizations maintain personal information about an individual and then choose to share that information with third parties in the course of doing business. GAPP defines the *disclosure to third parties* principle as follows: "The entity discloses personal information to third parties only for the purposes identified in the notice and with the implicit or explicit consent of the individual."

The criteria associated with the disclosure to the third parties principle are as follows:

- Including third-party disclosure practices in the organization's privacy policies
- Informing individuals of any third-party disclosures that take place and the purpose of those disclosures
- Informing third parties who receive personal information from the organization that they must comply with the organization's privacy policy and handling practices
- Disclosing personal information to third parties without notice or for purposes other than those disclosed in the notice only when required to do so by law
- Disclosing information to third parties only under the auspices of an agreement that the third party will protect the information consistent with the organization's privacy policy
- Implementing procedures designed to verify that the privacy controls of third parties receiving personal information from the organization are functioning effectively
- Taking remedial action when the organization learns that a third party has mishandled personal information shared by the organization

Security for Privacy

Protecting the security of personal information is deeply entwined with protecting the privacy of that information. Organizations can't provide individuals with assurances about the handling of personal data if they can't protect that information from unauthorized access. GAPP defines *security for privacy* as follows: "The entity protects personal information against unauthorized access (both physical and logical)."

The criteria associated with the security for privacy principle are as follows:

- Including security practices in the organization's privacy policies
- Informing individuals that the organization takes precautions to protect the privacy of their personal information
- Developing, documenting, and implementing an information security program that addresses the major privacy-related areas of security listed in ISO 27002:
  - Risk assessment and treatment
  - Security policy
  - Organization of information security
  - Asset management
  - Human resources security
  - Physical and environmental security
  - Communications and operations management
  - Access control
  - Information systems acquisition, development, and maintenance

- Information security incident management
- Business continuity management
- Compliance

 This list includes the ISO 27002 elements that are relevant to privacy efforts and, therefore, our conversation. ISO 27002 does include other recommended security controls that fall outside the scope of a privacy effort.

- Restricting logical access to personal information through the use of strong identification, authentication, and authorization practices
- Restricting physical access to personal information through the use of physical security controls
- Protecting personal information from accidental disclosure due to natural disasters and other environmental hazards
- Applying strong encryption to any personal information that is transmitted over public networks
- Avoiding the storage of personal information on portable media, unless absolutely necessary, and using encryption to protect any personal information that must be stored on portable media
- Conducting periodic tests of security safeguards used to protect personal information

Quality

When we think about the issues associated with protecting the privacy of personal information, we often first think about issues related to the proper collection and use of that information along with potential unauthorized disclosure of that information. However, it's also important to consider the accuracy of that information. Individuals may be damaged by incorrect information just as much, if not more, than they might be damaged by information that is improperly handled. The GAPP *quality* principle states that "The entity maintains accurate, complete, and relevant personal information for the purposes identified in the notice."

The criteria associated with the quality principle are as follows:

- Including data quality practices in the organization's privacy policies
- Informing individuals that they bear responsibility for providing the organization with accurate and complete personal information and informing the organization if corrections are required
- Maintaining personal information that is accurate, complete, and relevant for the purposes for which it will be used

Monitoring and Enforcement

Privacy programs are not one-time projects. It's true that organizations may make a substantial initial investment of time and energy to build up their privacy practices, but those practices must be monitored over time to ensure that they continue to operate effectively and meet the organization's privacy obligations as business needs and information practices evolve. The GAPP *monitoring and enforcement* principle states that "The entity monitors compliance with its privacy policies and procedures and has procedures to address privacy-related inquires, complaints, and disputes."

The criteria associated with the monitoring and enforcement principle are as follows:

- Including monitoring and enforcement practices in the organization's privacy policies

- Informing individuals about how they should contact the organization if they have questions, complaints, or disputes regarding privacy practices

- Maintaining a dispute resolution process that ensures that every complaint is addressed and that the individual who raised the complaint is provided with a documented response

- Reviewing compliance with privacy policies, procedures, laws, regulations, and contractual obligations on an annual basis

- Developing and implementing remediation plans for any issues identified during privacy compliance reviews

- Documenting cases where privacy policies were violated and taking any necessary corrective action

- Performing ongoing monitoring of the privacy program based on a risk assessment

ISO 27018

In addition to the GAPP principles, organizations may also wish to consider adopting elements of the ISO standard related to information privacy. ISO 27018 provides a code of practice for the protection of personally identifiable information in a public cloud environment.

Direct and Indirect Identifiers

Privacy information can take many forms. In some jurisdictions, under certain laws, a person's name, date of birth, and home address are considered PII; in other countries/jurisdictions, the person's mobile phone number and IP address are PII as well; this entirely depends on the laws of those jurisdictions. These PII elements are sometimes referred to as *direct identifiers*. Direct identifiers are those data elements that immediately reveal a specific individual.

There are also *indirect identifiers*, which should also be protected. Indirect identifiers are the characteristics and traits of an individual that, when aggregated, could reveal the identity of that person. Each indirect identifier by itself is usually not sensitive, but if enough are collected, they may provide sensitive information. For example, if we take a list of indirect identifiers that are not sensitive, such as a man born in New York and currently living in Indiana who owns a dog and performs work in the information security field, we might reveal the identity of one of the authors of this book and thus derive sensitive information (an identity) from information elements that are not sensitive (location, birthplace, pets, industry, and so on).

The act of removing identifiers is known as *anonymization*; certain jurisdictions, laws, and standards require the anonymization of data, including both direct and indirect identifiers.

Privacy Impact Assessments

With a personal information inventory in hand, the organization may now turn to an assessment of the current state of its privacy program. This assessment should use a standard set of privacy practices, derived from either an industry standard framework or the regulatory requirements facing the organization.

For example, an organization might choose to adopt the privacy framework from the International Organization for Standardization titled "Security techniques—Extension to ISO/IEC 27001 and ISO/IEC 27002 for privacy information management—Requirements and guidelines" and documented in ISO 27701. An excerpt from this document appears in Figure 9.1.

FIGURE 9.1 Excerpt from ISO 27701

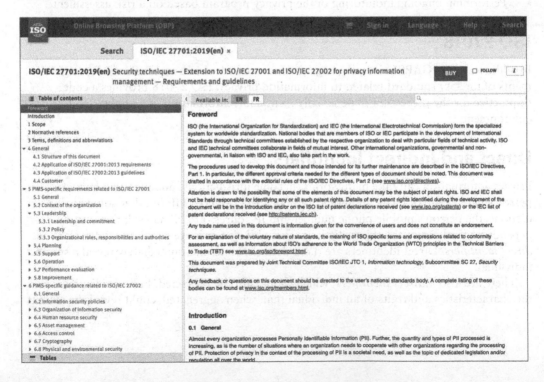

ISO 27701 is closely linked to ISO 27001 and 27002, the two ISO standards governing information security. This is another opportunity to align the interests of privacy and security programs. Annex F of ISO 27701 provides advice on applying the privacy standard in an organization that already uses the information security standards. These standards are also tightly linked to the National Institute of Standards and Technology's Cybersecurity Framework (CSF), allowing organizations to cleanly map controls between standards and frameworks that they adopt for both privacy and security.

The end result of the privacy assessment should be a *privacy impact analysis* that identifies any places where the organization's business practices handle personal information and describes the impact that those practices have on the organization's legal and ethical privacy obligations.

Cloud Forensics

Conducting forensic activity in a cloud environment is challenging. The nature of decentralized, off-premises data and its movement, storage, and processing across geopolitical boundaries all lead to a complex and perplexing environment when attempting to gather and analyze forensic data.

Forensic Requirements

The international nature of cloud forensics has created the demand for international standards that are applicable globally. Such standards help establish procedures across borders in an effort to limit the challenges to scientific findings.

ISO has developed a set of global digital forensics standards:

- **ISO/IEC 27037:2012:** Guide for collecting, identifying, and preserving electronic evidence
- **ISO/IEC 27041:2015:** Guide for incident investigations
- **ISO/IEC 27042:2015:** Guide for digital evidence analysis
- **ISO/IEC 27043:2015:** Incident investigation principles and processes
- **ISO/IEC 27050-1:2016:** Overview and principles for eDiscovery

Cloud Forensic Challenges

The distributed model of cloud computing presents a number of challenges in the area of forensics. Data location, collection mechanisms, and international laws are all factors when dealing with situations involving forensic investigations.

Do you know where your data is to start with? Are some parts of it on-premises or off-premises, and in either case, where is the data located? Is it distributed across multiple data centers, and if so, are those data centers across international boundaries? If so, do international laws hinder your ability to collect forensic information? For example, does the law in a certain country/jurisdiction prevent you from capturing certain types of data (detailed user activity records, for instance)?

Do you have a working relationship with your cloud computing vendors? Do your SLA or other contract elements delineate the rights and responsibilities for data collection and maintenance between the customer and provider? Are you authorized, as a cloud customer, to retrieve forensic data from the cloud data center? What happens if you accidentally collect another customer's data from a multitenant environment? Will your forensic tools be suitable for a virtualized environment? What level of cooperation is necessary on the part of the provider?

The answers to these questions will vary from vendor to vendor and will also depend upon the nature of the service offered, such as the service category and deployment model.

Collection and Acquisition

In traditional environments, forensic data collection is performed in a relatively contained environment (the organization's enterprise) with a single owner (the organization itself). The collection process is challenging in a traditional environment; care must be taken to ensure data is modified as little as possible and captured in a manner that is consistent, exacting, and repeatable. Certain techniques, like forensic imaging, are used to reduce the possibility that captured data is not affected while copies are made.

In the cloud environment, the practices and tools used in the traditional environment are not always feasible or useful. There are multiple owners of the resources; depending on the cloud service and deployment models, the cloud provider or the customer might have possession/ownership and/or administrative rights to certain systems/aspects of the environment. Moreover, the additional concern of third-party data (other cloud customers sharing the same underlying infrastructure) that might be affected by forensic collection complicates the process.

In many situations, forensic collection of cloud data will require the participation/involvement of the cloud provider; the customer will not be able (legally or technically or both) to capture the necessary material in a manner or with the detail required for the satisfaction of a court (where evidence gathered and analyzed forensically often ends up).

The ISO standards mentioned earlier (specifically 27037 and 27042) are excellent guides for collecting, preserving, and analyzing forensic data. However, most cloud customers (and most CCSPs) will not have the skills and tools necessary for defensible evidence collection and analysis readily available. It is highly recommended that cloud customers undertaking a forensic investigation in the cloud enlist the services of forensic professionals certified and licensed to perform those activities.

Evidence Preservation and Management

All evidence needs to be tracked and monitored from the time it is recognized as evidence and acquired for that purpose until the time it is delivered to a court or law enforcement agency. Clear documentation must record which people had access to the evidence, where the evidence was stored, what access controls were placed on the evidence, and what modifications or analysis was performed on the evidence. We call this record and the principles for creating it the *chain of custody*.

Being able to demonstrate a strong chain of custody, where only specific, trusted personnel had access to the material and with no gaps in the timeline or loss of control, is very important for making an argument in court using that evidence. Any discrepancy in the chain of custody introduces doubt as to the disposition and content of the evidence. Although this does not make the evidence inadmissible, it does allow an opportunity for opposing counsel to reduce the power of your narrative. Any doubt regarding a particular piece or set of evidence will make that evidence much weaker.

When creating policies for maintaining a chain of custody or conducting activities requiring the preservation and monitoring of evidence, it is best to get input and guidance from counsel and perhaps even to use specialized consultants who are trained and experienced in this practice area. You will also need to coordinate with your cloud providers to ensure that their chain of custody process integrates with your own.

The chain of custody provides *nonrepudiation* for the transactions detailed in the evidence. Nonrepudiation means that no party to a transaction can later claim that they did not take part.

e-discovery

Electronic discovery (e-discovery) refers to the process of identifying and obtaining electronic evidence for either prosecutorial or litigation purposes. Determining which data in a set is pertinent to a specific legal case can be difficult. Regardless of whether information is stored in databases, records, email, or files, identifying and locating applicable data can be quite challenging in the cloud due to the decentralized nature of the technology. Moreover, because cloud computing so often takes the form of a multitenant environment, there is added complication in finding data owned by a specific customer while not intruding on other customers' data that might be located in the same storage volumes, the same drives, or the same machines. Trained professionals certified in the practice of e-discovery are rare, and most organizations don't have these people in their employ. When faced with e-discovery activity, an organization probably would be best served by hiring an expert consultant who is licensed for the purpose. Anyone performing this activity should be extremely familiar with relevant industry standards and guidance, such as ISO 27050 (www.iso.org/standard/63081.html) and CSA guidance (https://cloudsecurityalliance.org/artifacts/csa-security-guidance-domain-3-legal-issues-contracts-and-electronic-discovery).

It is important for the cloud customer to be familiar with laws, SLAs, and other contractual agreements that can impact the user's ability to conduct e-discovery should the need arise. This is especially important if international boundaries are crossed in the process.

As demand for e-discovery capability increases, technology vendors have created products to meet this need. Some cloud providers offer SaaS e-discovery solutions in the form of cloud-based applications that can perform searches and collection of pertinent data (often in the provider's own cloud data center, for its own customers). There are also host-based tools that can be used to locate applicable information on specific machines (both hardware and virtualized).

Audit Processes, Methodologies, and Cloud Adaptations

An audit is a review of an environment in order to determine if that environment is compliant with a standard, law, configuration, or other mandate. The audit process in cloud computing, while very similar to the process in any other environment, does have some unique challenges, which we will explore in more detail.

Virtualization

Cloud computing requires virtualization; virtualization complicates auditing. The auditor is no longer looking at physical devices but at software instances or abstractions of devices. Even at the network layer, software-based virtual switches and routers are responsible for moving traffic around the cloud environment. That makes it hard for the auditor to identify all machines in the scope of the audit; the audit is not a simple matter of locating and enumerating tangible devices in a room, as in a traditional environment. At best, the auditor will have access to a management console with which to view the environment. This can at the very least be confusing and difficult for those unaccustomed to cloud computing.

There is also the need to understand the control mechanisms in play in a virtualized cloud environment. Virtualization requires a knowledge base that auditors unfamiliar with cloud technology will find confusing. One example is auditing access to the hypervisor. The auditor can view the accounts of the administrators but may not be able to speak to them, as they might reside in a different country.

Scope

Audit *scope* lists which elements, participants, and systems will be included in the audit. Scoping must be performed before the audit begins so that everyone involved (the auditors, the organization being audited, users, etc.) understands the breadth and depth of the audit, how long it may take, and what resources will be utilized/affected.

Defining the scope of an audit in a cloud-computing environment can also present challenges. Are you conducting an audit on the infrastructure of the cloud provider, the platform, or the applications involved? Depending on the service model you are using, audit scope can take many different forms. For instance, if you are simply using the provider as a software as a service (SaaS) vendor, should your audit scope involve the underlying infrastructure? Many vendors provide third-party audits of those services to satisfy this need so that customers' auditors can focus on the higher abstraction levels (that is, the providers' auditors will review the hardware in the data center, and the customers' auditors will review the application and usage).

Additionally, the scope of the audit may or may not be confined to geographical or geo-political boundaries. The auditor may only be auditing infrastructure as a service (IaaS) within the confines of a certain country. Anything outside these boundaries may be out of scope, depending on the engagement.

Gap Analysis

Once the audit has been completed, the audit results should show both where the organization is currently compliant and where it is not compliant. Auditors perform a control analysis against existing controls, compare those controls to a baseline standard, and then document any gaps between the existing controls and the baseline. The gap analysis is a review of the differences, in those areas where the organization is not yet compliant with the given standard/regulation. The purpose of the gap analysis is to aid in determining how to reach the desired end state (full compliance).

Generally, best practices dictate that the auditors do *not* take part in providing specific recommendations on how to close gaps—that auditors do not recommend particular technologies/systems/products for achieving compliance because this may lead to a conflict of interest (where the auditors take part in business functions, diluting their independence). Moreover, the affected departments within the organization should also not take part in the gap analysis; instead, personnel from outside the target departments should do the review, as they are more able to offer unbiased opinions and suggestions.

Restrictions of Audit Scope Statements

If an auditor feels that the organization has not disclosed sufficient information/artifacts/access for the auditor to perform a successful and fair audit, the auditor may issue a "scope limitation" statement or otherwise qualify the audit report/results. This indicates to any recipient of the audit that the auditor did not feel able to render a professional judgment due to the target organization's desire to withhold elements material to the audit.

For example, an auditor is hired to review Ostrich Inc. for PCI DSS compliance. The management of Ostrich creates an audit scope that does not allow the auditor to review the point-of-sale systems where customer credit cards are presented at the time of purchase. Because PCI DSS requires that cardholder data is protected from the time of collection, the auditor deems, in their professional opinion, that access to the point-of-sale systems is necessary to determine whether Ostrich is performing the data collection in a secure manner and whether Ostrich is compliant with the standard. When the auditor completes the audit report, they may issue a "qualified opinion," explaining that the report is not sufficient, in the auditor's estimation, to fairly and completely render a sound judgment. The auditor may also issue a "disclaimer of opinion," stating that the audit report is not complete and should not be taken as wholly accurate.

Many popular audit standards, such as Statement on Standards for Attestation Engagements (SSAE), published by the American Institute of Certified Public Accountants (AICPA), and the International Standard on Assurance Engagements (ISAE), published by the International Auditing and Assurance Standards Board (IAASB), require that auditors note any restrictions on audit scope that may materially impact the quality of the audit.

Policies

Policies provide a voice and expression of the strategic goals and objectives of senior management and play an integral role in forming the security posture of an organization.

Organizational security policies take the form of those intended to reduce exposure and minimize risk of financial and data losses as well as other types of damages, such as loss of reputation. Other typical policies include an information security policy, data classification and usage policies, an acceptable use policy (AUP), and a host of other policies related to software, malware, and so on. In addition, the CCSP should be familiar with disaster recovery and business continuity policies, vendor management or outsourcing policies, and incident response and forensic policies. All these policies are an expression of senior management's strategic goals and objectives with regard to managing and maintaining the risk profile of the organization.

In cloud computing, more emphasis may be placed on policies regarding access controls, data storage and recovery, and so on, where the cloud customer will have some semblance of control; many other policies that were applicable in the traditional IT environment (such as hardware management, personnel access to storage devices, etc.) may not be feasible in a cloud environment, as the customer does not have control over those aspects of the cloud. Those, instead, will be in the purview of the cloud provider. However, some policies that an organization may want to dedicate more time and resources to after migrating to the cloud include remote access, password management, encryption, and how duties and responsibilities are separated and managed, especially for administrators.

Audit Reports

When conducting audits or assessments of organizations that leverage the cloud, audit professionals run into some unique challenges. The use of virtualization and cloud computing raises unique assurance issues. The very fact that an organization is using service providers for the storage, processing, and/or transmission of some of its data expands the scope of the audit. If the organization is depending upon the security controls of its provider in some way (which is always the case in cloud computing!), then that provider's controls are within the scope of the audit.

This might lead you to think that the auditors would then need to travel to the cloud provider's site and verify the controls there, just as they would at the organization's own data centers. After all, they do need some assurance that the controls are functioning properly. But just imagine what that would mean. How would you visit the data centers of Microsoft, Amazon, or Google? They're distributed all over the world in different jurisdictions and, even if you knew where they were, they probably wouldn't let you in!

Even if you include a clause in your contract granting you the right to audit the controls of a cloud service provider, this is not a scalable approach. If the service provider allowed all customers to perform an annual audit, they would be constantly bombarded by auditors on a daily basis. They wouldn't be able to get any other work done!

SOC Reports

For this reason, cloud service providers conduct their own audits and provide the results to their customers. These audit reports are known as Service Organization Control reports, or SOC reports.

Exam Tip

We're going to talk about three different categories of SOC reports (SOC 1, 2, and 3) and then two different report types (Type I and Type II). This can be a little confusing, so be sure that you understand the differences before taking the exam.

SOC Report Categories

SOC 1 reports are the most common type of SOC audit report. SOC 1 reports are designed to provide customers with the assurance that they need from their service providers when conducting their own financial audits.

SOC 2 reports are designed to perform more detailed testing and evaluate the service provider's confidentiality, integrity, and availability controls. These reports often contain sensitive information and are not shared as widely as SOC 1 reports.

SOC 3 reports also look at confidentiality, integrity, and availability, but they contain only high-level information. These reports are designed for public consumption.

SOC Report Types

SOC 1 and 2 reports are further divided into types. The type of report differs based upon the type of work performed by the auditor.

Type I reports simply describe the controls that a service provider has in place and reports the auditor's opinion on the suitability of those controls. The auditor does not give an opinion on whether the controls are working in an effective way.

Type II reports contain the same opinions as Type I reports but go further and include the results of the auditor actually testing those controls to verify that they are working.

SOC Standards

The last thing that you should know about SOC audits is that they may occur under two different standards. In the United States, the American Institute of Certified Public Accountants publishes the Statement on Standards for Attestation Engagements 18 (SSAE 18) to guide SOC audits in the United States. Internationally, the International Auditing and Assurance Standards Board publishes International Standard on Assurance Engagements 3402 (ISAE 3402) for the same purpose. These standards are quite similar in scope and purpose and you won't need to get into the small differences between them on the exam.

Summary

As you have seen, the nature of international laws, standards, and regulations make cloud computing complex and at times difficult to comprehend. The International Organization for Standardization (ISO), the International Electrotechnical Commission (IEC), and the Organization for Economic Cooperation and Development (OECD) have promulgated what have become the de facto standards for information security and privacy for the vast majority of the international community outside the United States.

Inside the United States, auditors still work primarily with standards and regulations such as GLBA, PCI DSS, SSAE 18, and HIPAA. Agencies and governmental bodies continually generate these standards and regulations, making a consistent standard difficult to obtain. However, it is the CCSP's responsibility to understand all the challenges these present in order to provide sound advice when working with customers' and vendors' architectural, policy, and management efforts.

Exam Essentials

Explain the different sources of law in the United States.   Federal statutes are created by the legislative branch, after passing both houses of Congress and obtaining the signature of the president. The executive branch may create administrative law to assist in the interpretation and enforcement of statutes. The judicial branch reviews, applies, and interprets both legislative and administrative law, creating a body of case law.

Explain the difference between criminal and civil liability.   Liability is what allows one party to take action against another party in court. Criminal liability occurs when a person violates a criminal law. If a person is found guilty of a criminal law violation, they may be deprived of their liberty through imprisonment. *Civil liability* occurs when one person claims that another person has failed to carry out a legal duty that they were responsible for fulfilling.

Describe the four elements of the tort of negligence.   Negligence is a commonly occurring tort that occurs when one party causes harm to another party by their action or lack of action. The theory of liability for negligence involves four elements. First, there must be a duty of care. Second, there must be a breach of that duty of care. Third, there must be damages involved, and fourth, there must be causation.

Explain the chain of custody.   When gathering forensic evidence for possible use in court, investigators must document how and when they collected the evidence and every time someone handles the evidence between collection and presentation in the courtroom. This is known as documenting the chain of custody to demonstrate that evidence was properly managed at all times.

Understand the purpose of e-discovery.   When an organization is subject to a lawsuit, it must preserve any records related to the matter at hand. Electronic discovery e-discovery programs provide a process and mechanism for collecting and retaining that information. In cloud environments, eDiscovery may be guided by ISO 27050 and guidance from the Cloud Security Alliance (CSA).

Describe the types of sensitive information.   Organizations may handle many types of sensitive information in the cloud. This includes information about individuals, known as personally identifiable information (PII). It also includes information about healthcare, known as protected health information (PHI), and payment card information.

Explain the major laws that govern security and privacy in the cloud.   Security and privacy efforts in the cloud are subject to many different laws and regulations. Healthcare organizations are subject to the Health Insurance Portability and Accountability Act (HIPAA). Financial institutions are subject to the Gramm–Leach–Bliley Act (GLBA). Publicly traded companies are subject to the Sarbanes–Oxley Act (SOX). Organizations doing business in the European Union are subject to the General Data Protection Regulation (GDPR).

Review Questions

You can find the answers to the review questions in Appendix A.

1. Katie is assessing her organization's privacy practices and determines that the organization previously collected customer addresses for the purpose of shipping goods and is now using those addresses to mail promotional materials. If this possibility was not previously disclosed, what privacy principle is the organization most likely violating?

   A. Quality

   B. Management

   C. Notice

   D. Security

2. Kara is the chief privacy officer of an organization that maintains a database of customer information for marketing purposes. What term best describes the role of Kara's organization with respect to that database?

   A. Data subject

   B. Data custodian

   C. Data controller

   D. Data processor

3. Richard would like to use an industry standard reference for designing his organization's privacy controls. Which one of the following ISO standards is best suited for this purpose?

   A. ISO 27001

   B. ISO 27002

   C. ISO 27701

   D. ISO 27702

4. When designing privacy controls, an organization should be informed by the results of what type of analysis?

   A. Impact analysis

   B. Gap analysis

   C. Business analysis

   D. Authorization analysis

5. State data breach notification laws may require organizations to notify which of the following parties?

   A. Consumers impacted by the breach

   B. State regulatory authorities

   C. National credit reporting agencies

   D. All of the above

6. Which of the following is *not* a potential consequence an organization may face under state law following a breach?

    A. An obligation to provide free credit monitoring to affected consumers

    B. Enforcement actions, including penalties, from state attorneys general

    C. Civil actions brought by consumers under a private right of action

    D. Criminal prosecution of company employees who allowed the breach to occur

7. MediRecs Co. provides secure server space to help healthcare providers store medical records. MediRecs would be best described under HIPAA as which of the following?

    A. Service provider

    B. Business associate

    C. Covered partner

    D. Covered entity

8. Dimitri cashed a paycheck at County Bank three months ago, but he doesn't have an account there and hasn't been back since. Under GLBA, County Bank should consider Dimitri as which of the following?

    A. Customer

    B. Consumer

    C. Visitor

    D. No relationship with the bank

9. Which amendment to the U.S. Constitution explicitly grants individuals the right to privacy?

    A. First Amendment

    B. Fourth Amendment

    C. Fifth Amendment

    D. None of the above

10. What source contains much of the administrative law created by the U.S. government?

    A. U.S. Code

    B. Bill of Rights

    C. Code of Federal Regulations

    D. U.S. Constitution

11. During a negligence lawsuit, the court determined that the respondent was not at fault because the plaintiff did not present evidence that they suffered some form of harm. What element of negligence was missing from this case?

    A. Duty of care

    B. Breach of duty

    C. Causation

    D. Damages

12. Which one of the following elements is *not* always required for the creation of a legal contract?

    A. An offer

    B. Acceptance of an offer

    C. Written agreement

    D. Consideration

13. What category of law best describes the HIPAA Privacy Rule?

    A. Constitutional law

    B. Common law

    C. Legislative law

    D. Administrative law

14. Which statute addresses security and privacy matters in the U.S. financial industry?

    A. GLBA

    B. FERPA

    C. SOX

    D. HIPAA

15. The right to be forgotten refers to which of the following?

    A. The right to no longer pay taxes

    B. Erasing criminal history

    C. The right to have all of a data subject's data erased

    D. Masking

16. Which one of the following organizations is least likely to be subject to the requirements of HIPAA?

    A. Health insurance company

    B. Hospital

    C. Medical device manufacturer

    D. Health information clearinghouse

17. Which one of the following options is no longer valid for protecting the transfer of personal information between the European Union and other nations?

    A. Adequacy decisions

    B. EU/US Privacy Shield

    C. Binding Corporate Rules

    D. Standard Contractual Clauses

18. Which one of the following is not a law that would concern cloud security professionals?

    A. GLBA

    B. HIPAA

    C. PCI DSS

    D. SOX

19. What standard governs SOC audits that occur within the United States?

    A. SSAE 16

    B. SSAE 18

    C. ISAE 3402

    D. ISAE 3602

20. You are considering working with a cloud provider and would like to review the results of an audit that contains detailed information on security controls. The provider requires that you sign an NDA before reviewing the material. What category of report are you likely reviewing?

    A. SOC 1

    B. SOC 2

    C. SOC 3

    D. SOC 4

Chapter 10

Cloud Vendor Management

THE OBJECTIVE OF THIS CHAPTER IS TO ACQUAINT THE READER WITH THE FOLLOWING CONCEPTS:

✓ **Domain 1: Cloud Concepts, Architecture, and Design**

■ 1.5. Evaluate cloud service providers

■ 1.5.1 Verification against criteria (e.g., International Organization for Standardization/International Electrotechnical Commission (ISO/IEC) 27017, Payment Card Industry Data Security Standard (PCI DSS))

■ 1.5.2. System/Subsystem Product Certifications (e.g., Common Criteria (CC), Federal Information Processing Standard (FIPS) 140-2)

✓ **Domain 5: Cloud Security Operations**

■ 5.4. Implement Operational Controls and Standards

■ 5.4.10. Service Level Management

■ 5.5. Manage Communication with Relevant Parties

■ 5.5.1. Vendors

■ 5.5.2. Customers

■ 5.5.3. Partners

■ 5.5.4. Regulators

■ 5.5.5. Other Stakeholders

✓ **Domain 6: Legal, Risk, and Compliance**

■ 6.3. Understand Audit Process, Methodologies, and Required Adaptations for a Cloud Environment

■ 6.3.10. Policies (e.g., organizational, functional, cloud computing)

Vendor relationships are everything in the cloud. As organizations place critical business processes and sensitive business information in the hands of cloud providers, they must have confidence that the vendor is managing risk appropriately and will be able to fulfill their obligations.

In this chapter, you will learn the importance of managing vendor relationships as part of a broader enterprise risk management (ERM) program. You'll learn practical tools and techniques that you can use to build strong vendor relationships.

The Impact of Diverse Geographical Locations and Legal Jurisdictions

As discussed in Chapter 9, "Legal and Compliance Issues," the impact of the decentralized and geographically and geopolitically distributed model of cloud computing presents numerous challenges, including these:

- Data processing, storage, and computing, each occurring in different geopolitical realms
- Difficulties in assessing data actors
- Difficulties in locating data

A great deal of the difficulty in managing the legal ramifications of cloud computing stems from the design of cloud assets. They are necessarily dispersed, often across municipal, state, and even international borders. Resources are constantly being allocated and reallocated on a moment-to-moment basis. Also, specific control and administration of particular assets can be hard to ascertain and establish.

It is that transborder aspect that is most troublesome, in terms of allowing the cloud customer to maintain compliance with legal and regulatory mandates. As we discussed in Chapter 9, each jurisdiction can have its own requirements, which can vary significantly from jurisdiction to jurisdiction, and jurisdictions can overlap. A city is in a county or other municipality, the latter of which is in a state or province, which is in a country, and they might all have conflicting guidance and interests. Moreover, legislation and guidance is always in flux, especially in our industry. Lawmakers and standards bodies are constantly trying to catch up to the requirements and questions posed by new technologies and how those technologies are used. And these differences of law affect not only the cloud customer, in terms of how the customer must behave and respond to legal action, but also how the cloud provider must perform in response.

The governance used by both entities—the cloud customer and the cloud provider—must take all of this into account in order to operate reasonably with acknowledgment of legal risks and liabilities in the cloud.

It is important to not confuse the concepts of "governance" and "corporate governance." Governance refers to the legal and regulatory mandates of regions and countries. Corporate governance is the relationship between shareholders and other stakeholders in the organization versus the senior management of the corporation.

Security Policy Framework

An organization's *information security policy framework* contains a series of documents designed to describe the organization's cybersecurity program. The scope and complexity of these documents vary widely, depending on the nature of the organization and its information resources. These frameworks generally include four different types of documents:

- Policies
- Standards
- Procedures
- Guidelines

In the following sections, you'll learn the differences between these document types. However, keep in mind that the definitions of these categories vary significantly from organization to organization and it is very common to find the lines between them blurred. Though at first glance that may seem incorrect, it's a natural occurrence as security theory meets the real world. As long as the documents are achieving their desired purpose, there's no harm in using whatever naming system is preferred in your organization.

Policies

Policies are broad statements of management intent. Compliance with policies is mandatory. An information security policy will generally contain generalized statements about cybersecurity objectives, including the following:

- A statement of the importance of cybersecurity to the organization
- Requirements that all staff and contracts take measures to protect the confidentiality, integrity, and availability of information and information systems

- Statement on the ownership of information created and/or possessed by the organization
- Designation of the chief information security officer (CISO) or other individual as the executive responsible for cybersecurity issues
- Delegation of authority granting the CISO the ability to create standards, procedures, and guidelines that implement the policy

In many organizations, the process to create a policy is laborious and requires senior management approval, often from the chief executive officer (CEO). Keeping policy statements broadly worded provides the CISO with the flexibility to adapt and change specific security requirements with changes in the business and technology environments. For example, the five-page information security policy at the University of Notre Dame simply states:

> The Information Governance Committee will create handling standards for each Highly Sensitive data element. Data stewards may create standards for other data elements under their stewardship. These information handling standards will specify controls to manage risks to University information and related assets based on their classification. All individuals at the University are responsible for complying with these controls.

This type of policy allows an organization to maintain a high-level document and use it to guide the development of standards, procedures, and guidelines that remain in alignment with enterprise goals and objectives.

By way of contrast, the federal government's Centers for Medicare & Medicaid Services (CMS) has a 95-page information security policy. This mammoth document contains incredibly detailed requirements, such as:

> A record of all requests for monitoring must be maintained by the CMS CIO along with any other summary results or documentation produced during the period of monitoring. The record must also reflect the scope of the monitoring by documenting search terms and techniques. All information collected from monitoring must be controlled and protected with distribution limited to the individuals identified in the request for monitoring and other individuals specifically designated by the CMS Administrator or CMS CIO as having a specific need to know such information.

The CMS document even goes so far as to include a complex chart describing the many cybersecurity roles held by individuals throughout the agency. An excerpt from that chart appears in Figure 10.1.

This approach may meet the needs of CMS, but it is hard to imagine the long-term maintenance of that document. Lengthy security policies often quickly become outdated as necessary changes to individual requirements accumulate and become neglected because staff are weary of continually publishing new versions of the policy.

FIGURE 10.1   Excerpt from CMS roles and responsibilities chart

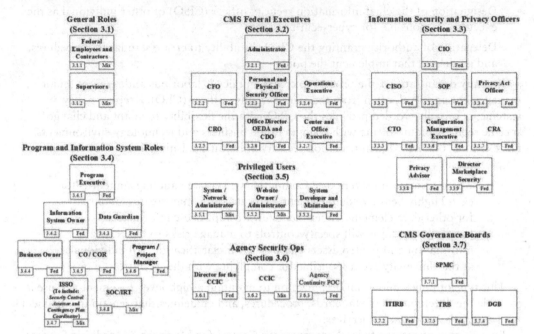

Source: Centers for Medicare and Medicaid Services Information Systems Security and Privacy Policy, May 21, 2019. (www.cms.gov/Research-Statistics-Data-and-Systems/CMS-Information-Technology/InformationSecurity/Downloads/CMS-IS2P2.pdf)

Standards

Standards provide mandatory requirements describing how an organization will carry out its information security policies. These may include the specific configuration settings used for a common operating system, the controls that must be put in place for highly sensitive information, or any other security objective. Standards are typically approved at a lower organizational level than policies and, therefore, may change more regularly. Organizations may choose to develop their own standards, adopt standards created by external groups, or use a hybrid approach where they modify existing standards to meet their needs.

For example, the University of California (UC), Berkeley maintains a detailed document titled the *Minimum Security Standards for Electronic Information*, available at https://security.berkeley.edu/minimum-security-standards-electronic-information. This document divides information into four different data protection levels (DPLs) and then describes what controls are required, optional, and not required for data at different levels, using a detailed matrix. An excerpt from this matrix appears in Figure 10.2.

FIGURE 10.2 Excerpt from UC Berkeley Minimum Security Standards for Electronic Information

MSSEI Controls	DPL 0 (TBD)	DPL 1 Individual	DPL 1 Privileged	DPL 1 Institutional	DPL 2 Individual	DPL 2 Privileged	DPL 2 Institutional	DPL 3 (TBD)	Guidelines
1.1 Removal of non-required covered data		o	√	√	√	√	√		see secure deletion guideline and UCOP disposition schedules database
1.2 Covered system inventory			√	√		√	√		1.2 guideline
1.3 Covered system registration			+	√		√	√		1.3 guideline
1.4 Annual registration renewal			√	√		√	√		1.4 guideline
2.1 Managed software inventory			+	√	o	√	√		2.1 guideline
3.1 Secure configurations	o		+	√	√	√	√		3.1 guideline
4.1 Continuous vulnerability assessment & remediation			+	√		√	√		4.1 guideline

Source: University of California at Berkeley Minimum Security Standards for Electronic Information

The standard then provides detailed descriptions for each of these requirements with definitions of the terms used in the requirements. For example, requirement 3.1 in Figure 10.2 simply reads "Secure configurations." Later in the document, UC Berkeley expands this to read "Resource Custodians must utilize well-managed security configurations for hardware, software, and operating systems based on industry standards." It goes on to defines "well-managed" as including the following:

- Devices must have secure configurations in place prior to deployment.

- Any deviations from defined security configurations must be approved through a change management process and documented. A process must exist to annually review deviations from the defined security configurations for continued relevance.

- A process must exist to regularly check configurations of devices and alert the Resource Custodian of any changes.

This approach provides a document hierarchy that is easy to navigate for the reader and provides access to increasing levels of detail as needed. Notice also that many of the requirement lines in Figure 10.2 offer links to guidelines. Clicking those links leads to advice to organizations subject to this policy that begins with this text:

> UC Berkeley security policy mandates compliance with Minimum Security Standards for Electronic Information for devices handling covered data. The recommendations below are provided as optional guidance.

This is a perfect example of three elements of the information security policy framework working together. Policy sets out the broad objectives of the security program and requires compliance with standards, which includes details of required security controls. Guidelines, discussed later in this chapter, provide advice to organizations seeking to comply with the policy and standards.

In some cases, organizations may encounter industry-specific standards. These best practices, developed by industry groups, are custom-tailored to the needs of the industry. In some heavily regulated industries, compliance with these standards may be required by law or contractual agreement. In other fields, the standards are just helpful resources. Failure to follow industry best practices may be seen as negligence and can cause legal liability for the organization.

Procedures

Procedures are detailed, step-by-step processes that individuals and organizations must follow in specific circumstances. Similar to checklists, procedures ensure a consistent process for achieving a security objective. Organizations may create procedures for building new systems, releasing code to production environments, responding to security incidents, and many other tasks. Compliance with procedures is mandatory.

For example, Visa publishes a document titled *What To Do If Compromised* (`https://usa.visa.com/dam/VCOM/download/merchants/cisp-what-to-do-if-compromised.pdf`) that lays out a mandatory process that merchants suspecting a credit card compromise must follow. Although the document doesn't contain the word "procedure" in the title, the introduction clearly states that the document "establishes procedures and timelines for reporting and responding to a suspected or confirmed Compromise Event." The document provides requirements covering the following areas of incident response:

- Notify Visa of the incident within three days.
- Provide Visa with an initial investigation report.
- Provide notice to other relevant parties.
- Provide exposed payment account data to Visa.
- Conduct PCI forensic investigation.
- Conduct independent investigation.
- Preserve evidence.

Each of these sections provides detailed information on how Visa expects merchants to handle incident response activities. For example, the forensic investigation section describes the use of Payment Card Industry Forensic Investigators (PFIs) and reads as follows:

> Upon discovery of an account data compromise, or receipt of an independent forensic investigation notification, an entity must:
>
> - Engage a PFI (or sign a contract) within five (5) business days.

- Provide Visa with the initial forensic (i.e., preliminary) report within ten (10) business days from when the PFI is engaged (or the contract is signed).

- Provide Visa with a final forensic report within ten (10) business days of the completion of the review.

There's not much room for interpretation in this type of language. Visa is laying out a clear and mandatory procedure describing what actions the merchant must take, the type of investigator they should hire, and the timeline for completing different milestones.

Organizations commonly include the following procedures in their policy frameworks:

- *Monitoring procedures* that describe how the organization will perform security monitoring activities, including the possible use of continuous monitoring technology

- *Evidence production procedures* that describe how the organization will respond to subpoenas, court orders, and other legitimate requests to produce digital evidence

- *Patching procedures* that describe the frequency and process of applying patches to applications and systems under the organization's care

Of course, cybersecurity teams may decide to include many other types of procedures in their frameworks, as dictated by the organization's operational needs.

Guidelines

Guidelines provide best practices and recommendations related to a given concept, technology, or task. Compliance with guidelines is not mandatory, and guidelines are offered in the spirit of providing helpful advice. That said, the "optionality" of guidelines may vary significantly depending on the organization's culture.

In April 2016, the chief information officer (CIO) of the state of Washington published a 25-page document providing guidelines on the use of electronic signatures by state agencies. The document is not designed to be obligatory but, rather, offers advice to agencies seeking to adopt electronic signature technology. The document begins with a purpose section that outlines three goals of guidelines:

1. Help agencies determine if, and to what extent, their agency will implement and rely on electronic records and electronic signatures.

2. Provide agencies with information they can use to establish policy or rules governing their use and acceptance of digital signatures.

3. Provide direction to agencies for sharing of their policies with the Office of the Chief Information Officer (OCIO) pursuant to state law.

The first two stated objectives line up completely with the function of a guideline. Phrases like "help agencies determine" and "provide agencies with information" are common in guideline documents. There is nothing mandatory about them, and in fact, the guidelines explicitly state that Washington state law "does not mandate that any state agency accept or require electronic signatures or records."

The third objective might seem a little strange to include in a guideline. Phrases like "provide direction" are more commonly found in policies and procedures. Browsing through the document, we found that the text relating to this objective is only a single paragraph within a 25-page document:

> The Office of the Chief Information Officer maintains a page on the OCIO
> .wa.gov website listing links to individual agency electronic signature
> and record submission policies. As agencies publish their policies, the link
> and agency contact information should be emailed to the OCIO Policy
> Mailbox. The information will be added to the page within 5 working
> days. Agencies are responsible for notifying the OCIO if the information
> changes.

As you read this paragraph, you'll see that the text does appear to clearly outline a mandatory procedure and would not be appropriate in a guideline document that fits within the strict definition of the term. However, it is likely that the committee drafting this document thought it would be much more convenient to the reader to include this explanatory text in the related guideline rather than drafting a separate procedure document for a fairly mundane and simple task.

    The full Washington state document, *Electronic Signature Guidelines*, is available for download from the Washington state CIO's website at https://ocio.wa.gov/sites/default/files/Electronic_Signature_Guidelines_FINAL.pdf.

Exceptions and Compensating Controls

When adopting new security policies, standards, and procedures, organizations should also provide a mechanism for exceptions to those rules. Inevitably, unforeseen circumstances will arise that require a deviation from the requirements. The policy framework should lay out the specific requirements for receiving an exception and the individual or committee with the authority to approve exceptions.

The state of Washington uses an exception process that requires that the requestor document the following information:

- Standard/requirement that requires an exception
- Reason for noncompliance with the requirement
- Business and/or technical justification for the exception
- Scope and duration of the exception
- Risks associated with the exception
- Description of any supplemental controls that mitigate the risks associated with the exception

- Plan for achieving compliance
- Identification of any unmitigated risks

Many exception processes require the use of *compensating controls* to mitigate the risk associated with exceptions to security standards. The Payment Card Industry Data Security Standard (PCI DSS) includes one of the most formal compensating control processes in use today. It sets out three criteria that must be met for a compensating control to be satisfactory:

1. The control must meet the intent and rigor of the original requirement.
2. The control must provide a similar level of defense as the original requirement such that the compensating control sufficiently offsets the risk that the original PCI DSS requirement was designed to defend against.
3. The control must be "above and beyond" other PCI DSS requirements.

For example, an organization might find that it needs to run an outdated version of an operating system on a specific machine because software necessary to run the business will only function on that operating system version. Most security policies would prohibit using the outdated operating system because it might be susceptible to security vulnerabilities. The organization could choose to run this system on an isolated network with either very little or no access to other systems as a compensating control.

The general idea is that a compensating control finds alternative means to achieve an objective when the organization cannot meet the original control requirement. Although PCI DSS offers a very formal process for compensating controls, the use of compensating controls is a common strategy in many different organizations, even those not subject to PCI DSS. Compensating controls balance the fact that it simply isn't possible to implement every required security control in every circumstance with the desire to manage risk to the greatest feasible degree.

In many cases, organizations adopt compensating controls to address a temporary exception to a security requirement. In those cases, the organization should also develop remediation plans designed to bring the organization back into compliance with the letter and intent of the original control.

Developing Policies

When developing new policies, cybersecurity managers should align their work with any other policy development mechanisms that may exist within their organization. The more that a leader is able to align cybersecurity policy efforts with existing processes, the easier it will be to gain traction for those initiatives. In any event, cybersecurity managers should follow a few key principles when working on policy development initiatives:

Obtain input from all relevant stakeholders. Think carefully about all of the leaders and teams that might be affected by the policy and work to understand their perspective while crafting the policy. This doesn't mean that everyone in the organization must agree with a proposed policy; it means that everyone should feel that their input was solicited and heard during the process.

Follow the chain of command.   Knowledge of the organizational structure is essential to the success of a policy initiative. Cybersecurity managers must be aware of the formal governance lines of authority as well as the informal mechanisms of the organization for getting things done.

Accommodate the organizational culture.   There's a good reason that there isn't a one-size-fits-all security policy that every organization can adopt. That's because every organization is different. Make sure the policies you create fit into the organizational culture and match the "tone at the top" from other leaders.

Meet internal and external requirements.   Cybersecurity programs are heavily regulated, both by internal governance processes and by external laws and regulations. In many cases, these requirements may dictate some of the contents of security policies. At the very least, security policies should not contradict these requirements.

After a policy is drafted, it should move through the policy approval mechanisms used by the organization. After the policy receives final sign-off, the cybersecurity manager may then communicate the policy to affected individuals and teams and begin the process of implementing it. Depending on the nature of the change, this may involve using a phased approach that allows the organization to gradually adapt to the new requirements.

Enterprise Risk Management

Organizations face an almost dizzying array of cybersecurity risks, ranging from the reputational and financial damage associated with a breach of personal information to the operational issues caused by a natural disaster. The discipline of risk management seeks to bring order to the process of identifying and addressing these risks.

We operate in a world full of risks. If you left your home and drove to your office this morning, you encountered a large number of risks. You could have been involved in an automobile accident, encountered a train delay, or been struck by a bicycle on the sidewalk. We're aware of these risks in the back of our minds, but we don't let them paralyze us. Instead, we take simple precautions to help manage the risks that we think have the greatest potential to disrupt our lives.

In an *enterprise risk management (ERM)* program, organizations take a formal approach to risk analysis that begins with identifying risks, continues with determining the severity of each risk, and then results in adopting one or more *risk management* strategies to address each risk.

Before we move too deeply into the risk assessment process, let's define a few important terms that we'll use during our discussion:

- *Threats* are any possible events that might have an adverse impact on the confidentiality, integrity, and/or availability of our information or information systems.

- *Vulnerabilities* are weaknesses in our systems or controls that could be exploited by a threat.

- *Risks* occur at the intersection of a vulnerability and a threat that might exploit that vulnerability. A threat without a corresponding vulnerability does not pose a risk, nor does a vulnerability without a corresponding threat.

Figure 10.3 illustrates this relationship between threats, vulnerabilities, and risks.

FIGURE 10.3   Risk exists at the intersection of a threat and a corresponding vulnerability.

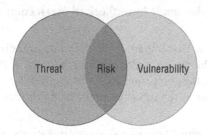

Consider the example from earlier of walking down the sidewalk on your way to work after parking your car. The fact that you are on the sidewalk without any protection is a vulnerability. A bicycle speeding down that sidewalk is a threat. The result of this combination of factors is that you are at risk of being hit by the bicycle on the sidewalk. If you remove the vulnerability by parking in a garage beneath your building, you are no longer at risk for that particular threat. Similarly, if the city erects barriers that prevent bicycles from entering the sidewalk, you are also no longer at risk. Of course, your new situation may introduce *new* threats, such as the parking garage collapsing!

Let's consider another example drawn from the cybersecurity domain. Organizations regularly conduct vulnerability scans designed to identify potential vulnerabilities in their environment. One of these scans might identify a server that exposes TCP port 22 to the world, allowing brute-force SSH attempts by an attacker. Exposing port 22 presents a vulnerability to a brute-force attack. An attacker with a brute-force scanning tool presents a threat. The combination of the port exposure and the existence of attackers presents a risk.

In this case, you don't have any way to eliminate attackers, so you can't really address the threat, but you do have control over the services running on your systems. If you shut down the SSH service and close port 22, you eliminate the vulnerability and, therefore, also eliminate the risk.

Of course, we can't always completely eliminate a risk because it isn't always feasible to shut down services. We might decide instead to take actions that reduce the risk. We'll talk more about those options when we get to risk management strategies later in this chapter.

Risk Identification

The *risk identification process* requires identifying the threats and vulnerabilities that exist in your operating environment. These risks may come from a wide variety of sources ranging from malicious hackers to hurricanes. Consider some of the different categories of risk facing organizations:

- *External risks* are those risks that originate from a source outside the organization. This is an extremely broad category of risk, including cybersecurity adversaries, malicious code, and natural disasters, among many other types of risk.

- *Internal risks* are those risks that originate from within the organization. They include malicious insiders, mistakes made by authorized users, equipment failures, and similar risks.

- *Multiparty risks* are those that impact more than one organization. For example, a power outage to a city block is a multiparty risk because it affects all of the buildings on that block. Similarly, the compromise of a SaaS provider's database is a multiparty risk because it compromises the information of many different customers of the SaaS provider.

- *Legacy systems* pose a unique type of risk to organizations. These outdated systems often do not receive security updates, and cybersecurity professionals must take extraordinary measures to protect them against unpatchable vulnerabilities.

- *Intellectual property (IP) theft* risks occur when a company possesses trade secrets or other proprietary information that, if disclosed, could compromise the organization's business advantage.

- *Software compliance/licensing risks* occur when an organization licenses software from a vendor and intentionally or accidentally runs afoul of usage limitations that expose the customer to financial and legal risk.

This is not an exhaustive list of all the possible types of risk facing your organization. It's intended to help illustrate the different types of risk that exist as a starting point for your own risk analysis based on the specific situations facing your organization.

Risk Calculation

Not all risks are equal. Returning to the example of a pedestrian on the street, the risk of being hit by a bicycle is far more worrisome than the risk of being struck down by a meteor. That makes intuitive sense, but let's explore the underlying thought process that leads to that conclusion. It's a process called *risk calculation*.

When we evaluate any risk, we do so by using two different factors:

- The *likelihood of occurrence*, or probability, that the risk will occur. We might express this as the percentage of chance that a threat will exploit a vulnerability over a specified period of time, such as within the next year.

- The magnitude of the *impact* that the risk will have on the organization if it does occur. We might express this as the financial cost that we will incur as the result of a risk, although there are other possible measures.

Using these two factors, we can assign each risk a conceptual score by combining the probability and the magnitude. This leads many risk analysts to express the severity of a risk using this formula:

$$\text{Risk Severity} = \text{Likelihood} \times \text{Impact}$$

It's important to point out that this equation does not always have to be interpreted literally. Although you may wind up multiplying these values together in some risk assessment processes, it's best to think of this conceptually as combining the likelihood and impact to determine the severity of a risk.

When we assess the risks of being struck by a bicycle or a meteor on the street, we can use these factors to evaluate the risk severity. There might be a high probability that we will be struck by a bicycle. That type of accident might have a moderate magnitude, leaving us willing to consider taking steps to reduce our risk. Being struck by a meteor would clearly have a catastrophic magnitude of impact, but the probability of such an incident is incredibly low, leading us to acknowledge the risk and move on without changing our behavior.

The laws and regulations facing an industry may play a significant role in determining the impact of a risk. For example, an organization subject to the European Union's General Data Protection Regulation (GDPR) faces significant fines if it has a data breach affecting the personal information of EU residents. The size of these fines would factor significantly into the impact assessment of the risk of a privacy breach. Organizations must, therefore, remain current on the regulations that affect their risk posture.

Risk Assessment

Risk assessments are a formalized approach to risk prioritization that allows organizations to conduct their reviews in a structured manner. Risk assessments follow two different analysis methodologies:

- *Quantitative risk assessments* use numeric data in the analysis, resulting in assessments that allow the very straightforward prioritization of risks.

- *Qualitative risk assessments* substitute subjective judgments and categories for strict numerical analysis, allowing the assessment of risks that are difficult to quantify.

As organizations seek to provide clear communication of risk factors to stakeholders, they often combine elements of quantitative and qualitative risk assessments. Let's review each of these approaches.

Quantitative Risk Assessment

Most quantitative risk assessment processes follow a similar methodology that includes the following steps:

1. *Determine the asset value (AV) of the asset affected by the risk*. This *asset value (AV)* is expressed in dollars, or other currency, and may be determined using the cost to acquire the asset, the cost to replace the asset, or the depreciated cost of the asset, depending on the organization's preferences.

2. *Determine the likelihood that the risk will occur*. Risk analysts consult subject matter experts and determine the likelihood that a risk will occur in a given year. This is expressed as the number of times the risk is expected each year and is described as the *annualized rate of occurrence (ARO)*. A risk that is expected to occur twice a year has an ARO of 2.0, whereas a risk that is expected once every 100 years has an ARO of 0.01.

3. *Determine the amount of damage that will occur to the asset if the risk materializes*. This is known as the *exposure factor (EF)* and is expressed as the percentage of the asset expected to be damaged. The exposure factor of a risk that would completely destroy an asset is 100 percent, whereas a risk that would damage half of an asset has an EF of 50 percent.

4. *Calculate the single loss expectancy*. The *single loss expectancy (SLE)* is the amount of financial damage expected each time this specific risk materializes. It is calculated by multiplying the AV by the EF.

5. *Calculate the annualized loss expectancy*. The *annualized loss expectancy (ALE)* is the amount of damage expected from a risk each year. It is calculated by multiplying the SLE and the ARO.

It's important to note that these steps assess the quantitative scale of a single risk—that is, one combination of a threat and a vulnerability. Organizations conducting quantitative risk assessments would repeat this process for every possible threat/vulnerability combination.

Let's walk through an example of a quantitative risk assessment. Imagine that you are concerned about the risk associated with a denial-of-service (DoS) attack against your email server. Your organization uses that server to send email messages to customers offering products for sale. It generates $1,000 in sales per hour that it is in operation. After consulting threat intelligence sources, you believe that a DoS attack is likely to occur three times a year and last for three hours before you are able to control it.

The asset in this case is not the server itself, because the server will not be physically damaged. The asset is the ability to send email, and you have already determined that it is worth $1,000 per hour. The asset value for three hours of server operation is, therefore, $3,000.

Your threat intelligence estimates that the risk will occur three times per year, making your annualized rate of occurrence 3.0.

After consulting your email team, you believe that the server would operate at 10 percent capacity during a DoS attack, as some legitimate messages would get out. Therefore, your exposure factor is 90 percent, because 90 percent of the capacity would be consumed by the attack.

Your single loss expectancy is calculated by multiplying the asset value ($3,000) by the exposure factor (90 percent) to get the expected loss during each attack. This gives you an SLE of $2,700.

Your annualized loss expectancy is the product of the SLE ($2,700) and the ARO (3.0), or $8,100.

Organizations can use the ALEs that result from a quantitative risk assessment to prioritize their remediation activities and determine the appropriate level of investment in controls that mitigate risks. This implements a cost/benefit approach to risk management. For example, it would not normally make sense (at least in a strictly financial sense) to spend more than the ALE on an annual basis to protect against a risk. In the previous example, if a denial-of-service prevention service would block all of those attacks, it would make financial sense to purchase it if the cost is less than $8,100 per year.

Qualitative Risk Assessment

Quantitative techniques work very well for evaluating financial risks and other risks that can be clearly expressed in numeric terms. Many risks, however, do not easily lend themselves to quantitative analysis. For example, how would you describe reputational damage, public health and safety, or employee morale in quantitative terms? You might be able to draw some inferences that tie these issues back to financial data, but the bottom line is that quantitative techniques simply aren't well suited to evaluating these risks.

Qualitative risk assessment techniques seek to overcome the limitations of quantitative techniques by substituting subjective judgment for objective data. Qualitative techniques still use the same probability and magnitude factors to evaluate the severity of a risk but do so using subjective categories. For example, Figure 10.4 shows a simple qualitative risk assessment that evaluates the probability and magnitude of several risks on a subjective Low/Medium/High scale. Risks are placed on this chart based on the judgments made by subject matter experts.

FIGURE 10.4 Qualitative risk assessments use subjective rating scales to evaluate probability and magnitude.

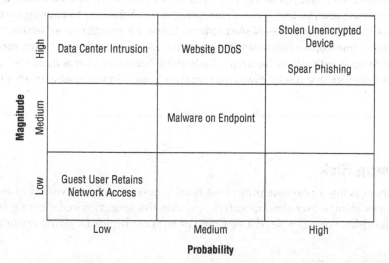

Although it's not possible to directly calculate the financial impact of risks that are assessed using qualitative techniques, this risk assessment scale makes it possible to prioritize risks. For example, reviewing the risk assessment in Figure 10.4, we can determine that the greatest risks facing this organization are stolen unencrypted devices and spear phishing attacks. Both of these risks share a high probability and high magnitude of impact. If we're considering using funds to add better physical security to the data center, this risk assessment informs us that our time and money would likely be better spent on full-disk encryption for mobile devices and a secure email gateway.

Exam Note

Many organizations combine quantitative and qualitative techniques to get a comprehensive perspective of both the tangible and intangible risks that they face.

Supply Chain Assessment

When evaluating the risks to your organization, don't forget about the risks that occur based on third-party relationships. You rely on many different vendors to protect the confidentiality, integrity, and availability of your data. Performing vendor due diligence is a crucial security responsibility.

For example, how many cloud service providers handle your organization's sensitive information? Those vendors become a crucial part of your supply chain from both operational and security perspectives. If they don't have adequate security controls in place, your data is at risk.

Similarly, the hardware that you use in your organization comes through a supply chain as well. How certain are you that it wasn't tampered with on the way to your organization? Documents leaked by former NSA contractor Edward Snowden revealed that the U.S. government intercepted hardware shipments to foreign countries and implanted malicious code deep within their hardware. Performing hardware source authenticity assessments validates that the hardware you received was not tampered with after leaving the vendor.

Reassessing Risk

Risk assessment is not a one-time project—it is an ongoing process. A variety of internal and external factors change over time, modifying existing risk scenarios and creating entirely new potential risks. For example, if a new type of attacker begins targeting organizations in your industry, that is a new risk factor that should prompt a reassessment of risk. Similarly, if you enter a new line of business, that also creates new potential risks.

Risk managers should monitor the internal and external environment for changes in circumstance that require risk reassessment. These might include changes in the threat landscape, evolving regulatory requirements, or even geopolitical changes. Organizations should maintain a set of *key risk indicators (KRIs)* that facilitate risk monitoring. These KRIs are quantitative measures of risk that may be easily monitored for situations where they exceed a defined threshold value or worrisome trends.

Reassessments of risk should take place whenever KRIs or other factors suggest that the environment is undergoing a significant change. Risk managers should also conduct periodic reassessments even in the absence of obvious changes to help the organization identify previously undetected issues. The results of these reassessments may prompt changes in elements of the organization's information security program.

Risk Treatment and Response

With a completed risk assessment in hand, organizations can then turn their attention to addressing those risks. *Risk treatment* is the process of systematically responding to the risks facing an organization. The risk assessment serves two important roles in the risk management process:

- The risk assessment provides guidance in prioritizing risks so that the risks with the highest probability and magnitude are addressed first.
- Quantitative risk assessments help determine whether the potential impact of a risk justifies the costs incurred by adopting a specific risk management approach.

Risk managers should work their way through the risk assessment and identify an appropriate management strategy for each risk included in the assessment. Managers have four strategies to choose from: risk mitigation, risk avoidance, risk transference, and risk acceptance. In the next several sections, we discuss each of these strategies using two examples.

First, we discuss the financial risk associated with the theft of a laptop from an employee. In this example, we are assuming that the laptop does not contain any unencrypted sensitive information. The risk that we are managing is the financial impact of losing the actual hardware.

Second, we discuss the business risk associated with a distributed denial-of-service (DDoS) attack against an organization's website.

We use these two scenarios to help you understand the different options available when selecting a risk management strategy and the trade-offs involved in that selection process.

Risk Mitigation

Risk mitigation is the process of applying security controls to reduce the probability and/or magnitude of a risk. Risk mitigation is the most common risk management strategy, and the vast majority of the work of security professionals revolves around mitigating risks through the design, implementation, and management of security controls. Many of these controls involve engineering trade-offs between functionality, performance, and security.

When you choose to mitigate a risk, you may apply one security control or a series of security controls. Each of those controls should reduce the probability that the risk will materialize, the magnitude of the risk should it materialize, or both the probability and the magnitude.

In our first scenario, we are concerned about the theft of laptops from our organization. If we want to mitigate that risk, we could choose from a variety of security controls. For example, purchasing cable locks for laptops might reduce the probability that a theft will occur.

In our second scenario, a DDoS attack against an organization's website, we could choose among several mitigating controls. For example, we could simply purchase more bandwidth and server capacity, allowing us to absorb the bombardment of a DDoS attack and thus reducing the impact of an attack. We could also choose to purchase a third-party DDoS mitigation service that prevents the traffic from reaching our network in the first place, thus reducing the probability of an attack.

Risk Avoidance

Risk avoidance is a risk management strategy where we change our business practices to completely eliminate the potential that a risk will materialize. Risk avoidance may initially seem like a highly desirable approach. After all, who wouldn't want to eliminate the risks facing their organization? There is, however, a major drawback. Risk avoidance strategies typically have a serious detrimental impact on the business.

For example, consider the laptop theft risk discussed earlier in this chapter. We could adopt a risk avoidance strategy and completely eliminate the risk by not allowing employees to purchase or use laptops. This approach is unwieldy and would likely be met with strong opposition from employees and managers due to the negative impact on employee productivity.

Similarly, we could avoid the risk of a DDoS attack against the organization's website by simply shutting down the website. If there is no website to attack, there's no risk that a DDoS attack can affect the site. But it's highly improbable that business leaders will accept shutting down the website as a viable approach. In fact, you might consider being driven to shut down your website to avoid DDoS attacks as the *ultimate* denial-of-service attack!

Risk Transference

Risk transference (or risk sharing) shifts some of the impact of a risk from the organization experiencing the risk to another entity. The most common example of risk transference is purchasing an insurance policy that covers a risk. When purchasing insurance, the customer pays a premium to the insurance carrier. In exchange, the insurance carrier agrees to cover losses from risks specified in the policy.

In the example of laptop theft, property insurance policies may cover the risk. If an employee's laptop is stolen, the insurance policy would provide funds to cover either the value of the stolen device or the cost to replace the device, depending on the type of coverage.

It's unlikely that a property insurance policy would cover a DDoS attack. In fact, many general business policies exclude all cybersecurity risks. An organization seeking insurance coverage against this type of attack should purchase *cybersecurity insurance*, either as a separate policy or as a rider on an existing business insurance policy. This coverage would repay some or all of the cost of recovering operations and may also cover lost revenue during an attack.

Risk Acceptance

Risk acceptance is the final risk management strategy, and it boils down to deliberately choosing to take no other risk management strategy and to simply continue operations as normal in the face of the risk. A risk acceptance approach may be warranted if the cost of mitigating a risk is greater than the impact of the risk itself.

WARNING   Risk acceptance is a deliberate decision that comes as the result of a thoughtful analysis. It should not be undertaken as a default strategy. Simply stating that "we accept this risk" without analysis is not an example of an accepted risk; it is an example of an unmanaged risk!

In our laptop theft example, we might decide that none of the other risk management strategies are appropriate. For example, we might feel that the use of cable locks is an unnecessary burden and that theft recovery tags are unlikely to work, leaving us without a viable risk mitigation strategy. Business leaders might require that employees have laptop devices, eliminating risk avoidance as a viable option. And the cost of a laptop insurance policy might be too high to justify. In that case, we might decide that we will simply accept the risk and cover the cost of stolen devices when thefts occur. That's risk acceptance.

In the case of the DDoS risk, we might go through a similar analysis and decide that risk mitigation and transference strategies are too costly. In the event we continue to operate the site, we might do so, accepting the risk that a DDoS attack could take the site down.

Exam Note

Understand the four risk treatment/response options (risk mitigation, risk avoidance, risk acceptance, and risk transference/sharing) when you take the exam. Be prepared to provide examples of these strategies and to identify which strategy is being used in a given scenario.

Risk Analysis

As you work to manage risks, you will implement controls designed to mitigate those risks. As you prepare for the exam, here are a few key terms that you can use to describe different states of risk:

- The *inherent risk* facing an organization is the original level of risk that exists before implementing any controls. Inherent risk takes its name from the fact that it is the level of risk inherent in the organization's business.

- The *residual risk* is the risk that remains after an organization implements controls designed to mitigate, avoid, and/or transfer the inherent risk.

- An organization's *risk appetite* is the level of risk that it is willing to accept as a cost of doing business.

These three concepts are connected by the way an organization manages risk. An organization begins with its inherent risk and then implements risk management strategies to reduce that level of risk. It continues doing so until the residual risk is at or below the organization's risk appetite.

Control Risk

The world of public accounting brings us the concept of control risk. Control risk is the risk that arises from the potential that a lack of internal controls within the organization will cause a material misstatement in the organization's financial reports. Information technology risks can contribute to control risks if they jeopardize the integrity or availability of financial information. For this reason, financial audits often include tests of the controls protecting financial systems.

Organizations can implement practices that address these concepts only if they have a high degree of risk awareness. Organizations must understand the risks they face and the controls they can implement to manage those risks. They must also conduct regular risk control assessments and self-assessments to determine whether those controls continue to operate effectively.

Risk Reporting

As risk managers work to track and manage risks, they must communicate their results to other risk professionals and business leaders. The risk register is the primary tool that risk management professionals use to track risks facing the organization. Figure 10.5 shows an excerpt from a risk register used to track IT risks in higher education.

FIGURE 10.5   Risk register excerpt

ID	Risk Statement	Risk Causes	Risk Impacts	Likelihood	Impact	Score
20	No coordinated vetting and review process for third-party or cloud-computing services used to store, process, or transmit institutional data	Lack of senior management support; lack of communication of central vetting process to staff/employees; failure to understand the need to protect institutional data	Multiple redundant services in place (inefficient and costly for the institution); institution unaware who its business partners are; institution unaware if institutional data are held by third parties; institution unable to ensure that third parties are following compliance requirements	1	2	2
21	Failure to create and maintain sufficient and current policies and standards to protect the confidentiality, integrity, and availability of institutional data and IT resources (e.g., hardware, devices, data, and software)	Lack of senior management support; failure to understand information security concepts; lack of funding to support policy development activities; lack of funding for training; lack of user training	Improper use of university IT systems and institutional data; failure of users to protect critical institutional data when using IT resources (leading to data breach); institution subject to regulatory violations and fines; institutional reputation loss; poor perception/reputation of IT	2	3	6
22	Data breach or leak of sensitive information (e.g., academic, business, or research data)	Lack of senior management support; complex regulatory environments impacting higher education IT systems and data (e.g., FERPA, HIPAA, GLBA, PCI, accessibility, export controls, etc.); complexity of IT systems, infrastructure, and services; lack of funding for data handling training; lack of user training; intentional user malfeasance; unintentional user error; hacking or infiltration by third parties	Institution subject to regulatory violations and fines; costs of breach notification; costs of redress for individuals; loss of alumni donations; loss of research data; costs to mitigate underlying breach event; institutional reputation loss; poor perception/reputation of IT	3	3	9

Source: EDUCAUSE IT Risk Register (`https://library.educause.edu/resources/2015/10/it-risk-register`)

The risk register is a lengthy document that often provides far too much detail for business leaders. When communicating risk management concepts to senior leaders, risk professionals often use a *risk matrix*, or heat map, such as the one shown in Figure 10.6. This approach quickly summarizes risks and allows senior leaders to quickly focus on the most significant risks facing the organization and how those risks might impact organizational goals and objectives.

FIGURE 10.6   Risk matrix

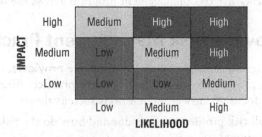

Circumstances will also arise where leaders and managers within the organization will need to understand changes in the organization's risk profile. These may be urgent situations based on an active emergency or slower-moving discussions based on the evolving risk landscape. Information security managers should establish a regular reporting rhythm, with periodic risk reports delivered at a regular frequency, as well as a mechanism for rapidly providing urgent updates. In all cases, risk managers should write their reports with a strong understanding of their audience, tailoring the content to the knowledge, needs, and specific concerns of each target group.

Enterprise Risk Management

As organizations seek to adopt a systematic approach to enterprise risk management, they should work to integrate risk management practices into normal business and information technology processes. Mature organizations don't treat risk management efforts as siloed projects but rather an integral component of their day-to-day work.

Here are examples of business areas that should incorporate risk management:

- *Software and systems development* efforts create and modify software and systems on a regular basis. New and modified systems are a potential source of risk to the organization, and integrating risk assessment and response practices into these development efforts helps ensure that the organization integrates security from the start and does not need to "bolt on" security controls after the fact in a costly and error-prone approach.

- *Procurement* processes bring new vendors and systems into the organization, another source of potential risk. Any new or renewing relationship with a vendor should include a formal risk assessment that identifies potential risks associated with the relationship and implements appropriate risk treatments before moving forward.

- *Project management* procedures govern much of the work performed in the modern organization and, like software and systems development, often result in change to business practices and technology. Project management procedures should incorporate risk assessments that identify new or changed risks that arise during the course of a project and address them appropriately.

The goal of integrating risk management into everyday business activity is to enable a consistent and comprehensive risk management program across the business.

Assessing Provider Risk Management Practices

As you conduct regular assessments of your cloud service providers, you should incorporate an assessment of each provider's own risk management practices. Examine their ERM programs, with a specific focus on answering questions such as these:

- What is the overall risk profile of the vendor and how do the risks they face impact your business and operations?

- What methodologies and policies does the vendor have in place as part of their own risk management efforts? Do they have a mature ERM program?

- What controls does the vendor have in place to mitigate identified risks? What level of residual risk remains? Is the vendor's risk appetite consistent with that of your own organization?

Answering these questions will help you determine whether the vendor's approach to risk management and risk tolerance are compatible with the needs of your own organization.

Risk Management Frameworks

Numerous risk management frameworks exist that are designed to assist the enterprise in developing sound risk management practices and management. However, for the purposes of the CCSP exam, we will only be discussing ISO 31000:2018, NIST SP 800-37, and the European Union Agency for Network and Information Security (ENISA) frameworks.

ISO 31000

ISO 31000 is an international standard that focuses on designing, implementing, and reviewing risk management processes and practices. The standard explains that proper implementation of a risk management process can be used to accomplish the following:

- Create and protect value
- Integrate organizational procedures
- Be part of the decision-making process
- Explicitly address uncertainty
- Be a systematic, structured, and timely risk management program
- Ensure the risk management program is based on the best available information
- Be tailored to the organization's business requirements and actual risks
- Take human and cultural factors into account
- Ensure the risk management program is transparent and inclusive
- Create a risk management program that is dynamic, iterative, and responsive to change
- Facilitate continual improvement and enhancement of the organization

For more information please visit `www.iso.org/iso/home/standards/iso31000.htm`.

NIST SP 800-37 (Guide for Implementing the Risk Management Framework)

NIST SP 800-37 is the Guide for Implementing the Risk Management Framework (RMF). This particular framework is a methodology for handling all organizational risk in a holistic, comprehensive, and continual manner. This RMF supersedes the old "Certification and Accreditation" model of cyclical inspections that have a specific duration (used widely in American military, intelligence, and federal government communities). This RMF relies heavily on the use of automated solutions, risk analysis and assessment, and implementing controls based on those assessments, with continuous monitoring and improvement.

NIST SP 800-37 is a guide organizations can use to implement the RMF. Although NIST standards are developed for use by the federal government, they have begun to be accepted in many nongovernment organizations as best practices. For instance, companies in the United States may use the NIST model and publications in developing not only their information security program but also their risk management program and practices. NIST publications and standards have the dual benefit of being widely acknowledged as expert and sensible but also free of charge (all NIST documents are in the public domain). It takes little effort to adopt and adapt the NIST materials from their intended use in the federal space into use in a private sector or nonprofit endeavor.

Keep in mind that these documents are not as accepted in international markets as are ISO/IEC standards. Therefore, if you conduct business outside the United States, you may want to investigate the other standards in more detail. Some overseas companies will not even do business with U.S. companies unless they subscribe to and are certified under ISO standards.

For a free copy of SP 800-37, as well as many other NIST documents, visit `https:// csrc.nist.gov/publications/detail/sp/800-37/rev-2/final`.

European Union Agency for Network and Information Security

You could think of European Union Agency for Network and Information Security (ENISA) as a European counterpart to NIST. It is a standard and model developed in Europe. While it could be considered international because it is accepted throughout Europe, it is not globally accepted in the way ISO standards are.

ENISA is responsible for producing *Cloud Computing: Benefits, Risks, and Recommendations for Information Security*. This guideline identifies 35 types of risks organizations should consider but goes further by identifying the top eight security risks based on likelihood and impact:

- Loss of governance
- Lock-in
- Isolation failure
- Compliance risk
- Management interface failure
- Data protection
- Malicious insider
- Insecure or incomplete data deletion

For more information about ENISA, please visit `www.enisa.europa.eu`.

Cloud Contract Design

As with any outsourcing relationship, agreements to obtain cloud services from a cloud service provider should use written contracts that define the parameters of the relationship. As you negotiate a new vendor relationship, you are documenting terms and conditions of that relationship that may seem insignificant in the moment but may become vital in later stages of the relationship. For this reason, customers should pay careful attention to the language included in cloud contracts.

Business Requirements

Before entering into any type of contract for cloud computing services, the organization should evaluate a number of things. First, there should be some compelling reason for engaging the cloud provider. Decisions should be made that assist the business in reaching its long-term goals. Decisions should never be made because they seem attractive or based on what your competitors are doing. You should have sound business reasons for deciding to use a cloud provider and for determining which one to choose.

As part of the due diligence in looking at cloud computing as a viable solution for the business, a few more items should be examined. Perhaps not all business units need to be involved in decision-making. Perhaps some changes will have little or no impact on them, in which case they do not need to be involved. This is called *scoping*, which is used to refer to including only departments or business units impacted by any cloud engagement.

Another important aspect of evaluating cloud computing solutions is that of regulatory compliance. It is vital that you investigate what regulators' expectations are with regard to cloud computing solutions and the additional or differing risks that engaging in a cloud solution will bring to the organization.

Last, you must look closely at the costs associated with any types of disaster recovery or outage situations and what you are able to withstand. Measurements such as recovery time objective (RTO), recovery point objective (RPO), and maximum allowable downtime (MAD) are critical in making decisions about choosing cloud computing solutions. You must be able to withstand a certain number of outages based on your risk profile, as they are bound to occur at some time. Knowing how to handle them and how your cloud provider will handle them is imperative.

Vendor Management

Vendors play an important role in the information technology operations of every organization. Whether it's the simple purchasing of hardware or software from an external company or the provision of cloud computing services from a strategic partner, vendors are integral in providing the IT services that we offer our customers. Security professionals must pay careful attention to managing these vendor relationships in a way that protects the confidentiality, integrity, and availability of their organization's information and IT systems.

Perhaps the most important rule of thumb is that you should always ensure that vendors follow security policies and procedures that are at least as effective as you would apply in your own environment. Vendors extend your organization's technology environment, and if they handle data on your behalf, you should expect that they execute the same degree of care that you would in your own operations. Otherwise vendors may become the weak link in the chain and jeopardize your security objectives.

Assessing vendor security controls is not a one-time process. In addition to any vendor assessments you perform at the beginning of a relationship, you should conduct periodic reassessments to validate that your original assessment remains accurate and that controls are still in place and functioning effectively.

Vendor relationships are absolutely critical in the world of cloud computing because these relationships inevitably include some degree of *vendor lock-in*—you're selecting a vendor that will be a long-term partner and it will be difficult to get out of that relationship quickly should conditions become unfavorable.

Because of this, you'll want to be sure to conduct *due diligence* to make sure that you're entering into a relationship with a vendor that is reliable and has solid finances. Researching the business viability of your vendors helps ensure that you aren't entering into a relationship with a vendor that is about to go bankrupt!

Vendor Management Lifecycle

Security professionals charged with managing vendor relationships may think of their jobs as following a standard lifecycle. It's not unusual for a large organization to add on dozens or even hundreds of new vendors in a single year, and organizations often change vendors due to pricing, functionality, or other concerns.

Step 1: Vendor Selection

The first step of the vendor management lifecycle is selecting a new vendor. Depending upon your organization's procurement environment, this may include anything from a formal request for proposal, known as an RFP, to an informal evaluation and selection process. In either case, security should play an important role, contributing to the requirements sent to vendors and playing a role in the evaluation process.

During your evaluation, you should also assess the quality and effectiveness of the provider's own risk management program. What controls, methodologies, and policies do they have in place to control risks that might affect your organization?

Step 2: Onboarding

Once the organization selects a new vendor, the *onboarding* process begins. This should include conversations between the vendor and the customer that verify the details of the contract and ensure that everything gets off on the right foot.

Onboarding often involves setting up the technical arrangements for data transfer, and organizations should ensure that they are satisfied with the encryption technology and other controls in place to protect information while in transit and maintain its security while at rest in vendor systems.

The onboarding process should also include establishing procedures for security incident notification.

Step 3: Maintenance

After the vendor is set up and running, the security team's job is not over. The vendor should then enter a maintenance phase where the customer continues to monitor security practices by conducting ongoing vendor assessments. This may include site visits and recurring conversations and the review of independent audit and assessment reports.

The maintenance phase will likely also involve the handling of security incidents that occur at the vendor's site. If the vendor never reports a security incident, this may be a red flag, as almost every organization occasionally experiences a security breach of some kind.

Step 4: Offboarding

All good things must eventually come to an end, and the reality is that even the most productive business relationships will terminate at some point. The offboarding process is the final step in the vendor lifecycle and includes ensuring that the vendor destroys all confidential information in its possession and that the relationship is unwound in an orderly fashion.

Depending upon business requirements, the lifecycle may then begin anew with the selection of a new vendor.

Exam tip

If you'd like to explore this topic in more detail, you may wish to review ISO 27036, which covers information security for supplier relationships. In particular, part 4 of the standard contains guidance on the security of cloud service providers.

Data Protection

As organizations begin to increasingly use vendors for services that include the storage, processing, and transmission of sensitive information, they must pay careful attention to the vendor's information management practices.

Data ownership issues often arise in supplier relationships, particularly when the vendor is creating information on behalf of the customer. Agreements put in place prior to beginning a new vendor relationship should contain clear language around data ownership.

In most cases, a customer will want to ensure that they retain uninhibited ownership of the information and that the vendor's right to use the information is carefully limited to activities performed on behalf of, and with the knowledge and consent of, the customer.

In addition, customers should ensure that the contract includes language that requires the vendor to securely delete all customer information within an acceptable period of time after the relationship ends.

One particular area of concern is data sharing. Customers should include language in vendor agreements that prohibits the vendor from sharing customer information with third parties without explicit consent from the customer.

The customer should include data protection requirements in the contract. This is particularly important if the vendor will be the sole custodian of critical information belonging to the customer. The contract should specify that the vendor is responsible for preserving the information and implementing appropriate fault tolerance and backup procedures to prevent data loss. In cases where the information is especially critical, the agreement may even include provisions that specify the exact controls the vendor must put in place to protect information.

Those controls may include data escrow provisions. Data escrow places a copy of your organization's data with a neutral third party who protects the data and will release it to you if the vendor goes out of business or otherwise fails to meet its obligations.

Negotiating Contracts

Negotiating vendor contracts is always a time-consuming process, and it's often quite different from the day-to-day work of most technologists. Contracts are, however, crucial to establishing strong partnerships with our vendors. They set forth the terms of an agreement in writing, ensuring that everyone is on the same page about the responsibilities of the vendor and the customer.

Contracts are especially important when it comes to cloud computing relationships. We are very dependent upon cloud service providers for the day-to-day operations of our businesses. If a cloud infrastructure provider experiences an outage, portions of our own infrastructure may stop working. If a cloud email provider suffers a security breach, it could cause a compromise of our own confidential information.

Common Contract Provisions

As you negotiate contracts with your vendors, you should be aware of some common clauses and sections found in cloud service agreements.

Definition of Terms

The contract should clearly define any terms that it uses. For example, if the contract uses the term *outage*, what specifically does that mean? If you can't access a single file that you have stored in a folder, is that an outage? If one office can't access services in their geographic region, is that an outage? Or does the entire service need to be down? The contract should answer questions like these by clearly defining terms.

Performance Metrics and Remedies

Contracts should also define clear performance metrics for uptime, availability, durability, and related measures. In practice, you might find that these metrics don't appear directly in the contract but instead appear in a service-level agreement (SLA) that the contract incorporates by reference. Cloud customers should adopt *service-level management* practices that include the active monitoring of vendor compliance with SLAs.

The contract should also specify the remedies that the customer has if the vendor fails to live up to its obligations. Is the customer entitled to a refund? If so, what portion of the fee will be returned?

Data Ownership

Cloud contracts should clearly state that the customer retains ownership of any data that it uses in the cloud service. Look for terms that cover access to that data and that cover export and destruction of the data at the conclusion of the contract.

Compliance Obligations

If you are subject to compliance obligations that you wish to pass through to your vendor, those requirements should be clearly spelled out in the contract. For example, if you are subject to HIPAA or PCI DSS, you'll want the vendor's compliance responsibilities for those obligations clearly outlined in the contract.

Assurance

You'll also want contract terms that provide you with the ability to implement assurance measures that allow you to verify that the vendor is living up to its obligations under the contract. For example, you might retain the right to audit the vendor to verify the presence of important security controls.

Indemnification

Watch for contract language covering *indemnification*. Under an indemnification clause, one of the parties to the contract agrees to cover losses incurred by the other party. If you are asked to indemnify the vendor, this could be a significant financial risk. On the other hand, you might want the vendor to indemnify you. These clauses, if present, certainly deserve scrutiny by your attorneys.

Termination

Contracts should also envision their own ending. How will the termination of the contract be handled? Does the contract automatically renew? How much advance notice must you give before terminating the contract? Is the vendor required to give you notice?

Litigation

We must remember that sometimes contracts go wrong. When we enter into a new business relationship, we expect everything to go well, but bad things happen and a small portion of the contracts we sign result in litigation. If this happens, where will the litigation take place? What jurisdiction's laws will govern the contract?

WARNING   Don't try to be an amateur attorney. When you're negotiating a contract, you should always have both technical and legal experts review the terms of the contract to protect your organization's interests.

Contracting Documents

Organizations may deploy some standard agreements and practices to manage these risks. Commonly used agreements include the following:

- *Master service agreements (MSAs)* provide an umbrella contract for the work that a vendor does with an organization over an extended period of time. The MSA typically includes detailed security and privacy requirements. Each time the organization enters into a new project with the vendor, it may then create a *statement of work (SOW)* that contains project-specific details and references the MSA.

- *Service-level agreements (SLAs)* are written contracts that specify the conditions of service that will be provided by the vendor and the remedies available to the customer if the vendor fails to adhere to the SLA. SLAs commonly cover issues such as system availability, data durability, and response time.

- A *memorandum of understanding (MOU)* is a letter written to document aspects of the relationship. An MOU is an informal mechanism that allows the parties to document their relationship to avoid future misunderstandings. MOUs are commonly used in cases where an internal service provider is offering a service to a customer that is in a different business unit of the same company.

- *Business partnership agreements (BPAs)* exist when two organizations agree to do business with each other in a partnership. For example, if two companies jointly develop and market a product, the BPA might specify each partner's responsibilities and the division of profits.

- *Nondisclosure agreements (NDAs)* protect the confidentiality of information used in the relationship. NDAs may be mutual, protecting the confidentiality of information belonging to both parties in the relationship, or one way, protecting the confidential information belonging to only the customer or the supplier.

Organizations will need to select the agreement type(s) most appropriate for their specific circumstances.

All things come to an end, and third-party relationships are no exception. Organizations should take steps to ensure that they have an orderly transition when a vendor relationship ends or when the vendor is discontinuing a product or service on which the organization depends. This should include specific steps that both parties will follow to have an orderly transition when the vendor announces a product's *end of life (EOL)* or a service's *end of service life (EOSL)*. These same steps may be followed if the organization chooses to stop using the product or service on its own.

Government Cloud Standards

Government agencies are subject to a wide variety of computing standards designed to protect sensitive government information. The U.S. federal government has three programs that are of specific interest to cloud security professionals: the Common Criteria, FedRAMP, and FIPS 140-2.

Common Criteria

The *Common Criteria* is actually an ISO standard (ISO 15408) that describes a certification program for technology products and services. The common criteria outline an approach for certifying that a technology solution meets security requirements, assigning it an assurance level, and approving it for operations. This program is almost exclusively used within government agencies and mostly applies to hardware and software products as opposed to services.

FedRAMP

The much more relevant program for cloud computing services is the Federal Risk and Authorization Management Program (FedRAMP). FedRAMP is a centralized approach to certifying cloud service providers. Run by the U.S. General Services Administration, FedRAMP provides a centralized certification process for the security of cloud services, allowing vendors to go to a single source for certification that then applies across the U.S. government.

You can find a complete list of FedRAMP certified cloud providers at https://marketplace.fedramp.gov. The FedRAMP Marketplace lists all of the cloud services that have been approved for use by government agencies. Users can drill down into specific entries in the FedRAMP database to learn more about the service and its certification status.

FIPS 140-2

Federal Information Processing Standard (FIPS) 140-2 describes the process used to approve cryptographic implementations for use in government applications. Government agencies and their service providers should ensure that they only use cryptographic modules that comply with FIPS 140-2.

Manage Communication with Relevant Parties

Both the cloud provider and cloud customers will have to establish durable, resilient lines of communication for business partners along the supply chain for a variety of reasons/purposes. Of particular interest are the following:

- **Vendors and partners:** Clear communications with vendors is necessary in order to ensure adequate quantities and types of resources/assets are available for operations. This can be especially true for emergency/contingency situations, where the immediacy/availability of resources is crucial (such as fuel for generators, replacement components for damaged systems, and so on).

- **Customers:** *Customers* can mean either individual end users of a product/service or a business that receives products/services in a supply chain. Communication with customers is essential to manage expectations (for instance, alerting customers prior to an interruption of service), maintain brand awareness, and ensure logistic needs are being met. Again, this is particularly true during disaster situations, where delivery may be delayed or interrupted. This might also be required by law, as in those situations involving privacy data, in jurisdictions affected by data breach notification laws.

- **Regulators:** In regulated industries, where a third party determines your ability to conduct business, maintaining communications with regulators is crucial. Regulators should be made aware of any situation where the organization might become noncompliant with pertinent standards or regulations (such as during disasters or in the aftermath of a crime). Regulators should be kept apprised of developments, potential solutions being considered by management, any stopgap measures or compensatory controls used in the interim, and the estimated duration until compliance resumes.

- **Other stakeholders:** Every organization operates in its own unique culture and vendor ecosystem. Make sure that you've included any other significant stakeholders specific to your organization in your communication plan.

For communications with all parties in the supply chain, secondary and even tertiary communications capabilities are highly recommended, especially for disaster situations. (Don't rely on the telephone to be working during a disaster.)

Summary

Vendors play a crucial role in modern IT environments, particularly when organizations make significant use of cloud service providers. In this chapter, you learned how organizations develop and maintain enterprise risk management (ERM) programs to manage these risks and adopt strategies of risk mitigation, risk transference, risk avoidance, and risk acceptance to maintain a risk profile that is consistent with the organization's risk appetite.

Exam Essentials

Policy frameworks consist of policies, standards, procedures, and guidelines. Policies are high-level statements of management intent for the information security program. Standards describe the detailed implementation requirements for policy. Procedures offer step-by-step instructions for carrying out security activities. Compliance with policies, standards, and procedures is mandatory. Guidelines offer optional advice that complements other elements of the policy framework.

Organizations often adopt a set of security policies covering different areas of their security programs. Common policies used in security programs include an information security policy, an acceptable use policy, a data ownership policy, a data retention policy, an account management policy, and a password policy. The specific policies adopted by any organization will depend on that organization's culture and business needs.

Policy documents should include exception processes. Exception processes should outline the information required to receive an exception to security policy and the approval authority for each exception. The process should also describe the requirements for compensating controls that mitigate risks associated with approved security policy exceptions.

Know how risk identification and assessment helps organizations prioritize cybersecurity efforts. Cybersecurity analysts try to identify all of the risks facing their organization and then conduct a business impact analysis to assess the potential degree of risk based on the probability that it will occur and the magnitude of the potential effect on the organization. This work allows security professionals to prioritize risks and communicate risk factors to others in the organization.

Know that vendors are a source of external risk. Organizations should conduct their own systems assessments as part of their risk assessment practices, but they should conduct supply chain assessments as well. Performing vendor due diligence reduces the likelihood that a previously unidentified risk at a vendor will negatively impact the organization. Hardware source authenticity techniques verify that hardware was not tampered with after leaving the vendor's premises.

Be familiar with the risk management strategies that organizations may adopt. Risk avoidance strategies change business practices to eliminate a risk. Risk mitigation techniques reduce the probability or magnitude of a risk. Risk transference approaches move some of the risk to a third party. Risk acceptance acknowledges the risk and normal business operations are continued despite the presence of the risk.

Review Questions

You can find the answers to the review questions in Appendix A.

1. Jen identified a missing patch on a Windows server that might allow an attacker to gain remote control of the system. After consulting with her manager, she applied the patch. From a risk management perspective, what has she done?

    A. Removed the threat

    B. Reduced the threat

    C. Removed the vulnerability

    D. Reduced the vulnerability

2. You notice a high number of SQL injection attacks against a web application run by your organization, so you install a web application firewall to block many of these attacks before they reach the server. How have you altered the severity of this risk?

    A. Reduced the magnitude

    B. Eliminated the vulnerability

    C. Reduced the probability

    D. Eliminated the threat

    Questions 3–7 refer to the following scenario:

    Aziz is responsible for the administration of an e-commerce website that generates $100,000 per day in revenue for his firm. The website uses a database that contains sensitive information about the firm's customers.

    Aziz is assessing the risk of a denial-of-service attack against the database where the attacker would destroy the data contained within the database. He expects that it would cost approximately $500,000 to reconstruct the database from existing records. After consulting threat intelligence, he believes that there is a 5 percent chance of a successful attack in any given year.

3. What is the asset value (AV)?

    A. $5,000

    B. $100,000

    C. $500,000

    D. $600,000

4. What is the exposure factor (EF)?

    A. 5 percent

    B. 20 percent

    C. 50 percent

    D. 100 percent

5. What is the single loss expectancy (SLE)?

    A. $5,000

    B. $100,000

    C. $500,000

    D. $600,000

6. What is the annualized rate of occurrence (ARO)?

    A. 0.05

    B. 0.20

    C. 2.00

    D. 5.00

7. What is the annualized loss expectancy (ALE)?

    A. $5,000

    B. $25,000

    C. $100,000

    D. $500,000

Questions 8–11 refer to the following scenario:

Grace recently completed a risk assessment of her organization's exposure to data breaches and determined that there is a high level of risk related to the loss of sensitive personal information. She is considering a variety of approaches to managing this risk.

8. Grace's first idea is to add a web application firewall to protect her organization against SQL injection attacks. What risk management strategy does this approach adopt?

    A. Risk acceptance

    B. Risk avoidance

    C. Risk mitigation

    D. Risk transference

9. Grace is considering dropping the customer activities that collect and store sensitive personal information. What risk management strategy would Grace's approach use?

    A. Risk acceptance

    B. Risk avoidance

    C. Risk mitigation

    D. Risk transference

10. Grace's company decided to install the web application firewall and continue doing business. They are still worried about other risks to the information that were not addressed by the firewall and are considering purchasing an insurance policy to cover those risks. What strategy does this use?

    A. Risk acceptance

    B. Risk avoidance

    C. Risk mitigation

    D. Risk transference

11. In the end, Grace found that the insurance policy was too expensive and opted not to purchase it. She is taking no additional action. What risk management strategy is Grace using in this situation?

    A. Risk acceptance

    B. Risk avoidance

    C. Risk mitigation

    D. Risk transference

12. Brian recently conducted a risk mitigation exercise and has determined the level of risk that remains after implementing a series of controls. What term best describes this risk?

    A. Inherent risk

    B. Control risk

    C. Risk appetite

    D. Residual risk

13. Joe is authoring a document that explains to system administrators one way in which they might comply with the organization's requirement to encrypt all laptops. What type of document is Joe writing?

    A. Policy

    B. Guideline

    C. Procedure

    D. Standard

14. Which one of the following documents must normally be approved by the CEO or a similarly high-level executive?

    A. Standard

    B. Procedure

    C. Guideline

    D. Policy

15. Greg would like to create an umbrella agreement that provides the security terms and conditions for all future work that his organization does with a vendor. What type of agreement should Greg use?

    A. BPA

    B. MOU

    C. MSA

    D. SLA

16. Which one of the following would not normally be found in an organization's information security policy?

    A. Statement of the importance of cybersecurity

    B. Requirement to use AES-256 encryption

    C. Delegation of authority

    D. Designation of responsible executive

17. Gwen is developing a new security policy for her organization. Which one of the following statements does *not* reflect best practices for policy development?

A. All stakeholders should agree with the proposed policy.

B. The policy should follow normal corporate policy approval processes.

C. Policies should match the "tone at the top" from senior business leaders.

D. Cybersecurity managers are typically responsible for communicating and implementing approved security policies.

18. Which one of the following items is *not* normally included in a request for an exception to security policy?

A. Description of a compensating control

B. Description of the risks associated with the exception

C. Proposed revision to the security policy

D. Business justification for the exception

19. A U.S. federal government agency is negotiating with a cloud service provider for the use of IaaS services. What program should the vendor be certified under before entering into this agreement?

A. FIPS 140-2

B. Common Criteria

C. FedRAMP

D. ISO 27001

20. The accounting department in your organization is considering using a new cloud service provider. As you investigate the provider, you discover that one of their major investors withdrew their support and will not be providing future funding. What major concern should you raise?

A. Vendor lock-in

B. Vendor suitability

C. Vendor security

D. Vendor viability

Appendix

Answers to the Review Questions

Chapter 1: Architectural Concepts

1. B. Programming as a service is not a common offering; the others are ubiquitous throughout the industry.

2. A. Quantum computing technology has the potential to unleash massive computing power that could break current encryption algorithms.

3. A. Service-level agreements (SLAs) specify objective measures that define what the cloud provider will deliver to the customer.

4. C. Security is usually not a profit center and is therefore beholden to business drivers; the purpose of security is to support the business.

5. D. Availability concerns arise when legitimate users are unable to gain authorized access to systems and information. The scenario described here is depriving a legitimate user access and is, therefore, an availability concern.

6. A. In this scenario, there is no regulatory agency mentioned. You are the cloud customer and you are working with a cloud service partner to implement a service offered by a cloud service provider.

7. A. Type 1 hypervisors, or "bare metal" hypervisors, are the most efficient form of hypervisor and the technology that is used in data center environments. Type 2 hypervisors generally run on personal computers. Type 3 and 4 hypervisors do not exist.

8. B. Risks, in general, can be reduced but never eliminated; cloud service, specifically, does not eliminate risk to the cloud customer because the customer retains a great deal of risk after migration.

9. B. Backups are still just as important as ever, regardless of where your primary data and backups are stored.

10. D. Interoperability is the ability of cloud services to function well together. Resiliency is the ability of the cloud infrastructure to withstand disruptive events. Performance is the ability of the cloud service to stand up to demand. Reversibility is the ability of a customer to undo a move to the cloud.

11. C. Vendor lock-in occurs when technical or business constraints prevent an organization from switching from one cloud vendor to another.

12. B. Cloud services provide on-demand self-service, broad network access, rapid scalability, and increased (not decreased!) elasticity.

13. C. Under current laws in most jurisdictions, the data owner is responsible for any breaches that result in unauthorized disclosure of PII; this includes breaches caused by contracted parties and outsourced services. The data owner is the cloud customer.

14. B. The business impact analysis is designed to ascertain the value of the organization's assets and learn the critical paths and processes.

15. A. Because ownership and usage are restricted to one organization, this is a private cloud.

16. B. In a public cloud model, the cloud service provider owns the resources and makes services available to any person or organization who wishes to use them.

17. D. In a community cloud model, customers all share a common characteristic or affinity and join together to create a cloud computing environment.

18. A. In a physical server environment, security teams know that each server runs on its own dedicated processor and memory resources and that if an attacker manages to compromise the machine, they will not have access to the processor and memory used by other systems. In a virtualized environment, this may not be the case if the attacker is able to break out of the virtualized guest operating system. This type of attack is known as a VM escape attack.

19. C. In software as a service (SaaS) offerings, the public cloud provider delivers an entire application to its customers. Customers don't need to worry about processing, storage, networking, or any of the infrastructure details of the cloud service. The vendor writes the application, configures the servers, and basically gets everything running for customers who then simply use the service.

20. A. Customers of *infrastructure as a service (IaaS)* vendors purchase basic computing resources from vendors and piece them together to create customized IT solutions. For example, infrastructure as a service vendors might provide compute capacity, data storage, and other basic infrastructure building blocks.

Chapter 2: Data Classification

1. B. All the others are valid methods of data discovery; user-based is a red herring with no meaning.

2. C. The data creation date, the data owner, and the date of scheduled destruction might be included in data labels, but we don't usually include data value because it is prone to change frequently and it might not be information we want to disclose to anyone who does not have a need to know.

3. B. While language may be useful for internal practices, it is not useful for lifecycle management or security functions. The source of the data, any handling restrictions, and the jurisdiction in which the data was collected or used are all useful when dealing with data that may move between different countries.

4. A. Credentials are not typically included in documentation and should be kept in a secured location. Hostnames, IP addresses, ports, protocols, and security controls are commonly documented in data flow diagrams.

5. B. Most cameras generate metadata about the images they create. Mei can rely on the metadata embedded in the original image files to conduct the discovery that she needs through her organization's files.

6. B. Packet capture is often impossible in cloud-hosted environments due to architectural and security reasons. Felix may want to identify another way to validate traffic flows for the data transfer.

7. C. In legal terms, when *data processor* is defined, it refers to anyone who stores, handles, moves, or manipulates data on behalf of the data owner or controller. In the cloud computing realm, particularly with software as a service tools, this is the cloud service provider.

8. D. Legal holds require organizations and individuals to retain data relevant to a court case. Organizations cannot follow their normal data destruction and lifecycle practices when data is impacted by a legal hold.

9. D. All the elements except transference need to be addressed in each policy. Transference is not an element of data retention policy.

10. B. Most cloud services don't provide physical ownership, control, or even access to the hardware devices holding the data, so physical destruction, including melting, is not an option. Overwriting and zeroization rely on access to a physical disk and only work when you can ensure that the entire disk or space containing the data will be overwritten, which cannot be guaranteed in a cloud-hosted, shared, and virtualized environment. Crypto-shredding is the only alternative in most cases when operating in the cloud.

11. A. Copyrights are protected tangible expressions of creative works. IRM rights management focuses on abilities like creating, editing, copying, viewing, printing, forwarding, and similar capabilities.

12. C. Traditional databases like MySQL are used to contain structured data. Unstructured data isn't stored in a defined format. *Tabular data* and *warehoused data* are not terms used for the CCSP exam.

13. C. Data classification activities often use sensitivity, jurisdiction, and criticality as inputs to determine the classification level of data for an organization. Crypto-shredding is a process used to destroy data, which may be required by classification at the end of its lifecycle. Data flow diagramming might note the classification level, but it's unlikely to show this level of detail, and tokenization is used to substitute nonsensitive data elements for sensitive data elements to allow processing without the potential for data leakage.

14. A. IRM provisioning capabilities are designed to provide users with rights based on their roles or other criteria. Data labeling is used to determine which data should be handled based on IRM rules but does not match roles to rights. DRM is digital rights management and is the technical implementation of controls—it does not match rights to files based on a role. Finally, CRM is the acronym for customer relationship management, an entirely different type of tool!

15. C. Moving large volumes of data from a cloud service can result in high egress fees. Nina may want to analyze the data using a tool in the same cloud as the data. There are no indications of issues that may cause low performance for retrieving the data, ingress costs are typically lower with cloud vendors because they have a desire for customers to bring their data and use storage services, and the data is unstructured and there is nothing in the question to indicate a need to structure it before analysis.

16. C. Jurisdiction and local law may create concerns for data discovery. Some data may require specific handling and needs to be accounted for before discovery and related actions are taken. Structured data is typically easier to conduct discovery against due to its well understood nature. While it is possible that the discovery process could overload database servers, Tej should be able to configure his discovery tools to not create issues and should monitor them when they are run.

17. B. Periodically testing data archiving, backup, and recovery capabilities is a key part of ensuring that they are successful in the long term. Classification and data mapping are useful to determine what should be archived and when it should be destroyed or discarded but are not critical to the success of the archiving process itself. Hashing is not critical to the archiving process, but it can be used to validate that data has not changed.

18. C. Certificates are commonly used to allow systems to authenticate and receive authorization to access data through an IRM system. Multifactor authentication typically requires an event and human interaction, making it less useful for system-based accesses. Neither TACACS nor LEAP is used for this purpose.

19. B. JSON is an example of semi-structured data. Traditional databases are examples of structured data, unstructured data does not have labels or other categorization information built in, and *super-structured data* is not a term used for the CCSP exam.

20. B. IRM tools should include all the functions listed except for crypto-shredding, which is typically associated with lifecycle management rather than rights management.

Chapter 3: Cloud Data Security

1. B. Data hiding is not a data obfuscation technique. It is used in programming to restrict data class access. Tokenization, masking, and anonymization are all obfuscation techniques.

2. D. SIEM is not intended to provide any enhancement of performance; in fact, a SIEM solution may decrease performance because of additional overhead. All the rest are goals of SIEM implementations.

3. C. The CCSP Exam Outline (Candidate Information Bulletin) describes three types of storage: long term, ephemeral, and raw. Lambda functions use storage that will be destroyed when they are re-instantiated, making this storage ephemeral storage.

4. C. Cloud hardware security modules, or HSMs, are used to create, store, and manage encryption keys and other secrets. Selah should ask her cloud service provider if they have an HSM service or capability that suits her organization's needs. A PKI is a public key infrastructure and is used to create and manage certificates, a DLP is a data loss prevention tool, and a CRL is a certificate revocation list.

5. A. Versions of executables for a service are not typically logged. While it may be useful to track patch status, versions of applications and services are not tracked via event logs.

IP addresses for both source and destination for events and queries and the service name itself are often logged to identify what happened and where traffic was going.

6. C. Scanning for credit card numbers using the DLP tool and a pattern match or algorithm is most likely to find all occurrences of credit card numbers, despite some false positives. Tagging files that have credit card numbers manually is likely to be error prone, finding them at destruction or deletion won't help during the rest of the lifecycle, and of course requiring users to use specific filenames is likely to lead to mistakes as well.

7. C. While privilege escalation is a concern, privilege reuse is not a typical threat. Privileged users will use their credentials as appropriate or necessary. Credential theft or compromise, infection with malware, and human error are all common threats to both cloud and on-premises storage.

8. B. In order to implement tokenization, there will need to be two databases: the database containing the raw, original data and the token database containing tokens that map to original data. Having two-factor authentication is nice but certainly not required. Encryption keys are not necessary for tokenization. Two-person integrity does not have anything to do with tokenization.

9. C. Data masking is very useful when testing. It doesn't provide features that help with remote access, least privilege, or authentication.

10. A. DLP can be combined with IRM tools to protect intellectual property; both are designed to deal with data that falls into special categories. SIEMs are used for monitoring event logs, not live data movement. Kerberos is an authentication mechanism. Hypervisors are used for virtualization.

11. A. Data labeling should be done when data is created to ensure that it receives the proper labels and can immediately be processed and handled according to security rules for data with that label. Labels may be modified during the Use, Store, and Archive phases to assist with lifecycle management.

12. D. Hashes can be created for both original copies and current copies and can be compared. If the hashes are different, the file has changed. Obfuscation, masking, and tokenization all describe methods of concealing data to prevent misuse.

13. C. Private keys used for certificates should be stored at the same or greater level of protection than that of the data that they're used to protect. Private keys should not be shared; public keys are intended to be shared. The highest level of security possible may be greater than the needed level of security depending on the organization's practices and needs.

14. D. All of these are key management best practices except for requiring multifactor authentication. Multifactor authentication might be an element of access control for keys, but it is not specifically an element of key management.

15. B. Tokenization replaces data with tokens, allowing referential integrity while removing the actual sensitive data. Masking replaces digits with meaningless characters. Randomization replaces data with randomized information with similar characteristics, preserving the ability

to test with the data while attempting to remove any sensitivity, and anonymization removes potentially identifying data.

16. B. The source IP address of a request combined with a geolocation or geoIP service will provide the best guess at where in the world the request came from. This can be inaccurate due to VPNs and other technologies, but having information contained in logs will provide Samuel with the best chance of identifying the location. Hostnames and usernames do not provide location data reliably.

17. B. The cloud data lifecycle is Create, Store, Use, Share, Archive, Destroy.

18. C. UserIDs are the most useful of these data elements when determining accountability for actions. If a UserID is paired with log entries, the individual (or at least their account) undertook the action in the log. Time stamps and host IP addresses are both useful, but without a UserID, they don't contain enough information to identify who performed the action. Certificate IDs may or may not be relevant depending on system and infrastructure design.

19. A. Masking replaces digits with meaningless characters. Randomization replaces data with randomized information with similar characteristics, preserving the ability to test with the data while attempting to remove any sensitivity. Tokenization replaces data with tokens, allowing referential integrity while removing the actual sensitive data, and anonymization removes potentially identifying data.

20. C. The first concern Greg will need to address with a large-scale web application environment with logging of all web requests is the sheer volume of the data captured. Once he has addressed how his organization will store, analyze, and act on those log entries, he can think more fully about the lifecycle and life span of the data. Geolocation can be performed with IP addresses in the logs, and secrets management may be required for services, but isn't a primary concern in this scenario.

Chapter 4: Security in the Cloud

1. D. Elasticity is the name for the benefit of cloud computing where resources can be apportioned as necessary to meet customer demand. Obfuscation is a technique to hide full raw datasets, either from personnel who do not have a need to know or for use in testing. Mobility is not a term pertinent to the CBK.

2. D. This is not a normal configuration and would not likely provide genuine benefit.

3. B. Background checks are controls for attenuating potential threats from internal actors; external threats aren't likely to submit to background checks.

4. B. IRM and DLP are used for increased authentication/access control and egress monitoring, respectively, and would actually decrease portability instead of enhancing it.

5. A. Dual control is not useful for remote access devices because we'd have to assign two people for every device, which would decrease efficiency and productivity. Muddling is a cocktail preparation technique that involves crushing ingredients. Safe harbor is a policy provision that allows for compliance through an alternate method rather than the primary instruction.

6. D. The cloud provider's resellers are a marketing and sales mechanism, not an operational dependency that could affect the security of a cloud customer.

7. A. State notification laws and the loss of proprietary data/intellectual property preexisted the cloud; only the lack of ability to transfer liability is new.

8. A. IaaS entails the cloud customer installing and maintaining the OS, programs, and data; PaaS has the customer installing programs and data; in SaaS, the customer only uploads data. In a community cloud, data and device owners are distributed.

9. C. NIST offers many informative guides and standards but nothing specific to any one organization. The cloud provider will not have prepared an analysis of lock-out/lock-in potential. Open-source providers can offer many useful materials but, again, nothing specific to the organization.

10. B. Malware risks and threats are not affected by the terms of the cloud contract.

11. C. DoS/DDoS threats and risks are not unique to the multitenant architecture.

12. B. Hardened perimeter devices are more useful at attenuating the risk of external attack.

13. C. ISP redundancy is a means to control the risk of externalities, not internal threats.

14. D. Scalability is a feature of cloud computing, allowing users to dictate an increase or decrease in service as needed, not a means to counter internal threats.

15. C. Conflict of interest is a threat, not a control.

16. A. One-time pads are a cryptographic tool/method; this has nothing to do with BC/DR. All the other options are benefits of using cloud computing for BC/DR.

17. C. Cryptographic sanitization is a means of reducing the risks from data remanence, not a way to minimize escalation of privilege.

18. B. Attackers prefer Type 2 hypervisors because the OS offers more attack surface and potential vulnerabilities. There are no Type 3 or 4 hypervisors.

19. B. Vendor lock-in is the result of a lack of portability, for any number of reasons. Masking is a means to hide raw datasets from users who do not have a need to know. Closing is a nonsense term in this context.

20. C. Software developers often install backdoors as a means to avoid performing entire work flows when adjusting the programs they're working on; they often leave backdoors behind in production software, inadvertently or intentionally.

Chapter 5: Cloud Platform, Infrastructure, and Operational Security

1. C. Internal audits typically attempt to test operational integrity and to identify areas for improvement. They may also validate practices against an industry standard. They are not typically done to provide attestations to third parties.

2. A. Geofencing is often used as part of a set of controls to prevent unauthorized logins. Auditing against logins that occur from new or unapproved locations and even preventing logins from unauthorized locations can be a useful preventative control. IPOrigin was made up for this question and both multifactor and biometric logins are used to prevent unauthorized access, not to check for potential malicious logins.

3. D. Alaina's best option to secure data at rest in the cloud for virtualized systems is to use disk or volume encryption. Hashing is one way, but it doesn't make sense for data storage. Ephemeral disks or volumes may be associated with instances that have a short life span, but they should still be encrypted, and read-only disks could still be exposed.

4. D. MD5 or SHA1 hashing is often used to check the hash of downloaded software against a published official hash for the package or software. Encryption and decryption are not used for validation, and rainbow tables are used for password cracking.

5. C. The CIS security controls are a security baseline adopted by many organizations. Naomi's organization should still review and modify the controls to match its needs. SOC is an auditing report type, and both ISO and NIST provide standards, but the CIS security controls aren't ISO or NIST standards.

6. B. Using dedicated hardware instances, while expensive, is the most secure option for protecting compute from potential side channel attacks or attacks against the underlying hypervisor layer for cloud-hosted systems. Memory encryption may exist at the hypervisor level, but cloud providers do not typically make this an accessible option, and virtualization tools are not a major security benefit or detractor in this scenario.

7. B. Removing anti-malware agents is not a typical part of a baselining process. Installing one might be! Limiting administrator access, closing unused ports, and disabling unneeded services are all common baselining activities.

8. D. While virtual networks in cloud environments are typically well isolated, Hrant's best choice is to use end-to-end encryption for all communications. A VPN for each system is impractical, and bastion hosts are used to provide access from less secure to more secure zones or networks.

9. B. Snapshots in virtual environments not only capture the current state of the machine, they also allow point-in-time restoration. Full, incremental, and differential backups back up the drive of a system but not the memory state.

10. B. A software as a service environment will not be able to provide operating system logs to third-party auditors since the service provider is unlikely to provide them to customers. Access and activity logs as well as user and account privilege information are all likely to be available.

11. C. Orchestration describes the broad set of capabilities that allow automated task-based control of services, processes, or workflows. It can handle maintenance and uses scheduling, but its uses are broader than both. Virtualization is a key component of the cloud, but does not describe this specific use appropriately.

12. C. To validate the software, she'll need VeraCrypt's public key. Fortunately, VeraCrypt provides the key and the signatures on the same page for easy access.

13. B. Bastion hosts are used to connect from a lower-security zone to a higher-security zone. Ting has configured one to allow inbound access and will need to pay particular attention to the security and monitoring of the system. The remainder of the answers were made up for this question, although network bridges do exist.

14. D. Common functionality of guest OS tools include mapping storage; supporting improved networking; and video output, sound, or input capabilities. They don't usually allow control of the underlying host operating system.

15. A. Type 1 hypervisors run directly on the underlying hardware or the "bare metal," and Type 2 hypervisors run inside of another operating system, like Windows or Linux. There are no Type 3 or 4 hypervisors.

16. B. Allowing access to their environments for auditors has the potential to lead to disruption of service for the wide range of customers they support. If they allowed audits for their multitude of customers, they'd also be in a perpetual audit process, which is costly and time consuming. Organizations typically do want to identify problems with their service. Not allowing auditors access is not required by best practices and would not be reported as a data breach.

17. C. A hardware security module (HSM) service will provide the functionality Michelle is looking for. A TPM, or trusted platform module, is associated with local system security rather than for organization-wide secrets storage and management. GPG is an encryption package and won't do what she needs, and SSDs are storage devices, not encryption management tools.

18. A. Security groups act like firewalls in cloud environments, allowing rules that control traffic by host, port, and protocol to be set to allow or disallow traffic. Stateless and stateful IDSs and IPSs were made up for this question, and VPC boundaries are not a technical solution or tool.

19. B. Honeypots are intentionally vulnerable systems set up to capture attacker behavior and include tools to allow analysis. The phrase *the dark web* is used to describe TOR accessible, nonpublic internet sites. Network intrusion detection and prevention (IDS and IPS) systems can be used to detect attacks, and while they may capture information like uploaded toolkits, they won't capture command-line activities in most scenarios, since attackers encrypt the traffic containing the commands.

20. C. Vulnerability scanners can't detect zero-day exploits because they won't have detection rules or definitions for them. Zero-day exploits haven't been announced or detected and thus won't be part of their library. Malware, known vulnerabilities, and programming flaws may all be detected by vulnerability scanners.

Chapter 6: Cloud Application Security

1. D. STRIDE stands for spoofing, tampering, repudiation, information disclosure, denial of service, and elevation of privileges, not exploitation.

2. B. Service providers manage authorization for their service and rely on the identity provider to authenticate users. Token provider is not a typical role in a federated identity arrangement.

3. D. Multifactor authentication needs to be made up of different types of factors: something you know, something you have, or something you are, like a biometric factor. A password is something you know and an application-generated PIN from a fob or smartphone is something you have. An HSM is not a factor, it is a storage method. Hardware tokens and magstripe cards are both something you have, and passwords and secret codes are both something you know.

4. C. Sandboxes are used to isolate code while it is running to allow it to be tested. Amanda is likely to encounter the sandbox as part of the testing phase when the organization wants to isolate its code while it undergoes QA and functional testing.

5. C. A typical secrets lifecycle starts with creation, moves on to rotation, may include revocation if needed, and ends with expiration of secrets at the end of their lifecycle.

6. B. Web application firewalls typically provide the ability to filter based on users, sessions, data sent and received, and application-specific context. Database activity monitoring (DAM) tools are used to monitor for privileged database use, among other useful data points for database security.

7. A. User acceptance is part of functional testing, not nonfunctional testing. Software quality, including its stability and performance, is tested by nonfunctional testing.

8. A. CI/CD pipeline and software supply chain flaws cover somewhat different areas, but SCA tools are used to address software supply chain flaws. Software composition analysis checks to see which open-source components are part of a software package and allows security professionals and developers to protect against issues in the software supply chain by knowing what components they're using and relying on.

9. D. Static code review involves reviewing source code to identify issues. Dynamic testing is done with running code. Interactive testing is done by interacting with the code or application as a user would, and black-box or zero-knowledge testing involves testing as an attacker would, without any knowledge or detail of the environment or application.

10. B. Docker is a container engine. Sandboxing is used to provide a safe, secure environment for testing or isolation. Microservices are small, independent services used to make up a larger service environment. Multitenancy is the concept of multiple users or organizations using the same infrastructure, typically through a virtualized management platform.

11. C. The last stage of the Waterfall model is the operational phase, which includes support and maintenance. Testing occurs in Phase 5, and business rule analysis is in Phase 2.

12. B. SSH keys are a form of secrets, and Jen knows that keeping SSH keys secure is an important part of secure secrets storage. Injection flaws can include XSS, SQL injection, and CSRF, among others, but not SSH keys. There's no mention of vulnerable components, nor is there mention of logging or monitoring issues, but Jen may want to ensure logging is enabled for privilege use associated with administrative accounts.

13. A. Scalability for cloud applications often relies on the ability to easily add or remove small instances to provide more resources as needed. Interoperability is the ability to work across platforms, services, or systems, and doesn't use many small instances to function. Similarly, portability allows software to move between environments without requiring specific APIs or tools and again doesn't rely on large numbers of small instances. API security attempts to prevent abuse of APIs and might leverage an API gateway instead of small instances.

14. A. Since cloud applications run on virtualized infrastructure in most cases, firmware vulnerabilities are not considered a common threat to cloud applications. Broken authentication, sensitive data exposure issues, and components with known vulnerabilities are all common threats to applications.

15. C. Stage 4 in PASTA involves performing threat analysis based on threat intelligence after Stage 3's factoring of applications and identification of application controls.

16. B. ASVS is composed of three levels, with Level 1 being the base level that relies on penetration testing for security validation, and moving on through Levels 2 and 3 with increasing levels of validation requirements. Selah's needs align to Level 1.

17. D. SCA is used to determine what open-source software is in a codebase. This helps to control risks by allowing the organization to know what components may need to be updated and which may be insecure, because they might otherwise be hidden in packages or installers.

18. C. IAST typically occurs in the test or QA stage of most software development lifecycles. It helps to ensure that testing occurs earlier and that errors are found and fixed sooner. Since code needs to exist before it can be tested, it cannot happen in design, and the code stage typically involves things like unit testing instead of interactive testing that requires a more complete application to validate. Finally, the maintain stage of the SDLC is more likely to use vulnerability scanning tools rather than interactive testing on an ongoing basis.

19. C. A DAM, or database activity monitoring tool, is a tool that combines network data and database auditing information to help identify unwanted or illicit activity. Susan's best bet is a DAM. A cloud application security broker is used to enforce policies on users of cloud services, a WAF is a web application firewall, and SDLC is the software development lifecycle.

20. A. API gateways are tools used to manage, monitor, and aggregate APIs, and typically have the ability to control authentication and authorization, provide traffic flow control features, and can filter based on API security best practices or rules. An IPS can be used inline to filter traffic and to prevent attacks, but they typically aren't designed to be API aware, and thus don't have the full set of capabilities that will meet Jason's needs. An IDS isn't inline and thus can't manage traffic, and API firewalls are not common security tools.

Chapter 7: Operations Elements

1. B. Much as with any package downloaded from the internet, Megan needs to validate the container. Ideally she should check the container's signature if one is provided and scan it for any malicious software. Running it or adding it to a repository without checking it is not a best practice, and decrypting a container does not validate it.

2. A. Significant data center usage usually makes building your own less expensive in the long term. For smaller deployments, third-party data center hosting companies can offer increased resilience, greater efficiency due to shared space and services, and greater flexibility as organizations grow until their needs exceed those of the commercial provider.

3. C. A honeypot is designed to be attractive to attackers and to capture their tools and techniques for later study. Firewalls and network security groups both block traffic based on rules but do not capture the tools or techniques in most cases. *Beartrap* is not a common term used in security work.

4. B. Multivendor pathway connectivity describes separate physical paths to different vendors for internet access or other services. Key elements of a multivendor pathway connectivity design include ensuring that the paths do not intersect or overlap, that multiple vendors are used, and that those vendors themselves do not have shared upstream dependencies. The remainder of the answers were made up for this question.

5. D. Network security groups, like firewalls, rely on rules to define what traffic is allowed to instances. Cloud watchers isn't a common term, but CloudWatch is an Amazon tool used to monitor Amazon resources, and both intrusion detection and intrusion prevention systems (IDSs and IPSs) are used to monitor for attacks, while an IPS can also be used to stop them.

6. A. Daniel has deployed a bastion host, a specifically secured device that allows external access from a lower-security zone to a higher-security zone. *Security gateway* is a broad term for network edge security devices. A span port is used to capture network traffic for analysis, and a VPC span was made up for this question.

7. B. Learning systems that apply data to improve their detection are considered artificial intelligence models. They may apply behavior-based analysis, pattern matching, and rules as part of their actions, but learning from those is a hallmark of AI-based systems.

8. C. Remote Desktop Protocol (RDP) is the built-in Windows remote desktop client that operates on TCP port 3389. Telnet is not encrypted, and `screen` is a Linux command that allows sessions to be paused without losing connectivity. SSH can be used to tunnel other services, but it is typically a command-line option.

9. A. While chilled water systems provide better cooling, the ability to switch to utility provider water in the event of an outage is a common capability for chilled water systems. None of the other answers address the need for water-based cooling.

10. C. Amanda should expect to use virtual desktops or applications hosted in the cloud or on servers, allowing all sensitive work to occur remotely via an encrypted connection. She should not expect local virtual machine hosting, and the problem does not indicate whether the organization uses a cloud-based server environment or a third-party managed data center.

11. D. While solar power may be used for a data center, it is not a common element in fully redundant power systems. Power from multiple providers on different physical paths, UPS devices in each rack, and multiple generators that allow maintenance to occur while still providing power to the facility during a power loss event are all common design features.

12. D. Enabling secure boot for guest systems does not help to harden the hypervisor itself. Restricting the use of superuser accounts, requiring MFA, and logging and alerting on improper usage are all examples of common hypervisor hardening techniques.

13. A. Using SSH with a jumpbox, requiring multifactor authentication, and using certificates are all best practices that Naomi should consider to provide a secure SSH solution.

14. B. Selah's organization is using dynamic optimization techniques to use data-driven, responsive adjustments in their environment to meet load-based needs. Distributed resource scheduling focuses on providing resources to virtual machines to ensure their needs are met and that maintenance can occur. Maintenance mode removes systems from a virtual machine cluster by shedding load to other systems so maintenance can occur. High availability can help with the scenario described but does not necessarily adjust to meet load conditions.

15. C. Frank will establish a security operations center, or SOC. A NOC, or network operations center, focuses on network management and monitoring, although SOCs and NOCs often have overlapping responsibilities. A SIEM, or security information and event management tool, is often used in a SOC, and IDSs, or intrusion detection systems, are used to gather data for a SOC.

16. D. Gary should set the system to maintenance mode, allowing the VM environment to move running virtual machines to other systems so that he can turn the server off and perform hardware maintenance. Distributed resource scheduling focuses on providing resources to VMs, dynamic optimization adjusts environments as demands change, and storage clustering is used to provide availability and performance for storage.

17. D. Clustering VM hosts, storage clustering for the underlying storage, and ensuring that resources are distributed appropriately will help improve the availability of guest operating systems. However, using a load balancer will help improve availability of a service, not the guest operating systems themselves.

18. B. IDSs, or intrusion detection systems, do not have the ability to block an attack. If Valerie wants to stop attacks, she should deploy an IPS.

19. B. Tenant partitioning is often done at the rack, cage, or bay level in data centers. Separate facilities are not common for tenant partitioning, since organizations that can fill a full facility or need one tend to acquire or manage their own.

20. D. Hu is employing data dispersion, which places data in multiple locations to ensure that a loss event or corruption does not destroy the data. RAID and mirroring are both techniques for data resiliency at the disk or array level. The term *data cloning* simply describes copying data.

Chapter 8: Operations Management

1. C. The full test will involve every asset in the organization, including all personnel. The others will have less impact on the organization because they do not involve actually activating the plan.

2. A. The tabletop test involves only essential personnel and none of the production assets. The others will have greater impact.

3. C. Liquid propane does not spoil, which obviates the need to continually refresh and restock it and might make it more cost-effective. The burn rate has nothing to do with its suitability, unless it has some direct bearing on the particular generator the data center owner has chosen. The various relative prices of fuel fluctuate. Flavor is a distractor in this question and means nothing.

4. B. Frustrated employees and managers can increase risk to the organization by implementing their own, unapproved modifications to the environment. The particular interval changes from organization to organization.

5. B. A data center with less than optimum humidity can have a higher static electricity discharge rate. Humidity has no bearing on breaches or theft, and *inversion* is a nonsense term used as a distractor.

6. D. The UPS is intended to last only long enough to save production data currently being processed. The exact quantity of time will depend on many variables and will differ from one data center to the next.

7. C. Generator power should be online before battery backups fail. The specific amount of time will vary between data centers.

8. B. Automated patching is much faster and more efficient than manual patching. It is, however, not necessarily any less expensive than manual patching. Manual patching is overseen by administrators, who will recognize problems faster than automated tools. Noise reduction is not a factor in patch management at all.

9. C. Checklists serve as a reliable guide for BC/DR activity and should be straightforward enough to use that someone not already an expert or trained in BC/DR response could accomplish the necessary tasks. Flashlights and call trees are certainly useful during BC/DR actions, but not for the purpose of reducing confusion and misunderstanding. Control matrices are not useful during BC/DR actions.

10. B. A data center that doesn't follow vendor guidance might be seen as failing to provide due care. Regulations, internal policy, and the actions of competitors might all inform the decision to perform an update and patch, but these don't necessarily bear directly on due care. This is a difficult, nuanced question, and all the answers are good, but option B is the best.

11. A. Regulators are not involved in an organization's CMB. The IT department, security office, and management all play a role in the CMB process.

12. D. Disk space, disk I/O usage, and CPU usage are all standard performance monitoring metrics. Print spooling is not normally incorporated into performance monitoring plans.

13. B. During maintenance mode, teams should remove all active production instances, prevent new logins, and ensure that logging continues. There is not normally a need to initiate enhanced security controls.

14. A. If the CMB is receiving numerous change requests to the point where the number of requests would drop by modifying the baseline, then that is a good reason to change the baseline. The baseline should not be changed due to power fluctuations, to reduce redundancy, or due to a natural disaster.

15. B. A UPS can provide line conditioning, adjusting power so that it is optimized for the devices it serves and smoothing any power fluctuations. It does not provide confidentiality, breach alerts, or communication redundancy.

16. A. All deviations from the baseline should be documented, including details of the investigation and outcome. We do not enforce or encourage deviations. Presumably, we would already be aware of the deviation, so "revealed" is not a reasonable answer.

17. A. The more systems that are included in the baseline, the more cost-effective and scalable the baseline is. The baseline does not deal with breaches or version control; those are the provinces of the security office and CMB, respectively. Regulatory compliance might (and usually will) go beyond the baseline and involve systems, processes, and personnel that are not subject to the baseline.

18. C. Joint operating agreements can provide nearby relocation sites so that a disruption limited to the organization's own facility and campus can be addressed at a different facility and campus. UPS systems and generators are not limited to serving needs for localized causes. Regulations do not promote cost savings and are not often the immediate concern during BC/DR activities.

19. D. The Uptime Institute dictates 12 hours of generator fuel for all cloud data center tiers.

20. C. The BC/DR kit is intended to be compact, and generator fuel is too cumbersome to include with the kit. All the other items should be included.

Chapter 9: Legal and Compliance Issues

1. C. One of the provisions of the notice principle is that organizations should provide notice to data subjects before they use information for a purpose other than those that were previously disclosed.

2. C. Kara's organization is collecting and processing this information for its own business needs. Therefore, it is best described as the data controller.

3. C. ISO 27701 covers best practices for implementing privacy controls. ISO 27001 and ISO 27002 relate to an organization's information security program. ISO 27702 does not yet exist.

4. B. The gap analysis is the formal process of identifying deficiencies that prevent an organization from achieving its privacy objectives. The results of the gap analysis may be used to design new controls.

5. D. While they vary by state, breach notification laws may require notification to consumers, state regulators, and credit reporting agencies.

6. D. While not all states impose all of these penalties, free credit monitoring, penalties sought by an attorney general, and civil suits arising from a private right of action are potential consequences for an organization. Unless some other criminal act has occurred, criminal prosecution of employees is highly unlikely.

7. B. Under HIPAA, business associates are third-party firms that participate in the handling of PHI for a covered entity. Covered entities are required to have a business associate agreement (BAA) with such companies that confer responsibility for HIPAA compliance on the third party.

8. B. GLBA distinguishes between customers and consumers. Customers are people like account holders who have ongoing relationships with the bank. Consumers may only conduct isolated transactions with the bank. This is important because the bank has fewer obligations to Dimitri under GLBA because he is not technically a customer.

9. D. This is a tricky question. The Fourth Amendment has been interpreted to provide individuals with some privacy rights, but it does not explicitly establish a right to privacy. The word *privacy* appears nowhere in the text of the Constitution.

10. C. Administrative law is commonly documented in the Code of Federal Regulations (CFR). The U.S. Code contains legislative law. The U.S. Constitution and its amendments (including the Bill of Rights) contain constitutional law.

11. D. In order to prevail on a negligence claim, the plaintiff must establish that there were damages involved, meaning that they suffered some type of financial, physical, emotional, or reputational harm.

12. C. Many states do have laws requiring that some contracts be in written form, but there is no universal requirement that a contractual agreement take place in writing, although written contracts are clearly preferable. The conditions that must be met for a contract to be enforceable include that each party to the contract must have the capacity to agree to the contract, an offer must be made by one party and accepted by the other, consideration must be given, and there must be mutual intent to be bound.

13. D. The Health Insurance Portability and Accountability Act (HIPAA) is legislation passed by Congress. However, the HIPAA Privacy Rule and HIPAA Security Rule did not go through the legislative process. They are examples of administrative law created by the Department of Health and Human Services to implement the requirements of HIPAA.

14. A. The Gramm–Leach–Bliley Act (GLBA) governs the security and privacy of personal information in the financial industry. The Family Educational Rights and Privacy Act (FERPA) applies to educational institutions. The Sarbanes–Oxley Act (SOX) governs the records of publicly traded corporations. The Health Insurance Portability and Account-ability Act (HIPAA) applies to healthcare providers, health insurers, and health information clearinghouses.

15. C. The right to be forgotten was first established under the European Union's General Data Protection Regulation (GDPR). It requires that, in many circumstances, companies delete personal information maintained about an individual at that individual's request.

16. C. HIPAA applies to three types of covered entities: healthcare providers (such as doctors and hospitals), health insurers, and health information clearinghouses. Medical device man-ufacturers do not fit into any of these categories and are unlikely to handle the protected health information of individual patients.

17. B. Organizations may transfer information between the European Union and other nations when there is an adequacy decision in place that the laws of the other nation comply with GDPR. They may also choose to adopt Standard Contractual Clauses (SCCs) or Binding Cor-porate Rules (BCRs). They used to be able to transfer data under the safe harbor provisions of the EU-U.S. Privacy Shield, but this was struck down by the *Schrems II* decision.

18. C. All of these regulations would concern cloud security professionals. However, the Payment Card Industry Data Security Standard (PCI DSS) is a private regulatory scheme, not a law.

19. B. SOC audits performed in the United States are subject to SSAE 18. The earlier SSAE 16 standard for these audits is no longer relevant. The ISAE 3402 standard governs SOC audits outside of the United States.

20. B. SOC 2 reports contain information on an organization's security controls and include detailed sensitive information. They are not normally shared outside of an NDA. SOC 3 reports contain similar types of information but at a level suitable for public disclosure. SOC 1 reports are normally used as a component of a financial audit. SOC 4 reports do not exist.

Chapter 10: Cloud Vendor Management

1. C. By applying the patch, Jen has removed the vulnerability from her server. This also has the effect of eliminating this particular risk. Jen cannot control the external threat of an attacker attempting to gain access to her server.

2. C. Installing a web application firewall reduces the probability that an attack will reach the web server. Vulnerabilities may still exist in the web application, and the threat of an external attack is unchanged. The impact of a successful SQL injection attack is also unchanged by a web application firewall.

3. **C.** The asset at risk in this case is the customer database. Losing control of the database would result in a $500,000 fine, so the asset value (AV) is $500,000.

4. **D.** The attack would result in the total loss of customer data stored in the database, making the exposure factor (EF) 100 percent.

5. **C.** We compute the single loss expectancy (SLE) by multiplying the asset value (AV) ($500,000) and the exposure factor (EF) (100%) to get an SLE of $500,000.

6. **A.** Aziz's threat intelligence research determined that the threat has a 5 percent likelihood of occurrence each year. This is an ARO of 0.05.

7. **B.** We compute the annualized loss expectancy (ALE) by multiplying the SLE ($500,000) and the ARO (0.05) to get an ALE of $25,000.

8. **C.** Installing new controls or upgrading existing controls is an effort to reduce the probability or magnitude of a risk. This is an example of a risk mitigation activity.

9. **B.** Changing business processes or activities to eliminate a risk is an example of risk avoidance.

10. **D.** Insurance policies use a risk transference strategy by shifting some or all of the financial risk from the organization to an insurance company.

11. **A.** When an organization decides to take no further action to address remaining risk, they are choosing a strategy of risk acceptance.

12. **D.** The residual risk is the risk that remains after an organization implements controls designed to mitigate, avoid, and/or transfer the inherent risk.

13. **B.** The key term in this scenario is *one way*. This indicates that compliance with the document is not mandatory, so Joe must be authoring a guideline. Policies, standards, and procedures are all mandatory.

14. **D.** Policies require approval from the highest level of management, usually the CEO. Other documents may often be approved by other managers, such as the CISO.

15. **C.** Master service agreements (MSAs) provide an umbrella contract for the work that a vendor does with an organization over an extended period of time. The MSA typically includes detailed security and privacy requirements. Each time the organization enters into a new project with the vendor, they may then create a statement of work (SOW) that contains project-specific details and references the MSA.

16. **B.** Security policies do not normally contain prescriptive technical guidance, such as a requirement to use a specific encryption algorithm. This type of detail would normally be found in a security standard.

17. **A.** Policies should be developed in a manner that obtains input from all relevant stakeholders, but it is not necessary to obtain agreement or approval from all stakeholders. Policies should follow normal corporate policy approval processes and should be written in a

manner that fits within the organizational culture and "tone at the top." Once an information security policy is approved, it commonly falls to the information security manager to communicate and implement the policy.

18. C. Requests for an exception to a security policy would not normally include a proposed revision to the policy. Exceptions are documented variances from the policy because of specific technical and/or business requirements. They do not alter the original policy, which remains in force for systems not covered by the exception.

19. C. All of these programs may play a role in the relationship, but the most important is the Federal Risk and Authorization Management Program (FedRAMP). This program applies specifically to cloud services and applies across the U.S. government.

    FIPS 140-2 certification is only required for cryptographic modules and there is no mention of these services in the question. The Common Criteria are generally only used for hardware and software, not services. ISO 27001 is a voluntary standard that is not required by the U.S. federal government.

20. D. While all of these concerns exist in any vendor relationship, the key issue in this question is that the vendor may not have sufficient financial support to continue operations. If there's a chance the vendor will shut down services before the end of the contract period, this is a vendor viability concern.

Index

Comprehensive Online Learning Environment

Register to gain one year of FREE access after activation to the online interactive test bank to help you study for your (ISC)² Certified Cloud Security Professional certification exam—included with your purchase of this book!

The online test bank includes the following:

- **Assessment Test** to help you focus your study on specific objectives
- **Chapter Tests** to reinforce what you've learned
- **Practice Exams** to test your knowledge of the material
- **Digital Flashcards** to reinforce your learning and provide last-minute test prep before the exam
- **Searchable Glossary** to define the key terms you'll need to know for the exam

Register and Access the Online Test Bank

To register your book and get access to the online test bank, follow these steps:

1. Go to www.wiley.com/go/sybextestprep (this address is case sensitive)!
2. Select your book from the list.
3. Complete the required registration information, including answering the security verification to prove book ownership. You will be emailed a pin code.
4. Follow the directions in the email or go to www.wiley.com/go/sybextestprep.
5. Find your book on that page and click the "Register or Login" link with it. Then enter the pin code you received and click the "Activate PIN" button.
6. On the Create an Account or Login page, enter your username and password, and click Login or, if you don't have an account already, create a new account.
7. At this point, you should be in the test bank site with your new test bank listed at the top of the page. If you do not see it there, please refresh the page or log out and log back in.

Do you need more practice? Check out *Official (ISC)² CCSP Certified Cloud Security Professional Practice Tests, 3rd Edition*, also by Mike Chapple and Dave Seidl. With hundreds more practice questions organized by domain, and with two additional complete practice exams, it's a great way to build your confidence and readiness for exam day.

SYBEX
A Wiley Brand